I PLEDGE ALLEGIANCE...

I PLEDGE ALLEGIANCE...

The True Story of the Walkers: An American Spy Family

by Howard Blum

WEIDENFELD AND NICOLSON
London

First published in Great Britain in 1988 by
George Weidenfeld & Nicolson Limited
91 Clapham High Street, London SW4 7TA

Portions of this book have appeared in a different form in *The New York Times Magazine* and *Life*.
The excerpts from *The New York Times* that appear on pages 371 and 412 are copyright © 1985/1987 by The New York Times Company. Reprinted by permission.
The author gratefully acknowledges permission from Elvis From Hell to reprint lyrics from "Wife of a Spy," pages 413–418.

ISBN 0 297 79319 5

Printed and Bound in Great Britain by
Butler & Tanner Ltd, Frome and London

This book is, appropriately,
dedicated with gratitude
to loyal friends:
Marcy and Peter Aschkenasy;
Ed Koch; Lindsay McCrum;
and, not least, Dan Wolf.

A NOTE TO THE READER

This is a true story. Every name, incident, date, and conversation is recounted as it occurred. To accomplish this, the author has relied on extensive interviews with members of the Walker family, their friends, federal and military agents, police officials, unpublished letters, confidential government documents, including FBI investigative reports and debriefings, and trial transcripts. A more detailed explanation of the author's method of attribution and a complete chapter-by-chapter listing of his source materials are included in a final note.

CONTENTS

THE WALKER FAMILY
AND THEIR FRIENDS

JOHN A. WALKER, SR. (The Night Walker), the head of the clan, and former disc jockey

MARGARET L. WALKER (née Scaramuzzo), ex-wife of John, Sr.

JOHN A. WALKER, JR. (Johnny, Jaws), their second son and head of the spy ring

BARBARA WALKER (Barb, née Crowley), Johnny's former wife

MARGARET WALKER (Mags, Maggie), Johnny and Barb's oldest daughter

CYNTHIA WALKER, their second daughter

THOMAS WALKER (Tommy), Cynthia's illegitimate son

LAURA WALKER SNYDER, their youngest daughter

PHILIP MARK SNYDER (Mark), her husband

CHRISTOPHER SNYDER (Chris), their son

MICHAEL L. WALKER (Mike), Johnny and Barbara's son

RACHEL WALKER (née Allen), Mike's wife

ARTHUR J. WALKER (Art), Johnny's older brother

RITA C. WALKER (née Fritsch), Art's wife

ANDREA, ERIC, AND CURT, their children

JAMES WALKER (Jimmy), Johnny's younger brother

GARY WALKER, Johnny's half brother

DOROTHY WALKER, Gary's mother and second wife of John, Sr.

JERRY A. WHITWORTH (Jer), Johnny's operative and best friend

BRENDA L. REIS, Jerry's wife

11

JUNE LAUREN ROBINSON (Laurie, née De Wolf), Johnny's partner in Confidential Reports, Inc., detective agency

HENRY ROBINSON, her husband

PAMELA K. CARROLL (P.K.), Johnny's girlfriend

PATSY G. MARSEE (Pat), Johnny's girlfriend

ROBERTA K. PUMA, Johnny's former employee

PHILIP PRINCE (Phil), Johnny's former partner in Confidential Reports

JOSEPH A. LONG (Joey), Johnny's boyhood friend

BILL C. WILKINSON (Billy), Johnny's shipmate and Ku Klux Klan head

DONALD C. CLEVENGER (Don), Johnny's shipmate

DANIEL RIVAS (Dan), sailor and former part-time employee of Confidential Reports, Inc.

SHALEL WAY, psychic and friend of Barbara Walker

MARIE HAMMOND, friend of Laura Walker Snyder

REV. PAT ROBERTSON, founder of the Christian Broadcasting Network and presidential candidate

ALEKSEY GAVRILOVICH TKACHENKO, Soviet embassy official in Washington who was Johnny's KGB postman

All happy families are alike, but an unhappy family is
unhappy after its own fashion.

Tolstoy, *Anna Karenina*

Live the adventure.

United States Navy recruiting slogan

DANCING IN THE DARK

Rachel Walker sat at a table in the back, her tongue playing with the salt along the rim of her margarita, and watched them take the stage. She had come because she needed to hear their song—the one about her. And she had come because there was still one final secret to be revealed. Her surprise, she called it.

The last time she had seen them, fourteen months and a lifetime ago, she had been the one performing. She was wearing her Rambo outfit: camouflage-colored G-string, khaki pasties, and a toy revolver stuck into a red plastic holster strapped loose around her waist. She was supposed to wave an American flag too, but she drew the line; she felt silly enough.

Still, all said, she had a good time. She got into the music, forgetting herself, getting reckless. That seemed to please the crowd at Donald's Go-Go no end; those guys, mostly squids from the Norfolk Navy

Base, could really whoop it up. And that was fine with her. "Pure Fantasy Land," she joked. Where was the harm?

A girl, though, had to watch out for herself. Rachel'd step down from the stage and an awful lot of guys would want to buy her a beer. Of course she knew where they were coming from: Here was this girl, twenty-one, you could see she made a point of staying in shape, and she put on a show like she wanted to hump the whole Seventh Fleet. "Sweet thing," these sailors would say, closing in on her, making their moves, grinning as they just about drooled out the words, "your ship has come in." She couldn't blame them for trying. Except it wasn't that way at all.

Because Rachel was in love.

In fact, the only reason she was dancing at Donald's was to earn some extra money so she could visit her husband, Mike. Just a month ago she had watched him, a surfboard under one arm, a duffle bag under the other, climb the gangplank of USS *Nimitz*. Her twenty-two-year-old yeoman first class. And he'd be off at sea for the next six months; hell, that meant—Rachel, who had a way with numbers, figured—nearly one-third of their entire married life so far would be spent apart! There was no way she could bear that. So she took the gig at Donald's, showing up after her classes at Old Dominion, and dressing up any way they wanted. It was pretty low-life, she admitted, but how else was she going to earn that kind of money? She needed to talk to Mike; she needed to find out what he was really up to. All that mattered was graduating in June, and then hooking up in Italy with her honey. Her showing up in Naples, that would blow Mike away for sure!

Rachel had a policy, then, of steering clear of the customers. She'd be sweet, but kind of distant. That was her rule. She only broke it once—on that April night in 1985. The last time she had met them.

They were sitting at a table, all five of them, and one of them, the one with lots of jet-black hair, called out and asked her to join them for a beer. She could tell straight off they weren't sailors, and maybe that made her feel safer. It certainly made her curious.

"What do you guys do?" she asked, coming over but still not sitting down.

"We're a band."

"Far out," Rachel gushed.

"Yeah," and she noticed that the one with all the dark hair was doing the talking, and that he really was kind of cute. "We're Elvis From Hell."

That clinched it. The name was just too much. It was just the sort of name Mike would really get off on. So she took a seat, and asked where was that beer they'd promised.

A lot of beers later, after listening to the bass player go on about how they were exploring a new sound—neo-Gothic death rock, he called it—Rachel couldn't seem to find a reason not to go back to the band's apartment. Besides, she later offered, part explanation, part apology, she was eager to hear them jam.

They were blasters, all right. Once at their apartment, they didn't waste any time. They plugged in their guitars, turned up the amps, broke into a riff, and Rachel felt as if the ceiling above her head were going to take off for outer space. No way she could sit still. Before she knew it, she was up and rocking.

That's when one of the guys in the band got the idea about the video camera: Get Rachel into her Rambo outfit; have her go through her moves while we're playing. It'd be a dynamite video. Something for MTV.

Rachel was reluctant. It was one thing to dance in a bar full of sailors; it might be something else again to do her number in an apartment with the guys from Elvis From Hell.

But then she thought about Mike.

He had written to her about the tape one of the guys on board had received from his wife. There she was, letting it all hang out in this sheer black negligee; it had really packed the squids in, the night it was shown on the wardroom VCR. Well, Rachel thought, maybe she could give that bimbo in the negligee a run for her money. And maybe it wouldn't hurt to give Mike a taste of what he had to look forward to. Keep him thinking of her.

Anyway, it seemed like a good idea at the time. "Why not?" she finally agreed, and went to change into her costume as the guys set up the camera.

At first it was a lot of fun. Then, and she would later take part of the blame, it started getting out of hand. She was doing her routine same as usual, a lot of bumps and grinds, but now she started thinking about Mike. Spacing out on him. That moved her to another level. Even she had to admit, things were getting kind of raunchy.

"Shake that th-aa-ng, mama!" someone from the band was yelling.

"Hump that wall!" another voice urged.

That's when Rachel realized things had gone too far. She immediately stopped dancing. Right away she got back into her clothes. She wouldn't listen to their attempts to patch things up; she simply hightailed it out of the apartment.

It wasn't until she was back in her own house that it occurred to her she had left without Mike's tape. She was cursing her stupidity when the phone rang. She figured it would be one of the guys from the band, probably the dark-haired one, wanting to know what he should do with the tape. She'd tell him, all right.

"Hello," she barked into the phone.

Only it wasn't Elvis From Hell; it was her father-in-law, Johnny Walker. And all at once she wasn't angry; she was scared.

In an instant, she had this truly terrible vision: Johnny Walker, the renowned private eye who was always sneaking around on some hush-hush case, had been tailing her all night. Now he was calling up to gloat.

But it wasn't that at all. It was just strange.

Johnny wanted to know what type of degree she'd be getting in June. It was after midnight; her father-in-law hadn't called her up in at least four months; and now he was asking about her major. What was this all about?

She had no choice, though, but to play along. A B.A., she told him. With a concentration in biology.

Not marine biology? he asked. She thought he sounded disappointed.

Well, she had taken a course in marine bio, but that wasn't her specialization.

But you've studied marine bio, right?

Yes, she agreed.

And you liked it . . .

Well enough.

Would you consider doing your graduate work in marine bio?

Well . . .

But he interrupted: I mean if I got you into this Navy program I heard about. You'd go to school for free. I know this guy who works in SOSUS development. That's the hydrophone system we use tracking subs. Real interesting stuff. I was bragging about my brainy daughter-in-law and he said she sounded just like what the Navy needed.

Figured you'd fit right in. If necessary, he'd pull a few strings. As a favor to me. How that grab you? You interested?

The last time Johnny Walker, the proud twenty-year veteran, had tried to get her to join the Navy, she just blew it off. That had made things pretty difficult between them. So this time she was more careful. Besides, he was Mike's father. He had a private plane, a houseboat; there certainly was no downside to humoring him.

So Rachel said, It might be just the thing.

Now that seemed to please her father-in-law tremendously. Great, great, he enthused. You'll send me your résumé in the morning?

First thing, she lied.

Then, after reminding her to be sure to drop it off at his office, he hung up.

It wasn't until she was in bed, finally, the long, strange night coming to an end, that she got around to wondering: What was Johnny really up to? What would happen to that tape? And when would she get to see her Mike?

She fell asleep before she had any answers.

Now, fourteen months later, watching Elvis From Hell take the stage, she had all the answers. And they were beyond anything she could have ever imagined.

She now knew that the tape, after being offered to the Christian Broadcasting Network for $50,000, would be confiscated by Agent Love of the FBI.

She now knew that Johnny had telephoned her because a KGB agent in Vienna had instructed him to do so.

She now knew that she would not get to see Mike for another twenty-five years—unless she visited him in prison, or he was pardoned.

And she now knew the Walker family secret: They were a family of spies.

Still, there was one last surprise: hers.

So she sat there, feeling weary, waiting for the band to sing its song. The one called "Wife of a Spy." She hoped it would help her find the final shove of will she needed. Maybe if she could grab on to some anger, she could do this one last thing. No matter how much it hurt. And then she would be free.

PART I

GAMES

I

Johnny Walker, a fifteen-year-old usher, was standing in the aisle of the Roosevelt Theatre when he saw the man leave without his rifle. The movie that night had been *From Here to Eternity,* and Johnny could understand how somebody could get really caught up in it. After the first couple of times he had seen it, he was telling anyone who would listen that it was the greatest damn movie ever to come to Scranton, Pennsylvania. He couldn't wait to tell his best buddy, Joe Long, about the scene on the beach, Burt Lancaster and Deborah Kerr just about doing it. Joey grabbed the free pass right out of his hand. The next afternoon on their paper route, the two boys had a lot of giggles over that. It was sexy, all right.

But now the movie was in its "third smash week," well on its way to breaking all the box-office records for 1953, and Johnny was getting bored. He passed his time in the dark theater playing Tit. The rules of the game—Johnny had both invented and christened the sport; his brothers Art and James along with Joey were his eager competitors—were simple: You got 25 points whenever you could spot some balcony Romeo trying to cop a feel, 50 points if he succeeded, and a bonus of 100 points if your hero actually managed to forage past the fortifications of sweaters, blouses, and whatevers to gain access to the Promised Land. Johnny, always imaginative, never failed to run up a big score. He claimed to see all kinds of things in the dark back rows of the Roosevelt balcony. That was how he had first happened to notice the man with the rifle under his seat.

It was hunting season, the autumn hills surrounding Scranton were running with deer, so it was a pretty common sight to see a coal miner toting a rifle or even a bow as he headed off after a buck for the winter freezer. The man in the balcony must have just come back from a Saturday in the woods; he probably decided taking in the movie at the Roosevelt would be preferable to getting through another evening with his wife. The feature had already started when Johnny watched the hunter take a seat toward the rear of the balcony. He shoved his rifle under his seat as matter-of-factly as if it were an umbrella. In his coat pocket he had a half-pint of something and Johnny saw him take a draw. That was all Johnny needed. He caught him with a stern beam from his flashlight. Its illuminated message: Drinking is prohibited. But the deer hunter was in no mood to be pushed around by a skinny teenager in a red usher's jacket. He just raised the bottle toward Johnny, a toast, really, and took a good long swig. Daring the kid.

Johnny lowered the flashlight instantly. He wasn't going to mess with a coal miner on a Saturday night in Scranton. And that was when the beam got a good look at the rifle. It was a goddamn cannon! More like something you'd use to go after bear or maybe even elephants. It had to be the biggest gun Johnny, who had done some hunting in his time, had ever seen.

The hunter, meanwhile, was getting bolder, just about chugalugging from his bottle. It was a challenge, but Johnny wasn't taking it. He decided this was not the occasion to push his authority. He shut off the flashlight and hurried toward the front of the theater. He convinced himself he had seen some kids smoking in the first row.

By the time the movie was over and the houselights were back on, Johnny had forgotten about the hunter. Then he saw the man heading out the front door. From the way he was weaving, Johnny decided it was a pretty good bet the hunter had drained one bottle and started in on another as a chaser. But there was also something else that Johnny, a born watcher, noticed—the man wasn't packing his cannon.

Johnny quickly went to the balcony. The gun was still under the seat, next to a dead soldier of Jim Beam. He thought about chasing after the man. Or at least taking the rifle to the front booth and leaving it with Mr. Kilcullen, the manager. Except he really didn't think about it too much. Straight off, he knew he had other plans.

He made sure he was the last to leave the theater that night, telling Mr. Kilcullen he'd lock up. When he went upstairs to the four-room apartment his parents had over the movie house, the gun was wrapped in his red usher's jacket.

"Where'd you get that?" asked James. The two brothers shared a bedroom and James, who was two years younger, worshiped Johnny because his brother was simply the coolest person in the world.

"Some hunter was drinking during the movie, so I grabbed him by the collar. Chucked him out. Then he tried to wise off, and I had to deck him. Figured I might as well grab the pussy's gun and teach him a lesson."

"Wow," said James.

Sister Rosario was standing by the blackboard explaining all about hypotenuses, but Johnny Walker wasn't listening. He had failed geometry last year, and figured he would fail it again this year, too. What good was geometry going to do him, anyway? When he turned seventeen he was going to quit school, say so long St. Patrick's High, and become a marine. He'd be off in Korea killing Commies. What did he care what the sister had to say about hypotenuses? Just as long as she wasn't waving that damn yardstick of hers in his face. Let her think I'm just eating it up.

So while the sister droned on, Johnny kept his head in his notebook by writing a note to his buddy Joey. He was eager to tell his friend about the hunter he had beaten up and the rifle he had taken. The date on the gun, Johnny wrote, was 1893. "It is an old army rifel, and only 1 shot. You have to open a *breach* to put the bullet in. Then you pull back the hammer. It's a powerful rifel." He signed the note, "Buzzzzz Saw Walker." And, as he always did, he drew a small saw after his signature.

That afternoon when Johnny and Joe Long picked up the evening edition of the *Scranton Times* to deliver, they decided that on Saturday they'd go up into the hills and see just how powerful that old gun really was.

Johnny spent the entire week planning Saturday's hike. It was the sort of thing he loved to do. In his mind it was no longer a trek through the foothills of Chinchilla, the town a few miles north of Scranton along Route 6. No, General Buzz Saw Walker was mounting a raiding party against a division of Chinese Communists bivouacked in a Korean mountaintop fortress.

His troops—Sergeant Joe Long (Topkick, the general called him) and Private James Walker—rode out on their bicycles first thing Saturday morning, ready for combat. The battle plan had been precisely outlined in blue crayon on a gas-station road map; each soldier was outfitted with camouflage-patterned canteens purchased from a downtown Army and Navy store; the general and his topkick communicated by a pair of walkie-talkies that Johnny had ordered last Christmas from an ad in a comic book; and strapped over the commanding officer's shoulder was a weapon with the date 1893 on its barrel. A bazooka, Buzz Saw told his men.

By midafternoon the assault on the hill was over. It had been a glorious victory for the Marines. The general, by his own count, had engaged in hand-to-hand combat at least a dozen times with the Commies, leaving a trail of broken Chinese arms and necks as he moved, undaunted, up the hill. As for the bazooka, it was a ferocious weapon. Not only did it actually fire, but it also was dazzlingly accurate. Every time Buzz Saw took aim at a rock or a tree, he claimed he hit a Red tank broadside. And that was pissing Joey Long off.

"You missed by a mile," Joey would complain, certain Johnny had not even come close to the tree he was aiming at.

"Like hell. Dead center perfect," said the general.

"Look, let's just check out the tree . . ."

"Hey, ask James if you don't believe me."

And James, loyal to his commanding officer, reported, "Course he hit it, Joey, Johnny's a great shot."

There was genuine dissension in the ranks by the time the troops were heading down the hill. The general and his sergeant were barely talking when James spotted the deer.

"Look at that. Off by the rocks," said James, careful to keep his excitement muffled.

About a hundred, maybe a hundred and fifty yards away, the boys saw a deer. It was a fine big buck just standing there.

"Let me take a shot," Joey whispered to his friend. "I can nail him."

But Johnny shook his head, brought the rifle off his shoulder, and took aim. The first shot was wide, and the buck was off and running. In his excitement, it took awhile to reload. The buck was deep into the woods when he got off his second shot.

"I wounded him," said Johnny confidently.

"Like hell you did," said Joey. He would have liked to have taken the meat home to his parents.

"I'm telling you I hit him," Johnny said. "I didn't have to work tonight, I'd trail that deer and show you."

The boys were still arguing as they rode their bikes into town. They stopped at Green Ridge Corners. The Roosevelt Theatre was there, the Walker apartment right above it. Joey got off his bike to give Johnny back his walkie-talkie. It was getting dark. It wouldn't be long before the lights on the marquee would go on.

"You're a rotten liar, John Walker," Joey shouted.

Johnny shouted back, "Am not. I hit that deer."

The two boys must have been going at it at the top of their lungs for a while when a man opened up the window above them.

"Goddamn you, you little bastard. I hear you raise your voice one more time, I'm gonna kick your ass again."

"I shot a deer today," Johnny boasted to the man leaning out the window.

His father, John Walker, Sr., hurled a bottle of whiskey at the boy. Johnny got his hands up quickly to protect his head, so the bottle bounced off his arm and crashed against the sidewalk.

John Walker, Sr., was still shouting something from the window as the two boys ran down the block.

Joey was shaking. But Johnny looked like he was going to cry.

"I'm gonna get that bastard someday," Johnny finally managed to say.

"Hey," said Joey putting an arm around his buddy, "what you complaining about, Buzz? You shot a deer today."

"I did," said Johnny Walker. "And that's more than my father's ever done."

• • •

During the last days of World War II, a war he spent fighting personal battles, John Walker, Sr., came home. He returned to Scranton, the town on the Lackawanna River where he was born and where he had met his wife. He came home because everything else had failed. He was out of work, broke, and had three sons to support. He was hoping maybe he'd get a break and an old buddy would give him a job playing piano somewhere. After six months, he settled for being manager at the Roosevelt Theatre.

It took another three years, but he finally got his break. A gig working the late slot on "The Voice of Scranton," radio station WARM. "Johnny Walker the Night Walker" he called himself, and he spun records for insomniacs and people working the lobster shift. Lots of Rosemary Clooney, Bing Crosby, Johnnie Ray. When he thought he could get away with it, he'd stick in some jazz and hope the squares wouldn't complain. Sometimes he'd fool around on the studio organ, ripping through a hot, improv verse of, say, a Doris Day song. Then he'd break straight into the record. It was a good gimmick, and the Night Walker had quite a following. "Johnny had the gift of gab, for certain," remembers George Gilbert who also worked at WARM in the early 1950s. "He had a smooth, smooth voice. A radio voice." He was even earning $85 a week. Yet by the time he threw the bottle at his son in the fall of 1953, John Walker, Sr.'s, life was falling apart at the seams. Again.

Many marriages are inspired by a glimpse of a larger life and then, as this youthful ideal is knocked down by circumstance, disappointment turns them nasty and unforgiving; and so it had gone with John Walker and Margaret Scaramuzzo. John was the oldest child of a large family of Irish immigrants who had wound up in Pennsylvania mining coal. Two generations later, John wanted something grander. He was playing piano in the roadhouses around Scranton when he met Margaret. She had grown up with seven brothers and sisters in a large white house on Allen Street. It was a home where Italian was spoken at the dinner table and a picture of the pope hung above the living room sofa. When the Scaramuzzo family wasn't in church, it seemed as if they were always at the family store, and, together, they made the Boston Fish Market on Penn Avenue in downtown Scranton prosper. Each of the four daughters would bring a $2,000 dowry with her to the altar; there would also be a place for their husbands in the family business. But by eighteen Margaret, with her jet-black hair, her church choir voice, and a hard laugh that (as it still would two generations later) ricocheted through conversations, felt there was something more ahead of her than a future in a fish market. She had the inkling that there was a whole other America beyond the foothills surrounding Scranton. When she met John Walker, she also met, for the first time, a fellow believer. He shared her faith: She'd be a famous vocalist, another Rosemary Clooney; he'd be the leader of a band of renown. Together they planned their escape.

For a while it worked. He got a job in Washington working for Warner Brothers. He was only a salesman, but at least it was, he convinced himself, show business. Most of the week was spent on the road, selling Warner films to movie houses throughout the South. On weekends he would try to make it home to his wife. But after a few years of driving his Ford down dusty southern roads, John Walker had traveled to some grim conclusions: Margaret would sing only in church; and, more painful, his band would play only in make-believe ballrooms. His show business career had peaked. Now when he returned to his new home in Richmond, Virginia, the house where Margaret was raising his three young sons—Arthur, John, Jr., and James —the journey only reinforced his woeful sense of losing something he had never really had. Regret led him to alcohol; and alcohol led him into despair. From there things got rotten.

It became the sort of household where the children quickly learned to stay out of their father's way. John, Sr., always seemed to have a drink in his hand and a chip on his shoulder. Anytime he decided the boys were wising off, he'd punch them. If he went after them with his belt, the welts would be visible for days. If he disappeared for a night and Margaret dared to call him on it, he wouldn't think twice about knocking her around, too.

Things go so bad that after one argument, Margaret took an overdose of sleeping pills. John, Sr., though, had been drinking, so maybe that was why he wasn't too upset. He just told Art, eight, and John, Jr., six, "Better keep her awake or she'll die." Then he left the house. The boys fed her coffee and kept her walking around the bedroom and she pulled through.

A year later, in 1944, the family wasn't so lucky. John, Sr., was heading down to Richmond on U.S. 1 from the Warner office in Washington when his Ford slammed head-on into a car pulling onto the highway. There was so much blood that the cops who rescued him from his ruined car were certain he wasn't going to pull through. But the accident didn't kill him. The lawsuit might just as well have.

There was some talk that John had been drinking before the collision on U.S. 1, and when the suit was settled John's savings were wiped out. The house in Richmond was sold off, too. Somehow, he lost the job at Warner's. John tried driving a cab for a while, but that didn't work out either. Drinking had become a full-time occupation.

It was at that point, cornered, that Margaret took the children and returned to Scranton. John followed. For a while the boys were farmed out to relatives, each to a different Scaramuzzo aunt. During the Christmas season, Margaret worked at a department store taking photographs of the kids sitting on Santa's knee. By Easter, however, John, Sr., got the job at the Roosevelt Theatre. He rented the apartment above the movie house. It was small, but the family now moved back together. He also joined Alcoholics Anonymous and, in time, found the will to confront his responsibilities. John, Sr., was soon feeling ambitious. That's how he wound up being Johnny Walker the Night Walker on WARM.

But all that fell apart, too. He started drinking again, smacking the boys around. Margaret was certain there were other women. When a hospital bill came in the mail for maternity care, she tore into him, but she paid it. John, Sr., just laughed at her. And that's pretty much the way things had gotten to be by the time he threw the bottle down at his son.

Late at night in his bedroom above the Roosevelt Theatre, Johnny would lay in bed with a Bakelite microphone near his pillow. A cord stretched from the microphone to the transmitter on a table near the window. The diffused, orangish glow from the candescent tubes was the only light in the room. Johnny had built the radio from a kit he had purchased with his paper route money. He had even climbed up on the roof and erected an antenna with a tall mast. When the weather was good, he could pick up stations as far away as Cleveland. Late at night, though, he would just tune in WARM, "The Voice of Scranton." He kept the volume low, only a whisper, so that James, in his bed across the room, could sleep. But while James kept his eyes closed, many nights he lay there awake in the dark, another listener. He, too, heard his father's easy, sensible voice, his radio voice, reaching across the night. And then he would hear another voice, closer, but still soft. A solemn child's voice whispering into a Bakelite microphone over and over again: "And this is Johnny Walker *Junior* the *real* Night Walker. . . ."

Art was the first to leave. When Johnny was a junior at St. Patrick's, his older brother decided he had had enough. Not that Art had ever made a big thing of his predicament. To the gang at Pantages, the malt shop on Main Avenue where the kids huddled in packs around the jukebox, he was simply happy-go-lucky Art, everyone's favorite. You had to like him: letterman in football and baseball, second trumpet in the band, lead actor in the school plays, altar boy, B plus average. Rita Clare Fritsch, the daughter of the night supervisor in the main post office, and a real looker, was his steady. But in the middle of his first year at the University of Scranton, Art, nineteen, told his friends he was quitting school to join the Navy. Everyone was surprised.

"Thought you were going to get your degree. Go to law school and everything," his old St. Patrick's classmate Vince Talberi challenged. Vince had use of his family's Olds 88 and Art and Rita would double with him and his girl just about every weekend.

Art didn't answer him straightaway. It was his way—his "big brother routine," James called it—to keep things inside. Years later after extraordinary circumstances had cost him his right to mysteries, Art would finally share a measure of what he had gone through: "My dad would come home, and I'd be the one who would have to go down and take the flak. The two younger ones would stay up there hiding and I would have to take whatever flak a drunk wants to give you, a whipping or whatever. I worked hard at masking emotions. . . ."

In those days in Scranton, Art still felt it was his responsibility to keep things under control. He told Vince, "I'm joining the Navy to see the world."

The world he was fleeing would remain his secret. He hoped.

• • •

Not long after Art had enlisted, Joey Long quit school, too, and
joined the Marines. Johnny Walker, always lonely, never the sort to
hang out at Pantages, no varsity letterman, and certainly not a student, now found himself completely alone.

The sixteen-year-old chased after his big brother and best friend
with letters. For a while he was writing three, four letters a week. A
typical letter, written on Roosevelt Theatre stationery, would begin:

Dear Joe,
  I just wrote a letter to Art, so I thought I would write you one
too . . .

St. Patrick's was the sort of institution that when anybody acted
up, Mother Vincent, the principal, would douse the offender with a
bucket of holy water and announce to the class, "The devil is in the
room." Johnny hated the place.

"Dear Joe"—he wrote in his loopy adolescent script—
"School is getting harder every year. I wish I could be at Parris
Island with you. Do you miss me?"

Mr. Kilcullen promoted Johnny to head usher at the Roosevelt. He
was making $24 a week. But with Art and Joey gone, the job had lost
a lot of its appeal.

" 'Powder Ridge' "—he reported in another letter to Private
Joseph Long—"is the movie tonight. We had a good picture in
Sunday and Monday. 'Stalag 17' was the name of it. It's about
prisoners of war (POW) in Germany (World war 2). Stalag means
prison camp in German. There is no one to use my passes in the
movie now."

Art always had his steady girl, Rita. Johnny, a short, skinny kid,
combed his thin black hair into a pompadour and made it a point to

smile a lot. He bought an old jalopy and played with the engine, he was good at that sort of thing, and then gave it a new coat of blue paint. The car really shined. He called it "The Blue Streak." Johnny wanted a girl, too.

"I got a new girl friend, her name is Marilyn. In your next letter tell me if you want me to send you a sexie one. You know."

—and just to make sure, the seventeen-year-old schoolboy decorated his letter to his buddy in the Marines with a sketch of a naked woman shaped like an hourglass.

"I got another girl friend"—he announced in a quick letter scribbled in pencil a month later. "She is from Mississippi, a southern state. The only thing is, she went back about a week ago, so I'm looking for another one."

"I don't remember"—began another note to Parris Island— "if I told you about my new girl friend or not, so I will tell you again. She is *very pritty,* has a nice face, and is *very sexie.*"

With his older brother and best friend gone, though, Johnny mostly kept to himself. He went to work at the Roosevelt or stayed in his room listening to the radio he had built. Some nights he drove The Blue Streak around looking for kids. But there was only James to lead on his hikes. And there was no one really to play his games.

"Art will *not* be home for Christmas. I won't have anyone to help with the trains. If you're home in time you can help me."

All he could hope to do was to share through the mail some of the secret world he was busy inventing.

"Well Joe boy, I have to go now. Don't show this top secret letter to anyone."

· · ·

It was only a matter of time before Johnny started acting out some
of his riskier fictions. On the night of May 27, 1955, opportunity
nudged him forward; and one of his games finally turned dangerous.

He was killing time that spring night at a candy store a few blocks
from his home, on Jackson Street, when the talk turned to cars. No
wheels in Scranton were faster than The Blue Streak, Johnny boasted.
Talk is cheap, answered a guy the kids called "Goat." Goat didn't go
to St. Patrick's, and he had a tough guy's rep, a real "rock." Johnny
had seen him around and had always been impressed. So before he
knew it, he and Goat were in The Blue Streak tooling it to Pittston, a
town about ten miles south of Scranton. Goat said he knew a girl
there.

But the girl wasn't home; or maybe there wasn't even a girl at all.
Goat had other things on his mind. The Blue Streak was pushing
eighty as Goat told his new friend about all the stores he had been
boosting. In the past two weeks alone, he claimed, he had pulled down
quite a score: $577, to be exact.

Bet you don't make that much in two, three months working the
Roosevelt, said Goat.

For certain, said Johnny.

Well, challenged Goat, you up for it?

Five hundred and seventy-seven dollars is an awful lot of money,
Johnny was thinking. And Goat kept at it. He taunted, You chicken?

So Johnny, without much consideration, fell into the next act of his
life. They were heading back toward Scranton when they stopped and
broke into an Esso station on Main Street in Duryea. The damn place,
though, had been closed up real tight for the night. There was nothing
to grab. The pair rode off empty-handed.

At that point, back behind the wheel of The Blue Streak and speeding down Route 6, Johnny knew he could call it quits. He had shown
Goat he had the balls. But climbing scared-assed through the window
of that dark Esso station—and this was something he would never
forget; there was many a late night ten and even twenty years later
when he, getting kind of grave, almost bashful, would share this indelible moment of self-awareness with his drinking buddies—Johnny
Walker had discovered something: He dug it. No way he was going to
stop now.

They were passing Marianelli's Esso station in Old Forge when they
decided to go for another score. They jimmied a door this time and

found $3 lying around. On the way out, they grabbed two tires to throw into the backseat of The Blue Streak. Down the block from the service station was old man Marianelli's used car lot. They were on a roll, so they figured why not. They grabbed whatever they could find —four quarts of oil, six cans of car polish. And then they struck pay dirt—a tin money box.

Except the money box only had business papers inside. Cursing, they gave the papers to the wind and drove The Blue Streak on toward Scranton.

The game, though, was getting good. When they drove by Cuozzo & Gavigan's, the clothing store on North Main, there was nothing to discuss. The Durkan Funeral Home had a lot next door and Johnny pulled in.

The front door of the clothing store was locked tight, and even though it was getting near midnight, the boys figured you might attract some attention jimmying a door right out on North Main. In the back alley, though, there was a ventilator that Johnny found he could pry loose. He climbed in, Goat followed. It was dark and spooky. But they kept on crawling, on hands and knees in the pitch black, a tight space, until they entered a room. One of the boys quickly hit the light —Christ, they were in the john. And when they tried to open the john door, they got nowhere. It was too thick to jimmy; after a lot of pushing and shoving, they realized it must be barricaded on the other side. They had no choice but to call it a night.

Johnny was crawling back out of the ventilator when, all of a sudden, he stumbled. His foot kicked a board, and the board flew off into the metal grate, which went crashing to the concrete sidewalk. It was a hell of a racket. Both boys jumped to the ground running.

But just as they were coming out of the dark alley, Officer William Shygelski spotted them. He had been heading up North Main to check out the noise.

Stop! the officer ordered.

Goat darted back into the shadows. Johnny kept on going. He took a running jump and started over the wooden fence surrounding the funeral home parking lot.

Stop! the officer repeated.

When Johnny didn't, the officer fired at him. Johnny was scared stiff, but he didn't look back. He didn't look at the officer and he didn't look for Goat. He made it over the fence and ran for all he was worth to his car. In a flash The Blue Streak tear-assed out of the parking lot.

Officer Shygelski saw the car take off and, revolver waving in the air, ran into the middle of North Main and stopped a passing car.

Follow that blue car, the officer told the driver.

Johnny, meanwhile, thought he had it beat. No cop on foot was any match for The Blue Streak. Johnny, nice and cool, the model citizen, had pulled up to a red light at the corner of North Hyde Park and Jackson. He figured—or so he would say when he told the story years later—that all in all it was a pretty wild night. Then, with no warning, he saw this crazy cop get out of the car behind him. Of course The Blue Streak started to burn rubber. Next Johnny, watching the whole incredible thing in his rearview mirror as if it were the big screen at the Roosevelt, saw the cop drop to one knee, take aim, and try to put one straight into his gas tank. The goddamn bullet went right through his rear bumper! Johnny, now genuinely scared, had his foot flat against the pedal. The Blue Streak was really moving. But, more amazing, the cop wasn't giving up.

The officer jumped back into the car he had commandeered and told the driver to give chase. Johnny was watching it all happen, but he wasn't believing it. It was better, he would someday joke, than any movie. And he was the star.

The Blue Streak hightailed it up Washburn, and the cop followed. Johnny cut over to Keyser, and he still couldn't lose him. But Johnny had a plan—he was heading for the highway. Nobody was going to catch The Blue Streak on the open road. And by the time he was running down the Morgan Highway, the needle on The Blue Streak edging past 90, there wasn't another car in sight.

It was just about then, though, that Johnny Walker realized he could have been killed—that crazy cop was firing real bullets!—over $3, four quarts of oil, and a couple of tires. All he could think about was why the hell was that cop making such a big deal? What was the harm?

He drove all night—"on the lam," he'd tell his buddy Joey—and found himself in Williamsport, a city about 110 miles southwest of Scranton.

It was in Williamsport that, while getting coffee in a diner, Johnny Walker, the seventeen-year-old fugitive, became friendly with a twenty-two-year-old housepainter. Johnny began to tell him some story about how he was in town, passing through on his way to his grandmother's. It didn't take Johnny long to weave the yarn together. By the time the coffee cup was drained, Johnny found that even he was believing it. And why not? He was always good at making things up, stretching reality.

Not that the painter cared. People, Johnny was learning, are easy to con. You want to park your car in my driveway and get some rest, the painter suggested to him, be my guest. For the next two nights Johnny kept The Blue Streak in the painter's driveway and slept inside the car. On the third night, the painter told him he could sack out on the living room couch. Johnny, grateful, gave him the two tires he had stolen from the Esso station in Old Forge. "Fair's fair," Johnny told him.

It was during his days in Williamsport, on his own in a strange town, that Johnny allowed his imagination to embroider circumstance. In his mind, his escape became something he had seen Jimmy Cagney pull off on the screen at the Roosevelt. He began to cultivate his self-image as Buzz Saw Walker, "Public Enemy Number One." Let the police come looking; he gave the dumb coppers the slip once, he could do it again. No problem. In fact, he felt just fine. And it was in this mood, full of his imagined self, that he made his big mistake—Johnny called a girl he knew in Scranton. Don't worry, he told her. Everything is great. And if you ever need me, he added in what he was convinced was the perfect touch, you can write care of a greeting card shop in Williamsport. He gave her the address.

The next day, June 1, 1955, the Williamsport police arrested John Walker, Jr., in front of the greeting card store. The girl had ratted on him. Two days later, after Johnny was returned to Scranton and locked in the county jail, it didn't take him long to give the police Goat's name.

It was another lesson that would last him a lifetime: Betrayal is a very repetitious habit.

"I can't see anything in favor of any one of you," Judge Otto P. Robinson told the two youths when they stood before him in Juvenile Court three weeks later. "You are just two crooks. The only thing in favor of you is that this is the first time you have been in court." The judge then sentenced John Walker and Goat to indefinite terms at the state correctional institution at Camp Hill.

But during the morning's recess Arthur Walker met with Judge Robinson in his chambers. Art, twenty, already a submariner, was in his Navy whites. He was erect, clean-cut, confident: a recruiting advertisement come to life. He told the judge what it was like growing up in the apartment above the Roosevelt Theatre. He also made a suggestion: Don't send Johnny to Camp Hill; let him join the Navy. The Navy will straighten him out.

That afternoon the judge brought the two seventeen-year-old boys back into the courtroom and he announced that he had decided to put them on probation.

"In a year or so," he lectured, "you boys will be in the service and when you go in there they will ask you if you have a criminal record. . . . The officer for the Army will ask us about you and we would like to say, 'Yes, they were in a little trouble but since then they were able to straighten themselves out.' The Army doesn't want crooks."

And the judge, concluding, gave them some advice: "This is a chance for you fellows to go straight. Don't make another mistake. You've got to be honest or you go to Camp Hill. Learn the Ten Commandments and obey them and you won't be in further trouble."

Johnny Walker, it seemed, learned another lesson, a schemer's Golden Rule: No jam was so tight that with a little shrewd prying, you couldn't slide your way out of it. A smart guy can always find an angle.

The waiting was the hardest part. Johnny did not return to St. Patrick's for his senior year and he also refused to go back, even for a month or two, to his job at the Roosevelt. That part of his life was over, he announced. He would simply wait. "I have decided not to get a job, just be a bum," he wrote Joey that July. So he spent the summer of '55 waiting first to turn eighteen, and then waiting for his naval enlistment papers to go through. He was bristling to get out of Scranton and into the world.

But his father, John Walker, Sr., beat him to it. Just days after his son's eighteenth birthday the Night Walker didn't show up for work. He didn't say anything to the radio station, or his wife, or his sons.

He left no note, and certainly no money. He just drove off on a fine August morning and never came back. It really wasn't much of a surprise when, after a while, the family heard some talk that a young woman, Dottie, had gone away with him.

Finally, ten weeks after his eighteenth birthday, on October 25, 1955, Johnny was on a bus heading to the U.S. Naval Training Center at Bainbridge, Maryland. As the bus sped down the highway, quick glimpses of the Pennsylvania countryside reflecting through his window like so many bad memories, he could not help wishing the bus would hurry up and get there, and he could begin his life as a man.

2

Barbara Crowley was nineteen years old and two months pregnant, but that wasn't the only reason she was in a hurry to marry Johnny Walker. She was afraid that if he kept dragging out this . . . courtship, he'd learn the truth. And then she'd lose her sailor forever.

It wasn't that Barbara had lied. Or, at least that was what she kept telling herself. It was just that maybe she had given Johnny the wrong impression. She knew too well how he could get, high-hatting people, cutting them all the time. So there was no way she was going to tell him the truth about her family. No way, because the reality left her ashamed and feeling dirty. The way sex sometimes leaves you dirty.

She had come of age in the sticks, more a cabin than a home. Things were very close, everybody always on top of each other. There were seven kids and no money. Shoes and clothes were passed down, from sister to sister. There were a lot of peanut butter and jelly sandwiches for dinner. Besides, the long Maine winter can be a heartache, no matter what.

When Barbara was nine, her father had died. That's when they

moved from East Boston to Mercer up in Maine and a hard life started
to get bad. Her mother had always been drinking, the kids had gotten
used to that as best they could, but now there was the partying.

There were lots of strange men hanging around. Lots of bottles, lots
of giggles. Other sounds, too. One time Barbara came home and found
her mother and some guy going at in the living room. They didn't stop
when she came in.

One of her sisters was like that, too. She'd pick up a fellow and
bring him to her bedroom, and Barbara, sleeping across the room,
would hear the bedsprings wheezing to beat the band for a good part
of the night. Sometimes Barbara, curious, would take a peek. She got
quite an eyeful. Or sometimes when she was sleeping, she'd get the
feeling there was someone's "date" watching her real close. Once,
asleep but feeling funny, she bolted out of a dream only to see some
guy scooting off her bed and dashing out of the room. Or perhaps it
was just part of the dream.

She must have been ten when her mother married a man everyone
called Smitty. He liked to hug the girls a lot. Maybe too much. Not
like a daddy, Barbara felt. Except he made a big point that the kids
should call him "Dad." Barbara refused; even as a child she had a
way of digging in her heels. You call me Dad, he ordered for what he
was determined would be the last time. But Barbara wouldn't give in.
So he slapped her. Smitty, she taunted back. So he just kept on belting
and belting and belting her. She missed two days of school, she took
that much of a beating. But she never called him "Dad."

Barbara always blamed Smitty for what she called "getting everyone's juices going." After Smitty moved in, a cousin of hers started
getting fresh. This cousin gave one of her sisters in particular a real
hard time. And Barbara knew this wasn't right.

Barbara's grandfather was a full-blooded Cherokee. People always
said there was never any doubt where Barb got her looks: She had his
jet-black hair, thick and shiny like a cat's, and Cherokee cheekbones,
sharp and high. He lived a couple of miles up the road, but she would
simply cut through the woods and get there in nothing flat.

He had spent a lifetime as a carpenter, and was good and careful
with his hands. He liked things done right. When he was seventy-two,

he happened to glance at one of Barb's algebra books and became curious. He went to the library, borrowed a book, and darned if he didn't teach himself algebra. People also said there was never any doubt where Barb got her brains, too.

The two of them would talk and talk, jawing on just about everything. It was her granddad who told her, "The only thing they can't take away from you is your pride." He also told her, "You find yourself a man, then you stick by him, little girl."

He lived till he was ninety-two, and while Barbara never got to see him very much after she moved away from home, she always said, especially after a drink or two, that there wasn't a day went by when she didn't think of her granddad; or about the things he had taught her.

She had just finished the ninth grade, only fifteen years old, but Barbara looked like a woman. Her cousins noticed the changes, too. Things were becoming tense. She knew the situation would only get harder; there was no way in the world she was going to put up with any of that stuff. So Barbara left. She didn't run away because, she would always make a point of saying, running away means there was somebody who wanted you to stay. She decided on Boston because it was all her experiences, at the time, had the imagination to desire: the capital of the world beyond the woods.

Barbara took a job in a department store, selling blouses. It was quite an education to see people spending that kind of money merely to look pretty. She didn't get jealous, really. Still, she did think about it, all those people spending all that money. She passed a lot of nights doing a lot of wishful thinking. That kind of thought is bound to breed ambition.

Yet, it was Barbara's roommate who really convinced her not just of the necessity, but also of the possibility of her life's becoming more than it had been. This girl was the first person Barbara encountered who had attended, for a while at least, college. She was also the first Jew Barbara ever got to know. Barbara, who took her Catholicism seriously, had grown up feeling Jews were different. But, she was to learn, not in the ways she had anticipated.

On Friday nights, her roommate's parents would have the girls over for dinner. They sat around a dining room table covered with a white, lacy spread. The dishes were a rose-patterned china and the knives and forks were real silver, heavy in your hand. Platters were filled with food, chicken usually, or maybe a roast. There was always plenty, and everyone seemed genuinely glad the more you ate.

The real discovery around the dinner table, though, was the conversation. Barbara didn't want to make too big a deal out of it, but she had never heard anything like this before: parents actually talking to their children, caring about them, people interested in each other. Things up north had just been nasty and loud.

Barbara, for the first time, got a glimpse of how comforting family life could be. Best of all, this girl and her family really took to Barbara, watching out for her, caring about her. It was natural, then, that Barbara returned their affection, treating them as if they were her parents. And in a way, she reasoned, they just about were. Especially since, she decided, she was more or less an orphan. In time, it became a convenient reality when asked about her folks to tell people, or at least give the impression, that her roommate's parents were really her own.

So when Barbara Crowley happened to go to a church dance and met a twenty-year-old sailor with a real sly smile, it was only natural that she described her family home as a big yellow clapboard house with a picket fence in Dedham. And by the time this Johnny Walker was getting really interested in her, when they were going roller skating on the weekends and ending up more often than not in the backseat of his Pontiac, when both of them were telling everyone it was "love at first sight," she realized things had gotten out of hand. The truth had been pretty well tattered. Except it was too late to do anything about it because Johnny Walker had fallen for it. There was no way of knowing how he'd feel after he learned the truth. Still, Barbara must have had an inkling.

Years later, decades after finally stumbling upon the truth about the Crowleys, John Walker would remain bitter. It stuck in his craw, even after circumstances had caught up with him. Sentenced to be in a prison cell for the rest of his life, Johnny, undeterred and unrepentant, would go on instead about how Barbara had lied to him. "Real shock!" he wrote. "Sick and disgusting family which would have prevented their relationship to have grown if JW knew them."

By that time, though, Barbara figured her lie was pretty meager in the scheme of things. Besides, all she had really done was invent a cover. The first of many.

3

It was one of the ironies of desire that while Barbara was stretching the truth a bit, so was her sailor. Johnny Walker, despite everything he was confiding to Barbara in the backseat of his Pontiac, figured there was no way he, a frisky twenty-year-old, was ever going to get married. Or, for that matter, even stay in the Navy.

At first, Johnny really took to the Navy. After what he had gone through in Scranton, the Bainbridge Training Center in Maryland might just as well have been summer camp.

"Well old pal," he wrote to Joe Long in October of 1955, "I have been in the Navy 1 week. I'm having the greatest time of my life. You were an idiot to join the Marines. This Navy boot camp is soft as hell. I was working harder in civilian life . . . The damn chow is better than at home. I have more free time than at home."

The competition with the other sailors seemed to spur Johnny on. It wasn't like St. Patrick's where doing well meant learning things, useless, obscure things, from books. At Bainbridge, a sailor could go to the head of the class simply by playing the sort of games Johnny had always played with Joey. For the first time, Johnny became familiar with success. He was really quite proud of himself.

"Yesterday I was made chief semaphore sender of the company," he informed his Marine Corps buddy, archly replacing the Roosevelt Theatre letterhead with stationery imprinted with the battleship *Missouri* blasting its 16-inch guns. "Semaphore is sending signals with those little flags. You must know what it is. Well they made me an instructor on it. When I see you, I'll teach you how.

"I already told you that I was second platoon leader, and on the staff. The staff carries cutlasses. So watch your ass when you come down, or I'll stab you."

Johnny was also busy taking all kinds of tests at Bainbridge. He scored particularly high for electronic aptitude. Maybe it was just that he had been putting together radios since he was twelve, so he had a real jump on most of the other sailors. The truth was, though, he genuinely enjoyed fooling around with all the equipment. Getting the various wires and tubes in the right place, he had told his brother James, was like solving a mystery.

The only problem seemed to be his eyes. The Navy, after checking his body out from stem to stern, had told him he had weak eyes. They wanted him to wear glasses. Johnny hated the heavy black-framed glasses they gave him. He told people they made him look queer, not at all like a sailor. Even if he didn't wear them much, he realized the Navy had him listed for now and forever in its records as a four-eyes. He knew that could limit his future assignments. Worst of all, it could very well interfere with his, as he called it, "master plan."

Still, it was a confident Johnny Walker who wrote to Joey as boot camp was ending: "I have been doing pretty good in my tests so far, and I might get a good school out of this Navy."

The Navy sent Johnny in the winter of 1956 to the Naval Schools Command in Norfolk, Virginia, which was just what he wanted: He was going to be trained as a radioman. In those days at Radio A school, the electronic technology was rather basic. Most ship-to-shore communication was done by high-frequency transmissions and Johnny, who boasted to his instructors that he had been playing around with radios forever, had no trouble mastering HF. The rest of the course was dull, the sort of skills that take a good deal of practice and only a little talent: learning to type, sending Morse, and getting down the official shorthand for Navy message traffic. Yet, Johnny was very gung ho and wound up being the second-fastest typist in his class. But that was something he didn't brag about; typing, he would explain years later to a teasing friend who watched amazed as his fingers darted about the keyboard, was like packing a gun in your back pocket—something a man doesn't advertise, but something that sure comes in handy when you need it. (And all the friend could think was only Johnny Walker could equate packing a piece with knowing how to type. How very Johnny.)

Another subject that the instructors spent a lot of hours on in A school was security. Nothing too technical; the special responsibilities that came with a knowledge of cryptography and top secret cipher machines would be disclosed only to those trainees who climbed up the rating pipeline. But the drill for E-1 was still substantially the same for the "tape apes" who wore E-9 patches: Loose lips sink ships.

A radioman, went the standard lecture, is the first on the ship to know what's going on. He reads all the messages that go in and out. If the sailors on board want to learn where the ship's going and when the ship's coming into port, the one they ask is the radioman because he's up on all the news. The radio room, the trainees are told, is a repository of secrets. The tape ape's job, his sworn duty, is to keep it that way.

Not all the training in Norfolk was in the classroom. Johnny started hanging out in the squid bars in Ocean View. A guy could always buy a good time. So Johnny learned to pay for sex. And he learned to get his money's worth.

Now when he wrote to his buddy in the Marines, it was as the swaggering sailor: "Hey, shit, I'll be home for Christmas for a 14 day leave. . . . See if you can get a leave at the same time so I can take you on a good old Navy liberty. Scranton better watch out because I'm going to wreck that town."

On that leave he got to know a nursing student he had first met in church. She had long red hair and, as Johnny told Art, "she sure knew how to fill a sweater.'' They spent a lot of time together, but on New Year's Eve she called and said she had the flu. Maybe it was true, but after that Johnny managed to spend the remainder of his leave without their paths crossing.

When he returned to Norfolk, he wrote Joey about her:

. . . I was going with a student nurse from the state for a while there. I met her on my last 15 day leave. We were going pretty strong for a while, but she got too damn serious so I ended it. I sure hated to give that stuff up, those nurses are pretty hot stuff you know. As she used to say, she knew what made me tick.

The letters sent while Johnny was still at radio school were all typed in big capital letters as if they were official naval communications. Joey Long got a real kick out of that, and he was pretty impressed by how well his buddy had learned to type. But what really caught his eye and set him thinking was the signature. No more ''Buzz Saw Walker.'' No more cartoon sketches of menacing blades. These days the letters were signed a terse (and unfamiliar; Johnny couldn't help testing out new identities) ''Jack.'' Everybody's growing up, Joey decided.

Now that A school was coming to a close and Johnny, nearly twenty, was certain he had become both a sailor and a man, his intention was to get on with his ''master plan''—submarines.

Part of the allure of submarines, even the old diesel subs, was that they were special. They weren't called ships like the other vessels in the Navy; subs were boats. And their crews, the men who wore the arm patches showing a boat's prow and conning tower flanked by leaping dolphins, weren't merely sailors; they were known throughout the service as submariners. It was a distinction that wasn't easily earned: A man had to have a good deal of guts and a bit of reckless-ness, too, to go down 400 feet beneath the sea. Johnny, who liked his share of romance and danger, was intrigued. It was the sort of rep he wouldn't mind bringing into a bar.

The other attraction—and this is what got him thinking about subs as soon as he finished boot camp—was that his brother Art was already a submariner. In fact, Art, now married to Rita for almost a year, had the look of what sailors call a "hot runner"—someone who slides up the rating's pole. Boosted by impressive evaluations from his executive officers, Art seemed to have quite a future in subs. Straight out of Bainbridge, the Navy had sent him to Fleet Sonar School in Key West, Florida, and then to Submarine School in New London, Connecticut. By the time Johnny was finishing up at Norfolk, Art had served on SSN *Torsk,* a diesel sub, for nearly two years. Just twenty-three, he had become the boat's senior sonarman. And Lieutenant Commander Siple, the *Torsk*'s CO, gave him the sort of evaluation that was bound to lead to more opportunities: "Walker is considered to be an excellent candidate for officer status."

The way Johnny figured it, there was no reason his older brother should be the only one grabbing the glory in the Walker family. Besides, if Art could make it, then it'd be just as easy for Johnny. Maybe easier: Having a brother in subs—and a hot runner at that—should help.

So when Johnny filled out his "dream sheet"—the Navy has sailors list their preferences for future assignments—he put in for subs. He wanted to be a radioman beneath the sea.

Johnny got his E-1 patch, but he didn't get his dolphins. The detailer at the Command Office read the naval surgeon's note about John Walker, Jr.'s, weak eyes on the trainee's 88, the standard medical examination report form. Boats, the detailer therefore decided, were out. Johnny was assigned to the radio room of the USS *Johnnie Hutchins,* a destroyer escort ship. His duties aboard the *Hutchins* were routine: Listening to the International Distress 60 at 500 kilocycles for any Morse Code SOSs; and tuning in to the International Life Code and Life Distress Circuit at 2182 kilocycles in case any civilian ships were in danger.

Twice a month, Chief Collins, the chief petty officer who ran the radio shack, put his team through the security drill. The emergency action plan, the Navy called it. The sailors called it "bash and trash." Each radioman was assigned a certain amount of equipment and matériel to burn, shred, or pound to pieces with a hammer. Whatever happens, the lecture went, don't let our secrets get in enemy hands. It could cost lives.

Johnny's assignment—come hell, high water, or the Russians, Chief Collins instructed—was to grab the wooden mallet that was kept on the wall in the radio shack and pound the cryptograph machine into smithereens. Hit it with all your might, Walker, the chief ordered.

Back in his bunk, Johnny, like a gruff echo, would amuse his shipmates by approximating the chief's bark pretty accurately. It got so that the entire radio room, after a day's work and a couple of beers, would join Johnny in a mimetic chorus of Chief Collins's favorite refrain, "Sailor, just don't let the Commies get their fuckin' red hands on it."

There's a joke, more or less, that the execs tell the squids whenever it's evaluation report time: Know what a 4.0 sailor is? A man who can walk on water and not get his feet wet. Joke or not, there weren't many people aboard the *Hutchins* who would have doubted that Radioman Walker was shooting for this ideal. In less than a year—no time at all by Navy standards—he had made E-2, his evaluations were "superior" in all categories, and he let it be known that he was a lifer, the Navy would be his career.

But—and this was Johnny's secret—he was just conning them. He would hide behind his smile, do his job, and let the fools think whatever they wanted. He had already make up his mind. He was going to put in his four and get out. He hated the *Hutchins*.

He hated his boring work; he hated doing a 4 to 8 and then putting in some rack time only to wake up and find himself having to eat goddamn meat loaf for "breakfast"; and he hated that the *Hutchins* was taking on reservists for training cruises. These spoiled rich kids, weekend sailors, really rubbed him raw. "These reserve training ships are a real racket," he wrote Joey, knowing his buddy, another guy who never had too many advantages, would understand. "I can't stand these shit head reserves."

Most of all, though, he hated his life on the *Hutchins* because it labeled him as ordinary. "I might as well be a shitty TV repairman," he complained to his brother James. Johnny missed the games. On the *Hutchins*, the reality was so oppressive that there was little room for even his imagination to help him invent escapes.

There was also something else—he still wanted subs. Just thinking about Art wearing dolphins, that really hurt.

• • •

Of course Johnny never told any of this to Barbara Crowley. He knew what kind of confident man rich girls like her wanted. From the first night, Johnny was certain he knew just how to play her.

The *Hutchins* had been harbored during the icy winter of 1957 up in Boston, and Johnny, along with a bunch of guys from the ship, found themselves one evening at a dance in a church basement. Barbara had been standing with a girlfriend across the room when Johnny spotted her. No way you could miss that black hair, black as coal. When there was a slow record, he asked her to dance. The rest was pretty simple. They danced. They talked. She told him all about her fancy job at the department store, all about her parents with the house up in Dedham. Johnny told her he, too, had big plans. Someday, he said, Admiral Walker. She didn't know whether to believe him or not, but then he let loose a smile that would stay in her mind forever. "His rascal's smile," she would fondly recall, enjoying the memory even when she was a grandmother. By the end of the evening both of them knew he was going to drive her home.

The roller skating was Barbara's idea. There was a rink near her apartment, and after some cajoling, she finally got Johnny to go. He had never skated before; it was not the sort of thing boys did in a coal-mining town, but he took to it right away. He got really good, learning, after only a couple of times out, to do figure eights. Mostly, though, his arm close to Barb's waist, his fingers putting a soft pressure on her hip, they would do slow, looping circles about the rink. They would skate for hours, skate and talk.

They talked about the future. Barbara wanted a home where she could raise a family, some place like her parents'. She promised to take Johnny up to Dedham one afternoon and introduce him. He told her a family would be nice, but these days being a sailor was too exciting. He had his career to think about. He was still going on about "Admiral Walker," and she still couldn't tell if he was *really* joking.

Then there was the time Barbara, who could get devout when she found herself talking about her Catholicism, asked Johnny if he believed in God. I was an altar boy, he told her. That's not an answer, she chided. "Do you believe in God?" she repeated.

He waited awhile; perhaps, she felt, playing in his mind with a quip. When he finally got the words out, though, there was a quality to his voice, a soft and somber Johnny Walker, that made her think he was really confiding something:

"Barb, when I was a kid my dad used to give my brothers and me a real hard time. It didn't matter what we did, whether we were right or wrong, if my dad was in the mood, he'd just haul off and tear into us. Now, why am I tellin' you this? Well, 'cause the fact of the matter is, sure, I believe in God. But He ain't the sort of God the sisters used to tell us about. The way I see it, He's more like my father. He's gonna give you a hard time no matter what if He's in the mood. So the trick is, go out there and do what you want—and just hope you get lucky."

Then, from out of nowhere, Johnny, the old Johnny, flashed her one of his rascal smiles; and once again she couldn't tell if he really meant what he was saying.

The spring day when she learned the *Johnnie Hutchins* would soon be leaving Boston harbor for a long cruise down the East Coast was the day Barbara finally decided to confront her sailor. She didn't know how he'd take to the news that he was going to be a father. She should have realized, though, that by now Johnny was just as much in love with her as she was with him.

"Well," he said, giving her belly a fond pat, "I guess we'd better get married."

They didn't tell anyone; and they never told each other that part of the reason was that there really was no one to tell. They just went to a justice of the peace in Durham, North Carolina. The justice didn't have an office or anything, just his grocery store. His wife was the witness. They were married on June 4, 1957. Afterward, Johnny decided to call his mother in Scranton. That night he went back to his ship. Barbara, as happy as she'd ever been, spent the night in the rooming house by herself.

. . .

"The best Christmas present ever," Johnny rejoiced. Because two days after Christmas in a hospital in Brooklyn, New York, Barbara gave birth to a baby girl. But it wasn't an easy birth. Barbara developed toxemia, and the Navy doctor told the new father to be prepared; he didn't think either the mother or the baby girl would pull through. Johnny sent for a priest; he couldn't think of what else to do.

Nature, however, worked its way. The doctor was Italian and he told Barb to drink a lot of red wine; that would make her milk richer. Johnny and she had a couple of laughs over the advice, but they decided they might as well give it a try, and it led to some interesting evenings. In time the baby was christened Margaret, after Johnny's mother. And Johnny, who was now a radioman on the aircraft carrier *Forrestal,* was quick to give out cigars to the guys in the shack. He even bragged to his chief that "I changed a diaper." Barbara, too, thought things had gotten pretty wonderful when she heard her husband tell one of his buddies, "I took one look at little Margaret and I fell in love forever."

The only problem seemed to be money. At least that was the only one Johnny, a twenty-one-year-old father, would talk about. He was earning $130 a month base, with another $77 a month added as a family allowance. It didn't go very far: Margaret's crib was a dresser drawer. They made up their minds not to have other children for a while.

There was something else, however unarticulated, that also ate away at Johnny. He wanted subs. Or he wanted out.

But things just didn't seem to go Johnny's way. This time when he requested subs, the Navy assigned him to a sub tender, the USS *Howard W. Gilmore,* based in Charleston, South Carolina. That was like, he told his brother James, a guy wanting to live like a rich man, so they make him a butler. He was pretty bitter about the whole thing and was counting the days till he could get out.

At home things had gotten out of hand, too. Johnny and Barb had made up their minds to have no more children, but one night, both of them a little tight, resolutions became more spontaneous. So Cynthia was born in Charleston in the winter of 1959. She was a sickly baby, always crying, and Barb, a twenty-one-year-old mother with another infant to care for, was overwhelmed. The more Cynthia cried, the more Barbara resented her. But that didn't help; the guilt only made things worse.

The breaking point, though, had to be when Barbara, just two months after Cynthia was born, found herself pregnant for a third time. Johnny told her to get an abortion, but she wouldn't hear of it. She was too much of a Catholic. Instead, she reached a compromise with her husband and the dogma: She would try to induce a miscarriage. She made a point of lifting heavy boxes. She carried a boxy club chair across their small living room. Once, after screwing up her courage, she even took a tumble, sort of, down a flight of stairs. But the baby was stubborn. In April 1960, their third daughter, Laura, was born.

That's when Johnny lost it. He had figured the only upside to this third child was at least the odds were pretty good he'd get a son. After two girls, he felt he was due. When the doctor congratulated him on being the father of a 7¼-pound baby girl, Johnny stormed out of the hospital. He didn't go see his wife, he just went looking for the nearest bar. He didn't come home for three days. By then, he was a mite contrite. But there was no use asking him where he had been; even he couldn't remember.

There was nobody Johnny could turn to but his big brother. Art had gotten him out of a jam with the judge in Scranton, and now Johnny needed him again. He had to believe Art, a boot ensign on a training submarine in Groton, Connecticut, would help him out. Johnny, for once, just put it to his brother straight: He was a twenty-two-year-old father of three baby girls and he was broke. A hundred bucks would sure help. Art, now a father himself, told him, "That's a lot of money." But the next day Art wired the $100.

Not that Art ever really had much of a choice. Looking back at the incident almost thirty years later, he would explain: "It wasn't always monetary. A lot of what was between us was protective feelings for one another in childhood, watching out for each other, protecting your brother, you know? It's what you did, what you were supposed to do."

So when Johnny, full of despair, confided to his older brother that not only was he broke, but also he didn't see how things would be getting better next year when he was a civilian, Art took the bait. Thought you were going to be a lifer like me, Art said. You? Johnny barked at him. You got it made—you're in subs. The goddamn Navy put me on a boat, I'd sign on for another four for certain.

Johnny tried to sound surprised when his brother suggested maybe he could help. Art said he'd talk to a few people he had met in Groton. Maybe one of them could do something.

Six months later, in October 1960, Johnny Walker, back in control once more, wrote to his Marine buddy:

Hi Joey,

Its been so long since we communicated, I can't remember what ship I was on or what I was doing. . . . I was pretty bitter at the Navy at the time and had decided to get out on 4 rather than ship over. However, I got to know some people after return- ing to the states who would help me get into submarines, so I shipped over after all. . . .

Sometime this week I'll be transfered again; this time to the USS Balo, a submarine here in Key West. So, I'll be finally making it aboard subs after wanting them since I enlisted.

4

At the start of every cruise, just as the tug was pushing the sub's bow toward the channel, Johnny Walker would sit at his desk in the radio shack with a roll of toilet paper. On each perforated square he would write a number. He'd start at one and continue, consecutively, to seventy: a square for each scheduled day of the voyage. Then, as the boat was beginning to feel the chop of the open sea, he'd carefully wind up the roll and position it, always, in the right-hand corner of his desk. It would be his way of keeping track of time.

Time for submariners was that makeshift. Once the hull began reverberating with the diving alarm, and the crew could hear the hard whoosh of rushing air as the vents on the top of the ballast tanks were opened, they knew they were descending, slowly, to a continuum without sunrises or sunsets. Underneath the sea, days became nights; nights became days. Even veterans could be spooked by this, it was so unnatural. The Navy, concerned, tried to impose a bit of structure: While clocks on surface ships were changed to conform to the local time zones, clocks on a submarine were permanently set to Zulu, or Greenwich mean time. Johnny's roll of toilet paper seemed to ease his buddies' anxieties more successfully, though. At the end of each twenty-four-hour period, the tape apes would gather round his desk. Then one of the guys, usually Don Clevenger, a big, beefy good-time Texan who shipped out with Johnny on a lot of boats, would pucker up like he was about to kiss his sister; but, instead, he'd break into a humming, put-on rendition of "Taps," while Johnny, getting into the mock ceremony, would rip off one of his flimsy, numbered squares. Another day was now officially done.

In this manner, for the next six years, his voyages were measured out. Yet if there ever was a perfect time in Johnny Walker's life, a time when his ambitions, talents, and even personality were appreciated and, better, encouraged, it was during his tours as a radioman on submarines. He threw himself into everything: the hot runner poring over tech manuals, determined to make chief; the submariner, proud of his dolphins, kicky with the dangerous thrill—and prestige!—of his profession; and the wiseass games player eager to invent diversions, now in the name of morale. All the levels he lived on, Johnny discovered to his profound satisfaction, could run loose in this narrow world under the sea.

Not that life on a sub, especially toward the end of a long cruise, couldn't grind on him. It was hard duty. Worst of all, though, was when he was just starting out in subs back in 1961 and he caught one of the last of the World War II–class diesels, the USS *Razorback*. He learned to hate the very smell of that boat, its air heavy with the high stench of machine oil and battery acid. In the summer, things on that boat could get really rank. Once down in Key West, Johnny was sitting at his desk in the shack in just his skivvies and a rakish beret— things were pretty casual in the diesel Navy—when the story started moving through the boat that a thermometer in the engine room had hit 130.

Johnny and the other eighty-odd submariners crammed into a steel can that was not much more than 300 feet long by about 27 feet across the beam didn't have much trouble believing the rumor. Nothing they could do about it, however. There were only two narrow stall showers on board: one was used as a storage bin for fresh vegetables, the other was for the officers. It got so the wardroom was known as "the goat locker." And it got so that a commanding officer was willing to look the other way if his crew got caught up in a little inspired mischief. Just the sort of fun that Johnny loved to instigate.

• • •

There was the incident, then, of what became known to the crew as "the tasty turd." It happened when Johnny decided a scheme was needed to get a boot ensign off everyone's back. The ensign had just come to the *Razorback* from the academy and was puffed up with a textbook vision of a spit-and-polish Navy. On the shakedown cruise, he didn't let up: The crew must be in proper uniform at all times, officers were to be saluted, and shifts were to start and end precisely on schedule. But when he went after their berets, that really ticked off Johnny.

It was during his first cruise on the *Razorback* that Johnny had begun sporting the black beret. He started wearing it about the time he grew his thin strip of black mustache; and also about the time he was becoming particularly troubled because he could no longer kid himself—he'd be bald by thirty. So he wore a beret, and he was convinced it looked pretty cool. The other tape apes must have thought so, too. A lot of the guys picked up on it; some even took the time to sew their dolphins on the cap. Now you'd enter the shack and just about everyone would be wearing a black beret. Except, the ensign informed them, it wasn't Navy. The berets had to go.

That's when Johnny decided the ensign should be taught a lesson. He and his buddies sat around until they came up with a plan that, spurred on by a couple of beers, involved the design and construction of a reasonable facsimile of a coil of human excrement. One of the tape apes volunteered that he was a bit of a sculptor. And he had told the truth: He was able to do really impressive things with peanut butter. But when the time was right, it was Johnny, always daring, who snuck the ugly little turd onto the ensign's desk.

"What the hell is this?" the ensign barked.

Radioman Walker, deferential and obliging, stepped forward. He looked curiously at the foul concoction for a moment. Then he stuck his thumb into it and, without a second's hesitation, popped his thumb into his mouth.

He took his time chewing; like an actor, he understood how to play a crowd. There was also a lot of pensive licking of his lips. Until, finally, he looked the ensign straight in the eye and with a big smile lighting up his face, Johnny announced, "Tastes like shit, sir."

Another time, when the *Razorback* was stationed as an open exhibit at the Seattle World's Fair in 1962, Johnny gave the crew some more laughs. This one, too, was Johnny's favorite sort of joke—some sucker was at the short end.

A group of civilians was working its way through the narrow boat, when one of them asked about a sign that read, FLOOD SAFETY.

The standard drill was that the sign would flash whenever the sub was rigged for a dive: A glowing FLOOD SAFETY simply meant the ballast tanks were being flooded with water.

Johnny, though, found it more enjoyable to invent another explanation; it was, after all, one of his little vanities, this gift of pulling stories out of nowhere. He told the inquisitive civilian that a flashing sign meant big trouble. When you see that sign flashing, he explained, you'd better practice your swimming because it means the sub is going "gray lady down."

That caused a couple of the rubes to gulp, and the submariners to share a couple of sly winks. It might just as well have been applause.

Now, encouraged, Johnny waited a minute or two, and as the procession of civilians was studying the sonar console, he flipped a switch. Immediately the big red letters started flashing: FLOOD SAFETY . . . FLOOD SAFETY . . .

That was Johnny's cue. He let loose with a bloodcurdling shriek, "Oh my God, that's it!" Then he tear-assed down the deck toward the ladder to the main hatch. He took the ladder two rungs at a time until his head was sticking out in the fresh air. And then, for the first time, with his buddies cheering him on, he looked over his shoulder and what did he see? Every one of those dumb-ass civilians, eyes bulging with fear, breathless, lined up behind him.

Or at least that's the way the tape apes, still hooting over the escapades of their prankster buddy, would tell it for the next twenty-five years.

Johnny was also particularly partial to a bit of fun if it had an edge of risk to it. There was the night, then, in Seattle when he and his buddies were returning to the *Razorback,* the boat still parked in its World's Fair berth, and they became intrigued by a gigantic blimp tethered across the way. Johnny made a slow tour of the silver blimp, kicking it here and there with all the curious concern of a man pounding the tires of a car he was thinking of buying. That gave everyone a laugh. Of course that only prompted Johnny. He was always quick to up the ante.

"Hey, let's cut her loose," he announced.

It was one of those late-night ideas that seemed pretty swell at the time. The guys cheered him.

He was on his knees, his pocket knife sawing through the thick tether, when a security guard noticed the crowd of sailors. The guard started to head toward them. "What the hell are you doing?" he demanded.

The guard's shout was signal enough for most of the submariners to head for the darkness. But not Johnny. He was digging the game; the risk only made it sweeter. He held his ground, cutting away.

It must have been when the guard got close enough to see the knife in Johnny's hand that he fired the first shot. Still, Johnny kept at it. Suddenly there was another shot. And only then did Johnny, whooping with delight, take off.

The blimp never had left the ground, but the way they told it the next day in the wardroom that didn't matter much: Crazy Johnny Walker had pulled off another one. Some old coot was firing away at him, but Johnny was determined to cut that sucker loose. That's one tape ape with brass balls.

Johnny, loving the spotlight, never felt prouder.

Not all the risks, however, were from gun-toting security guards. It wasn't always smooth sailing on the *Razorback*. "If a guy doesn't have what it takes, no way he's going to last in submarines," Johnny would still be boasting in the years when his days at sea were only a grandfather's memory. To prove his point, he passed more than a few Happy Hours entertaining people with the story of the time the *Razorback* "just about went gray lady down." Forever the actor, he'd get grim when he'd tell this one. Except some of his drinking cronies were willing to bet that macho Johnny had no idea how grim he came across in this yarn; or, to tell the truth, how just plain damn scared he sounded.

It happened in the water outside Seattle. The boat was cruising submerged at about 400 feet, merely a dozen feet above its maximum safety depth of 412 feet, when, all of a sudden, it started to dive. Uncontrollably. A freshwater pocket from the nearby Columbia River was playing havoc with the ballast of a boat rigged for saltwater oceans. The crew could hear the hull starting to creak. Millions of tons of water were shoving against the steel, pounding like angry fists. The creaking was getting louder, insistent: a steady groan. Something had to give. And the boat was still diving: 410 . . . 415 . . . 420 . . . 425 . . . "That was when I started praying," Johnny admitted.

Maybe his prayers were answered. Or maybe the boat simply passed through the freshwater pocket. But suddenly someone let out a cheer: The boat had started to rise.

Johnny, his tone also making a trip upward from its graver depths when he told this story, would unfailingly end with a glimmer of philosophy: "Once you heard the hull creaking, it's a sound you'll never forget. And once you heard that sound, like death calling to you, a man comes to realize he can go at any time—so why not grab it all while you can?"

In those days, "grabbing it all" largely meant one thing to Johnny —boomers. Any submariner worth his dolphins felt the same way. Boomers, as the nuclear-powered boats armed with nuclear ballistic missiles were called, were the hottest ticket in the Navy. With the launching of the *George Washington* in 1959, the first nuclear boat armed with solid-fuel thermonuclear missiles capable of being fired while a submarine was submerged, it was clear that boomers were the capital ships of the future. The potential for secrecy, surprise, and destruction would change warfare forever. Naturally Johnny, the hot runner and the games player, wanted to be part of the team Admiral Hyman Rickover was shaping into the nuclear Navy. "You got to understand," explained Bill Wilkinson, Johnny's buddy in the radio shack, "the guys on boomers were select, an elite bunch. They were something more than regular sailors. They were special. And that's what Johnny and I wanted to be. That's what we always talked about."

There was also something else goading Johnny. Something he wouldn't talk about to the guys in the shack. Sure, he was all for breaking out of the pack of sailors. He knew he was sharper than your average squid. But when it came down to it, there was really just one sailor in the entire Navy whom he was out there competing against— his older brother, Art.

Art was an officer, an accomplishment Johnny with his run-in with the law in Scranton had little chance of matching. But the way Art's career was shaping up, it seemed certain he was never going to make it to boomers. That made Johnny's desire really fierce.

Barb and the three girls were living in Vallejo, California, then. When he was first assigned to the *Razorback,* he had put in for Pearl Harbor—now that would have been something, Johnny dreamed— but the Navy wasn't eager to ship a family of five across the Pacific. Not that he was complaining. He was away at sea for months at a time, and when he was home the California sunshine made Scranton seem a million gray miles away. Johnny didn't mind that at all. And nobody could say he wasn't glad to get home to Barb, or that she wasn't head over heels over her sailor. He'd come back from a cruise, seventy days at sea, and they'd just about rush to the bedroom. They could have stayed between the sheets forever.

It was in Vallejo that Johnny was convinced his luck was finally catching up to him. Johnny always had this thing about destiny. He believed that he was a lucky person, that he was special. That's what got him through, he said, all the heartache in Scranton. As a kid he told himself he was just biding his time: My day will come. And now an adult, a husband, a father even, he found himself still waiting. He was just waiting, he told Barbara, for his luck to catch up with him. Maybe, he even admitted to her, he was getting a little tired of waiting.

Then things started to click. He was taken off the *Razorback* and assigned to an advanced radio school. That was a good sign: The Navy wanted the radiomen on subs to know not only how to operate all the equipment, but also how to repair the various machines; boats were crowded enough without having to find room for the electronic technicians who shipped off on surface ships. It seemed pretty clear, he felt, the Navy wanted to keep him in subs. He was all for that, too.

Then, when Barb got pregnant Johnny figured his fourth child *had* to be a boy. You spin the wheel four times, he told his brother James, you got to figure the odds are getting more on your side. This time he was right. On the first day of November in 1962, Michael was born. The moment the screaming infant was handed to his mother, Barbara took one look at his bald, pink head and told her husband, "Well, he's got your hair, that's for sure." Johnny, staring at his child, a son finally, was so damn happy, he couldn't help but laugh.

It was also while he was in Vallejo in 1962 that another of Johnny's wishes came true: He was selected to be a supervisory radioman aboard the maiden voyage of the *Andrew Jackson*. The *Andrew Jackson* was a boomer.

The *Andrew Jackson* was the largest and fastest submarine in the world when it was officially commissioned in 1963. It was 425 feet long and 33 feet in diameter, and if it wanted to sprint, the boat could, submerged, hit speeds approaching 25 knots. This boat was, especially after diesel duty, a submariner's dream. Its three levels had room for showers, man-size bunks (with foam mattresses!), a cafeteria that didn't run out of fresh vegetables, a radio shack that six tape apes could squeeze into, a library with a shelf of old *Playboy*s, and, once a week, a movie that a submariner might have heard of would be shown in the rec room. The *Jackson* didn't even smell like a submarine. Its 300 tons of air-conditioning equipment and charcoal granulated air scrubbers gave the boat a refrigerated, almost antiseptic smell. Test-tube air, boomer crews called it. But Johnny figured those guys had never been on a diesel boat in July. He breathed deep, and liked it just fine.

But all this was icing. The *Jackson* was designed and commissioned for one purpose only: to be the deadliest man-of-war in the history of the world. Its teakettle, as the crew called the 24,000-horsepower nuclear reactor that powered the boat, enabled the *Jackson* to leave its home port of Charleston, South Carolina, and proceed submerged to any ocean in the world. Its ultimate mission? The crew had no illusions about that: Beyond the conning tower were sixteen Polaris missiles with thermonuclear warheads. Each missile could be fired from 100 feet beneath the sea and could travel 2,500 miles in the air. Navy analysts put the kill estimate for a Polaris with, say, the Kremlin as its ground-zero target at approximately 500,000 humans. One missile could destroy a city; sixteen missiles could go a long way toward destroying the world. So there wasn't much a submariner could do but try not to think about it. "Sherwood Forest" was what the crew called the area where the missile silos rose straight up from the deck like so many thick primeval trees. That made the whole thing easier to deal with.

Of course, practicing to blow up the world was part of the game submariners played. The Navy called it "WSRT"—Weapons System Readiness Test. "Bingo time," Johnny called it.

The drill would start with the alarm bell ringing on the ELF radio in the boat's radio room. This signaled that COMSUBLANT, as the Norfolk-based commander of the Submarine Force in the Atlantic was tersely designated in all naval communications, was sending a Z flash—top secret and top priority. The radio room would immediately go on combat footing. And Johnny, the shack's supervisor, would be on the horn to the conning tower. In seconds the entire boat would hear the announcement: "All hands man battle stations . . . All hands . . ."

It takes, however, some time for a message to travel across the country and under thousands of miles of oceans. The *Jackson* was one of the first boomers to trail a lengthy wire antenna attuned to the Navy's extremely low-frequency transmitter hidden in the lonely woods of Michigan's Upper Peninsula. This ELF transmitter passed on its coded messages slowly, about one character every thirty seconds. Each message was sent in three-letter blocks. The duty radioman would record the message on tape. The whole shack would be watching him.

When the entire message was received and transcribed onto high-speed tape, the duty radioman would hand the six inches or so of tape to his supervisor, John Walker. ELF signals were not encrypted in standard code but in "onetime pad." This "pad" was a book distributed to all boomers every six months and filled with randomly generated transpositions for each letter of the signal. Each three-letter group in the message corresponded to a word or phrase in the book. The book was Johnny's responsibility. It was kept in the safe in the radio room vault. Johnny now removed it; and every man in the shack knew the loose-leaf book had the power to destroy the world.

Johnny did the deciphering by hand. It took about three minutes to unravel an ELF message. It was tense work. Three minutes was a

long time to live with the fear of discovering one awful phrase: This is
not a drill.

Johnny finished, quickly double-checked his work, and then rushed
to the boat's attack center. The captain and the executive officer
would be waiting. Both men carried keys around their necks at all
times. If the message in Johnny's hand matched the phrase inside the
sealed envelopes they had already removed from their safes, they
would have no choice but to follow orders: The captain would go to
the conning tower and insert his key in the Polaris console; the exec
would hurry to the Missile Control Center and insert his key into
another console. With a twist of their wrists, the countdown to World
War III would begin.

"Boom time" was the sort of drill that really got everyone on the
boat's juices going. From the moment the ELF bell sounded, it was a
race. Submariners were like athletes, always competing against the
clock to see if they could shave a second or so off their best time. The
entire procedure was monitored by computers; a digital display announced every passing second. But what really gave the game its
spark, Johnny would tell his drinking buddies long after he had ever
shipped off on a sub, was that until the moment when you waited for
the captain to reach for the key around his neck, you wouldn't know
if it was a game . . . or the end of the world. "Now if that doesn't
teach a man how to handle pressure," Johnny used to say with a grin,
"nothing will."

The other side to the pressure was the coming up with ways to
defuse it. Here again Johnny was a natural, a man born to play before
an audience. Everyone had a favorite Johnny Walker story. There
was the time in Charleston when Johnny tried to smuggle Peg Leg,
the one-legged hooker, on board in his duffle, or the one about the
grain alcohol and bug juice cocktail party he hosted in the shack, or
did you hear about the smiling face he painted on a tape ape's behind
to greet the sub's doctor who was coming around with his procto-
scope? Or how about when Johnny began spicing up the *Old Hickory
News,* the boat's daily paper, with the choicest snaps from the latest
Playboy, and when one of the officers complained, what does Johnny
do—he runs a picture of some naked guy in the next issue instead.
Or, talk about inspired mischief, there was the night at the sub base
in Rota, Spain, when Johnny ran off with a five-foot potted plant,
stowing it in the radio shack for the entire voyage, while each day he
ran an "AP" story in the *Old Hickory News* detailing Franco's des-

perate search for the missing plant—and wouldn't you know it, Johnny invented so many sidesplitting stories about that silly plant that the boat's captain gave him a commendation for keeping up morale. That was vintage Johnny, everyone agreed: the jester having the last laugh.

So no matter what the port, Johnny would be elbowed up to the bar, telling jokes, singing the raunchiest songs, winking at all the bargirls, the master of ceremonies till closing time. He'd weave on back to the sub, and in the morning he'd greet his buddies with the same line: Great thing about the *Jackson* is the 619 painted on its hull. Looks the same right side up or upside down. A pie-eyed submariner's bound to find his way home to this boat.

Loose crew, tight boat. That's the formula a generation of boomer skippers—all Rickover protégés and, therefore, comfortable with ambivalence—has used to command their boats. It meant awarding commendations for pranks. It meant looking the other way if your crew rolled in a little under the weather after a night of liberty. It also meant letting your crews have their small fun because once at sea they were playing against a real enemy.

While the other armed services routinely run exercises against allies or themselves, one side pretending to be the bad guys, there is no pretense under the sea. Every day, under 130 square million miles of ocean, U.S. attack boats are constantly playing hide-and-seek with Soviet ballistic missile submarines. The Navy calls this strategy "defense in depth." The objective is to be prepared, the moment a shooting war begins, to meet and destroy enemy submarines as far forward as possible before they reach their missile or torpedo launching areas.

It is a strategy that, explains Admiral James D. Watkins, former chief of naval operations, has resulted in an "era of violent peace." And it is a stategy that, explained John A. Walker, former chief radioman on two nuclear ballistic submarines, has resulted in "for sheer heart-in-your-mouth thrills, the best goddamn game anybody's ever come up with."

. . .

Sonar operators on a sub work six-hour one-in-three rotating watches. They sit by their instrument panel, headphones on, listening to the sounds of the sea. They listen to the glide of sharks, the whoosh of water currents, the honk of whales. They learn to discriminate and categorize. Yet all the time they are waiting for one telltale noise: the sound of a Russian boomer. It can be a noise that ranges in sonic magnitude from the ferocious rumble of a nuclear generator to the soft, but distinctive hiss of a collapsing bubble caused by a boat's propeller screws. When this revelatory sound is isolated and the identification of an enemy boomer is confirmed, the game begins.

The boat now begins to work the enemy sub. The drill is known as "sprint and drift." Once the crew spots a target, a boat dashes to a more concealed position; then, drifting quietly, the boat again makes sonar contact with its target; only to sprint once more as it rushes into firing position. It takes a navigator who can play the sea currents, and a skipper with a killer's instinct: a man who can lead his boat as if on cat's feet to his prey.

As soon as the boat is in a position to pounce, the fire-control team takes over. The range data—distance between the two boats, water depth, sea-current speeds—are fed into a high-speed computer. A shooting solution—the precise angle, the precise depth—is plotted. In a matter of moments the team has the exact running time it would take one of the boat's Mark 48 torpedoes with their half-ton warheads —wire guided, and able to hone in on the enemy with its own active sonar at about 50 knots—to reach the target. The enemy is a target dead in the boat's sights—except it is only a game.

All the skipper can do is rub it in. And maybe have some fun with his $150 million toy.

The order now is for "Yankee search." That's the ironic way one boomer captain announces himself to another. The enemy boat is immediately bombarded with active sonar. Each *ping!* is salt in a skipper's wounds. It's like sneaking up on somebody on tiptoes in the dark and whispering, "Bang! Bang! You're dead." It's the sort of thing that really rankles a boomer crew sitting there four hundred feet under the sea.

It's also a dare. The captain is announcing to his enemy that my boat is going to stay on your tail—unless you're good enough to lose me. So the game of shadowing begins. The two boats—hunter and roamer, that's how submariners designate the players—start to sprint and drift through miles of often uncharted ocean depths. It's a pursuit that continues until the roamer, now rigged for ultraquiet, silently maneuvers onto an undetected course; or the hunter goes off after game or prey; or one of the boats, speeding through the ocean at 30 knots, plunges head-on into a whale, or an iceberg, or the knife-edged ridge of an underwater mountain.

As Johnny said, "For sheer heart-in-your-mouth thrills, the best goddamn game anyone's ever come up with." And submariners play it 365 days a year.

Sometimes, though, it's a little too "heart-in-your-mouth." The *Andrew Jackson,* Johnny Walker supervising the radio shack during the winter of 1964, was heading submerged to a duty post in the Mediterranean. The mission was routine: maintain SLOC and URG; that is, in case shooting begins, provide protection for this vital sea line of communication and also give logistical support to the fleet already in position. In the meantime, she—submariners use the feminine pronoun to refer to an American or allied boat; Russian subs were always "he"—had standing orders to remain undetected.

She failed.

The boat was rigged for ultraquiet and drift, the teakettle switched to low, as it entered the Strait of Gibraltar. This was standard procedure: The Soviets usually have a boomer stationed somewhere along this fifty-mile-toll-booth strait to the Mediterranean. All a skipper can hope to do is tiptoe by him.

The first *ping!* caught the *Jackson*'s sonar chief by surprise. Then a series of *ping!ping!ping!* echoed through the entire boat. Now the whole crew knew it: They had been sitting in the sights of a Russian attack sub. That could really shake a skipper up; but suddenly there wasn't time for consideration.

"Conn, sonar," the chief now reported, "he just flooded his tubes."

It was a sound that a sonarman rarely hears in even a violent peace. The sound of a torpedo tube being opened is a sound that is a press of a button away from war.

Immediately the battle station alarms rang out in the *Jackson*. The skipper gave orders to turn rudder, hoping to give the Russians mini-

mum target profile. Fire control desperately tried to solve the chang-
ing target geometry. Johnny, though, doubted there was time; he sat
by his radio feeling that in a moment he'd be sending a Z flash—boat
under attack. And the entire crew, battle quiet, waited to hear the
pneumatic sound of a fish with a fifty-ton warhead closing in on them.

Except the Russian skipper let the *Jackson* drift on by. He was just
having fun. This time.

"Nothing like knowing you're about to die," Johnny always said,
"to make you know how to live."

5

Always, after a couple of beers, Bill Wilkinson would latch onto the same wistful memory. He and Johnny could be sitting elbows up in Newport News or even Hong Kong and, sure enough, Billy would get that mushy look in his eyes and start right in: "Ever tell you, padn'r, 'bout the best darn bar in the world? A little place in Houston, Texas, I used to frequent from time to time. They called it The House of Bamboo."

It got so Johnny—who had a right; he was the senior chief aboard their boat, the *Simon Bolivar*—would lose patience with his buddy. "Hell, Billy," he'd finally let loose, "put a cork in it. The way you go on 'bout that joint, you'd think they got gold on tap. It's only a goddamn bar."

"Might be just a bar to you, Chief," Billy would snap back, "but to those of us who been there, it's The House of Bamboo." He'd make sure to play with that syllable some, stretching that "booooo" just about across the length of the bar. And there'd be no backing off now. Instead, relishing his advantage, he'd throw Johnny a wallop of a wink, the sort of gesture that was drawn wide enough for a man to fill in the blank spaces as his imagination saw fit.

A seventy-day voyage on a boomer, weeks on end cruising deep below the sea, gives a man a lot of time to fill in the blanks. Johnny, always imaginative, got to thinking about The House of Bamboo quite a bit.

After he played with fantasy long enough, it started taking on the patina of a good idea. The way Johnny explained it, it seemed natural, logical even, that he'd want to open a bar. After all, wasn't Chief Walker—or "chiefie weefie" as the crew teased him, mimicking the yelping come-on of the Hong Kong bargirl who took a real fancy to Johnny—the fleet's favorite, the life of every party? Wasn't it Johnny who was always up for a little fun? Doesn't that sound like the sort of good-time guy who'd have the squids lining up shoulder to shoulder for any bar he'd open?

Not that Johnny was a juicer. Sure, he liked a beer or two, and if there was something to celebrate, he'd spring for a glass of harder stuff. "Bartender," he'd bark, "I'll have a shot of the scotch that's named after me—Johnnie Walker." He got a kick out of that line, all right; he tried it out in bars from Virginia Beach to Manila. But more nights than not, Johnny nursed his beer. He liked to keep in control, even when he was acting a bit wild.

Truth was, he hung out in bars because he liked to perform. He could walk into a bar in a strange city anywhere in the world and Johnny knew he could always find what he was looking for—an audience. Now twenty-eight, he was starting to realize he wouldn't be in the Navy forever. He'd need a new stage. Running a bar, his *own* bar, didn't sound like a bad idea at all.

Naturally, Billy Wilkinson was in the deal from the start. Both men had been in the *Bolivar*'s radio shack since the boomer's maiden voyage in 1965. All that close time under the sea gives submariners a chance to check each other out; by the end of a cruise, a sailor will tell you, you either want to break a guy's neck, or you'll risk your own for him. The way it worked out, Johnny and Billy had gotten pretty close.

It wasn't just that there was a lot of rascal in Billy, too. Sure, with his slow, smooth country-boy twang, and thick black pompadour— oh, how balding Johnny envied that mop!—Billy was always up for a night of honky-tonkying. But come the morning after, like his buddy the chief, he was all Navy. "Being on a nuclear sub," Billy was still bragging years after his last active duty, "meant we were the cream of the crop. We were special and we did special work. Johnny and me, we both were first-class radiomen. Real wizards.''

Like most of the guys in the shack who, when you came down to it, earned their living preparing to fight the Russians, Johnny and Billy also shared much the same way of looking at the world. Of course Johnny voted for Goldwater in '64; he even made sure Barb went out and gave the Republicans her vote, too. But sitting around jawing with Billy in the shack all day gave Johnny's instinctive hard-line politics a bit of refining. The way Billy went on, the Jews, Negroes, and Commie liberals were planning to take over the U.S. of A., while real Americans, guys like Johnny and himself, were risking their lives each day for their country. It was about time real Americans started standing up for their beliefs. That made sense to Johnny, too.

So just before Johnny was promoted to senior chief in 1966 and the Naval Investigative Service ran another background check on him, there were some new additions to Chief Walker's résumé. Under clubs and affiliations were listed the John Birch Society and the National Rifle Association.

Johnny's promotion was routinely approved. It was the hot runner's eighth jump in pay grades since enlisting. "Really remarkable," Johnny called it. He was also given a top secret/crypto clearance. He was now, as they say in the Navy, "cleared for the world."

While the two submariners, both billeted in Charleston, were on shore leave from the *Bolivar* during the spring of 1966, the plan for the bar really began to take hold. They spent their days shooting pool and scheming. Especially Billy. Now playing with the idea full-time, he came up with all kinds of notions. To his way of thinking, a bar was just the starting point.

The real money, he told Johnny, was in restaurants. Someplace in the country, a place with tablecloths, where a guy might drive his wife and kids on a Sunday afternoon for a fried chicken dinner—that was the ticket, he now insisted.

Johnny didn't know about that. He was thinking along the lines of a beer and shot joint. A real squid's bar. But that didn't slow down Billy. His imagination kept pumping. From out of nowhere popped up his best idea yet—Go-Karts. Put up a Go-Kart track right next door to their restaurant and people'll flock to their door like bees to honey. All they needed was the land. A couple of acres, say.

Acres? Johnny wasn't so sure about that at all.

Circumstances, though, helped him start coming around. Part of it had to do with how the Walkers were living in Goose Creek. All six of them were crammed into a bulky, gray, cinder-block cube—"genuine Navy ticky-tack," is the way the kids remember it—in Men Riv, the development named after South Carolina's Mendel Rivers, the chairman of the House Armed Services Committee. If you asked Johnny, though, "They should have named it after the guy they named that prison after—Sing Sing."

He felt cramped, all right. But it wasn't only the wailing of four kids packed into a couple of narrow rooms that was roughing up his calm. Things just didn't feel right. "Maybe I was never cut out to be a husband or father," he told friends. Or maybe he was starting to realize he needed room, room to live on all his different levels.

He did his best to blame it all on Barb. "Relationship turned sour in 7th year," he would write, looking back on those days as if he alone had been jilted by fate. He, the proud senior chief, was the "high achiever," while Barbara "tended toward lazyness and drinking." If you listened to Johnny, the kids—Margaret, a big-eyed redhead was the oldest at eight; Mike, the youngest, was a skinny three-year-old—might as well have been raising themselves. To hear Johnny tell it, Barbara spent her afternoons drifting through the waterways around Charleston in an old rowboat. She'd go with the current, a glass in one hand and his service revolver in the other. When she spotted a snake, she'd take aim and, in a flash, pop his head off. Course, Johnny would explain as he tickled the listener with the ironic edge of one of his big smiles, there was just one snake she really wanted to pop—but I've always been too fast for her.

The line always got a round of laughs, which might have been reward enough for Johnny. But that wasn't the only reason it got such prominence in his barroom repertoire. To Johnny's way of thinking, you tell a story often enough, it's as good as true. And that sort of truth sure made things a lot easier for him.

"You're only young once," Johnny would tell Billy, when he felt the need to justify his stepping out on Barbara. But Billy didn't fall for that. He was damn sure chiefie-weefie had made up his mind to stay young forever. Look at him: For 1,200 bucks, money he had scraped together, Johnny had just bought a bright orange MGB. Now a two-seater wasn't the most practical car when a guy has a wife and four kids. But there Johnny would be, top down, a beret or a baseball cap hiding his bald spot, tooling around Charleston. And squeezing his family into the car didn't appear to be a problem at all. He had other passengers.

Oh, did Johnny love to brag! He wanted his buddies to know he was a real stud. He'd get pretty graphic, all right. Making sure he told you how he did this to them, then that, before flipping them over for some of what they really liked. Maybe, Billy and some of the other guys got to thinking, the chief liked the telling better than the kissing. But then again, when you're stuck on a boomer for seventy days any story is a good one.

Almost any story, that is. One of Johnny's yarns truly got Billy's hackles up. The way Johnny told it, he was going hot and heavy with the wife of an old shipmate from the *Jackson*. Soon as her hubby shipped out, ol' Johnny made a beeline for his buddy's bedroom. The bed would still be warm, and Johnny would be cuddling up with his friend's wife.

"Johnny," Billy would remember coming down on his chief, "there are certain things a man don't do—and screwing a so-called buddy's wife is one of them."

"Hey," said Johnny, "all's fair in love and war."

Billy shot him a look. "This ain't war and it sure as hell ain't love."

Johnny nodded; he could be easy. "Well then," he said, "how about this— All's fair."

But Billy couldn't stay mad at Johnny. How can you get mad at a guy if you can never tell if he's giving you the gospel, or just putting you on? You never knew with Johnny. Besides, Johnny now was talking up the idea of a restaurant, too. The way he went on, a place in the country was his scheme from the start. Said it was just the thing Barbara and the kids needed. And again, maybe he meant it; or maybe he just thought it made sense to put them out in the sticks while he was tomcatting around Charleston. You never knew with Johnny.

They searched everywhere. Billy heard about a Go-Kart track somewhere south of Charleston, so one afternoon they jumped into

the MG and checked it out. The owner was friendly enough and he
had a bit of advice: You want to make a buck, these days miniature
golf is the ticket. So they began scouting miniature golf courses.
Awful lot of work setting up one of those things, they decided. And,
naturally, they were chatting up restaurant owners all over town;
Johnny could charm the pants off just about anyone. But he couldn't
change the facts: A restaurant was a damn expensive proposition, and
an iffy one at that. Gradually, their ambitions started narrowing: A
place where a guy could wash down his cheeseburger with a couple
of brews and still get some folding money back from the five he had
placed on the bar seemed more like it.

Johnny held on to at least a piece of the old dream, though. He
wanted enough land so that someday he could put a house behind his
restaurant for his family.

That's how they found the place in Ladson, a country town a half
hour's drive north of Charleston. It wasn't much: a one-story con-
crete-block house about the size of the wardroom on a boomer. But it
sat there next to an asphalt parking lot, clumps of weeds pushing
through the cracks; and stretching beyond this strip of concrete, another four acres or so of dry, sun-spotted fields went with the place.
That was the clincher.

"What do you think?" asked Johnny.

"The House of Bam-booo," said Billy.

And so it was settled.

Or, at least that's what the two submariners would have liked to
believe. Except now they had to talk money. Before, when it wasn't
real, price was never a serious consideration. "Ballpark figures" can
be squeezed tight enough to fit any conversation. Not that Johnny was
a worrier. He lived in the happy-go-lucky world of imagined profits,
not risk capital.

This time it served him well. For a while at least. The price was a
real steal—$16,000 for the house and the land. For $1,000 down and a
$95-a-month mortgage it was theirs. Only in America, Billy rejoiced.

Of course, you get what you pay for. The house was pretty much a
shell. But that seemed to encourage Johnny. It gave him a new world
to invent from scratch. He was full of industry, tearing down walls,

putting up new ones, splashing buckets of white paint all over the place. He even recruited some local teenagers to help him. Johnny paid them off in burgers and sea stories, and none of the kids felt cheated. They hadn't heard much about the sophisticated tricks of Hong Kong whores before Chief Walker came to town. Johnny, a master, played the kids just so. He got a kick out of watching the youngsters get fired up. Made a real Navy work crew out of them, he bragged.

When he wasn't running around with a paintbrush or a hammer, Johnny was off someplace wheeling and dealing. He moved throughout the state cutting bargains on a used pizza oven, a gas grill, Formica-top tables, dozens of chairs, even a pool table. Billy was getting a little anxious as these wondrous additions kept materializing. No way we're going to be able to pay for all of this, he complained. Johnny told him to relax; once the place was opened they'd be raking in the dough. We'll be able to pay off everything, he insisted. In fact, Johnny revealed, he was already thinking about expanding. There was a lot across the way that might be perfect. Think I'll talk to the owner, he announced.

It was a heady time, all right. Finally, when the paint was dry, the grill all set to fry, the pool table polished up, and a couple of cases of beer waiting in the cooler, the place was ready to open. Or so Billy thought. Except Johnny had one last touch. The way he explained it, there had been this bar in Hong Kong, an "A number one watering hole," he called it, that had rows and rows of amber plastic beads hanging down like curtains from the ceiling. When you walked into the place, you had to shove them aside, and the beads sort of cracked and tingled like pennies bouncing off a frying pan. It was a noise that always got Johnny excited, in a party mood. So God knows where he found them, but somehow he got them, and just before the place was to open he strung this long curtain of plastic beads by the door and another by the pool table. Some of his crew, the kids, thought it was pretty fruity. But Johnny paid them no mind. "You kids know shit about class," he lectured.

There was just one more last-minute change. From the start, when it was only a daydream, it seemed simple enough to call the place The House of Bamboo. A tribute of sorts, Billy and Johnny had figured. But now that the place, *their* place, was real, nobody was too happy about giving it somebody else's name. Especially Johnny.

Aren't there some kinds of laws that stop us from using a name some other joker's already grabbed? he decided. Copyright? Libel? Johnny wasn't too sure about the particulars. He just knew that he wanted something original. His own. So he came up with The Bamboo Snack Bar.

In October 1966, The Bamboo Snack Bar opened for business.

Even before the snack bar started serving, Johnny had bought a used house trailer and staked it down in a back corner of his four acres facing a stand of woods. His family moved in there during the heat of summer. It was tight quarters, not really better than Men Riv, with Margaret and Mike sharing one room, Cynthia and Laura in another, and Johnny and Barb camping out on the foldout sofa in what was supposed to pass for the living room. Still, maybe it was getting out of Goose Creek, or perhaps the upswing in Johnny's mood sparked everyone, but this was a happy time for the Walkers. They were a family again, and Johnny, for a while at least, had a go at playing daddy.

He had the knack, too. The childhood games player started playing games with his own children. The woods behind the trailer became a land of adventures: Johnny took the kids hiking; taught them how to build campfires; led them on overnights, mischievously spooking them with ghost stories; he even built them a tree house. There was nothing Daddy didn't know: He could explain the mystery of how the TV in the living room actually worked; or he'd take apart the radio and then, to everyone's cheers and amazement, put it back together again so that it played as good as new; and on a warm summer's night he'd line his crew up in front of the trailer and announce that all those stars up there were actually part of something called constellations— look, there's a bear, and a man . . . Everything was fun: On Saturday mornings the gang would watch cartoons, Daddy giggling the loudest; on Sundays he'd whip up a pancake breakfast; and if there was house- work to do, everyone pitched in, with Daddy leading the way, first making sure, though, that the jazz station—he loved bebop—was blasting through the trailer. He was the wisest, bravest man his chil- dren could ever imagine. Once, down at the shore, Laura, just a toddler, got carried off by a wave. She still remembers being kicked and tossed around, swallowing so much salty water that she simply faded out. And then, all of a sudden, she remembers being in her daddy's arms, her being able to breathe again, and everything being all right. Growing up, she tried to hold on to that memory for as long as she could.

One time, walking in the woods behind the trailer, Johnny told Margaret a secret. She was the oldest, a freckled-faced nine-year-old, so she figured she had a right to know important things. She listened carefully as her daddy told her something he said he had never told anyone.

"Know what I think is going to happen when we get this restaurant going?" he began. "I think that one day, out of the blue, your grand-daddy, my father, is just going to walk in. Course he won't know it's his son's place or anything, but he'll just be driving by and figure from the looks of it that it might be the sort of place he'd like to stop in for a beer. And when he walks in the door, there I'll be to greet him."

Johnny Walker, Sr., didn't drop in and, more noticeably, hardly anyone else did either. Johnny would sit at the bar waiting for his audience, but no one came. There were lots of theories: The snack bar was too off the beaten path; the local Baptists weren't the sort to cotton to roadhouses; foreigners from up North couldn't expect to move into the community and start coining money; and on and painfully on.

Failure hurt Johnny to the quick. He took it very personal. He'd walk into the empty place, and now the sound of the jingling curtain of beads cut him deep down inside. The empty silence worked on him. There was no way he could fit failure into the way he looked at himself. He was a hot runner, a submariner, a senior chief. Not some screwup. He'd have to invent a way out.

He started building a case against Barbara, and this indictment drained all his love. How could there be any profits, she was drinking them up. She was the one who couldn't even fry a burger, who kept the snack bar looking like a pigsty. She was the one who got them in trouble with the cops, she was the one caught drinking out front with Nora the cook on a Sunday afternoon in Baptist country and got slapped with a $50 fine. It was Barb who tore into the local college president, some Bible thumper, when he came to complain that she was serving his God-fearing students. "I'll serve anyone who's of age and got the fifty cents for a beer," she yelled back at him. That didn't help community relations at all, Johnny fumed.

Industrious and creative, he found it easy to work up quite an anger. In Johnny's mind the snack bar became Barbara's doing, and, therefore, it was her failure. So he just discarded them both. He couldn't wait to go off to sea; he was that eager to escape.

Johnny wanted to pretend it wasn't his problem, but when he came back from his cruise, the trailer was littered with past-due notices. The IRS was sending certified letters. He decided not to look at the mail; that made it easier. But Barbara also wouldn't let him forget. She was bitter; she figured he was screwing around, and that hurt. Vodka made things easier for her, until things got out of control. God, she would lash into him. And come the hazy mornings, embarrassed but still vindictive, she would plot her revenge.

Maybe, then, she led herself into it. She was working the bar, serving a customer or two and keeping pace herself, when the beer distributor walked in. He was in a mood, all right. Wanted his $200 or else. Barbara bought him a drink. Anything but a beer he said, so they laughed and that kind of broke the ice. They sat and had a couple. And at closing time he just came out and said it: You sleep with me, and I'll forget about the $200.

What surprised Barb even more was that she didn't slap his face or anything. She just walked away. Hell, maybe he thought she was thinking about it; and maybe she was.

But early the next morning, when Johnny came rolling in from God knows where, she was full of fire. She had reached quite a pitch, fueled by booze and anger and indignation. When she told her husband about the beer distributor's proposition, it was a teary confession.

Johnny, undaunted, looked her in the face and didn't miss a beat: "For two hundred bucks you'd be a fool not to fuck that guy."

He was beyond caring.

Things kept falling apart in bunches. Suddenly Bill Wilkinson decided he had to bail out. He had a right: The monthly nut was staggering, what with the mortgage, the beer bills, and the payments due on all of Johnny's fancy purchases. Worse, there were some family problems and Billy found himself in a real jam. He needed every penny he had. Johnny didn't think twice about offering to buy his buddy out. At the time it seemed like a good idea. He wanted Billy to like him.

Except he didn't have the money.

Johnny felt like doom itself. He had really wedged himself into a corner this go-around—drunken Barb, the four screaming kids, a stack of bills, the goddamn IRS, and now Billy, too. What the hell was he going to do?

Desperation, though, is a narrow domain: instinct commands. There was, after all, one person he could turn to. Johnny had gone running to him that time in Scranton when the judge was getting ready to throw the book; he had sought him out when three daughters, one straight after the other, had eaten away all of an E-2's savings; and he had talked to him, begging him just about, when it looked like he would never make it to subs and the only thing left to do was finish up and get out of the Navy altogether. Once again, the pattern held. Johnny reached out to his older brother Art.

As luck would have it, Art happened to be in Charleston. The two brothers had, until recently, not seen each other for nine years. If it had been up to the Navy, it would have been even longer. Art was a lieutenant on the *Grenadier,* one of the last diesel subs, and the boat was under way to the base in Guantánamo Bay, Cuba, when it developed propeller problems. The boat's orders were quickly rewritten: Put into Charleston for minor repairs. Minor repairs, however, stretched into a complete overhaul. The *Grenadier* was moored in Charleston from July 1967 to January 1968.

During those six months, Art was the engineer in charge. Commander George R. Robey, Jr., his commanding officer, thought Art did quite a job: "He has an almost uncanny ability to ferret out problems, often before they arise, and take timely and efficient action to correct them."

Johnny, as always, bought the first round. Put your money away, he insisted, Charleston is my port. Art, getting into the mood, drank to that. And why shouldn't they tie one on? he figured. They had a lot to celebrate: one a lieutenant, on the fast track from seaman to admiral; the other an enlisted man, but a senior chief on a boomer. So they drank to Scranton, to old times, to where they'd been, and to where their careers would take them. Lost time, sea stories, baby pictures—all were trotted out by the time last call came around. That had been the first night, the easy one, and Johnny played it as a prelude to what he really wanted to talk about.

The next time, no longer strangers, they took longer looks at each other. Art, now a father of three, bars on his shoulders, had filled out; it was as if he had become fleshy and adult with the responsibilities of command. Johnny, though balding like his older brother, still was a slight, thin presence, almost clownish with his shabby mustache. Which suited Johnny fine. He let his older brother tease him. He laughed at Art's jokes. He flashed his familiar warm smile. Johnny had, after all, become quite a performer.

When the moment was right, not the next time, or even the time after that, but when he felt the old ground was once more fertile with sentiment, he poured his heart out to his big brother. Art had no choice but to listen.

Perhaps he also had no choice but to bitch, hem and haw for a day or two, but then finally to surrender. Art, already well-noted for his "timely and efficient action," took a Household Finance Loan for $1,000 and gave the money to his little brother. But there was more to his generosity! Art, perceptive, a man also marked by his "uncanny ability to ferret out problems," had some brotherly advice. This, too, was meant as compensation, a secret down payment, brother to brother, on a hope for the future: a new adventure.

Art told Johnny a story. It was real; it was true; but since he kept it deliberately vague, it had the impact of a fable—you had to draw your own moral.

Back when he had been stationed on a training sub up in Groton, Art began, a lot of the guys were thinking about ways to make an extra buck. All sailors, he told his brother, manage to get themselves in a hole every now and then. Anyway, that's when a couple of the guys came up with the idea of selling the armature out of the electric motors. It was copper, and you could always get a good price for that.

They had it all worked out. There was a restaurant, Monte's, some of the guys would go to in Brooklyn on the weekends. The place was always packed. Great veal and peppers.

Mafia? Johnny interrupted, fascinated.

Who knows? Art continued. They didn't show you membership cards or anything. But they were willing to make deals. They'd buy copper, they'd buy anything. They were always friendly to sailors.

And that was the end of the story.

Johnny pressed Art, he nudged, he cajoled, but Art wouldn't give any names. Now don't jump to any dumb-ass conclusions, Art told him. I'm not saying I was involved in that or anything. It's just a story, sailor to sailor, brother to brother.

But for Johnny, given his mood, it was something more.

6

The ride, always a grind, had turned nasty. An unseasonably cold evening—January 23, 1968—had, as he drove north, become a chill, runny night streaked with sprinkles of wet snow. The five-hour trip up I-17 from Charleston to Norfolk had stretched into eight. And still he took it slow; he pulled into the right lane whenever he caught some cowboy in his rearview mirror gunning his rig and coming up tight on his tail. On a night like this he had a real fear of his little orange car, one taillight cracked and dark, being rear-ended by a galloping sixteen-wheeler. So it was after eleven—his crew would cover for him, he knew—when Warrant Officer John Walker finally drove his MG through the main gate of the Norfolk Naval Base. He downshifted to acknowledge the Marine guard's quick salute, and then headed to flag country.

It was a slow, twisting ride across the base. The wet, icy winds coming off the Chesapeake had made the road very sloppy. His defroster wasn't working, so he had, constantly, to use his hand to clear an oval out of the filmy condensation on his windshield. Not that there was much to see: The base, battened down for the storm, seemed deserted. Which suited him fine. He pulled into the parking lot across from the complex of squat, two-story concrete buildings off International Terminal Boulevard, the headquarters for the Atlantic Fleet, praying the late watch tonight would be easy duty. But it wasn't only the ride; after the last two days with Barbara in Ladson, Johnny figured he deserved it.

Out of the blue, nine months ago, as Johnny was finishing up a Mediterranean cruise on the *Bolivar,* a promotion came through. He received his commission—warrant officer. And then, before he had a chance to get used to his new stripes, a month later only, came the real surprise. Sure, he had known the Navy might take him off the *Bolivar;* detailers like to rotate the senior radiomen. He had hoped to serve, though, on another sub: Boomers were at the top of his last dream sheet, with diesels as his backup choice. A lot of good it did him. After twelve years in the service he had caught on that a sailor might as well believe in Santa Claus as believe in dream sheets, but he still hadn't anticipated the grand swings of Navy logic. In April 1967, he was pulled from all boats. He was ordered to report to COM-SUBLANT Operations. Johnny couldn't believe his luck.

It wasn't only that his being assigned to the commander of submarine operations for the entire Atlantic Fleet was Johnny's jump into high-command, hot-runner country, the sort of duty an ambitious 4.0 sailor likes to have on his roster. There was also something else: COMSUBLANT—along with the rest of the command under CINCLANT, the three-star admiral who controlled the Atlantic Fleet—was billeted on the Norfolk Naval Base. And Norfolk was 475 miles from four wailing kids, a moody wife, and a business that was sliding further downhill each day.

For a while, a couple of months at least, Johnny tried putting in his duty days in Norfolk and then, stoking himself up with caffeine, heading off on an all-night drive to Ladson. The ride gave him time to brood. He thought about Barb, the real hard case he felt she had grown into—and how she was dragging his life straight down; and he thought about the kids, the rug rats, he called them, and how they were always kicking and screaming and cutting into his Happy Hour money; and he thought about The Bamboo Snack Bar, how Barbara had screwed it up, drinking up the profits, scaring off the locals, shredding his future into small pieces as he, her victim, could only watch. By the time he'd reach Charleston, he'd be in no mind to deal with it all. Sometimes, it would be easier to hunt up a few old shipmates, buy a round or two for them, and get a nice soft buzz—a bit of attitude adjustment, he'd say—before pulling up to his battered trailer. Of course, that would only make things worse.

Then there were the confident times. Johnny would head down to Ladson determined to set things right. He'd make a go of the snack bar, put in pinball machines, a jukebox. He'd tell himself: A bar takes time to catch on, that's all. As for Barb, they were head over heels once upon a time; that's still got to count for something. But come the end of another tense evening, his hopeful thoughts would slam into reality. He'd close up the bar with three singles in the register; and rather than crawl in next to a wife who, wild and taunting, had shouted ''baldie'' at him—was that before or after he called her a lush? what did it matter anymore? he decided—he'd sleep in little Mike's bed.

It became easier not to make the trip. He'd just telephone Barb and tell her things were hopping at COMSUBLANT. My country needs me; let the old witch argue with that, he'd plot. And then he'd run off like a kid playing hooky from school.

A new buddy, Chief Marsh, was teaching him how to sail and Johnny, as he did with any game that grabbed his attention, threw himself into it. He passed many sunny afternoons on the bay, grinding winches, unfurling spinnakers, hoisting sails. Naturally, a little fun grew into another greedy fantasy: One day he'd buy his own boat, a real hot one, very fast. That's not all he told his new buddies: Johnny was getting a little on the side. While the wife was down in South Carolina managing his business—he had this bar that was raking it in, he boasted—he was also taking care of business. There was this hot number, a secretary on the base, who couldn't get enough of Johnny. She, too, became part of Johnny's barroom repertoire. The story went like this: I'm a married man, he had dutifully confessed after their first roll in the hay. Course I knew that, she answered pridefully. That's why I was so careful not to get any lipstick on your boxers. Now that's my kind of girl, Johnny concluded, *real thoughtful*. And a room full of sly laughter affirmed his judgment.

Still, as thoughtful as this secretary was, Barbara somehow had gotten wind of her. Or maybe, knowing Johnny, she was just playing out loud with her suspicions. Either way, it didn't matter. From the moment Johnny came home that third January weekend in 1968, Barb was on his case. They were broke, she shouted. He was a pig, a bum. So he came back at her. You're lazy, a lush, he snapped. But when she sneered he was a screwup, a failure just like his father, that was when Johnny, not even thinking about it, hit her. One quick slap. And that was that.

On the slow, sloppy ride back to Norfolk the next night, Johnny was really low. He felt there was just no way out of the life he had become caught up in. He hated Barb. He couldn't put up with the four kids. He was broke; the IRS was still demanding back taxes. Art's money, hard to borrow, had been too easy to spend; it was all gone. Maybe he was just like his father. And that realization, he would later claim, made him want to kill himself. Just end it all.

World weary, his sad conclusions his only company for the past eight hours, Johnny left the parking lot on that chill January night and walked to Building Two. There were Marine guards at the main door, but he was quickly buzzed in. He rode the elevator down a flight; the stairs would have been faster, but he was just too tired. In the basement, still in no hurry, he headed down a pale yellow corridor toward another pair of secured doors. Maybe he should have called in sick, he was thinking. But, always very Navy, he quickly let that excuse slide. Pep talk time, instead: C'mon, sailor, he lectured himself, Ladson, Barb, all that crap—stow it. Duty calls. Still, when he reached the doors—gray steel as thick and solid as a wall—he wasn't up for shooting his usual lines with the Marine guards. It must have been obvious. Without hesitation, Johnny was buzzed in.

The heavy doors opened; and right away the sudden bright lights and the active noise—the clickety-clack of high-speed printers, the fuzzy whine of radio transmitters, the voices of a dozen sailors—helped to bring Johnny around. Crammed into this cluttered space—an area not much larger than the end zone of a football field had been partitioned into four work stations—was the communications operations room for the entire Atlantic submarine fleet. If a submariner's wife had a baby or the President wanted to launch Polaris missiles at Moscow, the message would be sent from here. And as soon as he

walked through those doors, for the next eight hours, Warrant Officer
John Walker was in charge.

Most days, this was Johnny's kind of duty. He felt, he'd tell people,
as if he, a poor kid from Scranton, was close to all the secret doings
that were going on in the world. There was a big map at the front of
the room, he'd still be bragging a decade later, and on it were little
squares, blue for diesels, bright red for boomers: the location of every
one of our subs. Know what the Russians would give for that kind of
info? he'd challenge. Or for an idea at what those subs were up to?
That's why, Johnny would go on, just about all messages coming and
going to these boats would be in code. Before a message would be
transmitted, it would be encoded with a garbled text; and when a
message was received at COMSUBLANT a yeoman would have to
run it through one of the cryptograph machines to decipher it before a
clear text would appear on the printer. Not that all the messages were
top secret. Most of them were unclassified GENSER, general service
communications, the daily sort of messages that any ship might receive; communications including Familygrams from a wife informing
her submariner husband that their son had just cut his first tooth to a
NINKS announcement ("all submarines copy this message") that a
raunchy bar in Manila was now off-limits. The drill, though, was to
send these routine messages in code, too. It was another safeguard;
that way the Russians couldn't be sure if the garbled text they had
intercepted was a battle order or the announcement of the winner of
the World Series. Makes the game nice and complicated, Johnny
would explain with an insider's grin.

After the message had been received and deciphered at COMSUB-
LANT, part of Johnny's job was to supervise its routing. If it were
routine, a Familygram, say, it would be printed on white paper. Then,
one of his tape apes would put it through Autodin, the automated
switching system for military communications that works similarly to
a telephone exchange. A wife across the country would find her love-
sick submariner's telegram waiting for her with the morning's mail.
However, if the decoded message had a priority designation—confidential traffic would be printed on green paper, secret on yellow, and
top secret on pink—Warrant Officer Walker would check the message
personally for transmission garbles before logging it on the disclosure
sheet and sending it upstairs, usually by hand, to one of the admirals
in flag country. That way, there wasn't much going on in the Atlantic

Fleet, especially concerning submarines, that Johnny didn't know about. And, as he liked to say, he often knew it before most admirals.

To hear Johnny describe his job, he was right in the middle of a hush-hush, global—he was partial to that word; it sounded so author-itative—game. A keeper of secrets, he called himself. It was just the sort of occupation that suited him. Except tonight, after the woeful couple of days in Ladson, after his dredging over and over through his hopeless situation during that rough eight-hour ride, he just wanted easy duty. Let them move routine GENSER, Familygrams. He was counting on a couple of cups of strong coffee—there was a percolator outside the vault in the crypto room—and the time to thumb through a sailing magazine.

Johnny got his cup of coffee, but he never opened his magazine. At about 1:30 A.M.—the way he remembers it—the bell started ringing on the "hot" printer. A Z flash was coming in. It was the first of many. They were moving "yellow" just about nonstop for the next eighteen hours.

By the following evening, the flash information had spread way beyond the windowless basement room in Norfolk. It was all over the news: The USS *Pueblo* had been boarded by the North Koreans, one sailor dead, the crew captured. There were even published reports speculating that the ship had been on some sort of intelligence mission off the east coast of Korea when it had been attacked.

But that was just the half of it, Johnny was thinking when he lis-tened to Walter Cronkite the next night. After an endless watch in the communications room—bedraggled Johnny and his crew had been ordered to work a piggyback shift—he had no illusions: The *Pueblo* was a spook ship; of course it had been on a SIGNIT (signals intelli-gence) assignment monitoring transmissions from Soviet ships. Hell, that was how the game was played. He also knew for certain that the entire crew was in North Korean hands. That was rough, but it went with the territory. The real disaster, though, was still taking shape. Flag country knew it, and so did Warrant Officer Walker. In fact, all hands in the communications room had been grumbling about it from the moment COMSUBLANT had caught the first Z message from the *Pueblo*. It had been a vivid bit of raw intelligence:

"We need help. We are holding emergency destruction. We need support. SOS SOS SOS. Please send assistance. Please send assistance. Please send assistance. Please send assistance. SOS SOS SOS. We are being boarded."

The tape, forwarded from Pacific Fleet Operations, was played and replayed in flag country; and its analysis offered few consolations. The concern, it seemed, centered on the radioman's verb tenses. They were active. The boarding had occurred, if the panicky tape ape banging out the Z flash had been accurate, *in the midst* of "emergency destruction."

It was possible, then, that the cryptograph machines aboard the *Pueblo*—a KW-7 and a KL-47—were now in enemy hands. It was possible that the ship's TECHINs, the bulky repair manuals that explain precisely how these machines operate, were now being scrutinized by the North Koreans. And it was possible that the Russians would soon have their first chance to inspect a KL-47 cryptograph machine. The same sort of KL-47 machine that, standing in a corner of the COMSUBLANT crypto room about two yards from Johnny's desk, was used daily by the entire Atlantic submarine fleet to transmit and receive messages.

Before Johnny had been assigned to Norfolk, in the days when keeping secrets was simply his instinct, not his profession, the Navy had him do a term at its crypto school in Vallejo, California. Most of the training was mechanical; crypto machines can break down and a radioman, especially on a sub, needs to know how to repair them. However, during the first week of the course the Navy likes to reveal a little bit of what the instructors call "the big picture."

The standard overview lecture—and if Johnny didn't catch this one, the chances are the one he heard probably covered the same ground; every crypto instructor, after all, gets his brief from the National Security Agency—starts with, for the Navy, a surprising show of candor.

The instructor, usually a chief petty officer, is hulking over a lectern at the front of a room filled with attentive radiomen as he launches into his presentation. The best way to keep a secret, he barks out, is not to share it. Any husband knows that, the chief slips in mischievously; and one can imagine Johnny, the eager student of secrets, latching on to the joke and following right along.

The thing is, the chief continues, the Navy, same as most married men, doesn't always have the luxury of keeping its secrets to itself. So we settle for the next best thing: making sure our secrets are shared with only those we want to share them with. For example, when Op Orders are sent out over the air, we want only the ships in the battle group to pick up on them—not the Russians. Just as a sailor at sea has to be real sure the sweet promises he's mailing to the dish he met in some bar don't wind up in the same envelope he's sending to his wifey, adds the chief, once more ad-libbing; and once more, for certain, winning the squids over.

The chief, if he's been at it for a while, knows enough to wait a moment for the laughter to fade. Then, again all Navy, he gets into the heart of his lecture. So we protect our secrets with cryptography, he explains. What's cryptography? Cryptography—and now the chief is off and running; he's got his definitions down pat—is taking the text of a message, correspondence, or communication and placing that text in a form that is unintelligible to anyone receiving it other than those people who are its intended recipients. More simply put, he adds, cryptography is the language the Navy uses to communicate among itself. And it's impenetrable. What does that mean? It means we can send any message we want anywhere in the world, and if the goddamn Russians pick it up off the airwaves, all they'll have for their troubles is a bunch of electronics beeps. The code is impossible to break. Ivan'll get diddley.

At this point the chief usually turns his back to the class and draws three letters on the blackboard—NSA. Any of you tape apes got an idea what that stands for? he demands. And perhaps because most of them do—you don't get into the course unless you're a hot runner radioman—the chief generally answers his own question: That's the National Security Agency. They're the bright boys up at Fort Meade in Maryland who supervise this country's communication security. The whole show. All the crypto machines we use in the Navy, all the codes we run in the machines—the entire cryptographic system is designed by these whizzes up at Fort Meade. Millions of dollars spent, he says with a touch of true awe, just to keep secrets. And it's money well spent: The system works.

It works, that is, it's impenetrable—and now the chief is walking away from the blackboard and heading toward a chunky machine encased in a dull gray metal—because a cryptographic system consists of two components. The first component is something we call cryptographic logic.

And while he's talking, the chief, with a bit of furtive ceremony, is unscrewing the heavy steel lid of the crypto machine that's resting on the table next to his lectern. Sometimes this model is a KW-7, the machine that was used throughout the Navy for standard teletype communications; other times he might choose a KL-47, the machine that encrypts the messages sent over the fleet's submarine broadcast channel; but, for Johnny's lecture, the chief most likely demonstrated on a KWR-37, because that was the specific machine Johnny's class was being trained to repair. Once the chief has removed the top, he reaches into what he identifies as "the pregnant part" of the machine and extracts a circuit board.

Waving the foot-long circuit board to the class like a man who has just used it to return a serve, the chief points out the words at the top of the board: CONFIDENTIAL CRYPTO. Know why this piece of equipment is classified confidential? he asks. But again his challenge is rhetorical. That's because, he continues without missing a beat, this board, along with two others inside the machine, is programmed with a very powerful algorithm or mathematical formula that enables the user to encrypt the plain text of a communication. A bunch of scientists at NSA might have been holed up for four, five years working on nothing but the formula contained on these boards.

Now the chief—and every senior instructor is also a bit of an actor —turns grim as he shares a disturbing thought: If the Russians or whoever were able to get their hands on the information contained on all these boards, their bright boys would be able to construct their own machine that could receive our most sensitive communications. They'd be able to plug into our cryptonet, for sure. (And if a sailor should ask, the chief, putting on an air of sheer astonishment that anyone would have questions about the obvious, explains that a cryptonet is the term used to designate all the stations that employ the same crypto system to communicate.)

However, and now the chief switches moods dramatically and his voice is shrewd and triumphant, that would sure put Ivan close, but still no cigar. Ol' Ivan wouldn't be able to decipher or, as they say at NSA, decrypt what we're transmitting throughout our cryptonet unless he could get his hands on the other component of the system—the cryptographic key.

Once more the chief turns to his crypto machine and pulls open a smallish steel drawer. This here, he tells the class, is what we call the CRIB—the card reader insert board. It's where we insert the keying material. Now, the keying material for this particular machine comes in the form of an IBM-type computer card. Different machines, though, might use tapes, lists, or another type of card as the keying material. A machine that uses lists, for example, doesn't have a crib but a permuter tray on which the key list numbers are set manually. Regardless, the keying material is printed for all the machines by the NSA and then delivered by the ARFCOs—that's the Armed Forces Courier System, the chief adds—to all the users.

Now look closely at this card, he instructs his class, as he waves a flimsy, perforated key card toward them. See the inscription on it—TOP SECRET NOFORN. That means that these damn things are not only top secret, they're also not for distribution outside United States channels. And why is that? Well, sailors, that's because these pieces of cardboard are what set the codes. These little holes you see allow electrical energy to pass through certain spots so that the logic is fundamentally changed. The card tells the machine what circuit board to use or what direction to move a certain circuit board so that a message can be decrypted. And each day the Navy changes the key. We insert new cards into each Navy crypto machine every twenty-four hours. A sub sitting on the bottom of the Indian Ocean, say, might be tied into the Pacific Fleet cryptonet, but if it's a Tuesday and the radioman hasn't set his machine with Tuesday's key card, then all the sub's going to receive from CINCPAC is indecipherable mumbo jumbo.

These cipher cards, then, are part of the national treasure, sailors. And the Navy treats them that way. Cryptographic material probably has the most rigid control procedures of any material in government. Every monthly book of thirty key cards, each individual key card even, is serially numbered and relentlessly monitored from the day it is produced at Fort Meade till the day it is destroyed at the duty station by the CMS—the initials stand for Communications Material Security, the chief breezily adds—custodian. And even the CMS custodian has to round up another sailor at the end of a day to sign a statement that he witnessed the destruction of the keying materials.

Which brings us, sailors, to the bottom line: You men are now becoming part of the process. You men are being trusted to keep your country's most confidential secrets.

It's at this point that the chief more often than not pauses. But it's not mere theatrics; he now takes his time with each word for the simple reason that his life's work, everything the Navy has trained him to believe, resides in his final rhetorical question: What would happen if the Russians got their hands on both the logic *and* the key for any one of our machines? Well, he says, the best way to understand that kind of disaster would be to compare it to a poker game. A poker game where one side would be able to know what cards the other side was holding. Except, sailors, the stakes for this particular game of poker happen to be the future of the world.

One week after the *Pueblo* sent out its first SOS, a series of events began quickly to unfold which, when linked together by opportunity and circumstance, would go a long way toward shifting the odds in the chief's poker game. It started in Wakkanai, Japan. A radioman at this NSA-run station on the northern tip of the island was routinely monitoring the facsimile link between Pyongyang, the capital of North Korea, and Moscow. "All of sudden," a member of the intelligence station staff has been quoted as recalling, "there was this special transmission, and all these secret-code-word documents were coming across. All the *Pueblo* stuff was coming across. Everything was captured."

Of course by the time this information reached the basement operations room of COMSUBLANT, the role played by Source Wakkanai —as it was known at NSA—had been sanitized from all transmissions. Yet, the flash was all over Norfolk flag country: The *Pueblo*'s crypto machines and TECHINs were in Russian hands.

It was also around this period—the tail end of January 1968—that COMSUBLANT had a scare over a shipment of cipher cards. The CMS custodian receiving the delivery of February key cards noticed that the package's outer seal was undone. This was in violation of

NSA controls. Warrant Officer Walker was informed. An investigation was immediately begun.

Before the day was over, the situation was cleared up. The seal had not been broken; the cards had not been tampered with; the error was simply negligence. A new clerk at the manufacturing facilities in Fort Meade had failed to affix the outer seal to the package. Still, coming so soon after the capture of the *Pueblo,* the unsealed shipment of cipher cards had everyone talking.

The next link in this haphazard chain was forged a few days later in an Ocean View bar. The name of the bar has long since been forgotten; it could have been any of a handful of squid joints that are scattered across four seedy blocks less than a twenty-minute ride from the Norfolk Naval Base. But what remains indelible is that a bunch of sailors, tape apes, were sitting around having a few beers. And that Johnny Walker was one of them.

Not that Johnny was the life of this party. His troubles were still cutting into him. A ton of debts, a lush of a wife, four screaming rug rats—it was a hell of a woeful load he felt he was toting. Who could blame Johnny for looking to his buddies to help him kill the rest of another long night?

So the gang of radiomen had a few; and a few more; and, as is often the case when friendship is based on a common pride, the talk eventually found its way to their job. Naturally someone brought up the *Pueblo.* The feeling around the table was the crew should have gone down with the ship rather than let the Russians get their hands on the crypto equipment. That led to somebody's mentioning the panic over the cipher cards. From there it became just one long gripe: Hell, they're always screwing up the delivery of those damn key cards. It's a joke, the security. They just made a big deal of this time 'cause of the *Pueblo.*

That was when one radioman—and again his name is lost; it is doubtful that even the culprit could today, twenty years later, identify himself, so inconsequential were his intentions—finally came out and said it: Sailor wanted to, he could just make copies of those damn key cards. Who the hell would stop him? Tell me the Russians wouldn't pay good money to get their hands on those babies. . . .

Sure, all you do is call up the KGB, said one of the guys, trying to make the scheme seem wild and crazy and impossible.

But the schemer wouldn't be put off. You got it, he announced. Just call up the Russian embassy in D.C. Tell any one of those Ivans you got key cards. He'll listen, all right.

And then, just as quickly as it started, the conversation took another boozy turn. Again, no one really remembers why. The best speculation has it that there probably was a girl—was she the subject of a raunchy story? the punch line of some squid's joke? or perhaps the real thing, a live, in-the-flesh female who had caught one of the sailors' eye?—behind this development.

The truth is, it does not matter. What matters is that Johnny Walker listened very carefully to the conversation that night.

Later, as he lay in bed, Johnny played with all the pieces: his brother's strange story about a restaurant in Brooklyn, the capture of the *Pueblo,* the cipher card scare, a barroom scheme. And by and by, for the first time, he was beginning to imagine a way out.

7

Johnny couldn't find the Russian embassy. He kept walking down the street, but nothing looked right. He took the scrap of paper from his raincoat pocket and checked the address he had copied from the Washington phone book: 1125 16th Street. This was Sixteenth Street, all right. But the number on the building in front of him was already 1200 and something. He must have walked past the damn place. He had been looking out for a big, official sort of building. With a sign. Or at least a flag. He hadn't seen anything like that. Nothing he could do though, but turn around and backtrack. It had to be somewhere nearby. Still, the thought crossed his mind, they sure weren't making it easy for him to become a spy.

Up to that moment, everything had gone quick and smooth. Not that he had a real plan. It all just sort of happened. One night he was in Norfolk looking for a way out of his life. And come the morning, he had simply decided to invent a new one. Once he had reached that decision, instinct, the lure of a new game, took over.

On his first night back in the operations room, the barroom conversation goading him, he set out to steal a key list. It's hard to imagine, he would later try to explain, but there was no room in his plotting to consider what he was doing; his calculations focused only on the act: the challenge of pulling it off. He was charged with excitement. But after that first night Johnny knew he—he alone!—had them all beat. He went to the safe where the ready crypto was stored; shoved a key list sheet between the pages of one of his sailing magazines; and then, when no one was looking, oh so very calm, Warrant Officer Walker ran the cipher list, a month's worth of settings for a KL-47 machine, through the Xerox machine outside the vault. Ten minutes later—but each of those minutes pounded through him full-speed—the original was back in the vault, and the copy nonchalantly wedged between the glossy pages of *Sail*.

The game had moved forward so easily, the thrill of fear felt so much more invigorating than the dull, hopeless corner his life had become boxed into, that how could Johnny resist pursuing it to the next level? Truth was, he didn't even consider the possibility. The game was getting too good; the play was now the only thing.

With the copy of the key list in his back pocket, Johnny, on his first duty-free morning, set out in his orange MG. It was a four-hour drive from Norfolk to Washington, D.C., and Johnny used the time to flesh out his scheme. He thought things out step-by-step, the way the Navy had taught him, he would one day state, seemingly untroubled by the irony: He would drive up to D.C., head to a local gas station where he could copy the address of the Russian embassy from the phone book and get a downtown map that would help him plot out the route, and then he'd simply show up at the front door and tell them what he had to sell; cutting the deal would be the fun part. It was a simple plan, but then the game was still new.

It was only after he had written out the address from the Washington directory that Johnny, like any actor searching for the dimensions of his new role, tried to get clever. What if, it suddenly occurred to him, he had been followed from Norfolk? What if the FBI had the embassy staked out and spotted his car with its naval base stickers? What if on leaving the embassy the Russians followed him to his car and traced his real identity—he was determined to play his part under a stage name—through his license plate? All the what ifs ran through him like an electric charge. But Johnny might just as well have been glowing from all that energy. He enjoyed the idea of outsmarting people whom he felt were trying to get an edge on him. He added a new tactic to his plan: He would park his car about a mile from the embassy and then hail a cab to take him to Sixteenth Street. He would even walk the last block or so for added protection. That would throw off any tail, he reasoned. And he congratulated himself on this final shrewd touch.

In all that plotting, in all his hours on the road with a top secret key list in his back pocket, did Johnny Walker, a sailor for the past twelve years, ever really think about the friends or country he was about to betray? Years later he would greet the question with a limp smile and then a flood of genuine astonishment at his interrogator's naïveté. Finally, like a child giving in to a stern parent, he would offer an apology of sorts: "It was a desperate act," he said. But he might have added: Reasons? There was simply no reason not to. Allegiance? A man's allegiance is only to the game he's playing at any given moment. Betrayal? To betray something, a man has to believe in something.

These unarticulated responses and the sentiments that provoked them, though, were worlds away from Johnny's deliberations as he walked down Sixteenth Street on that evening in February 1968. His concern was finding the damn Russian embassy. It was dark, nearly five, and cold. If he didn't find the place soon, he figured he would give up. For good. Sashay down Sixteenth Street two days running, the FBI would be sure to get a beat on you.

That's when, down toward the end of the block, he saw a black iron gate being opened as a car pulled out and headed into traffic. Immediately he realized he had been standing in front of the freakin' embassy for the past few minutes; the building was protected by a fence and then set back from the street. That had to be the entrance at the corner; he had walked right by it. Feeling foolish, he hurried to the gate before it was once more slammed shut.

Johnny took one look at the man standing by the gate and instantly decided that if he wasn't the embassy chauffeur, than he sure looked like he was made for the job. It wasn't that the guy was in uniform; he was wearing a regular sport coat and a shirt, no tie, real casual. Except he did have on this silly hat with a visor, like a Navy officer's, only the guy's hat seemed a size or so too small, like a child's beanie or something. Whatever it was, it didn't make the guy appear to be too swift. Still, Johnny figured the guy with the hat would have to do. It was now or never.

"I want to talk with someone in security," Johnny announced. He had given his opening line some thought; he had wanted something that sounded authoritative, knowledgeable, but not too off-the-wall.

The guy with the hat just stared at Johnny.

Was he going to blow a whistle, call the police? Johnny wondered.

It was too late to run, though. Nothing Johnny could do but try again. Except this time his voice slipped: "I want to talk with someone in security."

The oaf didn't say a word. He just looked confused.

And that's when it occurred to Johnny that of course the guy would be confused: He didn't speak English. Why the hell hadn't he thought of that before?

But just when he was becoming edgy with panic, just as he was mulling whether to run like hell or to try in slow, careful Pidgin English to explain himself one more time, the man at the gate turned to him and without even a trace of an accent said, "Follow me."

Almost two decades later, Johnny would be asked to draw a diagram of the interior of the Russian embassy and his sketch would be applauded for its accuracy by a group of skeptical critics. "As if I ever could forget anything about that day," he shot back at them, eyes near bulging, raw temper showing; which frightened them, and told them something too, for until that wild moment they had only seen Johnny playing the good sport.

He would always remember, he told them, switching back to his accommodating role, walking into the embassy through the front door, the chauffeur leading the way. It was so dark, shadowy, inside the embassy that for a moment he felt disoriented and yet the sensation was oddly familiar. Then it fell into place: It was dark like a submarine. And that gave him a rush of confidence.

The chauffeur led him to the reception area and started to say something, it might have been in Russian for all Johnny could make out, to the woman seated at the desk. Johnny, though, was in a hurry. He didn't think it made good sense for an American naval warrant officer to stand around in the lobby of the Russian embassy. So he cut in, this time talking to the woman. "I want to see someone in security," he tried again. Maybe he had raised his voice, or maybe there was something in his tone. But as quick as he got the words out, a guy in a dark suit moved into position behind him. He was a big guy, solid. A bonecrusher, Johnny decided. Johnny figured it might be wiser just to stand there real quiet and wait.

And still nobody said a word to him.

Five, ten, an eternity of minutes later, Johnny was in a real state. What have I gotten myself into? he was wondering. Am I waiting for the cops? The KGB? Or some goon with a rubber hose?

The three Russians—the chauffeur, the receptionist, and the bone-crusher—just stood there watching him. Nobody said a word.

So, finally, when this guy came up to him, about thirtyish, nice suit and all, and asked how he could help, Johnny was grateful. Johnny flashed him one of his well-rehearsed gushy smiles and, feeling kind of dumb to keep repeating the same line, offered it once more: "I want to see someone in security."

This time it worked. The man led him down the hall, stopping at a wooden door that couldn't have been more than twenty-five feet from the reception desk. He gave the knob a twist; the door was unlocked, which seemed to surprise the Russian for a moment; and recovering, more cautious than polite, Johnny felt, he held the door open for his guest. Then he followed Johnny into the room and shut the door behind him.

"I'm an American naval officer," Johnny began, knowing that fudging the facts was the least of his sins today.

The Russian merely looked at Johnny dully. He was seated behind a metal desk and Johnny sat across from him in a chair of some sort of modernish design. It was a small room without a window. The bookcases were empty and the desk top was bare. There was nothing in the room to show that it was part of the Russian embassy, or that its occupant was a KGB officer. It could have been a business meeting, a salesman making his pitch to a disinterested prospective buyer. Except it wasn't.

When the Russian didn't respond, Johnny, tiring of a game where he was not in control, figured it was time to show the Russian what he had come to deal. That should shake up Ivan, he imagined. He reached into his back pocket and took out the 8½-by-10-inch photo-copy of the key list for the KL-47. He kept it tight in his hand, but he let the Russian get a good look at the classification at the head of the page: TOP SECRET NOFORN.

Then, uneasy and oddly unsure of himself, he went into his spiel.

He rattled nervously on about how the paper in his hand was the cryptographic key for an entire month of radio messages for the whole Atlantic submarine fleet. Better than that, he said, this crypto channel was used for only the most important messages, Op Orders at the very least. The traffic on this channel was so restricted, he insisted, that only a select few radiomen were allowed to transmit or receive it.

Everything Johnny said was the truth, but he knew he was sounding a bit out of control. Maybe he was trying too hard. But, Christ, that damn Ivan was spooking him. He just sat there listening, not saying a word. All stony-faced. Johnny couldn't tell if this was making any sense to the Russian, so the only thing he knew how to do was to keep trying harder; Johnny was, after all, inventing his role as he went on.

Finally, the Russian cut him short. He asked to see the key list.

Johnny, irrationally, he realized later, refused. How was he going to make the guy pay, once he gave up the list? Suppose the Russian was planning on ripping him off? No, he told Ivan. Let's make a deal. Tell me what it's worth to you, and then I'll let you see it.

I want to inspect the product first or we cannot cooperate, the Russian explained flatly. We will talk price later. Or not at all.

Johnny knew this wasn't a bluff; son o' bitch was holding all the cards. Ivan the Glum would get his way, or he'd walk for certain. And Johnny hadn't come this far to drive back to Norfolk empty-handed. Besides, there was something comforting about the way he talked about the product and cooperating. (Johnny, the actor trying on the role of fieldman for the first time, would remember the Russian's cool, precise use of English for the rest of his life. It was, he would one day insist, his first lesson in his new language.)

So since there was no choice, Johnny, always adaptable, folded. Without even a shrug or a whimper, he handed the Russian the cipher list. It was, he knew, the real thing: Let Ivan take a good, long look. What could Ivan pull?

Except the Russian *did* pull something. He took the list and announced, I want to study this in private.

Before Johnny could protest, the Russian got up from his chair and headed out of the room.

You wait here, he told Johnny.

And that was all Johnny could do.

. . .

When the Russian returned, it was as if Johnny had never given him a top secret key list. He could not have seemed less interested in access to the United States naval codes. He was, in fact, apparently interested in only one thing. And this insistence was scaring the bejesus out of Johnny.

Before we go any further, the Russian declared in his expressionless, no-nonsense way as he took his seat, I must know your name.

Johnny was prepared for this one. From the start he had been convinced that it would be wiser to keep his real name to himself; it'd be a level of protection in case things got nasty with the Russians. For a day or so, then, he had been trying on names the way he often tried on moods. Yet, instinctively he seemed to realize that the strength of a good cover was in how tightly the lie fitted around the truth. He needed, therefore, a name that was like Johnny Walker but was not Johnny Walker. He played with the problem awhile. Until it came to him: Johnnie Walker was a whiskey; wouldn't a brand by any other name do the trick? That's how he settled on Harper, I. W. Harper. I spell it just like the bourbon, he imagined himself saying. That would be a good joke, not unlike one of his all-time favorites, all right; and perhaps an even better one because he was certain the dumb Ivans would never get it.

Except, on the ride up to Washington Johnny realized that maybe he had outsmarted himself. I. W. Harper? What the hell does "I." stand for? The Russians are going to ask me that for sure. His mind started racing: Ira . . . Izzy . . . Isaac . . . Shit, they all sound too Jewish. No way the Russians are going to believe that I'm some Jew naval officer.

Time running out, Johnny settled on something familiar: a family name—his younger brother's. So when the Russian asked him to identify himself, Johnny, playing it cool and friendly and sincere, said, James Harper.

The Russian, impassive as a commissar, nodded. And then he asked, You have identification with you? Driver's license? Military papers?

Johnny had not counted on this, but he thought he could still hang on to his script. When all else failed, he told himself, fill the stage with indignation. He'd simply huff and puff a bit: Course I got a license. An ID. But we got to trust each other. How we gonna do business without trust?

I need to see proof that you are who you say you are, the Russian explained. He wasn't arguing; he was stating a rock-solid fact.

What about the key list? I want it back now, Johnny demanded.

The Russian chose to ignore the request. Instead, he repeated in the dullest possible voice, I need to see proof of your identity.

Proof! Johnny shouted, trying on a new tone for effect. I'm here. That's proof enough. And Johnny, desperate, let his histrionics lead this argument to all sorts of rhetorical heights until he was just plain exhausted.

When Johnny's performance was done, the Russian, low-keyed and dour, once more told the sailor the rules: I need proof of your identity, or we cannot proceed any further.

And by now Johnny, utterly dejected, believed him.

There is a certain moment in nearly every sort of transaction when, though the deal is not yet done, someone makes a slip, a concession, and both parties know full collaboration is only a matter of time—and who will be setting the terms.

So it was when Johnny dug into his wallet and pulled out his military ID card. There was his picture in the right-hand corner and beneath that, typed in block letters was his name: JOHN A. WALKER, JR. There was nothing he could do, though, but hand the card to the Russian.

He had to throw out one script, but he quickly set to inventing a new one. He reached now for a professional tone, one man of the world confiding in another:

You know how it is, he told the Russian. It wasn't that I was lying to you. I just thought I might protect myself some. Till I got to know you better.

The Russian did not let on that he had the slightest idea what Johnny was talking about. He simply took the card and, without even looking at it, placed it in his pocket. Then he stood up.

You will wait here, the Russian instructed, and once more he left the room.

· · ·

Now I've done it, Johnny moaned to himself as he sat there waiting for the Russian to return. They've got the key list. They know who I am. Now they're checking me out—with who, the goddamn FBI? A crazy scene played in his mind: Hello, Norfolk? You got some top secret communications man down there name of Walker, John A.? Sure do; and by the way, who wants to know? Oh, just the KGB. . . .

They kept him waiting in that little room for at least twenty minutes. He didn't know if it would be all right to get up and walk around. What the hell, he finally decided. He stood up and took a few steps. Then he looked out the door, sly like, and saw the bonecrusher standing there. On guard. So Johnny went back to his chair and sat down.

He was scared stiff.

"Why is this not signed?" The Russian had returned, and clearly intent on keeping Johnny off balance, brought with him a new mood —belligerence. He waved the key list toward Johnny and repeated, "Why is this not signed?"

Now it was Johnny's turn to be confused: He did not know what the Russian was talking about. Finally, uncertain of what else to try and hoping not to sound like he was pleading, Johnny told him the truth: "They're never signed."

In time the Russian believed him; or at least was appeased.

His manner retreated to its previous mechanical way. He was as proper as an undertaker, calm as a commissar. But he was now talking, asking questions. Lots of them.

Johnny knew they were getting down to business. At last.

The Russian wanted to know on what circuits the key list was used; and Johnny could tell the guy knew a bit about cryptography, but was no expert. He wanted to know about Johnny's former duty stations. How much longer he anticipated being posted at COMSUBLANT. Where he anticipated he'd next be billeted. Whether he thought he'd get a promotion. But most of all, the Russian wanted to know what secret codes, operation orders, and technical manuals a warrant officer had access to. And years later, an odd pride still ringing in his voice, Johnny would reconstruct his response to the Russian: "I was totally honest. Exactly what I had access to—which was everything."

He later added, perhaps thinking further explanation was necessary, "I was in charge of the entire communications while I was on watch."

All that remained, then, was to cut the deal. The Russian set the price for the copy of the key list. Was it $1,000? $2,000? It was the first of many deals, and a small one at that, and Johnny quickly forgot the exact amount. He does remember, though, that he took the money, all in cash, and stuffed it in his pocket. He also agreed to meet with the Russians again. Only now, Johnny, the quick learner picking up on their tradecraft, said he would "cooperate."

Which had been his master plan from the start: a steady new income, an exciting new game. And feeling pretty good about his foresight, he handed the Russian the schedule, his next month's Norfolk watch bill, that he had brought with him. Pick a day that's good for both of us and I'll drive on up, Johnny told his new friend.

The Russian chose a day about three weeks off, but he would not allow Johnny to walk into the embassy again. There is the question of security. I have a list of procedures for you. You are to listen and memorize them.

Johnny grabbed on to the new word, but the Russian's procedures were too complicated, and not that he wanted to make too much out of this, he was too damn scared to get it all straight. In the end though, he just had to come out and say it: I got to write this down. I'm too nervous to remember all of it.

So the Russian, making a disdainful face Johnny would never forget, violated all the rules of the trade and allowed him to take notes while listening to the instructions for the next face-to-face: It would be at a Zayre's department store just across the river in Alexandria; Johnny would carry a *Time* magazine; he would walk left, then right a hundred yards, and so on in a quick series of twists and turns; eventually an agent would contact him in the parking lot. Johnny was to bring with him another month's shipment of key lists. He was also to supply a written account of all the sensitive material that passed through his command.

You want a shopping list, so to speak, Johnny interrupted.

But the Russian ignored this attempt at a joke. He only added that the amount of Warrant Officer Walker's remuneration would be in direct proportion to the number and quality of the classified documents he produced.

And then, nearly two hours after Johnny had walked through the front door of the Russian embassy, the meeting was over.

He did not leave through the front door. First they bundled Johnny up in a bulky overcoat and put an absurd, wide-brimmed hat—the Russians must have a thing about silly hats, Johnny was thinking—on his head. For good measure, one of the Ivans, there were three new ones now, pulled the hat low over his eyes. In case someone outside is watching, he explained; and the possibility made Johnny want to tremble.

But before he could work himself up, they guided him out a rear door, the three Ivans leading the way like linemen on a sneak play and Johnny, of course, was the quarterback. In no time at all they crossed a tiny courtyard and Johnny was shoved into the backseat of a waiting car. One Ivan got in on either side of him; the third sat in the front next to the driver. They ordered Johnny to crouch down as they pulled out of the embassy compound; to this day he is not sure if they were trying to help him or simply show him that they meant business when they pushed him to the floor.

Once they had gone for a bit, Johnny was told he could sit up. That felt better. He explained to them where his car was parked. No one seemed to care. They just kept driving.

That's when Johnny started to panic. Where were they taking him? I'm going to be late for my watch, he tried. It's a four-hour ride back to Norfolk, he insisted. People might get suspicious if I'm late, he explained.

The Russians didn't say anything. They just kept driving. First slow for a block or two. Then fast. Johnny, trapped in the backseat between two mute hulks, watched as the car ran a couple of red lights. Then it slowed down again, allowing traffic to pass. The goddamn Russians, he realized, were crisscrossing back and forth about the city. And all the time Johnny couldn't help wondering where they were going to wind up. Or what they were going to do to him when they got there.

But, after nearly an hour's worth of stop-and-start driving, they didn't do anything to him. They simply pulled over about a block away from his orange MG, had him return the hat and coat, and then they sped off without even saying good-bye.

By the time he reported for duty that night as watch officer in the communications room for the Atlantic submarine fleet, it was way after 11:00 P.M. and Johnny was really done in. Still, as he sat at his desk near the crypto vault, a keeper of secrets now holding onto another one, it's not hard to imagine that he was silently congratulating himself. Because he had pulled it off—he had become a spy.

PART II

COOPERATION

8

Nearly ten miles outside Moscow, driving southwest toward the village of Tëplyystan, a two-lane road abruptly breaks off from the main highway. Exiting here, though, is discouraged. The large sign at this intersection is a warning: HALT! NO TRESPASSING! WATER CONSERVATION DISTRICT.

Still, if one were curious one could disregard the sign and follow the curving road. It is a beautiful drive, the road leading deeper and deeper into a thick forest, until suddenly a militia post blocks the way. Soldiers are aiming automatic weapons, ordering the car to a halt. And then it is only a matter of time before the trespasser learns that despite the high-collared *gymnasterkas* these guards are wearing, they are not the regular soliders of the Moscow militia. Their uniforms are a disguise, more cover. These are troops of the KGB.

The KGB, as the Komitet Gosudarstvennoy Bezopasnosti is commonly known, is the Committee for State Security for the Union of Soviet Socialist Republics. Its mission, both at home and abroad, is to preserve, defend, and expand the power of the Communist party. Its soldiers are a secret police force throughout the Soviet Union, its agents a secret army throughout the world.

If, however, one can convince these KGB guards he is on official state business, the gate is raised. The tree-lined road continues far into the forest; and then, just when one might suspect that it will go on and on through the woods, it all comes to a halt. It ends in a traffic circle. A sign orders all cars to be parked; fanning out around the circle are the lots. From this point, one is allowed to proceed only by foot.

It is a short walk from the parking lots to a high chain link fence. The fence is topped with barbed wire. A guardhouse protects the single entrance gate; turnstiles, similar to the ones in the Moscow subways, are just inside the gate. The bronze-colored plaque on the guardhouse says SCIENTIFIC RESEARCH CENTER.

To enter, it is necessary to have an official pass. The pass is buff-colored and has the bearer's photograph. Each pass is inspected by the armed sentries. The soldiers have blue stripes on their khaki service trousers and blue stripes on their lapels. There is no longer any pretense: These are the markings of the KGB Guards Division.

The path beyond the guardhouse cuts through a neatly manicured lawn; in spring and summer flower beds along the walk are bright with color. At the end of this walkway, a four-hundred-yard trip that seems much longer during the painfully cold winter months, stands a building shaped like a three-pointed star. It even appears to glow, too; its seven stories are faced in aluminum and glass, and the materials catch the sun. Which pleased its Finnish architects, and surprised the Soviet officials who hired them.

A set of double glass doors opens onto the building's entrance. Once again, it is necessary to show one's pass to an armed sentry. Then one can proceed across a wide marble lobby toward the elevators. The offices are on the upper floors; only a cafeteria—vodka is something of a tradition in most state canteens; however, beer is as close to a real drink as one can order here—and a newsstand share this ground floor. In the middle of the lobby, though, is a pedestal supporting a massive bust. Fresh flowers are placed daily in a vase beneath this sculpture. Regardless, it is a grim, rather stern sentry. But that is appropriate: It is the face of Feliks Dzherzhinsky, the first chief of the Soviet secret police.

And this is the headquarters for the First Chief Directorate of the KGB.

The First Chief Directorate conducts the committee's foreign operations. It is a highly bureaucratized organization, divided into three separate directorates and eleven separate geographic departments. These departments control the Line PR—the letters stand for the Russian words meaning "political intelligence"—agents who work out of the embassy KGB Residencies throughout the world. These Line PR agents, often under consular cover, are the fieldmen responsible for recruiting new agents and maintaining communications with agents already in place: devising the procedures for each meeting, servicing drop sites, and administering the transfer of funds from the Moscow Center bankers—as the accountants working out of the main KGB headquarters on 2 Dzherzhinsky Square are known—to their covert operatives. Each Line PR man is the "handler" of many "assets": part psychologist, part tough guy, part salesman, and part housekeeper.

There is, however, one instance when the Line PR officer does not run the agent in his territory. In fact, the operation will be handled so clandestinely that the KGB Residency will not be informed of the existence of this asset, or even the identity of his Soviet handler.

This is a Department 16 case.

Department 16, run from an upper floor of the First Chief Directorate headquarters, is the most compartmentalized of all KGB divisions. It is also the most secretive: its officers control only one case; its fieldmen, working under deep cover, handle only one agent.

Department 16 directs cryptographic cases. Its assignment is to steal foreign codes and ciphers.

On that evening in February 1968, as soon as Johnny Walker was hurried into the backseat of the embassy sedan, a process was begun that would entwine his life—and his family's—with irrevocable decisions made in the star-shaped building hidden in the woods near the village of Tëplyystan.

The Washington embassy Line PR officer—and there is nothing in subsequent events or reports to suggest he did anything but follow standard tradecraft—sent a coded flash message informing Moscow Center that he was in possession of possible American naval cryptographic material. A detailed report of his meeting with the American warrant officer—is there a tape?—and the procedures he had set for the next face-to-face would follow. Once this report was written and encoded (and it is difficult to imagine a KGB officer leaving his desk that evening until this was accomplished), both it and the 8½-by-10-inch copy of the key list would be folded into a metal container not much larger than a shoe box; the container—standard Soviet diplomatic issue—held a minute pyrotechnic charge that would explode if the box was improperly opened or even suddenly shaken. The KGB officer would then hand-deliver the container to the embassy's courier-in-residence. By the time Johnny finished his late watch at COMSUBLANT that night, his stolen key list might very well have been on an Aeroflot jet to Moscow. What is certain, though, is that there was no additional action by the embassy KGB officer. Moscow Rules: Back off after the initial pass. Promise the asset the world, but hold off till Center wires further instructions.

There were none. It is now known that the agent in the Washington Residency never heard another word about his report; presumably he reasoned that the Directorate cryptographic analysts had determined that the key material was of little value; or that they had come to the conclusion that the American warrant officer was actually an FBI CI-2 provocateur. This was not, however, the determination.

Within weeks after the key list had been received at Moscow Center, the decision was reached to make Warrant Officer John A. Walker, Jr., a Department 16 asset. A case officer was selected to control the operation. He would pull the strings; the handler, a fieldman, would make the asset jump. So a work name was taken off a computer list and assigned to another Department 16 operative. He was immediately posted to the Washington embassy's Ministry of Foreign Affairs. His instructions were to bury himself deep in the cover of his ministerial duties, stay clear of the KGB Residency, and beginning with the drop at the Virginia department store, to run Johnny Walker.

9

Johnny, trying out his new life as a spy, was in the parking lot when he heard the voice.

"Hello, my friend," it called.

Immediately, Johnny found the accent, guttural with intrigue, a real treat. Then, eager, and of course scared, he turned toward the voice. First thing he noticed, though, was the Russian's coat: It was a trench coat, belted, collar up. Just like in the movies. All that was missing, he later joked, was the background music. So what if he had to rely on the strings of his heart for the *dum . . . da . . . dumdum*? Johnny was having a blast.

What a day it had been! Full of the game, as meticulous in his organization as if he had been leading his gang on a hike in the foothills of Scranton, Johnny had moved through Zayre's department store. The Russian's dictated procedures were his gospel. The recognition signal, a copy of *Time*, was under his arm and he kept to the prescribed route: first one way, then another, up a flight, then down. With the passing of the years, the precise path of his maze would become blurred; and only Johnny's wiseass quip would survive: Would Ivan make his pass in ladies' underwear?

But Johnny made it through ladies' underwear, and through men's furnishings, across the entire ground floor, and was now heading outside. The procedures specified the parking lot, and Johnny, taking his time, reaching for a bit of nonchalance, headed that way. He worried he was being followed: FBI? Naval Intelligence? KGB bonecrushers? And he worried, always comfortable with contradictions, that he wasn't being followed: There'd be no meet, no money, no game.

Yet as he walked through the parking lot, from out of nowhere it seemed, came the voice. Johnny could have just about cheered.

At first.

Things started out fine. This new Ivan with his trench coat was very impressive. He knew about communications, and Johnny enjoyed talking spy business with him. They discussed the various crypto systems at COMSUBLANT—KL-47, KWR-37, KG-26 (whose keying materials, Johnny complained, were a bitch to steal; the cards were cut as they were put through this equipment), and the KL-7. The Russian also zeroed in on the different circuits and frequencies for these machines; and that seemed to Johnny the smart way of going about things: If you knew the specific broadcast frequencies for naval radio traffic, you wouldn't have to waste your time monitoring the airwaves. Ivan in the Trench Coat also seemed really impressed when Johnny offered that Annex Kilo documents for the Atlantic Fleet were available in the communications room; while Johnny, too, gave the guy points for knowing that Annex Kilos were summaries of operation orders and operation plans.

When the talk turned to money, the Russian, getting very military, had a bit of a lecture: The pay would always be in cash, usually in fifties; twenties were too bulky, he explained, and hundreds were recorded in banks after each transaction as if they were checks. The safest place for the new money he'd be making, the Russian instructed, was in a safe-deposit box. As for spending, the way Johnny was reading Ivan, the advice came down to this—don't. But if you did, keep your purchases simple. A Chevy, say, rather than a Cadillac. And use a cashier's check; it's a good way of washing cash. The last thing you want to do, warned the Russian, is to attract attention. Things could get complicated if anyone—including your wife—

started asking questions about where all this money was coming from. Johnny found himself quickly nodding in agreement; he didn't even want to think about that.

What the new spy did want to pursue, though, was something more immediate, and more comforting: How much was coming to him?

Ivan didn't beat around the bush. He just threw out the numbers: between $2,000 and $4,000 a month. It was a salary Johnny claims he never debated, which may, however uncharacteristic, be true; or, perhaps is just Johnny's way of dealing with his inability to nudge the bottom line a little higher. Regardless, the figures, of course, had been set by the Department 16 case officer back in his office in the woods and therefore were immutable.

Johnny, the way he tells it, focused on the gap. What did he need to do to earn $4,000 rather than $2,000 a month?

Quality, explained the Russian, was the key. If the product was tech manuals or crypto, the money would be good. If Johnny could obtain a full month of key list settings, the money would be very good. Naturally, the Russian added, Johnny would not be paid until after the product was carefully evaluated.

Which led Ivan into his next question: Where was the material Johnny had obtained since his visit to the embassy?

That was when things fell apart.

At the time, Johnny thought he was being clever. Resourceful, even. No one at the embassy had told him how he was supposed to deliver the documents he was copying at COMSUBLANT; so Johnny, embracing his new role, began playing with the problem. Course he could just put the documents in a bag, carry it right under his arm with his *Time* magazine as he walked through Zayre's. Which might be fine; unless he was followed by the FBI; or Naval Intelligence; or, and there was no way he was going to share this with Ivan, the Russians conked him one from behind and took away his bargaining chip—for free. So the master spy worked out his own set of drop procedures: He stored the copied key lists and cipher cards in a rented locker at Washington National Airport. Shrewd, huh?

No, snapped the Russian. It was not shrewd, it was stupid, danger-

ous. Didn't Johnny know anything about airport security? Didn't he
notice how well lit locker areas are? Worse, airport lockers are always
being checked for bombs, for guns. What would happen if some curious airport policeman started thumbing through a pile of papers
marked TOP SECRET NOFORN? Perhaps a squad of FBI men had the
locker already staked out, just waiting to see who was going to make
the pickup.

There was a long, thoughtful moment, and then the Department 16
fieldman tried something else out: Perhaps that was Warrant Officer
Walker's plan? Perhaps he and the FBI were working together?

The way Ivan in the Trench Coat posed the question, his words as
measured as a vow, quickly convinced Johnny that playing dumb just
might save this sailor's life.

God, did Johnny puff smoke. He charged full steam ahead reciting
all the real and imagined risks he was taking. Yet what did he get in
return? He's accused of working for the FBI. Incredible! Especially
when all he had done was something stupid. Hell, he was new to all
this; he's bound to make mistakes. So how about this: Why doesn't
he just go to the airport, pick up the documents, and meet the Russian
back at Zayre's. Okay?

And what do you know, the Russian agreed.

After all that, Johnny himself was pretty relieved when he returned
to the locker and he didn't hear some guy barking through a mega-
phone: We've got you surrounded. Put up your hands . . .

And by the time he was in the airport parking lot, the documents in
a bag under his arm, he was feeling a little put out about the prospect
of driving back to the department store.

Except now it wasn't necessary.

Without a word of explanation or excuse for this change in plans,
the Russian was waiting for Johnny. Perhaps Ivan in the Trench Coat
had followed him to the airport, Johnny guessed. Or had a KGB
surveillance team been on his tail all along? Instinct, though, told him
not to ask these questions. Instead, he simply handed the package to
the Russian.

In return, the Russian handed him a sealed envelope. Inside, the
veteran fieldman announced to his novice, were the procedures for

the next drop. Johnny was to follow these instructions precisely. It was too dangerous to continue meeting face-to-face. If there were extraordinary problems, a means of getting in touch with him was included in the procedures. Agreed?

No problem, Johnny proclaimed. Similarly, the date of the next drop was quickly settled.

It was only as Johnny was getting into his MG that the Russian handler, almost as an afterthought, asked his asset if he anticipated having any trouble obtaining additional quality product.

Johnny, not finding it necessary to lie or embellish for perhaps the first time that day, told him, "Easiest thing in the world."

How easy was it for a COMSUBLANT radioman, and a rather low-ranking sailor at that, to steal top secret key lists and tech manuals? It was a question that was later asked quite often of Johnny Walker; and one which he seemed proud to answer:

Q. How were you able to copy this material?

A. On the Xerox machine.

Q. How did you get access to it? What was it about your responsibility that made you able to copy this stuff?

A. Almost anybody could have done it. It's just a matter of going to the safe where the ready crypto was stored and taking it to the Xerox machine. Of course, it had to be covered or hid and put something on top of it. One could just walk to the copy machine with a book. It's just enough to conceal it.

Q. What did you do with the material you were copying before you made your next connection?

A. I just kept it in my room at the naval station where I was living and carried it to my next meeting.

So Johnny, used to living on many levels, now added another one. A shift as watch commander; a shift as spy. Loyalty never was much of a problem because Johnny, the games player, lived in a world where beliefs changed as quickly as the adventure itself: The rules of each game were inviolate for only as long as he was playing that particular bit of sport. The 4.0 sailor, therefore, set out to become the master spy. He devoted himself to his new task. There was so much his Russian handler gave him to learn:

Procedure for summoning me to an exchange

Normally a schedule of fixed dates will be set for every exchange. However, if for some reason we fail to conduct it on these dates or if you need to summon me to an exchange outside the pre-arranged schedule use please the following procedure:

Mark the signal of the appropriate shape (which as you know has to be changed after each successful call to an exchange) at one of sites you've got on hand on a Thursday night. The schedule of choices will be as follows:

> 1st Choice—First Sunday after the Thursday on which you marked the signal.
>
> 2nd Choice—First Saturday after 1st choice.
>
> 3rd Choice—Second Saturday after the second choice.
>
> 4th Choice—Second Saturday after the 3rd choice . . .

The current *shape of the signal to be used* to summon me to an unscheduled exchange is "K" (Letter "K") . . .

Procedure for a face-to-face meeting outside the country

(To be used if you need to see me urgently)
Mark the signal shaped like this—6 (Figure Six) on a Thursday night at one of the sites you've got on hand . . .

Procedure for an extraordinary face-to-face meeting in the country

(To be used only in case of an extreme emergency)
Mark the signal shaped like this—ʃ (the lightning) on a Thursday night at one of the sites you've got on hand. We'll meet then at 20:45 (alternative time 21:15, should one of us be late) at the telephones at the 7/11 store located in Fairview Plaza in Virginia at the intersection of Little River Tpke. (Rte. 236) and Tedrich Blvd. (on the right-hand side of rte. 236 if you are coming from

D.C.). For easier identification please hold small "Dart Drug" paper bag in your left hand while standing at the telephones . . .

Procedures for summoning you to a face-to-face meeting

If something extraordinary causes me to summon you to a personal meeting I'll use the following procedure: I'll mail you a card of the kind you know about . . .

If all this wasn't enough, Johnny only had to make a delivery to be informed in another block-printed, handwritten note that the signal site was being changed. Johnny had visions of Ivan in the Trench Coat driving around Washington and its suburbs (their playground, Johnny knew, was limited; travel for Russian diplomatic personnel was restricted to a twenty-five-mile radius around the city) looking for inconspicuous places for a warrant officer to place a chalk mark:

Draw your signal in white chalk or crayon on the wall of the Kitchen Korner store running along 16-th Rd. S.;
Draw your signal in red chalk or crayon on the first concrete post of the railing on the right hand side of the bridge on S. Walter Reed Dr. . . . ;
Draw the signal in white chalk at your waist level from the ground on the near wall of the house on the left side of the alley in the middle of the wall . . .

And so on. The instructions were so convoluted that Johnny got to asking himself, Don't these Ivans know English? Which only made him laugh, because of course they really didn't.

The best part of the game, though, was the deliveries. Dead drops, the Russians called them; and Johnny, too, wasted no time in picking up on the phrase. Yet what Johnny admired, marveled at, really, about these procedures was the way the Russians had them so well planned. It was—and here, too, Johnny was at home with the irony—very Navy.

The tradecraft for each dead drop was always the same. Weekends were the chosen time; the Russians believed the FBI, paunchy capitalists, put in only five-day weeks. So on a Saturday night Johnny would follow the map he would have received at his last exchange.

The map would lead him to some remote spot in the woods of Maryland or Virginia; the isolation not only allowing the fieldman to make his drop unnoticed, but also giving Johnny plenty of opportunities to look in his rearview mirror in case somebody was on his tail.

Yet if glancing over his shoulder and following the map wasn't enough of a job, there were also the photographs. The Russian, with a meticulousness that Johnny would never stop finding sort of insulting, had laid out the procedures for the drop in a series of photos. All along the route, the handler and his asset were to exchange safety signals—empty cans of 7-Up; no other soda, for reasons Johnny never could determine or dared to ask, would do. Therefore, on one photograph there would be a precisely ruled arrow pointing to, say, a telephone pole and the block letter instruction: I DROP MY INITIAL CAN HERE. Until, after often a half-dozen of these exchanges, Johnny would come to the photograph with the instruction: YOU DROP YOUR FINAL CAN HERE. Then there would be the dead drop. Johnny would leave a garbage bag packed with genuine trash; only under the garbage, in another carefully sealed bag, would be the treasure: a pile of top secret naval documents and key lists.

After Johnny made his drop, he, always scared stiff and always having the time of his life, followed the route to the final site. There, another garbage bag would be waiting. Inside would be his treasure: A "Dear Friend" letter evaluating the last shipment of material, a KGB shopping list for the next drop, and the cash.

All in all, Johnny thought it was a pretty good way to spend a Saturday night.

Not long after he met his handler at the department store, probably at his second or third drop, Johnny received his first piece of spy equipment. Inside the garbage bag was a Minox camera; and Ivan in the Trench Coat, always one to make sure of things, also included in the package a copy of the owner's manual.

Johnny, who really didn't know much about photography, now had a new activity to master. Not that he minded. He delighted in how the camera fitted just so into the palm of his hand; that made each practice session another round of intrigue. He was really into the game by now. He even destroyed the manual the Russian had given him—a touch of tradecraft Johnny thought up—and, instead, substituted his own, less suspicious handwritten instructions. "Parameters," he called these notes: Use black-and-white film, Plus X Pan, ASA 125; set camera to one one-hundredths of a second to photograph from 18 inches from the document; use a light bulb at least 75 or 100 watts; have light bulb one foot from the documents you're photographing.

He began using his new piece of equipment in the spring of 1968. It really helped production.

Q. When you used the camera, I assume that you were trying to copy as much material at one time as possible; it that a fair statement?

A. Yes.

Q. Where did you go in the message center in order to accomplish that?

A. There was a vault-type office as I recall in the crypto—in the on-line room that was available for use.

Q. You have to go in there and shut the door?

A. Yes.

Q. Was there any risk of detection by a superior officer or anybody else during that period that you were concerned with?

A. It's a risky business, yes.

Q. Approximately how long would it take to photograph an entire month's worth of keying material?

A. Maybe 20 or 30 minutes, depending on what system you were talking about.

Q. Let's say the KWR-37. Now: In that you'd have a separate card for each day of the month?

A. Yes.

Q. How long would it take you to photograph that using a Minox camera?

A. Three to four minutes.

The Minox camera, though, was run-of-the-mill when compared with the contraption he found in the garbage bag at his drop site a few months later. Inside was something the Department 16 whiz kids had designed especially for Johnny Walker. It was an instrument for decoding the internal wiring system of the KL-47 crypto machine. It, too, fitted into the palm of his hand, and, complete with battery, weighed about fourteen ounces. NSA scientists would later, with some admiration, call it a "rotor decryption device"; they estimated it cost at least $50,000 to manufacture. Johnny, with equal admiration, would someday boast that it was "real James Bond."

Rotors, since World War I, have been the key internal mechanism of many military crypto machines. They are wheels—gears, really—made of Bakelite or hard-rubber insulating material. Around the circumference of each rotor are twenty-six—one for each letter of the alphabet—evenly spaced electrical contacts. Each contact is connected at random by a wire to a contact on the opposite face; electrical current travels along this wire from one point on the circumference to another point on the opposite side.

The contacts on the starting, or input, face represent plaintext letters; those on the opposite, or output, face are ciphertext letters. To encipher, the radioman pushes the button which fires a burst of current into the rotor at the input contact of the desired plaintext letter, say, *h;* this current then runs along the wire and comes across the "hot printer" as the ciphertext letter, say, *b.*

The daily key lists, however, manipulate the turning of the rotors so that a current entering at a specific point will no longer emerge at the same point as before. A rotor, then, will produce as many cipher alphabets as it has positions; that is, twenty-six.

Naval crypto machines usually have more than one rotor. Five rotors, each with twenty-six positions, will create 11,881,376 cipher alphabets. Which comes down to this: There would be, cryptologist David Kahn has determined, a different alphabet for *each letter* in a plaintext far longer than the complete works of Shakespeare, *War and Peace,* the *Iliad,* the *Odyssey, Don Quixote, The Canterbury Tales,* and *Paradise Lost* all put together.

But a KL-47 doesn't have five rotors. It has eight. Which made its encoded messages impossible to crack. Until Johnny Walker began playing around with his rotor decryption device.

• • •

Johnny wasn't too keen on this piece of equipment. Like any cranky fieldman, he had quickly reached the point in his career where dumping on the bright boys, safe in their offices, was part of the trade. Still, he might have had a case when it came to using the rotor decryption device. It was a bitch to operate without anyone noticing, and that only made a risky business a lot more tense.

Sneaking the tiny device into the COMSUBLANT crypto room was the easy part. It was once he got inside the room that the process gave him the willies. Johnny would have to remove the rotor from the KL-47 and place it, like a record on a spindle, on his instrument. Then he'd fold out the two hinges from his machine, each copper-tipped hinge sticking out like the claws on a lobster. One "claw" would be placed on the input contact point of his machine, the other on each output point on the rotor until a light on his machine glowed: an electrical circuit had been completed; the logic had been revealed. Point one, say, on his device corresponded to point 5, say, on the KL-47's first rotor. And then he'd have to repeat the process for the twenty-five remaining letters. And then for the seven remaining rotors. And he'd have to make sure he was keeping an exact list of the corresponding contact points for each rotor. And all the time in the crypto vault, while he was checking the contact points with his little machine and writing his findings down on a page of notebook paper, Johnny couldn't stop feeling that any moment someone was going to pop in and ask him just what the hell he thought he was doing.

But no one ever did. Johnny, to his immense pleasure, was a perfect spy. In fact, things were going so well, what with the money coming in, and the game being such great fun, that Johnny, brimming once more with confidence, figured the time had come to have a go again at being a husband and father. He decided to move his family to Norfolk.

10

She might as well have been the big winner on one of those TV game shows. That was the only way Barbara Walker could understand it: One day she and the kids were living in a trailer; the next day they were living in Norfolk in a fancy apartment house with a doorman. She couldn't believe her luck.

All of a sudden, there was so much: fuchsia wall-to-wall carpeting; a teakwood dining table with matching chairs; a black-Naugahyde-covered bar and four Naugahyde stools; an electric broiler; a king-size bed with a fluted, gold-leaf, Mediterranean-style headboard; and even—Johnny's choice—a foot-high replica of Michelangelo's David to stand on the new dresser. She couldn't believe her luck.

No matter how hard she tried.

At first, when Johnny had come down to Ladson during the summer of 1968 and told her he had rented an apartment in Norfolk, all she could think about was no more grilling burgers and pulling drafts—it was about time! The Bamboo Snack Bar should have landed belly-up a stack of bills ago. Only Johnny announced he had no intention of closing the snack bar. He'd just hire a cook and a waitress, or maybe he'd rent the place out. Someday, he promised, the joint would be a gold mine. And not seeming to have a care or debt in the world, he was quite prepared to wait for someday. Very strange; but then again her Johnny was a man of many moods.

Finally, the car packed with boxes and stuffed with four kids, when the time came to make the drive to Norfolk she was just glad to be getting out of South Carolina; and she was hoping, now that she and Johnny were going to be back together again full-time, things might smooth out between them. She took a lot of daydreams, a lot of expectations with her.

They pulled up to this high-rise on Glenroie Avenue, the Algonquin House, and as her daughter Laura would remember, it was if they had stepped into a fairy tale. There was a doorman going, "Hello, Mr. Walker," and a somebody called a concierge, and the kids were all running off and bringing back excited reports that "Mommy, there's a pool out back" or "They even got a Ping-Pong table in the basement." Then the elevator ride up to the apartment with all the furniture, and the brand-new kitchen appliances, and the glass doors to the balcony where you could sit with a drink in your hand, and, after eleven years of a scrimping-and-saving marriage, just watch the river flow—it was all she had ever wanted. And, of course, impossible. This wasn't strange . . . it was wrong.

"Know how it is," she would try to explain a lifetime later, "when you're taking a shower and all of a sudden you feel this lump in your breast? Well, you could do something, go to the doctor, get an X ray, or whatever. Or you could just hope that tomorrow it'll be gone. Well, that's the way it was in the Algonquin House."

So Barbara did a lot of hoping about tomorrows; and a lot of drinking to get through the days. She didn't know what would be worse: Asking Johnny the question, or dealing with his answer. But either way she knew her life—and the life of her family—would never be the same. His secret terrorized her.

It was only a matter of time.

. . .

She had been drinking, which was a handy excuse. Not to mention that she just knew Johnny was screwing around; there had to be some sort of proof, a love letter or something lying around. That, too, seemed like a good enough reason. Or maybe it was just an accident. Or maybe there are no accidents.

Whatever the reason, not long after they had settled into the Algonquin House, Barbara found herself poking around Johnny's desk.

Johnny's desk. Even the phrase rankled her. Through their marriage, wherever they were living, Johnny always seemed to need a separate place, a place where he would do his business. A place—a corner, even—that tied him, and him alone, to the large world out there. A world, Barbara felt, where Johnny, the life of every party, was frolicking about, inventing new lives and alibis as he drifted into new bedrooms. While Barbara, a stranger in even this corner of her own home, was ignored.

At the Algonquin House, Johnny's space was the biggest yet. He had bought some sort of Chinese screen and used it to divide the bedroom in half: On one side was their bed, on the other was *his* desk. It was a real sore point to Barbara.

So one morning when vodka, or jealousy, or simply instinct started tugging on her, she decided to do some exploring. She crossed the bedroom and stepped into the wall-to-wall carpeted territory on the other side of the screen—Johnny's world.

There was a new desk, dark shiny walnut, and as big as the dining room table. On top of it was a stack of papers; a neat pile as was Johnny's way. Barbara rushed through them. But she knew she wouldn't find anything; clues are always hidden. That's why she tried the center drawer. It was locked. She pulled and pulled, defeat only making her more ferocious, more obsessive. And feeling this way, unable to walk away from the secret, she rushed into a decision: She would jimmy the lock.

It took only a couple of hectic minutes working with a screwdriver for the lock to give; then, like a rabbit pulled from a hat, the drawer slid open.

She quickly scattered handfuls of papers; until, as if drawn by some force, some intuitive magnetism, she reached deep into the drawer and found what she knew she had been searching for: a tin box; and, she never doubted, the fortress protecting Johnny's secret.

What should she do? Barbara could open it and have the answers to questions she did not even dare ask. Or she could put it back, walk away, top off her drink, and hope that life would just go on.

But of course there was no turning back. Life could not go on. Once the questions, the doubts about her wonderful, impossible new life had been announced in her own mind, there could be no pretending. The truth, however dangerous, was a compulsion. Curiosity, rage, even guilt—all conspired to push her forward.

So she opened the tin box.

Inside was money; $2,000 in cash, she counted. A puzzling, extravagant sum. But it got even wilder.

There was an envelope containing photographs of trees: a forest, perhaps. On each photograph a precisely ruled arrow pointed to a specific tree or rock. Written on each photograph in careful block letters—the script of an engineer? an architect? she wondered—were the strangest things. YOU DROP INITIAL CAN HERE. What could that mean?

There was also a map of Virginia, and underneath the map was a note. It was handwritten in capital letters, the same painstaking script as on the photographs. At the top of the page, printed in red, was an instruction: PLEASE DESTROY! The letter was addressed, "Dear Friend." She read the page, and then read it again.

She didn't understand it all, but it was pretty clear the writer was angry. He wasn't at all happy with the "quality" of the last "delivery." There were a whole lot of things he wanted his dear friend to get for that next shipment that sounded technical and scientific. Most of all, he made it clear he wanted information "on rotor."

Barbara wondered: What the hell is going on here?

It was all, she decided, beyond her. Probably something to do with Johnny's Navy work. At least they weren't love letters. Maybe he wasn't cheating on her. Now isn't that nice. So all she had to do was close the box, straighten up the desk, get on over to the other side of the Chinese screen, and not give it another thought because it only proved one thing—there was no other woman. Things weren't so bad after all.

She clutched onto this way of thinking with all her might. For as long as she could. In the end, though, it just ripped in two under all that pressure.

It was an evening perhaps two weeks after her discovery. She had been drinking; she always seemed to have a glass in her hand these days. Johnny was home, the kids were in bed, and it just sort of snuck up on her. There was a squabble. Something she said? Something Johnny said? So much dirty water has passed under the bridge since then, the specifics are bound to be muddied. But all at once, as if on command, she couldn't hold back and everything fell into place.

"Traitor," Barbara shouted at her husband.

Johnny did not look surprised. Only angry.

"You're a spy," she accused. Hoping he would deny it.

Instead he punched her. Once, in the face. And when she cried out, he hit her again.

He did not want the neighbors to hear, he whispered.

It was as much of an apology as she would get.

Was Johnny hoping to recruit her? Was it pride? Was it relief at finally having an audience for this huge last laugh he was having on all the squares? Or was Johnny, the great manipulator, simply casting his net, sucking her in, scurrying in those first moments for the tone, the angle of persuasion that would restrain his wife from turning him in? By now, even Johnny Walker is no longer sure; besides, his motives are never simple.

Both of them remember, though, how after the crying and the screaming had run their course, in this lull full of false calm and real danger, Johnny, taking advantage of the competing pulls of these contradictions, took the stage to share his secret.

He had been snowed under with debts, he said without a trace of embarrassment as he started in. He had no choice. So he grabbed the only thing he could think of to shovel himself out—his Navy job. What harm did it do? It was all a big game, government against government. People, sailors, friends—these were real things that didn't enter into it at all. Besides, he purred, a lot of people were doing it. As for the drops, the tradecraft he had learned, the risks he was taking, the money he was earning for his family—now that was something! Who else could have pulled it off but Johnny Walker, he proclaimed, as if begging for a round of applause.

Later, as they lay in bed before going to sleep, he asked her again, You understand how it is?

She told him she did. Which was easier than wondering how she would wake up in the morning and explain her two black eyes; or how she would live with the knowledge that her husband was a Russian spy.

Yet, two days later, she seemed to resolve things. Johnny read her decision his own way:

Q. What was her stated reason for going along with you on the drop . . . ?
A. Like most alcoholics, she would drift between love and hate during those periods. She wanted to work with me and be a good spy, and then the next day she would revert to the other self. I have no idea.

For Barbara, however, her logic was single-minded:
"I suggested it," she said. "I wanted him to know how much I cared."

It was, the way Barbara remembers it, a routine Department 16 dead-drop exchange:

"We rented a car, and we flew to Virginia, rented a car at the airport, drove to a motel, stayed there for a little while, and we got in the car and drove around.

"John was following directions from a map. We drove for some time, I don't recall how long.

"We went back to the motel. He waited. It was dark by then. He made a phone call. Then he told me it was time for us to go.

"We followed the same route that we had followed earlier. John stopped at a designated spot and left a bag that appeared like it had trash in it. He got back in the car, and we drove a very short distance, a matter of feet, got out again, picked up something, got back in the car. We went back to the motel."

Q. Did you know what it was that John Walker picked up?
A. Money.

The next day, in her kitchen at the Algonquin House, Barbara set up her ironing board while her husband unpacked the trash bag. Inside were rolls and rolls of $50 bills bound with rubber bands. Every bill had been so tightly rolled that even with the rubber band removed, it still curled up in your hand. That spooked Johnny; the fieldman in him figured it was something the FBI might pick up on. So he wanted Barbara to iron each of the fifties until they were nice and flat. Normal, he called it.

It took her maybe a minute or so to press each bill. Still, she had to be very careful, holding a corner of the bill down with one hand as she moved the iron back and forth over the rest. All the time she was ironing, her husband was warning her, Slow now. A fifty can go up like *that*.

She had finished off nearly a bottle of vodka by the time she was done ironing. It didn't help.

That night, as Johnny did his watch in the operations room, Barbara sat by the phone. At last, she picked it up.

"Operator," she managed to say into the receiver, "can you give me the number for the FBI?"

"One moment, please. . . . "

But Barbara, utterly helpless, hung up the phone.

And in that way, her decision was made.

The secret became part of both their lives, something rarely mentioned, something always there. It was what made them different; and no one knew it.

Johnny could handle it. He simply thought up a new script and, naturally, cast himself in the leading role. That way when one of his buddies suggested, Hey, Johnny, living a little high on the hog, ain't we? there was no problem. Reaching for the check, Johnny would brag that The Bamboo Snack Bar was raking it in. Just as a shrewd businessman like ol' Johnny Walker knew from the start. And best of all, this bit of cover allowed him to present himself to his kids and the Happy Hour crowd as the man he would have liked to have been if things had worked out.

Barbara, though, was no match for her husband. She was having a rough time. She couldn't handle the guilt.

And since neither of them could dare to talk about what was really eating away at their marriage, any small problem could rush off full-pitch in a flash. More often than not, by the time it was done playing itself out, the kids would wind up in the middle.

Those kids—Maggie the oldest at ten, Cynthia, Laura, and Mike, the youngest, five—got quite an education. Like the time their mom smashed their dad's brand-new tape recorder to the floor, and he's bellowing he'll fix her all right she don't make things right; so, drink in hand, she has to get the four of them out of bed and beg them to help her put the damn machine back together again. Or the time Mom and Dad came back from this Caribbean cruise, which must have been no vacation at all the way they were going at each other as they walked in the door, and the sitter said she had had her hands full, and that was all their father, full of fury, needed—he took his Navy belt to each of them. Or the time on their dad's new sailboat, Johnny, the teacher, tying a rope around Laura's waist, as she floated along learning to swim, when all of sudden Barbara threw a bottle at him, and after that it was all downhill. All those days; all those nights when the kids lay in bed and heard the shouts and sobbing from the bedroom, and all they could do was just lie there, afraid of what might be coming next.

Johnny blamed it on Barbara's drinking. Barb, worse off, could only blame it on herself. But since she couldn't set things right without destroying what little remained of her life, all she could settle for was revenge.

That's how, not long after her first drop, she started having an affair with Johnny's older brother, Art.

Was their pillow talk full of love? Passion? Or was Barb merely trying on Johnny's way of living—betrayal?

Whatever. In time it became just another dirty secret she was holding onto. That didn't help things at all.

Which is only one way of looking at it. The other way was that Lieutenant Commander Arthur Walker, husband, father of three, was shacking up with his younger brother's wife. That wasn't a pretty picture, either.

Art, though, didn't seem to pay it much mind. Like Johnny, he was simply taking advantage of a situation that had happened to come his way. Loyalty didn't enter into things as long as he was getting his share.

Besides, also like Johnny, he was used to playing roles. He was stationed at the Atlantic Fleet Anti-Submarine Warfare Tactical School in Norfolk. His assignment: He was the orange submarine commander in the large-scale tactical exercises conducted by the entire Atlantic Fleet senior commands. The orange team was the enemy.

He was so good at it that the Navy in September 1969 detailed him to the National Cryptologic School at Fort Meade to teach NSA analysts a course in sonar/antisubmarine warfare tactics. His presentation, according to the commandant of the school, "demonstrated professional ability of the highest order."

On the home front, Art was getting good marks, too. He and Rita seemed to have the perfect marriage; he was the ideal father. One commanding officer at the ASW school, Captain R. H. Ewing, concluded Art's fitness report with the judgment that "LCDR Walker and his wife are a definite asset in the social activities of the command. He has evidenced all those qualities desired for command and he highly is recommended for promotion." The next commander at the school, Captain A. F. Blair, was also full of praise, noting that "LCDR Walker is active in community affairs. He coaches Little League baseball and football and is a member of the board of directors of the community swim club."

Even Johnny's kids couldn't help thinking about how different Uncle Art and his family seemed from their out-of-control way of life. Laura, then nearly nine, remembers her time in the Algonquin House this way:

"We lived in the same area as my uncle Art who would often come to visit with his three kids who were roughly our age. We always felt we couldn't measure up to our cousins because they seemed so perfect, so good, such a happy family. We had been taught to believe we were bad, dirty, disorganized, and unworthy of love."

Yet all along Art, burying himself in deep cover, was keeping a dirty secret just like Johnny. One was betraying his country, the other his family. For both brothers it was a habit that would become a way of life.

· · ·

Meanwhile Johnny, the 4.0 sailor, was having a difficult time following orders from both the U. S. Navy and the KGB. The pressures took their toll. On September 9, 1969, after nearly a year and a half of spying, he received a poor fitness report. It was his first in fourteen years in the Navy:

"Chief Warrant Officer 2 Walker is an individual with excellent potential as a communications specialist. However, during this reporting period he has allowed his performance to fall below his previous level. The apparent lack of interest in his job, with the consequent reduction of reliability of his performance have contributed directly or indirectly to numerous serious mistakes . . . "

Johnny, though, was simply wrapped up in another game. He was doing much better at this new one.

Q. How much were you getting paid at your pickup points during this period?

A. I'm not sure. I think it was three thousand a month. Possibly four thousand.

Q. Now, starting with the time that you made your arrangement with the Soviets at the embassy in 1968, approximately how many months' worth of crypto key lists material were you able to copy . . . ?

A. A year's worth . . . Close to 100 percent on the KWR-37, and to a lesser degree on the remainder.

Still, instinct was telling Johnny not to press his luck. His CO was on his case, the last evaluation made that clear. Warrant Officer Walker would get a real careful going-over from now on. That was the last thing Johnny needed. Besides, Barb was all over the place. With her drinking, there was no telling what she might wind up doing. Or whom she might talk to.

Maybe the whole Walker family needed a change, he decided. So he called his detailer and asked for an early transfer.

It came through in October 1969. The radio school at San Diego, California. Which suited him fine: Sun. Sailing. And the chance to spy on the Pacific Fleet.

II

Johnny, who never failed to be positive when things were still new, had big plans. All the long way across country, nothing seemed to detour his schemes and dreams. The car was packed with four antsy kids; Barb was jumpy from all the Cokes she was drinking, another good intention gone awry; and he had to watch his foot on the pedal because he was dragging his twenty-four-foot sailboat, *The Dirty Old Man,* behind him. Still, Johnny started out each day on that trip during the fall of 1969 believing his future was as bright as the southern California sun. "We're coming in from the cold," he constantly rejoiced to Barb, sharing both a private joke and a wish; and when they reached their last stop, San Diego seemed to bless his ambitions by giving him a big, brilliant day with the temperature shooting past 80.

That first warm night, they camped out with an old submarining sidekick, Don Clevenger, and Johnny, full of glee, didn't hold back. With the westerlies coming off the Pacific, a glass of his namesake for attitude adjustment, and a buddy to impress, he was tireless. He gave Big Don a picture-window look into the good life his newfound income from the snack bar was going to help him buy. Big Don, the perfect audience, did nothing but gush, which only encouraged Johnny. "A man can sink his teeth into life out here," Johnny, hungry as ever, predicted to his former shipmate.

While Barbara, sticking to oceans of Coke as her own act of faith in the regenerative powers of southern California, kept her tongue. Though she did think: My Johnny, he'd be searching for the angle at his own hanging. Then, just as quick, she let her conscience tiptoe around the secret for at least the millionth time while she hurried to convince herself that her small joke had nothing to do with the life she was living—or the future.

From his first day at his new post, Johnny, never a man to quibble, embraced it. True, love was just a flash of temper away from boiling hate for Johnny. But this new job and title fulfilled a pet ambition—authority. It was quite a kick, his prancing around as assistant director of the Practical Applications Laboratory (or PRACTEC as they called it in keeping with the Navy's tradition of making a mouthful of jargon as sleek and as menacing as a frigate). His empire, just two hangarlike buildings at the San Diego Naval Training Center, was a mock-up of the real thing: training laboratories built to resemble the radio rooms on two separate destroyers and also a shore station. Yet for Johnny, the whole artificial setup gave his job the dignity of theater; and, so inspired, he truly got into the performance of his newest role—teacher. He devoted himself to being the model chief, the "fount of all wisdom," as they say in the Navy, the squid's best and wisest friend. If you couldn't get the hang of a piece of crypto equipment or a transmitter, you wouldn't have to blink before Chief Walker would be right there waiting to take you through it one more time.

A less receptive audience, however, were the fifty or so instructors Johnny had under him. Some of these senior radiomen didn't take too well to Johnny's operational belief that an opinion was just as good as a fact. They got a little perturbed when their boss would be the fount of all wisdom, even when he didn't have the slightest idea of what he was talking about. No matter what the topic, from the intricacies of Autodin to the size of tits, Chief Walker had to get in the last, definitive word: Johnny always knew best, or at least he was always willing to tell you he did. It got so, the way radioman Michael O'Connor, one of Johnny's instructors recalls it, that there were a couple of nicknames for Chief Walker flying around PRACTEC. Johnny's drinking buddies, those who would put up with his bragging for a laugh or two, called him "the dingdong." It was a name they felt suited a man who was so quick to ring his own bell. The radiomen like O'Connor who couldn't stand Johnny no way at all called him "the shithead."

Not that Johnny cared. He was, after all, the boss; the rumblings of underlings simply served to remind him he was on top. No, his job was just fine. The problem was his trade was awful.

There was plenty of crypto gear at PRACTEC—a KWR-37, a KG-14, and a KY-8 machine. But, as Johnny discovered, those machines were not for active military communications. They were training machines—with training key lists. Message traffic, classified SECRET at best, a couple of tech manuals—that was all Johnny, sneaking around in the dead of night, could focus his Minox C on. Pretty slim pickings for a master spy.

Still Johnny, the dutiful agent, enthusiastically played the game. Every six months or so he'd catch the red-eye on a Friday night to Washington National Airport, rent a car, and then go for a drive in the woods leaving a trail of 7-Up cans behind him. By Sunday, he'd be back in San Diego, the typical jet-setting executive coming home after a quick look at his business interests out East. Only he'd be carrying an attaché case stuffed with bundles of tightly rolled $50 bills..

These days the attaché case didn't have much heft to it; the quality of product he was delivering was worth only $2,000 a month. That was a disappointment; but one that Johnny, never as greedy for money as he was for excitement, could have put up with till his next posting. What was working him over, though, were the letters Ivan in the Trench Coat was leaving at the drop site. They were addressed "Dear Friend," but they weren't friendly at all.

For any control officer, the most difficult part of running an agent is gauging his asset's mood. The officer, working from his desk, has to

make judgments about an agent—a man he's never even seen or met
—off in the field. At best, this is a tricky bit of tradecraft; at worst, it
is the stuff of wild hunches. Changes, good or bad, make case officers
suspicious.

From the distorting perspective of distance, it is almost impossible
to determine whether the sudden decline in the quality of your asset's
product is due to bad luck, or to the fact that the FBI is now helping
him snap the pictures. And this conclusion is only a shrewd deduction
away from another: Maybe the FBI or Naval Intelligence had been
behind this source all along.

A control officer who spends his time exploring these dark alleys
can get pretty jumpy: Is his asset going to come to the drop with a
piece of gold, or with the FBI?

By the spring of 1970, this was the dilemma confronting the Department 16 control. Yet all he could do was instruct his fieldman, the
handler working out of the Washington embassy, to keep probing the
asset.

And, more troublesome, the responses they were getting from Warrant Officer Walker were not very reassuring.

Consider the case Johnny, more rash than shrewd, was building
against himself: He was instructed not to inform anyone of his espionage activities. But Warrant Officer Walker abruptly admitted in his
next "Dear Friend" letter that he had told his wife. Alarm bells rang
in Department 16, but their outward response was fraternal. "Be careful," Ivan in the Trench Coat wrote his agent. And, he asked a few
questions: Your wife, is she loyal, courageous, and steady as a rock?
Johnny, afraid to lie—who knew if they were watching his house,
testing him?—wrote back that Barb was an off-the-wall alcoholic. But
don't worry, everything was under control. Which must have really
reassured Moscow Center.

Then, just as Johnny was delivering shipments of solid gold—
months' worth of key lists, rotor settings, Op Orders—he wrote that
he was leaving COMSUBLANT. For a radio school. And he was
leaving a year early. Why not just announce he was working for the
FBI, that he'd become a double agent?

Perhaps even more incriminating—and here one has to rely on the
informed insights of the teams of intelligence agents, the backbeaters,

who would re-create the history of every moment of Johnny Walker's professional life—was the timing of their agent's sudden decline: It was just as the Navy was expanding its role in Vietnam.

On September 30, 1968, when Vice Admiral Elmo R. Zumwalt, Jr., the first naval officer of three-star rank to be assigned to Vietnam, took command, the personnel strength of the Navy forces stood at 38,386. Under his leadership, as the Paris Peace Talks dragged into 1969, the Navy moved to pressure the enemy in Nam Can with Operation Market Time, Silver Float, and Sea Float. Before these missions were launched, the Vietcong sent English-language leaflets on wooden rafts down the Cua Lon River in Nam Can vowing they would "blow the American Navy out of the water." Their promise was horribly enforced; casualties were high. It was almost as if, commanders said at the time, "the Vietcong knew when we were coming and were waiting for us." Two decades later, military analysts would theorize that was exactly the case. They would blame Johnny Walker.

Then suddenly in 1970 Johnny stopped providing the Russians with access to naval codes. It was another clue in the pattern Department 16 was tracking, a clue leading to a dangerous conclusion: Warrant Officer Walker had turned on his Russian masters.

So they began threatening Johnny. First they cut his money in half, but that was just a slap on the wrists. When Johnny didn't respond, they got tough. We are losing confidence in you, Ivan in the Trench Coat wrote to his dear friend. You must win us back, prove yourself again, Ivan instructed. Or else there might be "grave consequences." And the word "grave" was underlined twice.

For the first time since Johnny had begun cooperating, he suddenly realized he could be killed. It was as if the precisely ruled lines under the word "grave" were two spears aimed at his heart. He was overrun with fear.

He had no choice but to take more chances. Dismissing instinct and tradecraft as weak sisters, Johnny, believing he was fighting for his life, wrote a memo to his CO. No copy of this note still exists (which perhaps was precisely Johnny's intention); one can only imagine the passion that lay beneath the bare bureaucratic facts. The memo, as reconstructed, went something like this:

As assistant director of the Practical Applications Laboratory,

Chief Walker was dedicated to ensuring the best and most complete education of apprentice radiomen. To facilitate this goal, however, Chief Walker needed to be knowledgeable about the latest advances in naval communications. Therefore, he was requesting that he be appointed the Registered Publication Supervisor.

Against all odds, the request was approved. Johnny was given access to the latest top secret naval communications manuals. And so were the Russians. Which made both Johnny and his Department 16 control breathe a little easier.

It was natural, too, that Johnny's shaky mood had its effect on Barb and the kids. Life in their little dream ranch in San Diego became a real roller-coaster ride. One night Johnny would come back from the training center full of jokes and stories, giving his daughters ten cents each for back rubs or a quarter if they played barber and ran a comb through his thin strands of hair. The next night he'd come home barking, "Do you know what silent contempt is, young lady? That's when just the way you're eyeballing me is plain, rank insubordination." And then he'd go after them—Margaret mostly; she was the oldest, nearly thirteen—with his belt. Or he'd punch them, right in the chest, as if they were a man. Only little Mike could escape these sessions. Even when Mike, almost eight, had been caught shoplifting, Johnny didn't want to hear about it. "Boys will be boys," he decided. Same as Mike's sisters didn't complain when night after night, waking up full of bloodcurdling shrieks from one of his nightmares, Mike would crawl into one of their beds. He was so cute, after all. How could they help but spoil him?

With Johnny all over the place, every day acting from another script, it was no wonder Barb's resolve broke. Or maybe she just missed her drink. No matter. The fact was, not long after they had settled into the house with the yard and the pool table in the family room, Barb began topping off her Cokes with something extra. From there it was just a short what-the-hell to drinking her vodka straight. That's when things got bonkers.

There was the time, then, when Cynthia threw sand in another child's face and Barbara, wild with rage, decided to teach her daughter a lesson. She taped Cynthia's eyes shut and made her sit all day on the front lawn; that way she'd know what it was like to be blind.

Or that first Halloween in San Diego when Barb, out of the blue, decreed that her kids were not allowed to trick or treat. Instead, they were ordered to sit in the living room, and when other kids rang the bell, no one was to answer. The Walker children had to sit there nice and quiet, learning some sort of lesson. Until finally when their door bell wouldn't stop ringing, their mom, beside herself over something, ran outside and yanked the bell straight off the door.

And so on, and so on.

Guarding the secret was costing Barbara. Somedays she felt she just couldn't pay the price any longer. It was such a burden. Even she didn't know what might happen next, and that scared her.

One night, taking herself by surprise, she picked up the phone and called the FBI in San Diego. She began with a question.

"If someone knew someone was spying," she asked the man who answered the phone, "could they give that person protection?"

He said, "No."

"Well, forget it," Barbara shot back. And she hung up the phone.

Except, she couldn't forget it.

So their life in San Diego, despite all their hopes, quickly became just another wish that didn't amount to anything. Unless you count what the Walker girls would call "the shooting incident."

It happened on a tropical San Diego night when Barb, fed up with Johnny's catting around, decided the time had come to teach him a lesson. She'd ambush him in the living room and give the two-timer a greeting he'd remember—with his service revolver.

She waited, the gun in one hand, a glass in the other. And she waited; until sleep got the better of her anger. When Johnny came rolling in near dawn, he found her passed out on the living room couch. Still clutching the revolver.

Which pissed him off no end. He decided to give her the fight she was looking for.

Did they go at it! The kids heard yells and screams and curses like it was the end of the world. Margaret, being the oldest, led them all into the bathroom. It didn't make any sense, but at least they were together.

All four of the kids were huddled, crying and shaking, when they heard their father taunt, "Go ahead, Barbara. Pull the trigger."

She didn't, and he came right at her. There were some real loud slaps. When they pulled apart, Johnny was holding the gun. Now Barbara was pleading, "No, Johnny. Please. Don't."

Suddenly there was a shot.

Margaret, working on instinct, knew she had to get help. She climbed out of the bathroom window. Crying, she ran down the street in her pj's, heading toward the neighbor's house. Yet before she got there, she stopped. She realized what she was doing: Suppose her father had shot her mother. And suppose she told the neighbors and they called the police. Why, then she'd be turning her father in. There was no way she could do that. All she could do was return home. And hope things got better.

Johnny was only aiming at the ceiling that night. The next time, though, was a worry. He decided to move into bachelor quarters at the naval base for a while. So perhaps things did get better.

At least he thought so. He spent most of his time during the fall of 1970 at PRACTEC or down at the San Diego Yacht Club on *The Dirty Old Man*. That was how on a November Saturday just before Thanksgiving he happened to ask one of the new radio instructors if he'd like to go for a sail. Maybe have a couple of beers afterward.

"Sounds great," said Jerry Whitworth.

12

Jerry Whitworth was seventeen when he tracked down his father. That feat meant a lot to him, and it was a story he often told close friends. Then again, Jerry only had best friends; it was as if he collected them.

Way back in 1957, Jerry would begin as though launching into a fable, he had joined the Navy to see the world. He wound up stationed as a storekeeper at the Hunter's Point shipyard in San Francisco. Yet you didn't catch him complaining, no sirree. He had busted out of Paw Paw Bottoms, Oklahoma, and that was good enough for this sailor. No more granddaddy's house with the chickens running helter-skelter in the dirt yard and the flat acres of soybeans out back as far as your eyes can see; no more waking up on Sunday mornings to the sounds of "We Shall Gather at the River" coming from the New Covenant Free Will Baptist Church next door; no more pumping gas at Billy Phillips's after school and on weekends; no more, he groaned, "staring plum into a future that was just plain hickey." He was a kid, only seventeen, but he knew there had to be a lot more to life than perching your buns ten hours a day on a John Deere Tractor, or make-believing that come Friday night you might finally meet the gal of your dreams at Beverly's Drive-In over in Fort Smith. Get right down to it, he'd take being a sailor, even a storekeeper third class, ten out of ten times over being some dust-kicking Okie. At least a storekeeper had a chance at a future. And some good times.

The other thing about the Navy, Jerry, in no hurry since he truly loved to weave a story, went on, was the people you got to meet. Guys from all over the U.S. of A. Educated. Not like the ragtime cowboy rednecks he had hung out with at Muldrow High. Sailors were men who were hunting for an experience or two. Case in point was Roger Olson, who these days was living on a Chinese junk in Papua, New Guinea, but back then in Hunter's Point was already everything Jerry wanted to be.

Naturally, since Rog was his best buddy and at the very least the brother he should have had, Jerry from the start poured out his life to him. A woeful piece of business, for sure: Jerry never had a real family. His dad had only married his mom to give their kid a last name. Just a month after Jerry was born, Johnie Ike Whitworth skedaddled to California. Jerry's mom then up and married a drunk, an ornery drunk, who had no use for another man's son. So Jerry was shipped off to his grandparents' farmhouse. Which was okay . . . but when you stopped and thought about it, not okay enough.

To hear Jerry tell it, his problems caused his buddy Rog no end of pain. Rog, one of life's romantics, wanted to make things right; and maybe he was a little curious, too. Anyway, he asked Jerry, "Whereabouts in California your old man settled?"

Jerry wasn't sure. "My uncle Willard said Ike Whitworth promised to keep on running till he came to the ocean."

"That all you know?" Rog pressed.

Jerry was never one not to try and please a best friend. He gave it some thought. Till it came to him: Uncle Willard once mentioned that Ike Whitworth had built himself a restaurant. Named it after some Okie hash house up in Saddlesaw . . . The Blue Moon Cafe, that was it. Running it with his new wife, if Uncle Willard had the skivvy.

"All right," said Rog. "We got a name. Now we need a place. C'mon, Jer. Think."

But all Jerry could come up with was that the town started with an *M*.

Rog, though, would not be thrown. He was a California boy, raised south of Fresno, in the valley, so he knew his way around. He just started rattling off names. Modesto? Moorpark? Maxwell? Mendota?

"Mendota," Jerry repeated. "Yeah. That sounds kinda familiar."

And when they called Mendota information they were told there was a Blue Moon Cafe on Crescent Street.

Which left them both pretty excited. Rog, because it was something the way after all these years he had solved the puzzle; while for Jerry it was, he'd admit to you straight off, a bit more complicated: He was closing in on the chance to grab the one thing he had missed most in his entire life—to be part of a family.

So on their first weekend pass the two sailors followed the signs pointing the way to MENDOTA—THE CANTALOUPE CENTER OF THE WORLD. Galloping down Highway 99 in Rog's Dodge Charger, it was certainly a quest; and the Blue Moon Cafe held the grail.

When they got to the restaurant, Jerry—whose voice at this point usually took on the portentousness of a drum roll—saw him. There, behind the counter, was his spitting image, though a little older of course: tall, fence-post lean, and with the sort of broad, high forehead that leads folks to think a quiet man is thoughtful rather than slow on the uptake.

Jerry had worked out what he was going to say, but when he saw his father plans fell by the wayside. He just rushed up to the counter and blurted, "You don't recognize me, do you?"

Which was, Jerry always would be the first to volunteer, not the swiftest thing to say. A look should have told him Ike Whitworth was not the sort to play games. He was also pretty busy.

"Can't say that I do," Ike answered, and headed for the kitchen.

Jerry, though, stopped him. "Well," he said, "I'm from Paw Paw Bottoms and I'm your son."

Ike looked at him, studying him sort of, and then growled, "How the hell I'm supposed to recognize you? You grown some, boy." He was laughing as he said it; it had been seventeen years after all. But it wasn't the greeting Jerry had expected.

And then Ike, dishes in his hand, told his son, "Step aside now, boy. Have a seat. We'll get around to talking when I take my break."

Four, maybe five hours passed before Ike got a chance to get away from behind the counter, Jerry would tell you, his face even today collapsing into a pile of ruins as he spoke. Worse, by the time father and son were finally sitting together there didn't seem much to say.

When Jerry walked out of the Blue Moon Cafe he made sure to pay for his meal. No one argued.

There wasn't much to knock around on the way back to the base. Though these days when he told the story, Jerry, wiser, would say, "I guess things never really work out the way you imagine them to." And he'd repeat what he told Rog as they pulled into Hunter's Point: "It's good to be home."

"So it was just a stroke of luck I got to meet my father," Jerry, who prided himself on being thoughtful and therefore knew a good yarn should have a moral, would conclude. Then he'd try on one of his half smiles, tug for a beat on his beard, and, very deadpan, flick off his punch line—"Bad luck."

Johnny Walker, Jerry's newest best friend and boss, was in the Lighthouse, a San Diego jazz joint in the winter of 1971, when he heard this tale. A bunch of the PRACTEC radio gang was around—George Moore, Mike O'Connor, a couple of others—and nobody really knew if Jerry's story was aimed at Johnny, or another best friend, or all of them. You couldn't tell if Johnny was hearing this for the first time or the fiftieth. But what everyone is sure about is that Johnny, who knew a bit about iffy fathers, and escapes from small towns, and dicey luck, was not sharing a thing. He held on to his confidences; grandstanding always seemed to get in the way of any sort of genuine revelations. Most he offered that night in the Lighthouse when Jerry finished was a raised glass and a bit of philosophy: "Life's a bitch, ain't it?" Which most people read as a toast; but then again, knowing Johnny, it might have been a challenge.

Still, there was no denying that Jerry Whitworth from Paw Paw Bottoms had been shaped by some of the same hard traveling and fanciful thinking as Johnny Walker from Scranton. Maybe that's what interested Johnny; or maybe it was just convenient to have someone around; or maybe it was friendship, though such a natural emotion seems too easy an explanation for anything Johnny did. The fact was, though, that after their first day on *The Dirty Old Man,* the two sailors spent a lot of time together. They'd be out on the boat, crewing in the Wednesday-afternoon yacht club beer can races; and at command parties; and taking flying lessons from Bruce Beazley at Lindbergh Field; and listening to jazz at the Lighthouse; and finishing off a pitcher at Boom Trenchard's. And all the time Johnny would be picking up the rest of Jerry's story in pieces. "Probing," he would later call it.

A lot of what Johnny discovered was sort of what you'd expect in a petty officer, first class, assigned to a naval training center: The hot runner radioman, a onetime Sailor of the Month with a file of impressive fitness reports, coming to PRACTEC after a billeting on the USS *Arlington,* a state-of-the-art communications relay ship. On board the *Arlington,* Jerry had quite a tour, participating in communications support for the recovery of the Apollo 8 and Apollo 10 manned spacecrafts and in President Richard Nixon's summit meeting at Midway Island. He'd come a long way, Jerry would tell you, from the soybean fields of his hometown.

Johnny, however, knew too well about disguises to leave it at that. So he kept digging a little deeper, and the yield got a bit more interesting.

On this ambiguous level—which was familiar turf to Johnny—there was a Jerry Whitworth who wanted something more than the Navy. He had a collection of scattered, but rather intellectual ambitions: Maybe he'd become an engineer, or he'd go off and study geology at the University of Arkansas, or perhaps he'd become a stockbroker and live on Knob Hill. He didn't talk about it much, but he had left the Navy for a spell. Enrolled at Coalinga College, roomed with Rog Olson, and drove a school bus to help make ends meet. But the responsibilities that went along with these dreams were too demanding and, shamefaced, he chucked it all, settling instead for a career as a radioman. At least on the surface.

Yet Jerry, despite his tail-dive in college, saw himself as real brainy. It was one of his vanities. Like the way he'd find the time each day to do the crossword puzzle—in ink!—and then he'd make sure that the rest of the radio gang would ooh and aah. Or he'd be always reading something, *U.S. News & World Report, The Wall Street Journal.* And there'd be a paperback, *The Fountainhead,* mostly, in his back pocket. Always going on about Ayn ("Not Ann," Jerry kept correcting his boss) Rand, Jerry was. Johnny, who had no time for books

since reality was adventure enough, shrugged off Jerry's egghead routine as a lot of smoke. Especially after Jerry announced that he was a
card-carrying member of the Libertarian party. However, when
Johnny, who didn't mind a discussion, started pressing him on how
could he hold with that sort of freewheeling mumbo jumbo and still
"yes sir" his way through the Navy, Jerry, flustered, backed off. The
way Johnny figured it, Jerry paid his Libertarian dues for the same
cockeyed reason his buddy had grown his beard: The fool wanted
people to think he was a heavy thinker, a sixties sort of guy. But
Johnny was never one to make too big a thing out of this; aspirations,
he knew, were almost as good as the real thing.

Not that there wasn't, for sure, a bit of the free-spirit rebel in Jerry.
When he wasn't threatening to chuck the Navy to become a stockbroker or a geologist, he'd be confiding his plan to restore a Chinese
junk with Rog Olson and sail around the world. Just as he'd be smoking a joint one moment, and spit-polishing his shoes the next. Yet who
was Johnny to call him on the contradictions?

Besides, Johnny, a little wayward himself, was real impressed with
this reckless, gung-ho side of Jerry's. He found a lot to admire in
Jerry's tales about scuba diving along the California coast to get a
front-row look at the migrating whales. Or, calling themselves the Red
Baron and Snoopy, the two of them would go at it over Lindbergh
Field seeing who could get the most tricks out of a pretty tame Piper
Cub. While on *The Dirty Old Man,* the two buddies sailed into a few
storms, only to come out of the rough weather still talking to each
other, which, both sailors knew, meant a lot.

Then there was Johnny's forever favorite topic of conversation—
sex. One can imagine his devotion to this round of vetting. Leering
like a carny barker, that would be Johnny's style, he began to ferret
out the clues. He'd build bridges, getting down and dirty as he boasted
about all the time he had put in exploring sin. Course for Johnny,
daydreams often would get confused with explicit memories of some
world-class partying. But Jerry, who needed heroes, didn't know that.
He was impressed, and agreeable, and as malleable as a novice at a
confessional. It didn't take him long to spill his lifelong secrets to his
new, probing best friend.

First of all, there was Jerry's short-lived marriage. He had been
twenty-eight when he married Evelyn Woodhouse, a nineteen-year-
old San Diego State University student. He had met her at a Libertar-

ian party meeting (now Johnny saw the upside to reading Ayn Rand) and next thing Jerry knew, they were married. And the next thing he knew after that was they were divorced. The marriage officially lasted ten months, but most of the time Jerry was at sea. Evelyn served Jerry with papers while he was on board the USS *Ranger* and she wouldn't even tell him why. That still hurt.

But, as Johnny learned, Jerry didn't give up chasing women. Especially younger women. In fact, it was thanks to Johnny that his thirty-three-year-old buddy got to meet a real special sixteen-year-old.

It was Chief Warrant Officer Walker, assistant director of the Practical Applications Laboratory, who assigned his ace instructor to chaperon a group of high-school science winners. The students came to San Diego from around the country, and Petty Officer Whitworth was detailed to them day and night. By the end of the week, Jerry, always on the lookout for new friendships, made three of the kids promise to write him; and for years all three dutifully corresponded. But Jerry, as he announced to all his closest friends, was only in love with one of them—sixteen-year-old Brenda Reis, from Kintyre, North Dakota.

Which struck Johnny as plenty odd. But not as odd as when Jerry told him it wasn't just young girls who caught his fancy—he had a thing about young boys, too. That blew Johnny's mind, and he couldn't wait to tell Barb about the weird games Jerry was playing. Yet after a while, Johnny began thinking about it some; and he worked it over in his mind until he saw it as just another experience out there worth having, another disguise to try on at least once. So he did.

Jerry's heart, no doubt, was a pretty complicated treasure chest. But as Johnny was sorting through the goodies, he made one discovery that above all others got his canny fieldman's mind running with possibilities. It happened on a sunny Saturday afternoon at the San Diego Yacht Club. Johnny was rigging *The Dirty Old Man* for an afternoon's cruise when Jerry, as planned, came aboard. Only he brought a date with him. "I want you to meet my boss," Jerry, still small-town polite, said as he made the introductions. Johnny found himself shaking hands with a Navy nurse who, he later offered, "is a real dumpling." All afternoon Johnny kept on checking her out. But that didn't seem to bother Jerry one bit. In fact, as they were tying up at the dock and making plans to have a sundowner or two, Jerry took his friend aside and, not making too big a thing out it, whispered,

"You want her, I'll disappear." And he did. But not before Johnny realized that above all the pulls of sex and romance, Jerry Whitworth was simply a guy looking to be liked by his friends. The sort of guy who'd maybe do anything for a best friend. Even help him get lucky for a night, which, Johnny bragged, he did.

Yet the intensity of Johnny's probing began truly to grow when, as he put it, he uncovered the existence of "larceny in Jerry's heart." The evidence—not too large a file; Johnny would only need plenty of convincing if the object of his attention proved honest—was centered around two seemingly casual conversations.

First, Jerry happened to tell his friend that he was ripping off the Navy. Each month he was drawing his married serviceman's allowance, only he had been divorced for four years. This, clearly, was small-time. But Johnny, the master thief, appreciated the attitude.

By the time he had maneuvered Jerry through another apparently aimless bull session, Johnny was convinced he had found a fellow traveler. It happened out on the boat. Johnny, the outlaw, was praising Jack Nicholson. Jerry agreed he was the real thing. You see *Easy Rider*? Johnny threw in, a natural question; but he was upping the ante. Loved it, Jerry answered. So Johnny, as if it had just come to him out of the blue, asked, What about the dope deal Nicholson and those other guys tried to pull off? You ever figure you'd be up for something like that? And Jerry, shooting the breeze with his best friend, didn't have to think twice before admitting, "A onetime score. I'd be up for that, all right. I'd take the money and know what to do with it."

Which was just what Johnny wanted to hear. It was the one bit of evidence that allowed him to assemble all his other clues into a pattern. Because all along, Johnny was talent spotting. His friendship was real; but it was also an operational strategy. Johnny had, it seemed, reached a troubling conclusion: His days as a spy were numbered. What with the Russians on his back over the poor quality of his training center product, what with Barb saying God knows what to God knows whom, what with the hassle of having to crisscross the country on weekends to make drops—it was all going to blow up in his face. Unless he got help. He needed someone who was smart. Someone who had access to top secret crypto. Someone who had larceny in his heart. Someone who'd trust him like a best friend.

But before Johnny, reluctant but resigned, could make his pitch, the Navy intervened. He had requested early transfer from shore duty, notifying his detailer that he wanted to serve in Vietnam, and the Navy Department suddenly agreed. In December 1971 he was ordered to report to the USS *Niagara Falls,* a combat supply ship assigned to the Pacific Fleet. His orders also stated that Chief Warrant Officer John Anthony Walker, Jr., would serve as the ship's Communications Material Security custodian.

And that meant Johnny, to his great delight, was back in business. Alone.

13

What a cakewalk it was! What easy trade Johnny had! Like a fox guarding the chicken coop, it was all there for his, the CMS custodian's, taking: ship-to-shore KW-7 key lists; broadcast crypto punch cards for the KWR-37; and booklets thick with ninety days of cipher settings for the KL-47, the KW-47, and the KY-8 crypto machines. Not to mention tech manuals, Op Orders for the Pacific Fleet, and top secret message traffic. There was nothing to it; the ship's crypto vault was Johnny's private library. His and his Minox C camera.

Q. During the three years that you were on the *Niagara Falls*, how successful would you estimate that you were in terms of the percentage of crypto material that you were able to obtain for these five different machines?

A. Near 100 percent.

Security was a lock waiting to be picked; on board ship it was never a clever spy's headache. The Navy and the NSA had spent their

153

energy and money devising sensible precautions to deter foreign intelligence organizations; the traitor, or "cognizant agent" as they insist on saying in the trade, was never considered a likely possibility. "It wasn't that we didn't lock the barn door," a member of a NSA damage assessment team explained. "We locked it, all right—but only after we put Johnny Walker inside the barn." Outsmarting these trusting boobs wasn't even much of a game for Johnny.

Take the security procedures for top secret key lists. A booklet of key lists—a month's worth of ciphers—for a crypto machine would be sealed immediately after its manufacture at Fort Meade. Then Armed Forces Couriers would deliver the packages to the *Niagara*. If a seal was found broken before the ciphers were to be used, the drill was to gather up the radio gang, and get ready for the captain's personal investigation. Johnny, the make-do spy, had no problem sidestepping these precautions. He'd saunter into the vault, slice the official seal with his pocket knife, photograph his product, and then reseal the packages with Scotch tape. Or, if that wasn't handy, masking tape. Either would do the trick.

Same as the Navy put a lot of stock in its Background Investigations Review Procedure. Every five years the Naval Investigative Service was required to update the BI of anyone holding a top secret or crypto clearance. A way of weeding out the apples that might have gone bad. Yet there wasn't much to it, really. Get a NIS agent to accept your pledge of anonymity and he'll throw you a helpless shrug and then admit: "We ring a few doorbells, telephone a few COs. Basically, we're looking to see if a sailor has started flying the hammer and sickle on his front lawn or has come into sick bay complaining of a slight case of heroin addiction. Anything a bit more subtle has a good chance of falling through the cracks."

Still, Johnny was nervous. It didn't take much arithmetic for him to determine that his BI update would take place in 1972. And the more he thought about some ramrod NIS investigator asking a vodka-sipping Barb if she happened to notice anything unusual lately in her husband's behavior, the more he got the willies. No way, Johnny decided, he could take a chance on that. So he conducted his own BI update. It cost him $2.98.

The money was spent on a replica of the official NIS stamp. He had it made at a stationery store. After that, it took a bit of boldness, but Johnny didn't falter: He lifted a standard pink-colored BI form from supply; typed in that a 1971 reinvestigation of Chief Warrant Officer

John Anthony Walker, Jr., had determined no derogatory information; gave his handiwork a firm embossing with his lookalike stamp;
and, when the coast was clear, slipped the sheet into his service record. At his next drop he billed the Russians for the $2.98.

Even the Navy's special precautions for "hot" wartime messages
and Op Orders seem foolhearted. Battle plans and intelligence reports
were often too lengthy and complicated to transmit over secure radio;
speed and accuracy were best served if an ARFCO—an Armed
Forces Courier—picked up the sealed messages at Command in Saigon and delivered them by hand to outlying bases or ships.

Johnny, while on board the *Niagara Falls,* served two tours in
Vietnam: the first for ten months, the next for eight. On each of these
tours he was an ARFCO. ". . . made frequent trips to Da Nang &
Saigon. Carried courier material to U.S. ships in the Tonkin Gulf,
being dropped from a helo on a sling. Was shot at in the helo and
encountered a rocket attack in Da Nang," he would brag, still full of
the thrill, in a letter written years later to his oldest daughter.

Course he couldn't tell her the best part. There was Johnny, bullets
flying—though probably more ferociously in the retelling than in the
heat of battle—as the chopper lowered him over the bouncing ship.
Swinging in the breeze, he'd jump from the sling, hit the deck running,
and make straight for the exec with his package. He'd get a priority
message from ComNavForV in downtown Saigon to a ship in the
Tonkin Gulf in twelve hours flat. With a photographic copy to the
Russians within six months.

That was Johnny's only operational problem, the lag between his
collecting the product and the drops. With the *Niagara* on long combat deployments in the Pacific, it was impossible for Johnny to sneak
off for a drive through the Virginia woods every three months or so.
All he could do was wait, and continue shooting pictures. He'd store
the film in cigarette packages. Each roll of Minox film had thirty-six
exposures. After a little practice, he could wedge six rolls of film, one
on top of the other, in a Marlboro package. When the *Niagara* docked
in Alameda, California, Johnny'd walk down the gangplank with his
Samsonite attaché case in his hand. Inside the case would be three
packages of Marlboros concealing eighteen rolls of film. The 248 photographs would be developed in a Department 16 darkroom.

· · ·

The game was going so good that Johnny, daring and greedy, decided to take a few risks. It was in 1973, after almost two years on board the *Niagara,* that he figured there was just no point in waiting so long between drops. These delays were, at the very least, bad business: The Russians were paying $4,000 a month; however, when he'd return from a cruise, shoot across country, make his delivery, and pick up his garbage bag filled with, say, nine months of salary, it'd be a flat $36,000. Not a penny of interest! For those nine months the Russians had use of his money. That wasn't fair at all.

So he decided to do something about it. Johnny, who could pump up a cover story in the same time it took to flash one of his salesman's smiles, gave his CO a hard-luck saga. Seemed his restaurant in South Carolina, which had been going great guns, Johnny offhandedly slipped in, was suddenly a little rocky. And the only thing he could reckon, he confided to his captain, one man of the world to another, was that his managers were up to a little hanky-panky. To put it bluntly, sir, they're stealing me blind while I'm off serving my country.

The next thing a giddy Johnny knew, he was at Saigon Airport waiting to catch a military flight to San Francisco. He had a ten-day emergency-leave pass in his pocket, and his attaché case in his hand.

As soon as Johnny got off the plane from Saigon, Barbara noticed his hair—it was all there. Incredibly, he had a full head of shiny black hair.

"My plastic hair," he explained. "Bought it in Hong Kong. What do you think?" he asked, for once seeming unsure of himself.

"Makes you look younger," Barb said, which was the truth. And it makes the top of your head look slick and flat like the deck of an aircraft carrier, which also was the truth, but no way was she going to say that. She hoped.

Johnny came home to the new house in Union City, California, a stranger, really, after so much time away, and walked into a very unhappy family. His three girls, now teenagers, had grown up into a way of seeing things he didn't even have the slightest chance of understanding; not that he tried. Drugs, alcohol, and sex had been called on to fill a lot of vacant spaces; but these gaps just kept on expanding out of control, until each of the girls, like their mom, was floating freely, nothing to hang on to. Everyone had a grudge; and a pile of pain; and everyone was sorry.

To hear Margaret, then fifteen, tell it, she was always spoiling for a fight, a victim ready to take her parents on. Her mom would order her not to see a certain guy, she'd go out of her way to walk arm in arm with him down the street. Then her dad with his goddamn strap would get into the act; but the next morning, her arms and back a gaudy black and blue, she'd wear a tank top to breakfast. Let 'em see she had been beaten, but she wasn't giving in. Yet all her daddy had to do was talk about the Filipino girls, how pretty they were with their long, straight hair sliding down to the small of their backs, and Maggie would start ironing her hair and letting it grow. Not that her dad ever noticed. Still, plenty of guys did. She was quite a looker, and she did a lot of running around.

Laura was unhappy in her own way. A pudgy thirteen-year-old, she didn't have any real boyfriends. Which is not to say she didn't hang around with a fast crowd. Dopers, mostly. She was high a lot of the time; toking up seemed like the easiest way to get through the day. Naturally, her mother noticed. Barb, at least once, even tried to rescue Laura from the riffraff she was running with. She caught up with her daughter at a neighbor's house and started issuing commands. When Laura didn't swing into gear quick enough, her mother took off her shoe and began pounding her with the heel. Blood was pouring down her face, the way Laura remembers it, and she was screaming for her mother to stop. "You're killing me," Laura pleaded, but her mother kept on hammering. Until at last Barb, exhausted, stopped. She walked off and left her bloody daughter to take care of herself.

Things got so that Laura began thinking about just ending it all. She went to her mother's night table where the guns were kept. There were five revolvers, but she chose the one with the ivory handle. It weighed heavy in her hand, and then felt ice-cold as she let the nozzle touch her forehead. Slowly, she started to pull the trigger. But as soon as she felt it give, in the instant that it all became real, she dropped the gun and ran from the room. Still, thoughts about suicide were always around back then.

While now, another woman living in another world, she thinks about something else that happened in those Union City days. She remembers Johnny really tearing into Maggie, whipping the living hell out of her, because Barb told him his little baby was sleeping around. And she remembers being furious at her mom for ratting on Maggie; and then her mom, staring her down before announcing, "We don't keep secrets from one another."

But, despite the varieties of denial, there was a secret. One time in Union City, Barb came back from her shift at Cecilia's, the hamburger joint she was working in, only to find a sailor waiting for her. When he said he had something to tell her, she began to prepare herself. "It's bad news," he went on and she poured herself a drink and got ready to deal with the day she knew was going to turn up eventually. So when the sailor revealed that Johnny was having an affair with his wife, Barb, who had gone on the warpath a couple of weeks ago after she found a pair of ladies' suede boots in the trunk of the new MG, could only laugh. The sailor was glowering at her, yet Barb was laughing into her drink, and wanting to tell him, Buddy, you don't know the half of it.

By the time Johnny came home on emergency leave, then, things were pretty far gone. Battle lines had been drawn; but Johnny, who saw nothing in his family worth fighting for, wouldn't allow himself to be pushed into the fray. Instead, rather than do without the pleasure of an audience, he went out and bought one—a German shepherd puppy. Sailor, Johnny named him. "My favorite child," he'd say; maybe it was true, but every time he repeated it, the words caused a lot of hurt.

Johnny, though, hadn't flown halfway across the world simply to buy a puppy. It was a business trip. And already jet-lagged and combat weary, he decided he needed his wife's assistance. "Help me," he asked. So she agreed.

They flew out of Oakland on a pleasant, warm Friday afternoon, and that cold night checked into a Holiday Inn in Fairfax, Virginia. The change in weather seemed to signal that they were entering a new territory; one with new rules.

The next morning, waking up to a sky full of autumn, he told Barb, "You drive." It would be easier, Johnny said, if he navigated; he'd keep the Russian's directions in front of him and call out the twists and turns for her.

"Me?" she said.

"Why not? You like to drive."

On the long plane ride across the width of the country, she had prepared herself, she believed, for everything. *Help me,* Johnny had asked. It was that simple. She could handle what she was about to do because she had one life to live and one man to live it with. She would stand by him; and pledge her allegiance to her family and their future.

Except she wasn't prepared to drive. She hadn't brought her license. And she was afraid to tell her husband, the spy and the tyrant.

So she drove through woods blazing with fall colors, woods like those in Maine. She became a little homesick; one of her sisters, the youngest, an artist, had died recently and she was in Barb's thoughts a lot these days. Her sister, only thirty-one, had been fine one day, in bed with a brain aneurysm the next. That was how it went. And until it did, family was all there was. *Help me,* Johnny had said. There was no choice. Just action. And then, her mind here and there, it was suddenly night. Johnny said he would drive now.

The headlights of the rented car bounced across the woods. She had the drop procedures in her lap, and she was calling out the directions to her husband. But it wasn't necessary. After the morning's dry run, Johnny, the smartest man in the world, seemed to have the maneuvers down pat. He moved through it all very swiftly, finding one 7-Up can, leaving another. The woods—tall, leafless trees—looked thin and fragile and vulnerable when silhouetted by the headlights. For some reason that bothered her.

Back in the Holiday Inn, Johnny scooped up fistfuls of $50 bills from the garbage bag; he might have been grabbing popcorn from a tub, there was so much. He was really very happy. He told her she did good. She wanted to believe there was something tender in the way he said it.

The next morning Johnny had an idea. Or maybe he had it all along, but waited until now to share it. He told Barb he was concerned about getting all that money back to California. Suppose, he said, they searched his bags at the airport. It made more sense, he explained, for Barb to carry the money; they were less likely to frisk a woman.

While Johnny watched, she sewed the money into the lining of her coat. But there was just too much; $36,000 in $50 bills is quite a bundle. Whatever couldn't be stuffed into the lining was placed into Holiday Inn envelopes. She then taped the envelopes around her waist. With her sweater on nobody would notice, Johnny told her.

Still, with the envelopes of money pressed against her waist and wearing her long coat on top of that, she felt as if she were carrying a heavy load. It really weighed on her.

On the plane, she quickly ordered a vodka. Then another. To celebrate, she told Johnny when he gave her a look. But suddenly the vodka wasn't good enough and everything she had previously decided was so much sand and she knew once and for all she hated him; and she hated herself. She felt like she was going to be sick. That's when she started sobbing.

Get a hold of yourself, Johnny warned. And his eyes, daggers, were darting around the cabin.

So she managed to; or maybe she kept on with her dribble of clenched sobs all the way across the country and no one noticed or even cared. All she remembers was that by the time they were back in Union City, she couldn't wait to get out of her coat, rip the money off her skin, and jump into a bath.

She would have stayed in the bathwater forever if she could have convinced herself it would make her clean. When that failed, she tried to believe a bottle of vodka would be an easier way toward salvation. That got her nowhere, either.

In a couple of days Johnny returned to the Pacific. They parted without saying a word.

A quick footnote—or so it seemed at the time—in the growing itinerary of Johnny's more significant travels, both domestic and foreign, was logged three months later. In February of 1974, the *Niagara Falls,* on deployment in the Western Pacific, made a supply stop at Diego Garcia.

The men stationed at Diego Garcia called it "the Rock." This was a cranky, but appropriate description of this lonely strip of coral atoll located in the Chagos Archipelago, about a thousand miles off the southern tip of India. It was also an assessment the Navy, rarely

1

After Johnny's father deserted the family, his mother helped make ends meet by taking photographs of children on a department-store Santa's knee. Here is fourteen-year-old Johnny with Santa.

2

Barbara and Johnny Walker's three daughters—Margaret, Cynthia, and Laura—in a snapshot mailed to friends for Christmas, 1961.

Warrant Officer John A. Walker, Jr., at about the time when he walked into the Soviet embassy in Washington with a KL-47 key list in his pocket.

Johnny, the happy-go-lucky "tape ape" aboard the USS *Niagara Falls*. He was also the ship's CMS custodian and was delivering nearly 100 percent of its crypto material to the Russians.

The Department 16 KGB handlers meticulously mapped out their most important asset's drop route according to Moscow Rules.

3

YOU DROP IT HERE

THE STOP AHEAD
SIGN

3A

YOU DROP IT HERE

5

YOU DROP YOUR FINAL
CAN HERE

YOU GO
THIS WAY

7

When Jerry Whitworth was late for the meet in Hong Kong, Johnny missed his face-to-face with the KGB. The fallback in Casablanca was a week off, so the jet-setting spy flew to Manila to kill time with the local lovelies.

8

Johnny and his mom. He took her to Europe for her birthday; going through customs on the way home, he made her wear a money belt stuffed with cash he had received from the KGB.

Margaret, the oldest daughter, moved out at seventeen. She had the carpenter she was living with become her legal guardian.

"Johnny's Jewels": P.K. Carroll (*r*) who wore his "unengagement ring," and Laurie Robinson, his favorite detective.

11

Laurie Robinson, cover girl. She wanted to be one of Charlie's Angels, but she wound up working, unknowingly, with a KGB spy.

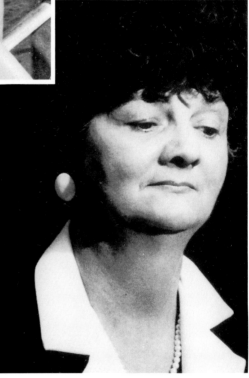

Barbara Walker's dilemma: Either she could betray her country; or she could destroy her family.

12

13

Mike Walker on his dad's houseboat. He took his surfboard on board the USS *Nimitz*, where he stuffed his duffle bag with classified documents.

14

Father and son: party animals and spies.

15

Rachel Walker. "Choose, Mike," she begged her husband. Choose us; or choose your dad.

16

Perfect cover. Johnny Walker, private eye, was hired by defense contractors to sweep their offices for electronic bugs.

Johnny, the spymaster, enjoyed the rewards of international espionage. He bought himself a plane . . .

17

18

. . . and a houseboat, a van, and land in Florida and the Bahamas. Meanwhile Barbara was living off food stamps in the backwoods of Maine.

19

The FBI, angry and vindictive, ripped the toupee off Johnny's head moments after his arrest.

Aleksey Tkachenko, the Soviet embassy official in Washington who was Johnny Walker's KGB postman.

20

Johnny in chains. Still clowning and now a celebrity.

23

Art Walker, with and without his toupee. He bought a gas barbe-cue, new brakes for the car, and a new hairpiece with the $12,000 he received for passing classified documents to his brother. He called it his "Happy Hour money."

22

24 Mike in his jeans, red Converse hightops, and chains as he arrived at Andrews Air Force Base.

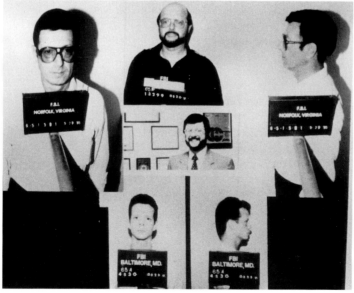

A family of spies.

26

Laura Walker Snyder, her son Christopher, and Pat Robertson at a taping for the CBN "700 Club" show. Johnny Walker's grandson refused to talk to the TV evangelist.

Jerry Whitworth, who grew up in Paw Paw Bottoms, Oklahoma, dreamed of the big time, and wound up full of remorse.

27

28

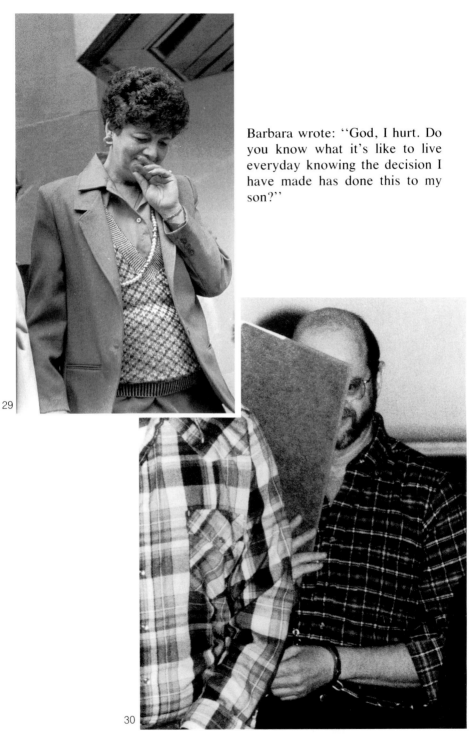

Barbara wrote: "God, I hurt. Do you know what it's like to live everyday knowing the decision I have made has done this to my son?"

29

30

Johnny Walker about to have his last laugh at his best friend's trial. Betrayal is easy, a fact of life.

sympathetic, didn't debate: A tour on "the Rock" was type-3 hard-ship duty, volunteers only, for usually just eight months at a time.

Yet starting in October 1972, after an agreement was reached by the governments of the United States and Great Britain, which had formal administrative control over the island, Diego Garcia became the site of the Joint US/UK Limited Communication Facility. Which was an-other way of saying that the island was to be turned into a floating spook house: It would be a ground station for spy birds, both Classic Wizard ocean surveillance satellites and White Cloud satellites capa-ble of monitoring radio communications and radar emissions from Soviet submarines and ships; an acoustical intelligence (ACOUS-TINT) installation of underwater hydrophones for tracking Soviet boomers was to be laid in its waters; and a storehouse for a variety of nuclear weapons, props for the very last act of any Asian conflict, was to be built.

Among the first volunteers for duty on Diego Garcia, in February of 1973, was Petty Officer, E-5, Jerry Whitworth. Jerry, the individ-ualist and adventurer, saw an opportunity to "go native" on the eleven-square-mile island populated with Quonset huts, four hundred or so sailors, and enough nuclear bombs to blow up the planet.

By the time his old buddy Johnny Walker happened to stop by, he was dying for a best friend to talk to.

Two days of R and R for Warrant Officer Walker. Sun, calm water, and nearly forty-eight hours of nonstop talking. What did the two friends discuss? By now, both men have forgotten. Oh, no doubt Jerry gave Johnny the grand tour—his steel barracks, the reef where he scuba dived, the beach where he took his evening strolls. Did he tell Johnny, as he had written to nineteen-year-old Brenda Reis who was off attending a Farm Bureau Citizenship Seminar, "Spiritually, I can really get to it . . . "? Or did he simply talk, more to Johnny's interest, of the English teacher he was carrying on with in Singapore?

Most probably, though, Johnny, eager to command, set the tone: telling jokes in his syrupy Happy Hour voice, bragging about the money The Bamboo Snack Bar was raking in, and all the while tap-ping another source. "Probing," as he called it. For a spy never has a day off. He simply gathers information for the far-off day when he might need it.

   Six months later, that far-off day, much to Johnny's regret and amazement, was at hand. By August 1974 his assignment as CMS custodian aboard the *Niagara Falls* was history. His "exceptionally high level of performance," as his last fitness report described his work, had won him a tour back in Norfolk flag country. And that was, as past experience had taught him, a slippery hunting ground for even a surefooted fieldman. Especially one with a wife one drink away from turning on him. Caution and instinct were telling Johnny to come in from the cold. Just as greed was signaling only a fool would give up the garbage bags full of loot. But what really convinced him to give his long-bubbling plan a try was the death of Sailor. The German shepherd had been put to sleep while Johnny was away at sea; the dog had quickly turned wild and mean growing up in an out-of-control home. At first Johnny raged. He accused Barb of destroying the one thing he loved. But, in time, Johnny—the ex-altar boy could be religious when it suited his purposes—saw the death of Sailor as a sign, an omen of sorts: He would be his family's next victim. Unless he protected himself.

14

Boom Trenchard's Flare Path doesn't seem like a sailor's sort of bar. There's a forest of woody-grained, milk-chocolate-colored Formica until, stretching bountifully across a long rear wall, there's the salad bar; a pair of gold link chains suspends a sheet of clear plastic like a protective cloud over the goodies, so you can be sure a stray bit of gunk won't land in the chunky blue cheese or the Bac-Os. While its wacky name, honoring a World War I British ace, is a nudge and wink because—get it!—large picture windows look straight out on a contemporary flare path—the landing strip of San Diego's Lindbergh Field. It's the kind of place where the wine list wedged in between the salt and pepper shakers on each table offers, in a breezy IBM Selectric script, the helpful reminder that rosé goes equally well with meat, fish, or fowl. And when you order a beer, the bartender makes a show of pouring it down the side of your glass.

Yet night after night, Boom's draws the radio gangs from the Naval Training Center. They come because there are rows of jacks embedded along the bar and in the tabletops. Just ask, and the waitress'll hand you a set of Bakelite headphones; plug 'em in, and you got the tower across the way at Lindbergh Field coming in loud and clear. You can be sitting there, nursing a cold one, and all the time eavesdropping on some traffic controller talking in a Cessna or a jumbo jet. The best of both worlds, for sure. Besides, what tape ape didn't feel more at home wearing a pair of 'phones?

That's how Johnny Walker, the resourceful recruiter, happened to settle on Boom's for his meeting with Jerry Whitworth. Two sailors sitting over a couple of beers, or even going at it hard and loud if things turned dicey, wouldn't require too much of a cover story. And after all, Boom's was an appropriate place for talking someone in. Though Johnny, reliving the discussion, called it his "sales pitch." Which might have been ironic since what he was asking his best friend to sell was, quite truly, his soul; or, knowing Johnny, it just might have been his flat, businesslike way of looking at things.

So they met at Johnny's suggestion on a September afternoon in 1974. It was in that valley of restaurant time after lunch and before cocktails, and Boom's was nearly empty; which, of course, was precisely what Johnny had hoped.

He arrived first, and chose a table in a lonely row smack up against the window. He ordered a scotch, then thought twice about drinking on duty, and told the waitress to make it a beer instead. When she headed toward the bar, he began looking out the window. But Johnny wasn't paying any real attention; the landings and takeoffs were a background performance to the heavy traffic flying through his anxious mind.

About twenty minutes later, Jerry made a point of shaking Johnny's hand before taking the seat across from his friend. For Jerry, this was everyday Paw Paw Bottoms politeness, but the gesture always rankled Johnny; there was something, he believed, of the politician in it. This afternoon, though, he was all smiles. "Hey, Jer, ol' buddy," he said as they clasped hands, "long time no see." Jer, dressed in a pair of khakis and a blue golf shirt with a fox running across his left breast, was grinning too. Though Johnny was thinking: Strip him of his petty officer's whites, and Jer seemed to shrink some. Not that Johnny had any problems with that.

Jerry, a jogger, ordered a Lite beer. But by the time the waitress brought it over, he was going on so that he didn't even notice. Normally, Johnny might have cut him short, telling him to drink up before his beer went stale. These soul-searching routines were another thing that didn't play too well for Johnny. Truth was, he thought it was kind of fruity, Jer's carrying on like a teenage girl telling all to her diary. But this afternoon, Johnny, the most obliging pal in the world, just let him gush. Of course, it helped that everything Jerry was confiding to his best friend was only proving Johnny's first-glance insight—the time was right.

Since filing his retirement papers last May after his tour at Diego Garcia, Jer had been doing a little of this and little of that; or, as Johnny who was only between duty stations summed it up, "Jerry was drifting between lives."

A lot of Jerry's squid dreams, the kind of last-laugh thinking that's only too easy with an exec riding on your back, were coming up short. A case in point was The Great Escape to the South Pacific fantasy. Just before retiring, he told Johnny, he and Rog Olson had made up their minds to chuck it all and sail to the South Pacific. But after a summer of dry-run cruising around Mexico's Baja, California, Rog decided another year's teaching high school might make a lot more sense; and Jer, though he had nothing better to do, had to admit that he was having second thoughts about a lifetime on a twenty-foot boat.

These days Jerry, putting a whole list of grander plans (stockbroker? geologist?) on the back burner without a word of explanation, was keeping himself in beer money by spotting sailfish. A dentist, Dr. Johnstone, had hired him. He'd get up with the sun each morning and fly a little two-seater job over the Gulf of California. The trick, he explained in his slow, labored way, was to be on the lookout for their big dorsal fins. Those mothers ride high through the water like the conning towers on a sub. Even from the air, if you look careful, you can't miss 'em.

Johnny greeted this information with only a thin grin, which Jerry, who knew his buddy some, found a bit of a puzzle. Wasn't like Johnny Walker, who had something to say about everything, not to jump in with a put-down. But, the way Jerry was coming to see it, either Johnny couldn't have given a hoot about his problems; or he was too busy plotting his next move like some chess master; or—and this possibility was most hurtful—he simply figured there wasn't much sport in going after a man that far gone. Still, Jerry didn't feel like retreating. I got no complaints, he insisted with the wistfulness of a man with at least a million. When that floated by, Jerry shot off a quick volley of other likely stories: I mean, I get out in the open; I get to fly; it's not like I'm stuck behind a desk or anything. Until finally, near about at his wit's end from the silent treatment Johnny was dishing him, Jerry came right out and said it, "I mean, what else am I going to do?"

So Johnny decided to tell him.

Not even now, though, did Johnny rush into it. He gave Jerry, wisely, some room; he played coy even; yet all the time he held out the prospect of adventure. "What I'm offering," Johnny started in, "is an illegal activity." "Even discussing it," he went on as he also tried to decipher the big-eyed look Jerry was giving him across the table, "is illegal." "If you want to talk about it, we will. If you don't, we won't. That'll be the end of it."

The decision to go on, Johnny repeated, was Jerry's. And then he sat back and waited: waited for Jerry to run off screaming for the cops; waited for the NIS agents to run out of the kitchen and grab him; waited for a hundred years to pass.

But all of a sudden there was nothing to wait for because Jerry, eager and excited, didn't have a second thought: "I'm interested," he said.

And yet—years later he would still congratulate himself on this touch—Johnny still held back. A small piece of theater, playground make-believe straight from his days as a twelve-year-old ringleader in Scranton, was hauled out to bind Jerry even tighter.

"I want you to swear a blood oath," Johnny announced. If, after hearing the proposition, Jerry didn't want any part of it, he had to swear on his life that he would not turn Johnny in.

"Will you swear?" Johnny repeated.

Not that he placed great weight on the sanctity of Jerry's pledge. He was shrewd enough to realize that an oath of allegiance from a man who you figured was ready to betray his country wasn't necessarily a promise carved in stone. But nobody understood better than Johnny how contradictions are the stock-in-trade of a wayward mind, or what the oath was really holding out to Jerry. It was an initiation rite into a world of intrigue. And it was a way of offering Jerry something else he had always wanted: to be a part of a family, even a secret one.

Of course Jerry swore the blood oath.

So Johnny, selecting only a few choice bits of the truth to throw into his stew, served up an explanation of sorts. He told Jerry he had been involved in selling classified material for a number of years, that it was profitable, and that he thought Jerry was "a perfect candidate" to build into the business.

The time was right, said Johnny, the big thinker, for expansion. He envisioned—and that was one of his favorite words; it had a real sweep of power and destiny—a two-man operation. He needed a partner, someone who would also be in a position to gather the right material. Johnny would then become, he said, more of a "go-between"; he would collect the material from this associate and deliver it to the buyers.

"You interested?" Johnny asked.

Jerry didn't answer straight off. He had a whole host of questions, and Johnny handled them with a repertoire of moods; candor, ignorance, and indignation were all trotted out in the course of the performance. He even stuck to the truth when it served his purpose. But mostly he had himself some fun.

So when Jerry asked how many years he had been involved, Johnny, with all the pride of a magician, revealed it was going on right under Jerry's nose at PRACTEC. As to when he had started or how, Johnny grumbled that Jerry had no right to ask that. And when Jerry asked how the deliveries were arranged, Johnny interrupted. We call them drops, he said, knowing full well that this keyhole peak into a James Bond world was going to leave his buddy begging for more. But Johnny wasn't talking. As if insulted by the prying, he announced that he simply would not comment on any of Jerry's other questions about procedures. Though he did share a bit of tradecraft, and told Jerry about the Minox C. He described how the camera fitted into the palm of your hand, real easy to use. He knew Jerry, who had a radioman's fondness for gadgets, would get a charge out of that. And he was right.

Jerry's big question, though, the one he kept pressing Johnny on, was, "Who are the buyers?" He made it clear he wanted to know from the get-go who was paying money for classified material.

Since this was so important to Jerry, Johnny told his buddy he would tell him the truth.

"I'm not sure," he said. The buyers were, he explained, simply people he had met. Who they precisely were, well, just between best friends, Johnny did have his suspicions: Maybe they were the Mafia, or some allied country like Israel, or maybe even a private defense organization like the people who published *Jane's Fighting Ships*. But when you got right down to it, Johnny admitted with a hint of embarrassment, he just didn't know for sure.

That seemed to satisfy Jerry. In fact, Johnny took it as a real good sign that Jerry was curious, but not too fussy.

The time had come, then, for Johnny to play his ace—the money. He told Jerry he was proposing a "fifty-fifty split." "A fair deal," was how Johnny described it; and he made the offer with such sincerity that Jerry had little choice but to believe that Johnny wasn't the sort to cut any other kind of deal.

Each month, Johnny explained, Jerry could count on making anywhere from $2,000 to $4,000. Pay was based on "the quality of the product"; crypto material, however, was a consistent money-maker. But don't expect low-level crypto like KY-8 key lists to go for as much as broadcast circuit or KW-7 ciphers. The people he was dealing with knew the ropes.

And there was one other thing. Naturally, Johnny added as if it were the most natural thing in the world, before I could cut you in on the deal, you'd have to reenlist.

But rather than let Jerry run too long with that thought, he quickly pulled out another of his, as he called them, "selling points." "There's no risk," Johnny declared. "The chances of getting caught are about nil." Proof of this, he went on, was the fact that he had been involved for a while and no one was ever on to him. If one guy can do it, why not two? "There's no reason why we should ever get caught," Johnny reasoned.

Jerry, giving it a moment's consideration, was tempted to agree.

Yet Jerry, now getting into the game, and clearly more than halfway there, had two large concerns.

The first was Johnny's wife. Jerry had seen enough of Barb—he had even visited her twice up in Union City while Johnny was off in Nam—to know she was real stormy weather. With a few pops in her, who knew what she might do.

Johnny, who had exactly the same worry, told Jerry the situation .was under control. As long as Barb continued to be "adequately compensated," she shouldn't be a problem.

Jerry agreed; since he had no money, he was willing to believe it could solve any problem.

Which left only one last fear: Would Johnny promise never, under no circumstances whatsoever, to reveal Jerry's name to the buyers?

"Sure thing."

"Never," Jerry insisted.

"Never," agreed Johnny Walker.

And that was that. The deal was done. To be sure, there were still a few things to arrange—Jerry's reenlistment, his new duty assignment, the date of his first payment. But these were small matters that could easily be worked out among friends. And partners. And spies.

So Johnny called for another round; there was a coy toast to the future; and as Boom's became thick with the Attitude Adjustment crowd, both men fell into deep cover. It was Jerry's first chance to practice living two lives.

Nearly a month later, on October 10, 1974, Jerry signed his reenlistment papers. The Navy, glad to have him back, promoted him to an E-6 rating and guaranteed that he would be assigned to an advanced radioman school in January. Jerry was hoping for satellites; that would be money in the bank.

Johnny, meanwhile, was driving with his family across country to Norfolk.

At first, Barbara refused to go. She called the kids into the living room, and as they sat before her on a row of barstools, she announced she was getting a divorce. She had put up with enough, and the girls saw her point. Besides, everyone was wrapped up in their California lives; they didn't see any reason to traipse across America simply because their father had a new duty station. The family would do just fine without him.

Except that wasn't what Johnny wanted. When Barb told him her decision that night, he wouldn't buy it. He grabbed her by the arm, and, with the girls watching, led her into the bedroom. Then he closed the door. This time there was no shouting; the girls only heard their father talking softly, carefully, like a doctor, one of them said. In the morning Barb announced to the kids that there would not be a divorce. The family was going back to Norfolk together.

It was a pretty rocky trip. They rode in a van with a motorcycle strapped over the rear tire, and they were towing *The Dirty Old Man* behind them. There was a lot of yelling, a lot of screaming. Real catfights. Then Barb started complaining she wasn't feeling well. They were crossing Texas when she started hemorrhaging; in no time flat she was sitting in a puddle of blood.

Johnny pulled the van into a rest area. The girls wanted him to take their mother to a hospital. But Johnny said it was nothing to worry about; besides, he was on a tight schedule. And he told his wife, "C'mon, Barb, get your act together. Don't die on me."

Barbara obeyed; by nightfall the bleeding had mostly stopped. On Saturday they checked into a motel outside Washington. Just as Johnny had promised the Russians he would.

That evening, while his wife and four children waited for him in their room, he drove off into the Maryland woods. After a while he dropped a garbage bag next to a telephone pole. Inside the bag was Johnny's last haul from the *Niagara Falls*. There was also a letter written to his "Dear Friend." Johnny announced that he had taken it upon himself to recruit another agent. The new man was his best friend, a career radioman, a petty officer—Jerry Alfred Whitworth.

There was no reason, Johnny had decided, to keep the name a secret.

15

After a month in a motel, the six of them camping out in a room crammed with cots, Johnny found the house he had always wanted. It was a boxy two-story Colonial on Old Ocean View Road in Norfolk, and Johnny bought it for $1,500 down; the remaining $45,000 was covered by a GI mortgage. The Walkers moved in just after Thanksgiving, 1974, and Johnny was very proud. It was the biggest house he had ever lived in, and certainly the grandest he had ever owned. From the outside, it was two-tone, like one of those half-and-half cookies Mike was forever munching: The top floor was white clapboard, while the bottom level was all red brick. The window trim was a contrasting jet black, nice and dignified, which was important to Johnny. And along the front walk, there was a row of germander hedges pruned so that they nestled close to the lawn like a line of green gumdrops; Johnny liked that touch, too. Best of all, though, there was room for a family to spread out—a living room, a family room big enough for a pool table, and, Johnny's pride, his first real den.

The only thing was, the house was haunted.

The Walkers spent their first night in the new house sleeping on the floor. The furniture hadn't arrived, but anything was better than another crowded evening in that dingy Little Creek motel. Besides, it was going to be fun, all of them huddled on their bedrolls like they used to do in the woods behind the trailer in Ladson. Except Laura heard a noise. Something creaking upstairs. Johnny went up, but couldn't find anything. Crazy thing was, the creaking got louder. So Johnny grabbed a flashlight and went poking around the basement. Nothing, he reported back. Only the creaking turned fiercer, like it was laughing at them. That's when Cynthia started to cry. Mike, too. Everyone was hearing the creaking, if that was what it was. It kept on, a steady, high-pitched whistle, like the sound kids make when they put their lips tight over an empty bottle of Coke and blow deep.

Laura, scared stiff, didn't know what else to do, so she started humming. Soft, at first. The only song she could think of was "The Star-Spangled Banner." It was silly, she knew, but she kept at it. And then Maggie joined in. But now they were all singing. Johnny, too. All of them were singing, "O say! can you see . . . " Their voices growing strong, like a choir, Laura thought, and they all sang together, louder and louder, until they couldn't hear the creaking.

That's how the Walkers got through the first night.

The presence didn't go away, though. One time Johnny and Mike were in the kitchen when, looking through the doorwell toward the family room, they saw a spiraling wisp of gray smoke. They hurried over, but they couldn't find anything. No fire, and certainly no smoke. Barb, meanwhile, was always smelling it. It followed her around the house, creeping up on her with the same sweet fragrance. It smelled like a juicy apple when you first bit deep into it, except now this aroma gave Barb the creeps. She knew it was an evil presence. And one afternoon Laura was in her bedroom when she saw it standing in the doorway. It was a big shadow, foggy, but definitely something. Suddenly, the radio on her dresser turned itself on and the music started building, filling the room, while the shadow started vibrating, dancing to the song. Laura, beside herself, started praying: "Our Father, who art in Heaven . . ." Her voice got louder, and the music grew softer, and the figure slowed down until everything was back to normal. For the time being.

So from the first, the Walkers took it for granted that the house on Old Ocean View Road was haunted. In time they all agreed that it was cursed, too.

Night after night, Barbara, a drink in hand, would sit in the family room staring at the TV. She would draw the blinds and make sure the lamps were off; the light from the screen would be the only illumination in the room: It was a cave of shadows.

Sometimes she would sit there talking to herself, pleading. "Please stop, please stop," she would beg. Nobody knew what she was talking about.

Another time she dumped all the contents of her purse into an ashtray and lit a match. Flames jumped up from the pile, but Barbara didn't budge. If one of the kids hadn't rushed in to put it out, the whole place might have gone up.

Johnny just wrote her off.

One of the first things Johnny did after moving in was install a dead bolt on the door of his den. The den was, he informed the kids, his "inner sanctum." No one was allowed to enter without knocking. It was paneled in a light walnut wood and there were red, white, and blue curtains dotted with little anchors on the windows. There was a book case holding the eighteen volumes of *The World Book Encyclopedia* and a large collection of *National Geographics*. On the walls were framed photographs of all the ships and submarines Johnny had served on; he had put a lot of effort into gathering this collection and he was glad he finally had a room where he could display it. It showed people how he had spent the last nineteen years of his life, and he thought it was quite a testimony to all he had seen and done. Of course, it only told part of the story.

There was a wall socket behind his desk that was easy to unscrew. Inside this hollow he kept the souvenirs from his other life—drop procedures, meeting signals, Minox film. It would have been something, he used to think, if he could've framed all of this and put it up on the wall, too. Show people the whole story.

There would be Johnny, then, locked into his "inner sanctum," while at the other end of the house, Barbara would sit in the darkened family room staring at the TV. That left the kids pretty much on their own. It wasn't the best of situations.

The girls always seemed to find themselves landing in hard places, and then would wonder why their luck was so thin. Part of the answer, they knew, was the drugs; they were stoned a good deal. Also, the guys they were running with made trouble easy to find. They hung out at a downtown pool hall. Maggie, seventeen, and Laura, fifteen, were pretty bold, too. There were a lot of one-night stands. Everything was fast and loose. "They weren't boyfriends who really cared about me, just guys that I was sexually attracted to. Sexual attraction became my criteria. I had to be turned on or I wouldn't go out." That's the way Laura remembers it. It was a time, she says, "when we were trying to push things farther and farther until it would all blow up in our face." "We were just looking for a chance, an opportunity to start anew."

Everyone wanted out. Everyone wanted to run away. Laura ran off to Wisconsin, and then to California. They brought her back each time, but she still kept trying. On her third try, Cynthia and another friend came along. They were singing "California, Here I Come" when the cops caught them on a bus outside Washington, D.C. Which was a real bummer. That night, back in the house on Old Ocean View Road, Laura and Cynthia tried to burn it down. Barbara freaked and called the cops.

So they spent a night in a detention center. They were put in separate cells. Each cell had a bed, a toilet, and a sink. In the morning, a judge remanded Cynthia, who had a pending court appearance involving a stolen bicycle, to a home for teenage girls; Laura was released in her mother's custody. Only Barb, full of tears, told the judge, "I don't want her." So Laura spent the next month in the correctional home, too.

"That was rock-bottom," said Laura.

Margaret was the only one of the girls not to run away. When she was seventeen, she simply moved out. Her father told her, "Go if you want to," and her mother drove her to the bus.

She went to Hayward, California, and moved in with a twenty-seven-year-old guy, a carpenter. There was a problem straight off when she couldn't enroll in the local high school because she was a minor without parental supervision. But Maggie, never one to give up, worked that one out: She had the guy she was living with become her legal guardian. She even got Johnny and Barb to sign the papers. And at first it was a hoot, the idea of shacking up with your guardian;

but then, when she thought about it some, it brought her down to think how easily her parents had—literally—written her off.

Things with the carpenter also soon got out of hand. It seemed he liked to smack her around. He'd get stoned and moody and the next thing Maggie knew he was slapping the daylights out of her. She'd be scared and hurting, but the irony didn't escape her: She had left a father who liked to go after her with a strap only to move in with a guy, her guardian, too, who got his jollies tearing into her.

One night the pounding just got to be too much. She wanted out, but she needed help. So she went to the cops. An officer came back with her, to protect her while she packed. Only while the officer was watching her, he also happened to spot her stash of grass. She wound up in jail that night. The next day she was on a bus back to Norfolk. Going from one prison to another was the way she looked at it.

Johnny, too, was only biding his time. After nineteen years as a sailor and seven as a spy, he was preparing for the next stage of his career. He had big plans, but he realized he first had to get his network, as he called it, in place. Meanwhile, he shoved aside all the unhappiness in his home because it had little to do with the lives he was living; and he kept his hand in trade.

He had a brief assignment, just two months, as communications officer on the staff of the commander of Atlantic Fleet Amphibious Forces. Then he was transferred to the staff of the commander of Surface Forces.

Q. Did that particular office then provide you with access to pretty much all of the operations of the surface Atlantic Fleet?

A. I would say the majority of it.

There was only one crypto system, a KG-13, at this duty station and it was set with key cards. At the beginning of each month, Johnny would find an excuse to wander into the vault and in about twenty minutes he could photograph a month's worth of cards.

A. It was simple enough to do . . .
Q. Were you able to copy nearly or approximately 100 percent of the material for that particular machine?
A. I'd say maybe 85 percent, roughly.
Q. What was the reason for your not being able to accomplish a full hundred percent?
A. Just inability to get my hands on the book or being absent in the beginning of the month.

Johnny was also always on the lookout for Op Orders or war game evaluations. The Russians were real hot for any information on naval tactics, so he'd always make a point of snapping these documents. Once he got his hands on a paper that detailed how U.S. surface ships would set up a barrier to block Soviet subs in case of war. Sub deployment strategies were another product his "Dear Friend" was constantly requesting, so Johnny figured that might earn him a bonus. But mostly, especially after the *Niagara Falls,* it was pretty slim pickings. The Russians must have thought so too; they cut his pay down to $2,000 a month.

Yet things began to look up for Johnny when on January 2, 1975, Jerry Whitworth was assigned to the Satellite Communications Agency training program at Fort Monmouth, New Jersey. It was a five-week course and strictly hot runner country. The Navy was in the process of switching its primary communications system from high-frequency radio transmission to an ultrahigh-frequency satellite network. Four satellites—one for each of the naval communications areas—would orbit over the earth at an altitude of 22,300 miles and would serve as relay stations for messages sent between ships and shore communications centers. The men who were trained in Sat Com technology would be controlling naval communications for the rest of the century. A man could get sizably rich given that kind of run, Johnny realized.

But he also understood that an agent in place is not the same as a "hot" agent; only crime, not intentions, pays. So Johnny, the master spy hoping to become the spymaster, summoned his recruit to a face-to-face in Norfolk. Jerry arrived from Fort Monmouth on a warm February weekend full of false spring. The glorious weather was cover story enough—a chance to sail, have a few beers, two old buddies unwinding in the sun. But if anyone had cared to check, they would have found that the two friends spent most of the sunny weekend behind the locked door of Johnny's den, the red, white, and blue curtains drawn tight.

It was a spy school. Johnny tried to teach Jerry all he had learned after seven years in the field. It was a curriculum filled with the details of a thousand behind-the-lines missions—how the Minox worked best without a flash; how the photocopy machine would do for key lists, but key cards came out a bit blurry; how a Q-Tip box could conceal a stash of film cartridges; how the click of the shutter fills a crypto vault with thunder. And through it all, there was a fieldman's heartfelt refrain—it's the risk that makes it fun; it's an adventure that never ends.

But Johnny was also shrewd enough to know that war stories, tradecraft, and a bit of philosophy might not be enough to bind Jerry, a man whose ambitions were always in flux, to the game. So he took an uncharacteristic gamble—he advanced Jerry $4,000 of his own money. The Russians still had not responded to Johnny's letter announcing the new recruit, Jerry still had not come up with any product, but Johnny figured he'd take the chance. Sometimes you first have to spend money before you can make it. He paid his agent $3,000 in $50 bills for the month Jerry had already put in at Sat Com school—education was a legitimate business expense, Johnny decided—and another $1,000 as an advance against February's salary.

Not that Johnny didn't get anything in return for his money. Jerry gave him a copy of the school's *A Tactical Satellite Communications System Preliminary Tech Manual*. It wasn't a classified document, but the gesture filled Johnny with hope: His recruit seemed eager. And it would give Johnny a chance to bone up on satellites; after all, the first rule of selling was to know your product.

Jerry had some good news, too. In March, after he graduated, he'd be starting another tour at Diego Garcia. He'd be the petty officer running the Satellite Communications Division of Naval Communication on the island. And that meant he would be in charge of all classified and crypto material in his command; the CMS custodian would deliver the monthly draw directly to Petty Officer Whitworth.

• • •

But all a handler can do is send his asset out into the field. Only the agent can act. His is a solitary deed.

So Johnny, trying out the role of control officer, his millionth disguise in a million lives, taught himself patience. He did his job, he continued his trade, he stayed with his family. But all the time he was waiting, waiting for the sign that he could go on to the next stage of his career—a grander and maturer treason.

Months passed, and still Johnny didn't panic. He made plans, but he didn't execute them. He had schemes, but he didn't try them out. The model deskman, he simply worried and hoped for word from the field.

And then in July he received a letter from Jerry on Diego Garcia: "I finally made my first dive. It was real good. My future dives don't look very diverse. Will have to wait and see. Most of these things are so dated."

It was precisely what Johnny had been waiting for.

Before the month was over, he moved out of the house on Old Ocean View Road. He didn't tell Barb or the girls where he was going, he simply came by one night and loaded up the van. It took awhile. There were boxes and boxes he carried from the house, and the slamming screen door signaled his comings and goings. It was a horrible rhythm; everyone in the house heard it, but no one said anything.

When he was done, Johnny called for his son. The boy was crying. His father told him to walk with him toward the van.

"Stop whimpering," Johnny ordered.

Mike tried, but it was no use.

"Look," Johnny said at last, "I'm going to tell you something. A secret."

The van was a wall between them and the house; Mike was standing by the door on the driver's side when his father revealed the address of his new apartment.

"Got to promise me you won't tell anyone," he made his almost thirteen-year-old son pledge. "Not your mother. Not your sisters. No one."

"You can trust me, Dad. It's our secret." Mike had stopped sobbing; the knowledge gave him confidence.

Satisfied, Johnny got behind the wheel. The engine was revving.

Mike called out, "I won't tell on you."

And Johnny, like a proud admiral, threw his son a sharp salute. Mike, the best little recruit in the world, returned it, holding his salute until his father's van had disappeared down the length of Old Ocean View Road on a sticky summer's night.

PART III

NETWORK

16

In the spring of 1976 an Air Force Titan IIID rocket was launched under strict security from the Eastern Test Range at Cape Canaveral, Florida. Its payload was a Lockheed Keyhole-9 (KH-9) satellite. The launch crews, however, called the satellite "Big Bird." The crews were working under orders from the National Reconnaissance Office. This organization, a joint CIA–Air Force group, had no nickname. Even its existence was classified information.

Big Bird was launched into a north-south polar orbit. Its flight had an apogee of approximately 155 miles and a perigee of about 100 miles. Every three and one half days Big Bird completed an identical ground track route. For accuracy, though, each segment of the route was overflown twice a day—once in daylight and once in darkness. The satellite's inclination was approximately 96.4 degrees. This took Big Bird directly over the Soviet Union and China.

Big Bird was an orbiting spy station. It weighed twelve tons and was fifty-five feet long. Infrared scanners on board were capable of detecting underground missile silos, the silos' temperature being warmer than the surrounding earth. Its multispectral scanners were able to reveal camouflaged equipment. But the core of the satellite was a superhigh-resolution camera. This camera could distinguish objects eight inches across from a height of ninety miles.

For this particular mission, a slight ellipicity was programmed into Big Bird's orbit, which allowed the satellite to maintain a somewhat longer "dwell time" along its northern ground track. This was a territory which included the Union of Soviet Socialist Republics Northern Fleet submarine base at Polyarny, the ice-free seaports along the Kola Peninsula, and the shipbuilding yards at Svererodvinsk.

At the completion of its ground track circuit, Big Bird jettisoned its canisters of film. As these reentry vehicles floated toward earth, they were recovered in midair by Lockheed C-130s stationed at Hickam Air Force Base in Hawaii. From Hickam, the film was then routed by special Air Force jet across the country to Langley Air Force Base in Virginia. At Langley, the package was transferred to the custody of an armed CIA courier. Approximately forty-five minutes later, the courier delivered the package to an official in a cement building in the rear of the Washington Navy Yard. The building was tall, had few windows, and was painted a jarringly bright yellow. It was the headquarters of the National Photographic Interpretation Center.

At the NPIC, teams of photo analysts began processing the film. Computers disassembled the developed pictures into millions of electronic Morse code pulses. Each spot was manipulated; intensity and contrast of color were programmed through hundreds of combinations. When the image-enhancement process was completed, the resolution of the photographs of the Soviet submarine fleet was vividly clear—clear enough to confirm Naval Intelligence's latest operational hypothesis, and, in time, lead some analysts toward another, more frightening theory.

Over the past eight months, the Office of Naval Intelligence had been coming to the conclusion that there was a new class of Soviet attack subs in the water.

The first clue was the mission reports being logged by dispirited U.S. sub drivers. Soviet boats in the North Atlantic and the Mediterranean were having remarkable success in eluding their American shadows. The scenario for each confrontation was disturbingly similar: The Russian boat would just sit as if daring the enemy to come and get him; then, once a boat accepted the challenge, the Soviets would outmaneuver her. The Soviet boats could not only dive deeper, but they could also sprint faster than anything the United States threw at them. Computer simulations at Norfolk were estimating that these Soviet boats were capable of running submerged at 48 miles an hour and their depth limits were 2,500 feet; American attack boats, including those still under construction, were designed to reach at most 35 miles an hour, at maximum operating depths of about 1,475 feet.

Also, there were the SOSUS reports. There was an entirely new noise under the sea—an extremely loud noise. One of the primary laws of submarine construction was that noise increases in geometric proportion to speed: the faster the boat, the greater the racket. "The Russians would put the pedal to metal on a boat in the Barents Sea," a COMSUBLANT ASW expert recalled, "and we'd get a Flash from a SOSUS station in Bermuda." "It had to be something new."

And now the Big Bird photographs confirmed it. The Russians had built a submarine with a new hull. This hull was snub-nosed, more bluntly shaped than the American boats' rounded lines. But even more significant than the hull's configuration was its metallurgy. An analysis of the infrared photographs of these new boats revealed the hull was made of titanium. Titanium is an extremely strong, yet low-density, highly corrosion-resistant metallic element. It had previously been used by military engineers in jet fighter designs; other military applications had seemed too expensive or farfetched. Yet it was these titanium hulls—a significant technological advancement—which made the Soviet Alfa class attack boats the fastest, deepest-diving submarines in the world.

At first, though, ASW tacticians were not overly concerned by the Alfas. The key strategic element in submarine warfare is stealth, not speed. It is the ability of a boat to sneak up on its target, rather than outrace it, that makes the nuclear submarine such a remarkable war machine. In fact, as initial reports from Office of Naval Intelligence analysts indicated, U.S. scientists had experimented with titanium hull metallurgy, but had rejected the technology after computer analysis demonstrated that the boats would be extremely noisy. The Soviet navy, naval analysts concluded, had commissioned a sub fleet that was fast enough to outmaneuver even the newest Mark 48 torpedoes, but was of limited strategic value because its cavitation sounds echoed through the oceans like the sirens of ambulances shrieking through city streets.

Which meant the Soviet Union had wasted hundreds of millions of dollars in the design and commissioning of this new submarine.

Or—one intelligence analyst finally dared to say—it meant that Soviet naval tacticians no longer had to include acoustical detection as a factor in their strategic thinking. Soviet boats, despite the racket they made, could sneak past American SOSUS lines *because they knew precisely where these hydrophone nets were deployed.* Soviet Alfas would not have to creep up on tiptoes to shadow U.S. boomers *because the Soviet navy already knew where these boats were positioned and where they were proceeding.* If this analysis was correct, with the commissioning of the Alfas capable of dodging U.S. torpedoes, the Russian Navy's strategic advantage was complete: The Soviet Union could successfully initiate a first strike against the United States and survive retaliation to a greater extent than previously imaginable.

But this doomsday theory, naval analysts hurried to convince themselves, was based on an incredible hypothesis: U.S. naval secrets had been completely penetrated.

Which was impossible.

Or was it?

While officers of the Naval Intelligence Command in Suitland, Maryland, anxiously investigated these conflicting theories, intelligence agents in the star-shaped building in the woods outside Tëplyystan were exploring related concerns. They—in a much more specific way, of course—were also wondering what Johnny Walker was up to.

Ever since Warrant Officer Walker had announced that he had recruited another operative and that he was planning to retire from the Navy, Department 16 officers had been debating the implications of his message.

To some in the KGB, the obvious conclusion was that Walker had been turned. The FBI had caught him, and now planned to run him as a double. The new recruit was clearly an FBI agent who would feed Walker a steady flow of disinformation. Walker's planned retirement, this theory deduced, was further evidence that American counterintelligence agents were now running the operation: A civilian Walker would never have direct access to top secret material and, therefore, would be unable to double-cross his CI-2 squad controllers; or as the spooks, at home with convoluted plot lines, worked it out—it was insurance that their double could never be turned and then run as a triple agent. There was, these Department 16 officers argued, only one secure course of action—terminate the operation.

Another school of KGB thought, however, focused on the psychology of their star asset. What would be more logical, these agents argued, than Warrant Officer Walker's aggrandizing, even entrepreneurial gambit? What else would one expect from a capitalist spy? His leaving the Navy, these supporters argued, was only proof of his concern for security. Termination, this view held, would result in the unnecessary disruption of an operation that could help the Soviet Union win World War III.

In the end, the Department 16 debate was settled, as are so many operational analyses in intelligence bureaucracies throughout the world, by a compromise. The new policy would be communicated to Walker in a "Dear Friend" letter at his next drop. All the opposing KGB theorists could do in the meantime was await Walker's reaction.

And so as spy satellites focused their high-resolution cameras on Soviet submarines and KGB agents tried to second-guess their American counterparts, Johnny Walker, oblivious to the global speculations he was creating, remained doggedly active in Norfolk. He was busy proceeding with the next stages of his own, as he called it, "master plan."

On April 9, 1976, Johnny withdrew $18,000 in $50 bills from his safe-deposit box. The next day he met with Jerry Whitworth on *The Dirty Old Man*. Jerry had just completed his tour on Diego Garcia; he was on a seventy-day leave before his assignment to the USS *Constellation*. As the sailboat drifted through the Chesapeake Bay, Jerry gave his handler two Q-Tip boxes; each box contained Minox film cartridges packed one on top of the other like fingers in a fist. Johnny, in return, gave his agent two 8-by-10-inch manila envelopes. The envelopes held the money from his safe-deposit box: $2,000 for each of the past nine months of "dives." This payment, like the previous one, had not been authorized by his Soviet control. It was simply Johnny, the investor, planning for his future.

Two months later, on June 22, 1976, Johnny finalized another preliminary step toward the realization of his scheme. His divorce from Barbara became official. Citing "irreconcilable differences," the court decree ordered John Walker to pay $10,000 in cash to his wife, and $500-a-month child support for his three minor children; Barbara Walker was also granted her husband's share of the home on Old Ocean View Road, undeveloped property in Florida, and a leased 1976 Chevrolet Monte Carlo. Johnny signed the agreement, but then, always thinking, made Barb a separate offer—he would buy back the house and its furniture from her. Barb, who had enough of that haunted house, and enough of Norfolk, and enough of her husband, was glad to make the deal. She and the four kids would move in with her sister up in Maine. Perhaps, she hoped, the change would do everyone in the family some good; after all, Margaret had just had an abortion, while Cynthia was pregnant and not saying a word about marriage.

On the first Thursday in July, then, Johnny came over to the house to help Barbara pack up the Chevy, and also to get her to hand over the key. Except when he got there, the house was empty. Completely. Not a stick of furniture. Not a sheet. Not a towel. Not a bar of butter in the refrigerator. The night before Barbara and the four kids had taken everything from the house. Including the furniture Johnny had purchased. It was the family's last laugh at Johnny; and it was also their first conspiracy against him.

Little made Johnny more vengeful than inconvenience, but as he proceeded toward his ultimate goal he had no time for smaller plots. On July 31, after nearly twenty-one years in the Navy, Chief Warrant Officer Third Class John Anthony Walker, Jr., retired honorably from the Navy. He was thirty-nine years old and the holder of the Navy Commendation Medal, three Good Conduct ribbons, the National Defense Service Medal, and the Vietnam Service Medal. And he had loved the Navy even while he was betraying it.

He refused his retirement party, telling his friends, with unappreciated irony, that there was nothing to celebrate. Instead, he went home to the empty house on Old Ocean View Road. His only company was a bottle of his namesake. Johnny sat cross-legged on the hardwood living room floor in a house haunted, for this night at least, by a lifetime of memories. He would tug on the bottle, and scenes from a dozen ships in a dozen ports would tug on his mind. He was filled with an unanticipated and powerful sadness. For an entire melancholic night—a night when spy satellites orbited across the heavens and Alfa-class subs sprinted under the oceans at remarkable speeds—he was, he naively believed, alone with all his past lives, all his past secrets.

17

It was the goofiest come-on Roberta Puma had ever heard. Guys were always coming up with some kind of line, but this one won the prize. A business deal, he called it. Sure. A trip up to Maryland. A late-night drive through the woods. And then—surprise!—a quick jump on her bones when they get back to the motel. Leave it to Johnny Walker to work up a kooky ploy.

Of course she should have seen it coming. Ever since last spring when Roberta had taken the job as manager of the apartment house he had just purchased in Willoughby, there was no doubt that Johnny Walker was on the make. She knew the type: ex-Navy, ex-husband, and now ex-citing. God's gift to women. Some of these old-salt Casanovas a girl had to watch out for. But Johnny, he was nothing more than silly. An ass patter just waiting to be put in his place. Which was exactly what Roberta had done whenever he got out of line. And oh would he look cowed.

Still, you had to give Johnny Walker credit. That man could talk a blue streak. Always had a new gimmick, her boss did. Like the time over lunch when he launched into that weird game of twenty questions.

"Suppose," he had started in, "someone offered you some money. Would you be willing to spend a month in jail, say, for ten thousand dollars?"

Roberta shot him one of her give-me-a-break looks, but Johnny was not going to be reined in that easily.

"Well then suppose," he went on, "someone offered you fifty thousand. Would you be willing to spend two months in jail for that kind of money?"

Roberta didn't answer. What was the point? Johnny Walker was simply the strangest man she had ever met.

So Johnny kept at it; and since he was her boss and was buying lunch, Roberta let him.

Finally, when Johnny's eyes seemed near to glowing with a shifty sparkle and his voice was silky sweet and his smirk might just as well have been that of a man savoring a real indecent gulp of fantasy, Roberta decided this had gone far enough. He had just asked if she'd be willing to spend a year in jail for $500,000. And all of a sudden Roberta was truly uncomfortable.

"No," Roberta said, her tone packed with authority, "I wouldn't spend a weekend in jail for any amount of money. Any amount."

That settled things. Until today's goofy proposition. "A sleuth-type operation," Johnny called it. He told Roberta they'd drive up early Saturday morning to Maryland; she'd help him out with a hush-hush job he was conducting ("I can't really explain what it's about," Johnny apologized, but somehow managed to imply he had sworn this oath of confidentiality to at least the President); and she'd make a nice bit of money for her time. Naturally. And in the morning with his toupee on the nightstand, he'd be asking was it as good for you as it was for me.

Roberta told Johnny, who after all was paying her salary, she'd give the idea some thought. For about the next thousand years, say; but she kept that part to herself.

Except that night when she was entertaining one of her girlfriends with the details of her boss's Mission Impossible proposition, it started to take on dimensions of a real sidesplitter. Now she knew who Johnny reminded her of—Peter Sellers. As Inspector Clouseau. She could almost imagine Johnny Walker, the great detective, asking her to "come into my rhume." It was really, when she looked at it this way, too funny.

Her friend was cracking up, too. "You gotta go along with him," she urged Roberta. "It'll be worth it just to see how far the charade will go."

So the next day, keeping a straight face, Roberta told her boss she was available for his secret mission.

On April 4, 1977, a week before he had recruited Roberta for the "sleuth-type operation" in Maryland, Johnny was busy with another furtive assignment. For this role, he followed a separate, much more direct script; though, of course, it was simply one more act in the same grand plot he was living.

This scene opened in the den of his house on Old Ocean View Road. There was a new, larger desk to replace the one Barbara had dragged off to Maine. Johnny sat behind the desk in a leatherette swivel chair. Despite the jeans and Frye boots he had taken to wearing these days, Johnny read his lines as though he were an officer in dress whites; after twenty-one years in the Navy, he had, if nothing else, picked up the tone of command. Opposite him, sitting rigidly in a wooden ladder-back chair—Johnny chose his props as carefully as any stage manager—was his agent, Jerry Whitworth.

Life had been smiling on Jerry these days. It seemed he had the best of both of the double lives he was leading. Five months ago, he had been promoted to chief petty officer aboard the aircraft carrier *Constellation*. He was now "the fount of all wisdom"; if there was a question in the radio shack, the bottom line was "ask the chief." He enjoyed his new position for its power, and for its access.

Jerry was now awarded a top secret clearance. He was put in charge of the maintenance and operation of the carrier's satellite communications systems and its cryptographic machines. He was cleared for the world, and, therefore, had the world on a string. Since his return from Diego Garcia, he and his handler had had two previous meets, both in San Diego. He had given Johnny Q-Tip boxes crammed with film cartridges, and in return he had received a total of $16,000. Jerry had flown through the money: $1,017.71 for Chinese lamps and velour couches from Trend Furniture, $4,437 in cash at the Fun Bike Center for a BMW motorcycle, $900 for scuba equipment at New England Divers, $2,000 cash down for a red Fiat Spyder.

His annual Navy salary was $8,960. That year he spent $8,822.22. All in cash.

So there were trips through the mall. Madcap, screw-the-price shopping sprees. But best of all, Jerry, the loner, now had someone to impress with all his accumulations. Last April on the way back to San Diego from his meeting in Norfolk, the $8,000 he had received from Johnny still in his duffle bag, he had stopped off in North Dakota to visit with Brenda Reis.

Brenda was now twenty-one, a student at the University of North Dakota at Grand Forks. For the past year she had been writing to a lonely sailor, nineteen years her senior, living in the middle of the Indian Ocean on an island she had never previously known existed. It was an improbable courtship; and perhaps that in itself was the only clue to the mystery of its success.

"In many ways I envy you, Jerry. You have traveled so extensively, seen so much of this world and life, and have had time to do adventurous things," she wrote him.

Or she could be coy: "I will feel much safer when I know how to defend myself; this campus has its share of sex-crazed males!"

Sometimes she was spiritual: "Are you a Christian . . . ? Your answer will certainly have no influence on our relationship, I just want to know how and why you feel as you do."

Other times, sentimental: "In order to do all of that, you had to give up having a so-called 'home,' didn't you? Does it bother you that you don't have roots planted deep someplace, or do you?"

But, always, Brenda was solid: "One more comment. You wrote, 'The thought has occurred to me that someday this correspondence with me could become an obstacle to you . . .' I thought you knew me better than that! Only society's materialistic people forget friends —remember, I'm not part of society and I consider your friendship as one to be highly valued."

When Jerry, the newborn spy, arrived in North Dakota, he asked Brenda to marry him. They were married a week later in a wedding chapel in Las Vegas. The only witnesses were the chapel employees; their names were stamped on the license.

Jerry decided not to tell Johnny that Brenda was his wife. He thought his handler would be more impressed by his agent's shacking up with a twenty-one-year-old. Besides, he was quickly learning one of the essential rules of his new trade: Truth is capital; fiction, a much more convenient currency.

The meeting in Johnny's den moved quickly. Some handlers use gossip as cement, but Johnny, gauging his asset, ran a tight ship. The preliminaries were brief. Yes, Johnny lied, retirement was a blast. The wholesale car radio business he had started with his brother Art (who had put in his papers back in 1973) was taking off, which was another lie. And, yes, Johnny the new bachelor was getting all the action he could handle, which, oddly enough, was true. Then with the small talk out of the way, Johnny fell out of his smarmy Happy Hour voice and found the blunt, no-nonsense bark of a chief warrant officer. "Now let me see what you have," he ordered.

Jerry handed him the rolls of Minox film and then, familiar with the routine, immediately started into his report. He was a meticulous fieldman; the Navy had trained him well. He talked carefully, with knowledge and precision, about all the material he had collected since his last meet with Johnny. It was a long speech, but Johnny gave Jerry center stage for as long as he needed; a clever control learns the facts before trying them out. When Jerry finished, only then did Johnny's debriefing begin.

Johnny's, too, was a disciplined performance. Going slowly, scratching out notes with a ballpoint on a schoolboy's lined, three-hole paper, he went back over all the key lists and crypto machines in Jerry's command. Question after probing question.

Johnny, though he tried not to make too big a deal out of it in front of his agent, was pretty shook up by what he was hearing. There had been so many innovations since his days in the presatellite Navy. Like the KG-36 crypto machine Jerry had mentioned. That was a new one on Johnny. So, taking on the manner of an alert salesman quizzing a supplier about his new line, Johnny dutifully bombarded Jerry with a bundle of questions, and then wrote: "KG-36. Programmable Insert. Sat High Data Rate. (KL and picture of reader and access to TM)."

Q. Would you tell us what the notes refer to?
A. Mr. Whitworth was describing to me a little bit about how the equipment was set up.

He's telling me that the key list is put into the equipment using a programmable insert and that the equipment worked on satellite with a high data rate.

In parenthesis, Mr. Whitworth is saying to me that he has the "KL," which is the abbreviation for the key list and picture of the reader.

The reader would be the item that the crypto would be set up into.

And, lastly, "access to TM." "TM" means technical manual. And Mr. Whitworth was saying he had access to the technical manual.

Q. And what was the significance of the fact that he had access to the technical manual . . . ?

A. Well, the technical manual then went on the shopping list. I would talk to my contact about it and see if they wanted it. If so, Mr. Whitworth would photograph it.

When the debriefing was over, Johnny handed his friend $8,000 in $50 bills. And, one spy to another, he told Jerry things were going just great. The sort of quality product Jerry was coming up with would make the buyers jump up and applaud.

Which was a lie . . . and a prayer. The Russians still had not responded to Johnny's announcement of his new recruit. And that made things iffy at best. These days Johnny was going around thinking he saw a hulking Ivan waiting for him in every shadow. Some bone-crusher wanting to powwow about the new recruit. Or maybe wanting to do something more than talk. As for Jerry's new material, Johnny was certainly banking on that. He was only afraid he might have to use it to bargain for his life.

"This is mobile one, proceeding to accident scene." Roberta was speaking into the CB microphone in Johnny's car and was trying, with some difficulty, to be the perfect straight man. Though the six-packs she had been putting away all evening, she realized, might have something to do with the problem. Still, any way you sliced it, it had been a long, kooky day.

They had driven to Maryland that afternoon and first off Johnny had insisted they stop at the airport to rent a car. Next thing she knew, he took off in the rented Ford and told Roberta to take his car and tail him. That was kind of a lark, playing follow-that-car just like in the movies. It was only when she realized where Johnny was leading her that the game wore kind of thin—the Rockville Ramada Inn.

Soon as they pulled into the parking lot, she jumped out of the car and didn't waste any time letting Johnny Walker know he was fooling with the wrong girl. Boss or no boss, this was not the sort of "sleuth operation" she had in mind. Only she could have saved her breath. For once she didn't have to beat Johnny off with a stick. He was odd, sort of serious. As if he was really into the silly game he still insisted on playing.

He gave her a bunch of photographs of country roads and a set of instructions, "procedures," he called them, she was to follow to the letter. In fact, just to make sure she would have everything down pat, they were going to take a trial run. Right now, he ordered. So with Roberta driving and Johnny sitting next to her cradling the photographs, they headed off into the Maryland woods.

"This is it," Johnny said after a half hour's twisting drive. His arm was indicating a stand of trees hugging the dirt road up ahead. In the photograph on his lap an arrow shot from the word HERE and was aimed directly at the foot of a tall beech. The identical beech that Johnny was now pointing to. "This is where you look for the first 7-Up can."

But there's nothing there, Roberta corrected.

"Don't worry," he promised, "the can will be there tonight."

It really was the craziest thing, Roberta decided. But at least he was keeping his hands to himself. What was the harm of playing along with him?

And now tonight, the game had gotten even weirder. She was alone in the car (if you didn't count the six-packs she had brought along for the adventure). Johnny said he had to be "out in the field." Roberta figured that was another way of saying he was parked over a cold one in the Ramada Inn lounge. But what the hell, she had gone along this far. And not to make too big a deal about it, she was kind of curious to see how all this drama was going to end up.

Ten minutes later when she spotted the first 7-Up can precisely where it was supposed to be, she figured Johnny was going to an awful lot of trouble just to do a number on her, but she played along. "This is mobile one, proceeding to the accident scene," she announced into Johnny's CB.

She waited for a moment, nearly laughing out loud at how ridiculous all this would seem if anyone were watching; and, a chaser to her embarrassment, she treated herself to a slug of beer. When there was no return transmission, she followed the plan to "proceed at normal speed" to the location of the second can.

Wouldn't you know it, the damn 7-Up can was now there too. That Johnny Walker was too much. So, getting off on all the silliness, she obeyed the next procedure and returned to the Ramada Inn. Johnny had told her to wait by a pay phone in the lobby, and that was exactly what she did.

At midnight the phone rang. Roberta picked it up and listened as Inspector Clouseau informed her that she was to proceed at normal speed to the drop site and deliver the package.

Which had to be the dopiest line of hokum she had ever heard. But probably not any dopier, she imagined, than her 10-4ing the call and agreeing to drive once again into the pitch-black woods. She followed the route to the telephone pole Johnny had pointed out earlier that afternoon; and next, the model accomplice, she reached into the back-seat and took out the package. It was a goddamn plastic garbage bag! You could see the trash in it, paper cups and everything. But, trying to pretend there was nothing unusual about leaving a bag of smelly trash by a telephone pole at 12:30 on a Sunday morning, that it was the sort of dream date every girl should have once in her life, she made the drop. What a horny fruitcake that Johnny was! There had to be easier ways to impress a girl. She was smiling all the way to the airport as she, obeying her nutty boss's final order, drove to the ren-dezvous site.

When she caught up with Johnny at the rent-a-car counter, he was still into his hotshot Mission Impossible routine. He was very grave, wanting to know if she had had any problems following the proce-dures, if the drop had gone down without complications. Roberta, who guessed that by now she had put away a keg of beer, was having fun. She was yes-sirring and no-sirring Johnny, making out like she hadn't caught on that this was nothing but a wacko's scam. It was really pretty funny.

And, just as she had been expecting all along, Johnny finally put on the moves. C'mon, Roberta, he began in that little boy's whine of his that he must have thought was kind of cute, what say we spend the night at the Ramada? It's been a bitch of a day. Why should we knock ourselves out by driving back tonight? Let's say we get a good night's sleep, eat a big breakfast, and then drive back in the morning.

And let's say, Roberta swiftly informed him in no uncertain terms, we don't. Five minutes later they were back on the interstate.

It was only now as they were heading toward Virginia that the thought crossed Roberta's mind that Johnny didn't put the moves on her until after he was assured the drop had been completed. Could he have really been taking all this seriously? Now, *that* was too weird even to think about.

When Johnny dropped Roberta off at her apartment, he gave her an envelope. "This is your share," he said. A polite escort, he then waited until she had disappeared inside the building before driving off.

Roberta didn't give the envelope too much thought. She washed up and changed into her nightgown. Then she got around to opening the envelope. Inside was $1,500. Roberta was stunned.

What was going on? Maybe it was one of her boss's tricks. Perhaps, she wondered, Johnny was testing her, trying to see if she was honest enough to volunteer that she had been overpaid. But then again, for all she knew it was just another of his attempts to impress her. Whatever it was, Roberta was certain she didn't like it. She telephoned Johnny right away.

"There must be some mistake," she said into the phone. And Johnny, for once, didn't put up too much of a fight. He quickly agreed to come by tomorrow and pick up most of the money. Roberta went to bed feeling she had outsmarted her boss once again.

Of course, there was no way for her to know that by the time she had spoken with Johnny, he was wrapped up in other, larger problems. He had just finished reading, and then rereading, the "Dear Friend" letter he had retrieved while Roberta was off on her own in the woods. The Russians were not pleased at all by the unauthorized recruitment of another agent. The time had come, the letter said, for a face-to-face meeting, the first in nearly a decade. Johnny was to travel to Casablanca to explain himself.

18

The smell was terrible. As soon as they got out of the big Monte Carlo, tired and bitching after two days on the road, the smell near about knocked them over. There was chicken crap, and hog slop, and horse manure all over the front yard, and the July sun had made it sharp and ripe. They were ready to get back in the car and keep on driving. Except there was no place for Barbara Walker and her four kids to go.

The end of the line was a farmhouse in Anson, a community along the Kennebec River just outside the mill town of Skowhegan, Maine. It was the Nelsons' farm, Barb's older sister, Annie, and her husband, Bob. Not that it was much of a farm; Bob was working these days as a logger; it was steady pay, and he had let the farm go its own way. The neglect was starting to show.

The arrival of Barb and her four kids swelled the crowd inside the farmhouse to eleven. It was a big house; it rambled willy-nilly across a flat stretch of dirt-brown land that had been cleared from the forest a couple of generations ago. Since it was an old place, and money had always been hard to come by, it wasn't too comfortable. The Nelsons hadn't gotten around to putting in a toilet till 1965, and there still wasn't a shower. There was a bathtub, but the well was a problem; once the tub was filled, everyone had to use the same water.

Hardscrabble, then, was one way of looking at it. Except coming from the brick house on Old Ocean View Road with its family room with the pool table and color TV, and the wood-paneled den, and the three bathrooms, the Walker kids were more direct. "White trash" was how Margaret saw it. It was about the only thing the kids could agree on.

Barb didn't much like the way things were working out, either. Anger and bitterness had once made running off to the woods of Maine seem like her last shot at salvation. She had figured a stretch of rugged country between her and that bastard Johnny Walker might give her some peace. And, of course, there was the secret. She was hoping, praying, she could escape from that too.

It just wasn't that easy. She was still paying the price. She was hiding out in these godforsaken woods at the end of America, and still the secret found her. That only made her feel double-crossed. Especially when she thought about Johnny living in their old house in Norfolk. Shacking up with someone new, if she knew her Johnny. Hell, the last she heard, he was even talking about buying his own plane. It wasn't fair, and most days she could work herself into a real vengeful state. But even in all her fury, the guilt wouldn't let up, staying close, cutting through her like sin.

Vodka was her best friend. She was miserable.

The kids found solace in pot. There was a lot of home-grown up in the backwoods, and it was dynamite grass. Mike, now fourteen, was a real head. The girls, too, were into smoke. They would meet in the woods at night and turn on. It was one of the ways they showed everyone that they were city kids, not hillbillies.

It wasn't the best way of making friends.

Sometimes, though, people got too friendly. The marriage of one of their Nelson relatives was on the skids, so this cousin moved back into the farmhouse. From the start, he had his eye on Laura who was nearly seventeen and had a way about her. As Laura tells it, he jumped her one night after everyone else had gone to bed. He was kissing, and pawing, and trying to climb all over her. And she couldn't stop thinking that he was filthy, and gross, and her cousin.

That just about settled it. So after nearly seven months in the farm-house in Anson, they moved to a house in Skowhegan on French Street. It was real narrow, with matchbox-size rooms. It was also, if you asked Laura, "piss yellow ugly." The rent was $87 a month, which might not have been too bad if Johnny had been keeping up with his child support. But he wasn't. Food stamps helped out some, though.

Margaret never moved into the house on French Street. She had enough of Maine, and, instead, moved in with her uncle Frank and his family in Boston. She got a job in a department store, like her mother had almost twenty-five years ago. But this was only stopgap. Maggie had dreams of being a commercial artist, of someday working, per-haps, for an advertising agency. She was simply putting together a nest egg. The way she had it mapped out, she would move back to Norfolk and enroll in college. Take some business courses; that would give her an edge. By the year's end, she had done it, too.

Getting her life together, as Maggie called it, was a real obsession to her. After all the rough times she had put up with, she was very serious about wanting something more. She was a looker, with a red-head's shoot-first temper, and she was determined to do things her way. A lot of her hard-nosed attitude grew out of her not trusting anyone, for which she sure had her reasons. But even if you took the time to understand where she was coming from, she still could be quite a handful. Maggie was a girl packing a lot of anger.

There still were four of them in the little "piss yellow ugly" house. Cynthia, eighteen, had given birth to a son, Tommy. When she first arrived in Maine, she had written to his father in Norfolk. But the father never answered. The story she heard from one of her Virginia girlfriends was that he was denying the child was his, and anyway he had gone off and enlisted in the Marines. After Tommy was born, Cynthia wrote to the marine's parents. They answered. They wrote that the last they had heard, their son had gone AWOL. He also, Cynthia should know, wasn't really their son, but a foster child they had sort of adopted. And, though they didn't put too fine a point on it, they made it clear that an illegitimate grandson just wasn't their problem.

Which Cynthia decided was their loss. She was a watery-eyed, vaguely blond, rail-thin girl. A pale presence. She was so thin and colorless, in fact, that it was as if all fun itself had been boiled out of her. In her calm, matter-of-fact way, Cynthia moved through her life without any great expectations; that way she was never disappointed or surprised.

Since Cynthia and her son needed their own room, Mike and Laura had to double up. A blanket was strung between their beds as a gesture toward privacy. It worked out fine, though, because the two teenagers were real good friends. They hung out with a lot of the same crowd, went to the same parties, and, naturally, spent a lot of time getting high.

Laura was still into sex. She was sleeping around some, that never stopped, but these days she was having second thoughts. Making some guy just wasn't the be-all or end-all it once was. And that was confusing her.

All this running around didn't leave too much time for school. Laura was doing well at Skowhegan High. Only thing was, she wasn't showing up all that often. There was talk she wouldn't be able to graduate.

Mike, an eighth grader at the Skowhegan Area Junior High, wound up getting suspended. The way his principal, Royce Knowles, saw the problem, Mike "was different." "He didn't dress or behave as our kids did." The way Mike saw things, he was just a whole lot hipper than these backwoods hicks. He'd let his freak flag fly, and if they couldn't put up with it, that was their tough luck.

But it was Mike who, finally, was given the boot. He was transferred to an alternative tutorial program run by Marti Stevens out on her farm. Barb couldn't pay for the tutoring, so Mike had to feed Marti's thirty cows and clean out her barn. It didn't make him like his classes any better.

．．．

Complaining about things, Barb came to realize, was like howling at the moon. It didn't get her nowhere. So, instead, she tried to take a giant step away from her misery and went looking for a job. The Dexter Shoe Company hired her. It was tough going: forty hours a week at the factory cementing outer soles. She'd come home bone-tired, glue splattered over her clothes, the high, sharp smell still strong in her nostrils, and all she could do was sack out on the couch until it was time to go off to work the next morning. Once while working on the line, exhaustion snuck up on her like a mugger and knocked her right out. She was unconscious for only a minute or so, but the experience left her shook. Still, a half hour later she was back cementing.

The good thing about the job was the pay. She brought home as much as $300 some weeks. It wasn't easy money, but it sure made life easier.

She used the money to get out of that tiny house. The baby's crying had become a real strain on all of them; so when they moved to the larger apartment on Maple Street it was as if they had escaped from something dangerous. Everyone was really very relieved.

But, looking back at things, what made the move something to be remembered was their new neighbor.

He was an Army recruiter.

That man had a mighty sensible way of looking at things, the way Laura figured it. Hang around Skowhegan, where was she going to wind up after graduation? Cementing shoes like her mother? Taking care of some fatherless baby like her sister? Or maybe she'd go around with a buzz all the time like her brother?

The way this neighbor kept on selling it, the Army was her ticket out of the boondocks. Her chance to make something out of her life.

Not that her father didn't have anything to do with the way her mind was starting to run. She had a picture of her dad in her room, and just looking at it used to give her a thrill. There was Johnny in his dress whites, cap square on his head, standing at attention. Everything was so clean, and precise, and razor-sharp. Everything her life was not. And so it became everything she wished for.

There was also something else. She wanted to please her father. Johnny had always been telling her that the military was a way to see the world, to live the good life. You could do a lot worse, he had lectured her, than doing a hitch in the armed services.

So on career day at school, just as she was finishing up her junior year, when her neighbor got up on the auditorium stage and gave his pitch for the Army, Laura decided then and there to sign up. There were a lot of tests and medical exams she had to go through first, she knew that. And getting her diploma next June was no foregone conclusion, what with all her cut classes. But her mind was made up: After graduation she was going to enlist in the Army. She had her heart set on becoming a radio officer.

A decision like that was too good to keep a secret, and Laura phoned her dad in Norfolk. "I'm so happy you're doing something with your life," Johnny told her. "I'm really happy you're going into the military."

When she told him she planned to go into communications, Johnny was near to gushing with pleasure. Laura had never heard him like that before. It made her feel loved.

Before hanging up, Johnny repeated to Laura that he was very proud of her. He had to go out of town, but as soon as he got back, he'd call.

"Where you going?" Laura asked.

"Nowhere special," said her father. "Just a business trip."

19

Johnny flew into Casablanca on a midmorning flight from Cairo and took an airport bus to town. It was an extremely bright, dusty August day, the high sun already drenching the city in sweat, and Johnny, adding to his misery, imagined surveillance teams following his every move into enemy territory. The fact that he was late, the fallback tonight was the best he could do, didn't help his mood any. It also wouldn't win him any points with the Russians. And that, he knew, could be dangerous.

Johnny had traveled across the world—the ticket in his pocket read Norfolk to New York to Tokyo to Hong Kong to Bangkok to Tehran to Cairo to Casablanca—and though finally at the end of his trail, he was still lugging a bundle of doubts about the purpose of this mission. The Russians, as moody as his ex-wife, had sent him such contradictory signals. First the note announcing they were on the warpath: You have violated procedures and you're hereby summoned to a face-to-face in Casablanca to explain yourself. Then, at his next drop, the "Dear Friend" letter was actually friendly: Whitworth's product was quality material, enclosed you'll find all his back pay, and we look forward to shooting the breeze with you in Casablanca.

That note had set Johnny, who was quite familiar with changes of heart as well as false promises, thinking. Either the Russians had come around to understanding the beauty of the network he was creating; or, the suspicious fools had set a honey trap: Shower him with money, feed him a line, do whatever it takes to lead Johnny Walker smiling and greedy into a dark alley in the Casbah. Where a Moscow Center hit squad will be waiting. One more American tourist killed for his traveler's checks wouldn't even rate a line in the *International Herald Trib*.

So that's why Johnny decided to take some insurance with him to Morocco. And that was why he was late. Though, it really wasn't his fault. The way Johnny looked at it, if you had to blame anyone, you might as well blame the U.S. Navy.

For two days, Johnny had waited in room 802 of the Hong Kong Holiday Inn. For two endless days he watched Kung Fu movies on the TV, ordered room service, and spent a lot of time looking at the view toward the harbor. He wouldn't leave. Whenever he got up from the bed and paced about the room, he could feel the money belt under his shirt rubbing against a tire of fat. The door was locked and bolted, but he wore the belt, as tight as a goddamn girdle, he ranted, at all times; he even slept with it under his pajama top. There was $8,000 inside the belt. The money was very important to Johnny. He planned to use it to buy the bargaining chip that could save his life in Casablanca. Except the seller had not shown. The seller was now two days late; and each hour's passing left a spy in a foreign land feel as if his future was drifting further and further away from home.

Then, on August 12, 1977, the house phone rang.

"Where the hell you been?" Johnny barked. But before Jerry Whitworth could answer, Johnny instructed him to come right up.

Relax, Jerry told his control as Johnny closed and then locked room 802. The *Constellation* had engine problems outside of Subic Bay; we just anchored in Hong Kong this morning. But Johnny didn't relax until Jerry, sitting on the bed opposite him, had finished his report on the product he had collected over the past four months. Only then, the Q-Tip boxes crammed with Minox film cartridges scattered across the bedspread, did Johnny come around to believing that the two days killed in a Hong Kong Holiday Inn had been time well spent.

It was quite a haul. Jerry had photographed tech manuals for the KW-7 and the KWR-37 cipher machines, months worth of key lists for these machines, and a foot-high stack of classified message traffic.

But the real gold was the information on two new, experimental systems. The first was the KY-8. This new version of a standard Navy crypto machine tied battle group commanders at sea directly to Norfolk flag country or even the Situation Room in the White House. It was ultrasecure, a voice link to be used in wartime operations; and Jerry Whitworth had photographed a TECHIN diagraming the system. The KY-8 might just as well have been a party line.

The other twenty-four-karat find—and Johnny's jackpot bargaining chip—was the details of a top secret research project being conducted on the *Constellation*. The project involved establishing a new, intricate frequency pattern for broadcast communications from ships at sea. These lower-wattage transmissions were designed to prevent the Soviets from vectoring in on the locations of American vessels. Petty Officer Whitworth was deeply involved in the project; and now it was only a matter of time until the Soviet navy was too.

When the debriefing was finished, Johnny grew confident. Jerry—his discovery! his trainee!—was a master thief. The Russians would serenade Johnny with a thousand balalaikas, toast him with cases of vodka. In this euphoric mood, the fact that he was sitting in a Holiday Inn in Hong Kong on the very day he had an appointment in Casablanca did not seem too troublesome. He could make the fallback in plenty of time. In fact, now that he thought about it, there was enough time to make a little detour. He remembered from his last WESTPAC cruise a girl in Bangkok who had long, straight black hair that reached to her waist. He remembered how she rocked on his lap, dainty, light as a feather. And he remembered what she did with her hair. That settled it. Johnny booked a night flight to Thailand. The fallback was days away; not to worry. Besides, all work and no play would make Johnny a dull spy.

. . .

The taxi driver told him there must be some mistake. It was nine days later, Johnny's first night in Casablanca. He was sitting in the backseat of a cab in front of his hotel, and he had just given the driver an address that had been left for him six months ago in the Maryland woods. But the driver, despite the rough time he was having with English, was emphatically telling Johnny it was a mistake. You not want to go there, mister, the driver insisted. It not good for foreigners. Not safe at night.

To Johnny, an agent on his own behind the lines, the warning loomed like a promise. Suddenly all his doubts hardened into terror. His "insurance," the golden bargaining chips of Minox film clanking in an envelope in his pocket, abruptly felt like little more than loose change. Hong Kong, Bangkok—those sort of confidences and good times were scenes from another life. Tonight, in an instant, Johnny was petrified.

But, he also knew, there was nowhere to run. An alley in Casablanca, an alley in Norfolk. A bullet is a bullet. After a moment he told the driver there was no mistake. He repeated the address.

The meet was to be played by Moscow Rules; the KGB had set the tradecraft in the last "Dear Friend" letter. Johnny left the cab, the driver shaking his head grimly, at a dark street corner whose name he instantly forgot. He continued on foot, as ordered, along a route that led him through a maze of narrow streets. He walked, he estimated, at least a half-mile; and for the entire distance he was certain pavement artists echoed his footsteps, watchers eyed him from parked cars, and hit men targeted him in their sights. A bit of body talk, a magazine, was clutched in his left hand.

The recognition signals, word code, had also been established six months ago. "Excuse me, didn't I meet you in Berlin in 1976?" was the opening. Johnny's response: "No, I was in Norfolk, Virginia, during that hectic year."

But on this August night, the Department 16 handler, as nervous as his agent, ripped up the script. Eagerly he called out from the darkness, "Welcome, friend. We have been worried about you."

But not as worried as I've been, Johnny felt like saying.

His glasses were fake. That was the first thing Johnny noticed. And he thought: a real nifty disguise. If that was the best the KGB could come up with, maybe there was reason for everyone to worry. But once the Department 16 agent started talking, Johnny became a little more impressed.

He was bigger than Johnny, nearly six feet, and had a spy's face—pleasant, the kind that gets lost easily in a crowd. His English was accented, but it came out effortlessly; he didn't speak in cumbersome, literal translations of Russian sentences. Best of all from Johnny, the salesman's, vantage point, the Russian was knowledgeable about communications. This Ivan, Johnny was certain after throwing him a few leads, had been in a radio room or two. He'd know gold.

But just as Johnny was beginning to lead the Russian through his sales pitch, the KGB man cut him short. "Do you have something?" he demanded.

Johnny did not hesitate. He gave the Russian an envelope containing the Minox cartridges he had collected from Jerry. He waited for the Russian to hand him his payment; it should be about $30,000, Johnny guessed. Instead, the agent, clutching Johnny's envelope to his side as if it were a holster, started to walk off. There was nothing Johnny could do but follow. And as they walked, a man with fake glasses and a man with fake hair taking a late-night stroll through the near-empty back streets of Casablanca, they talked, naturally enough, spy talk.

"Why were you late?" the Russian pressed.

All day Johnny had been debating how he would deal with this question. Yet when the moment came, all the master inventor could think of was the truth.

Look, he argued, though not too desperately, he hoped, the delay was worth it. What would have been the point of coming all the way to Casablanca without first stopping off to pick up a shipment in Hong Kong? It wasn't his fault the *Constellation* had engine problems.

The Russian, however, threw a fat hand through the night as if literally to brush aside this explanation; he had no interest in discussing mechanics. Rather, he came to a halt; and, fixing a face as stern as any worn by the ruler-waving nuns at St. Patrick's back in Scranton, he got to the heart of the matter. He began to reprimand Johnny for recruiting Jerry Whitworth.

It was only then that Johnny realized that he was home free. There wasn't going to be a bullet in the back. There wasn't going to be an end to all the fun and games. There was just going to be a dressing down from Ivan Four-Eyes. After eight years with the sisters and another twenty-one in the Navy, Four-Eyes couldn't lay a glove on him. So Johnny, newly confident, adopted one of his favorite roles: He came out fighting.

"The setup is perfect," he said, cutting the Department 16 officer off without an apology. "I know Jerry. I know what I'm doing."

By the time Johnny had finished his barrage, the Russian was retreating, and Johnny felt like a champion.

"Please do not do it again. Consult us first. Please," asked the Russian a little helplessly.

Johnny didn't argue. Neither did he make any promises he didn't intend to keep.

The stroll continued, and the talk turned to security. The Russian, putting on his nun's face again, began a catechism Johnny had been hearing from the KGB for the past nine years: If it's not safe, don't do it; watch how you spend your money; don't buy anything flashy; use safe-deposit boxes, not bank accounts; and, once again, the KGB Golden Rule—don't take chances.

Johnny had mastered all these lessons long ago. It was not only insulting, he felt, but it was also a waste of time. Here he was in Casablanca with a genuine Russian agent and they were feeding him grade-school stuff. He wanted something sexier, real spook tradecraft straight from Moscow Center. So, one professional to another, he asked Ivan Four-Eyes, Isn't there something I could read to learn about surveillance techniques. A KGB manual or something?

The Russian considered the request for a moment. And then, as if confiding a state secret, he told Johnny Walker, There is something I can suggest. It gives a very good description of how to tail someone.

. . . Yes? begged Johnny.

Finally, the KGB operative broke down and told him: It is a book. *The French Connection.* By Robin Moore. It's even in paperback, I think.

Johnny didn't laugh. But he no longer wondered where the KGB had picked up their phony-glasses disguise trick: There must be a pile of Superman comics in Moscow Center, too.

The conversation had continued for nearly an hour when the KGB man, as though determined to give a dutiful five minutes to every topic on his prearranged list, began an attempt at exploring the heart and mind of his companion. "Are you a Communist?" he asked.

Johnny tried to look insulted. He stared hard and said nothing. It was a question that did not deserve an answer.

Ivan Four-Eyes, though, would not be deterred. He went on about all that Johnny was contributing to the Russian people, to the cause of socialism.

Johnny nodded; it was a gesture meant to signal, Say what you got to say, Ivan, but don't expect me to buy it.

So Ivan, a flexible control, tried out another bit of KGB logic: It's people like you who are helping the cause of world peace. As long as the superpowers are able to keep track of each other's military machines, world peace can be preserved. You are a world patriot.

A world patriot! Now that was a lie Johnny would gladly live with. Thank you, he told the Russian, as pleased as any emperor with a new set of clothes.

After the money was exchanged—$30,000 in $50 bills can be stuffed into a package about as big as a lunch box, Johnny learned—there remained only one last order of business on the Russian's agenda. A final surprise.

From this evening on, the Department 16 case man, putting on his official voice, announced, we want to conduct meets abroad on a regular basis. Now that you are retired, you are free to travel?

Sure, said Johnny who had just been paid $30,000 for having the adventure of his life.

Good, said his handler. Is there any country you would prefer?

Johnny's mind started previewing possibilities, but all his ideas quickly funneled down to one very important bottom line: You'll pay all my travel expenses? Including what it costs me to meet with Whitworth?

Of course.

Johnny, then, could be equally generous: Anywhere in the world you want, I'll be there.

Well, suggested the Russian, would you like India?

India? For Christ sake, why do you want to meet there?

Fine, the Russian decided in an instant. We will meet in Vienna.

As if to seal the bargain, he promptly handed Johnny an envelope. Inside were two pages of handwritten instructions for a January face-to-face in Vienna. The document was titled "The Vienna Procedure." Did he have, Johnny wondered, another envelope in his pocket with "The New Delhi Procedure"? It was a question Johnny never asked.

A moment later, the two spies parted. Johnny, always careful, glanced over his shoulder and saw his new friend, Ivan Four-Eyes, offer an oddly affectionate wave before he disappeared into the Moroccan night. Then Johnny, as self-satisfied as only a man who has won himself a future full of riches and excitement can be, walked a bit before finding a taxi to take him back to his hotel.

A decade had to pass before a more fitting parting scene would be suggested to Johnny. Would have thought, said the wag, that someone with your sense of the dramatic, Mr. Walker, would have turned to the KGB man and vowed, "I think this could be the beginning of a beautiful friendship." Then the two of you, arm in arm, could have waltzed off into a foggy Casablanca night.

That really cracked Johnny up, especially since laughs these days were hard to come by. He liked this rewrite so much, in fact, that the next time he gave an account of the Moroccan meet he included a final scene exactly as had been suggested. Which was just Johnny's way of playing along; or, then again, he might have convinced himself that it really had happened that way.

There was, however, good reason for Johnny's parting from the KGB man to have been a pretty rushed business. Johnny had someone waiting for him in his hotel room. That afternoon Pat Marsee had flown in from Norfolk. Johnny had bought her ticket. She was thirty-five years old and was in charge of curriculum preparation at the Armed Forces Staff College. She was cleared for handling "Secret" and "Confidential" documents. And she believed that Johnny Walker was an international businessman and that he loved her.

20

In the months that followed his trip to Morocco, Johnny, the brilliant manipulator of the Great Game, began to transform his network into an international organization. All his previous doubts and suspicions were, typically Johnny, yesterday's small concerns; today he was in spy heaven, the KGB's star agent. Of course, he still held on to a few fears—that man behind him in the bank line; was his the same polished pink face that had followed him into McDonald's this morning? the couple going at it in the Mustang parked on Old Ocean View Road; were they simply two kids who didn't want to say good night?—but these were small, occasional throbs. And when these jitters snuck up on him, Johnny, never consistent, often welcomed them: They were part of the drama, the rush, that made the game his life had become worth playing.

On the calendar Johnny kept in his den, the calendar where "Dent" meant his teeth were due for a cleaning and "Oil" was a reminder that

213

the van was due for six new quarts, the box for January 21, 1978, had a more cryptic notation: "F/F-1." Johnny carefully penciled in this reminder as soon as he had returned to Norfolk. It meant: face-to-face meeting with the KGB in Vienna. It was four months off, and there was so much to arrange.

His operative had to be notified. A letter to Jerry c/o USS *Constellation,* Pacific Fleet, made the most sense. Have you still been collecting souvenirs? Johnny wrote. Would love to see them as soon as possible.

Jerry, a hard worker, had a bundle, but the problem was he was off in the Pacific while Johnny was in Virginia. What about meeting on Thanksgiving in San Diego? Jerry replied. Fly out for some turkey and I'll throw in a peek at my souvenirs.

So two months later, after Jerry had carved the bird, and Johnny had put away a pile of dark meat, a drumstick, a mountain of stuffing, and two slices of Brenda's homemade pumpkin pie, the two friends went for a ride. They drove toward the beach. It was Johnny's idea to conduct their meeting in Jerry's Fiat; houses, the master spy explained, were a cinch to bug. Jerry, the skinny apprentice still hungry for a bit of tradecraft, happily devoured this tidbit. He drove to a roundabout where they could park the car and stare out at the Pacific. Sunset came, and it was a beautiful spot for a debriefing.

Q. Did you receive anything from Mr. Whitworth in San Diego in November of 1977?

A. Yes, sir. Normal exchange. I received some cryptographic and other materials.

Two days later, Johnny was back in Norfolk. He was a very active spy. He strung red, yellow, and green Christmas lights along the eaves of his house; argued with some long-haired weirdo hawking Christmas trees for at least twenty minutes before convincing the kid to knock his price down; lugged the tree home in the back of his van and set it up, lights and all, in the family room; went Christmas shopping for his mom and James still in Scranton, and Art living across town; stopped in every other day or so at the apartment house he owned; decided to screw Art's advice, and expanded Walker Enterprises so that it now sold retail as well as wholesale car radios; spent a night locked in his den writing a "Dear Friend" letter itemizing Jerry's Thanksgiving shipment; and found a travel agent to book tickets for his Viennese holiday next month.

It was in the midst of this hectic season that Laura called from Maine with a problem: She had cut too many classes; it didn't look like she was going to graduate in June. And no diploma, she reminded her father, meant her preenlistment agreement with the Army was out the window too. She could forget about a posting in communications.

How can I help? her dad quickly volunteered.

Well, Laura explained, pretty certain that this was going to get her nowhere, there is one thing. I can enroll in a correspondence school to make up the credits I'm missing. It'll be a lot of work, but I'll get my diploma in June.

Terrific, Johnny rejoiced.

He sounded so genuinely pleased that Laura was even able to dare to tell her father the reason she had called in the first place: The thing is, Dad, these correspondence courses are expensive. They want a hundred dollars.

I'll send a money order off today, Johnny said without even waiting for her to ask.

And the next day when it arrived in Maine, Laura felt like the luckiest girl in the world: Her father loved her so very much.

Johnny was convinced the whole operation was going to go up in smoke over an order of pancakes. He was furious. But all he could do was sit there in this fleabag hotel dining room and curse the goddamn KGB. The cheap sons of bitches! None of this was his fault. How the hell was he supposed to know a stack of pancakes could cause such a crazy fuss?

Things had started falling apart not long after Johnny arrived at Schwechat Airport on the morning of January 20, 1978. He hurried through passport control (when the immigration officer asked, "Business or pleasure, sir?" Johnny truthfully boasted, "Both"), swore that he had nothing to declare (except, under his shirts, an envelope stuffed with Minox C cartridges), and headed out of the terminal searching for the bus that would take him into Vienna.

That was his first mistake. Austria was freezing. He had on his J. C. Penney car coat and a pair of jeans: Norfolk winter clothes. He didn't own a scarf or a pair of gloves, and these days he wasn't partial to hats—they messed up his rug. It never occurred to him that Vienna in January could be a bone chiller. But now he felt the icy wind whipping right through him, and it didn't help his mood, always a bit on edge before a meet, one bit.

Still, as instructed, he took a drafty bus—the goddamn heater must be on the blink to boot, he decided—to the center of town and then hailed a taxi. He gave the driver the address of the hotel the KGB had chosen and settled into a corner of the cab; it was good tradecraft never to give the watchers too clear a target.

He had been scrunched on a plane—Soviet agents, he had been told, do not fly first class; or at least not at Moscow Center's expense —since 3:20 yesterday afternoon, and now he was glad to be heading to his hotel. He had his day all planned: Have room service send up a burger. Cuddle up in a nice warm bed. Put in some serious rack time. And then, a bright-eyed and bushy-tailed spy, he'd give the Vienna Procedure a dress rehearsal run; work out all the kinks before show-time tomorrow.

So much for plans. As soon as he got to the hotel, Johnny, full of rising fury, chucked even his modest hopes. The place was a dump. More a boardinghouse than a hotel. One quick look and he knew he could cross off any ideas about room service; he'd be lucky if he could get them to change the sheets. But what really had him going was that nobody in the whole place spoke English. No one knew what he was talking about.

Checking in became an international incident. The guy at the reception desk, his face locked in a loony smile, kept repeating, "Dank you, dank you, mein Herr." But he obviously hadn't the slightest idea what Johnny was attempting to explain. Guests were summoned to consult. It was a madhouse of Pidgin English and sign language. Johnny, dumbfounded, just fumed. The tiny reception hall was filled with what seemed like a dozen voices blabbering in some thick gut-tural language that had to be Austrian or German or whatever the hell they spoke in this part of the world. All Johnny could do was stand there; yet all the time he was certain the natives were busy asking each other what Herr Valker was doing in this flophouse and not the Hilton like a genuine American businessman. Finally—it seemed like years—a boy who had to be playing hooky from grade school showed Johnny to his room. He was led into an ice-cold closet painted a cheery battleship gray. Johnny figured it was the secret agent suite. So much for plans. And so much for cover.

The next morning, though, after a frosty, but good night's sleep, Johnny was once more the gung-ho agent. He hurried downstairs, his heart set on a big breakfast.

There was a dining room of sorts, and whitish cloths were covering the tables. That was encouraging. A heavyset woman brought over a brief, typed menu that Johnny didn't have the least hope of understanding. He just tossed it aside, and, full of good cheer as he headed into his big day, ordered coffee, black, and a stack of pancakes.

The waitress smiled knowingly and disappeared. Minutes later she returned with a cup of coffee bubbling with steamed milk and a piece of pastry.

No, Johnny corrected her, shaking his head a couple of times so she'd get the point. A bl-ack cof-fee and pan-cakes, he repeated. He emphasized each syllable thinking that might clear up the confusion.

The smiling waitress returned this time with a cup of coffee floating with whipped cream like a goddamn ice-cream soda and a slice of chocolate layer cake resting on a doily.

And that's when Johnny lost it. Or, at least it seemed that way to him at that tense time. He began barking at all the numbskulls in this poor excuse for a hotel, tearing into the silly waitress, and repeating in a voice that was much too loud for cover, "Pancakes, goddamn it. I wanted pancakes." Then he stormed out of the dining room leaving behind a very confused waitress; and for some unknown reason, the guy with the loony grin from the reception desk trailed after him repeating, Johnny swore, "Dank you, mein Herr. Dank you." While all the time Johnny was thinking, I've blown it now. The CIA should be pulling up to the door in a minute.

But the CIA didn't come. Instead, Johnny, hungry, sulked in his room till lunch. Then he went out and found a café where he managed to have a sandwich and a Coca-Cola without incident.

It had started snowing, softly at first, early that afternoon and by the time Johnny was preparing to leave the hotel for his meet, the snow was coming down in flurries. Johnny considered waiting till the fallback, two days off. But the prospect of being holed up in his closet of a room left him colder than the weather. With the Vienna Procedure in his pocket and his car coat collar turned up, he went out into the storm.

At 18:15 p.m. . . . walk from Schönbrunn Palace and Park Grounds on Schönbrunner Schlosstrasse and its continuation Schönbrunner Strasse to Ruckergasse . . . Johnny, punctual to the minute despite the weather, followed the KGB route exactly. The palace with its pale yellow facade, rows of deep green shutters, and its roof packed with fresh white snow seemed something out of a happy child's coloring book. He hurried by the main entrance, two tall obelisks crowned with eagles standing guard; the gilded birds were dusted with snow. *. . . stop at the window of the "Komet Küchen" store . . .* Which Johnny did. He also tried searching the reflection in the store window, but a fat lot of good that did him; all that was mirrored was a dense screen of white. Still, the moment's pause allowed a thought to jump into his head: The signal for a crash meet in the United States was a white chalk line drawn on the wall of the Kitchen Korner store on Walter Reed Drive. A coincidence; or were kitchen stores with alliterative names standard KGB handwriting? *. . . for easy identification, please carry your camera bag on your left shoulder and hold a small paper bag in your hand . . .* But who the hell was going to make out these safety signals in a blizzard, Johnny cursed . . . *You'll see a Stadtbahn Station . . .* And there it was, ominously empty on a stormy night like this . . . *Cross it when reaching this intersection. Turn around and walk back one block on Meidunger Hauptstrasse, then left and one block on Neiderhof Strasse, right and one block on Viventogasse, right and one block on Reschgasse to Meidunger Hauptstrasse . . .* And why don't you have me do cartwheels, too, while you're at it? Johnny fumed. His toes, he was certain, were near to freezing and his toupee was wet with snow . . . *At 18:55 p.m. stop at the men's apparel store "Bazala Internationale Kleidung" . . .* Johnny arrived there to the minute and discovered, to his joy, that the store was in an arcade . . . *Browse around its window displays inside short passages in the corner section of this building from 18:55 to 18:58 p.m. . . .* That was two minutes longer than Johnny generally spent looking at clothes, but at least his toes were starting to thaw . . . *You'll be contacted at the "Bazala" store or somewhere on your* *route* . . . And, as promised, while Johnny tried to look interested in what the well-dressed Austrian man was wearing these days, a familiar voice called from the darkness, "Greetings, friend."

It was Ivan Four-Eyes, the KGB man from Morocco.

"Have you something?"

Johnny handed over the cartridges of film he had picked up from Jerry at Thanksgiving.

"You will wait," Ivan ordered.

So Johnny, stomping his feet to keep warm, his hands deep in his pockets, waited in the breezy arcade. Ten cold minutes passed. Worse, when the Russian returned—without the package, Johnny observed—he wanted to go for a stroll. Like Casablanca, he explained. Except it was 900 degrees in Casablanca, Johnny wanted to scream. There wasn't a goddamn blizzard raging like tonight. But, the obedient asset, he said nothing. For the next forty minutes he walked, talked, and shivered.

The Department 16 control had many questions about Jerry. He wanted to know about his personal life: Does he drink? Use drugs? Is he happily married? Is he a homosexual? Johnny quickly invented answers he hoped would reassure the KGB. The way Johnny told it, his agent was brave, loyal, courageous, and true . . . he just happened to be a traitor in addition to all that.

Ivan listened; and perhaps he believed all he heard, or perhaps he simply decided to move on to his next series of questions. Tell me about Jerry's tradecraft, he asked. Where does he take the photographs? What precautions does he take? Why is his access so good?

Here Johnny, the fieldman who had worked a similar source for years, didn't need to lie. He described how radio rooms on board ship were designed. A chief petty officer and a CMS custodian doesn't have to answer to anyone, he explained. He can walk into the crypto vault anytime he wants. The keys to all the military secrets in the world are his for the taking.

The Russian seemed to agree. He told Johnny they were having no trouble decoding naval communications. Actually, he corrected himself, almost no trouble. KWR-37 messages were not "breaking." Could Johnny think of any reason why this should be?

Johnny, who took pride in doing his job well, considered this for a moment, but couldn't come up with an explanation. I'll ask Jerry, he suggested.

Suddenly Ivan got all official. No, you will not ask Whitworth. We do not want to discourage him. You are not to tell him we are having problems with any system. Understand?

Sure, said Johnny, though he felt a little wounded. After all, he was just trying to help.

The flurries began to taper off. The streets were empty. The two spies' footsteps were soft, almost soundless, cushioned by the fresh-fallen snow. The rooftops were etched in white. The night was intensely still. Ivan Four-Eyes gave the same lecture he had in Casablanca about not taking risks or spending money lavishly. Johnny nodded, trying not to look too indifferent. The Russian next trotted out his line that Johnny was a "world patriot." Again Johnny tried to show a bit of enthusiasm, but after shivering in the cold for nearly two hours he no longer cared much about saving the world; he just wanted to get warm. Then, at last, the Russian handed Johnny a package stuffed with $50 bills and the instructions for their next meet.

Vienna in July. Is that all right with you? he asked Johnny.

Johnny said that was fine. He did, however, have one request. He refused to stay in the same hotel the KGB had booked him into for this meet. Let them pay for a Hilton or a Holiday Inn. Some place that knows how to treat Americans. Some place where I won't stick out like a foreign agent.

Ivan said he would see what he could do.

Precisely how Johnny's request was reviewed is a secret still buried deep in the files of Moscow Center's espionage bureaucracy. But an incident that occurred on the very day—January 24, 1978—that Johnny returned to Norfolk perhaps had some influence on its disposition. It was on that day that the COSMOS 954, one of the Soviet Union's nuclear-powered radar ocean surveillance satellites, malfunctioned. The multimillion-dollar satellite fell to earth over Canada, spreading a wide cloud of radioactive debris with its descent. The Russians were embarrassed; the Canadians were furious; and Soviet naval intelligence had lost a valuable source of monitoring the U.S. fleet.

Against this costly disaster, the extravagance of a four-star hotel, a place where a spy could have his pancakes, might have seemed a small price for even the normally stingy Moscow Center bankers to pay. Especially if they considered the scope of naval intelligence this agent was providing.

That March at a drop outside Washington, Johnny received a "Dear Friend" letter informing him that he was welcome to stay at the Vienna Hilton. The KGB would pick up the tab.

21

Still, one thing was missing from Johnny's world. Its absence was as painful as an unreturned love. Which, when he thought about it some, seemed to sum up the problem pretty neatly: There he was an actor on a secret stage throwing his heart into the performance of a lifetime; only, there was no audience—unless you counted the KGB; and Johnny didn't count them at all—to stand up and cheeer. Johnny needed to hear the sound of applause. To walk into one of his favorite watering holes, The Lone Pine Inn, say, and feel the admiring gazes and hear the envious whispers that his entrance created—that's what was missing in Johnny's life.

To make matters worse, Johnny had few illusions about the figure he was cutting to his Happy Hour buddies: The old salt put into dry dock; let him buy you a drink and he'll flood you with tales of submariner glory. Hell, even Johnny was getting seasick of these same old stories; and the depressing truth that he hadn't set foot on a boomer since 1967—eleven years ago, and on another planet—didn't bring him any cheer, either. All that people saw, Johnny brooded, was a middle-aged hustler trying to make a buck pedaling car radios. *Car radios?* That was some way for a secret agent to earn his living. And an awful job got shabbier when, after the IRS posted $31,000 worth of liens on the door, there was no way Johnny could continue to dust off the usual lies and brag that he was working a gold mine.

Even Jerry Whitworth—who was just a legman when you came right down to it—knew something was missing. At the last exchange in San Diego, Jerry began whimpering, "Doesn't it bother you that we'll both probably die without anybody knowing how good we were?" Johnny felt like shouting, "Bother me? It breaks my heart. And by the way—what's this 'we'? This is my network." But he kept his thoughts to himself; a shrewd handler reveals little to his asset.

No, Johnny decided, he needed something that would give his public life the same sort of star quality that made him glow so brightly to a secret few. He needed, he realized with full understanding of his dilemma, a lie that was an equal to the truth.

There was also something else Johnny needed. He required an explanation for the high life he was living on a warrant officer's pension. Thirteen thousand a year didn't get you sailboats, a plane, a van, land in the Bahamas, an eight-room Colonial, and still leave enough left over to buy the next round for the house. Especially when your only other source of income, Walker Enterprises, was going belly up. How much vague talk of "clever investments" and "killings in the silver market" could he get away with?

Not to mention all the trips he was always taking. Oh, Johnny worked up some story about a pinball machine business he owned with a partner on the Coast—even Johnny was amazed when that piece of nonsense popped magically into his head—and that helped to explain his trips to San Diego. A bit. But all his trips to Europe? The Far East? North Africa? Oh, I was just off selling a few car radios in Casablanca. Johnny, who never had any problems with any lie, knew he'd have a rough time with that one.

What Johnny needed, then, was a pretext story that made sense. Or, as they say in the trade, a good cover.

Good cover, field agents are taught, is a lie that runs pretty close to the truth, yet is flexible enough to be stretched over a multitude of fictions. But for Johnny, whose requirements were always something more, cover had to be not just a rationale, but also a calling. He wanted an explanation for all the mysteries of his life; and even more urgently, he wanted a role where he could take a bow or two. Once again he wished to be chief warrant officer, to lead James and Joey Long on hikes through the hills of Scranton, and to make Art see that his little brother was sitting on top of the world.

That would be good cover. Leave it to Johnny Walker to find the perfect cover. One that solved all his problems.

In the winter of 1978 Johnny applied for a job with Wackenhut Security in Norfolk. He had decided to become a private investigator.

Phil Prince, Wackenhut's director of investigation, conducted the interview. He took to Johnny straight off. Phil had put in twenty-two years with the Marines, won a battlefield commission in 'Nam, was wounded three times, and had received the Silver Star. Johnny Walker was a 4.0 sailor for twenty-one years, had top secret clearance, and had served on nuclear subs and as a naval intelligence courier in Saigon. What was there not to like? They were two old Navy boys, and Norfolk was a Navy town. He hired Johnny on the spot.

Before starting work, though, Johnny had to get his private detective's license. He enrolled in a course at Thomas Nelson Junior College, and that was kind of a lark. The way Johnny looked at it, it was like, say, Merle Haggard—who was far and away the wisest man Johnny could imagine—having to take songwriting lessons.

Still, the course did have something going for it: Johnny Walker, PI, had no trouble getting a pistol permit.

He chose a .38 Smith & Wesson. "It ain't the biggest gun, but if you know what you're doing," he explained to the Attitude Adjustment crowd at The Lone Pine, "it'll get the job done." He wore it in a waist holster, butt out. Seemed like he never took it off. There he'd be shooting the breeze with some square in white loafers and a matching white belt and ever so casually, Johnny'd let his jacket sort of slip open just enough for white shoes to get a peek at his .38. Would that loser's eyes pop! Cracked Johnny up every time.

• • •

Once he started at Wackenhut, Johnny, never one to do things halfway, put in a lot of time. He took all kinds of cases—he tracked runaways, cornered cheating husbands, searched for missing heirs. But out of all the work that came his way, one type of case became his specialty—workmen's compensation claims.

It was a real charge, Johnny told his PI pals, to go one-on-one against some schemer who thought he had what it takes to mastermind an insurance rip-off. These jokers would claim all kinds of illnesses, invent the flimsiest of injuries—all to make a buck. They'd get away with it, too. They'd be laughing at the dumb-ass insurance companies all the way to the bank. Until Johnny came along.

Sure, the phonies were smart. Only Johnny Walker was smarter.

The flashy plots Johnny would launch to trap his archenemies! He had a closet full of disguises, a file full of scripts.

There was The Cowgirl Gets Her Man:

She'd be done up in a wide-brimmed white Stetson, white pointy-toed boots, and matching gold lamé blouse and pants. The pants were real tight. Johnny, aiming his telephoto lens through the one-way smoked-glass window of his Chevy van across the street, would joke that he could make out the date on the nickel in her back pocket.

As soon as the cowgirl—one of Johnny's "operatives," of course —rang the doorbell, Johnny'd start clicking off photos: He'd get the mark flashing a half-moon grin as he collects the two tickets he "won" to a downtown country and western joint; then, the shots now a little grainy, you see the mark sitting in the cowboy bar, clinking glasses with the tight-panted cowgirl; and finally, there's the mark, his face lit with the good time he's having, two-stepping with the cowgirl across the dance floor.

The next day the mark'd be hauled in front of the workmen's comp board: The fall from that ladder last month really messed up your inner ear. Can barely walk, huh? But dancing's another thing? Look at these photos, buddy. Case closed. Stop the disability checks.

Or, The Ton of Fun:

At about 4:00 A.M. one morning, two 50-pound bags of cement just happen to fall out of a speeding truck and land right on the front lawn of a Virginia Beach split-level. Another bit of happenstance, naturally, is that the owner of this house is having a patio built and cement is

one of the things he can use most in the world. But, still one more
quirk of fate, the guy has a bad back; he injured it so severely while
driving his rig that he can't even work. Lucky for him, though, he still
gets his disability checks.

So much for his luck. In the morning, when the homeowner discov-
ers the two bags of cement on his front lawn, he does what any able-
bodied trucker would do. He hoists the 50-pound bags, one over each
shoulder, and carries them to the patio site.

How was he supposed to know that Johnny Walker was in the van
across the street taking pictues the whole time?

Or, The Eat Your Heart Out:

Mr. Johnson? This is WPIC, Norfolk, and we've called to tell you
the good news—you've won $50 worth of groceries. Just come on
down to the Bi-Lo market within an hour and it's yours.

So an elated Mr. Johnson would jump out of his sickbed and trot
off to Bi-Lo's. There the checkout girl—who bore an uncanny resem-
blance to the operative in the cowgirl suit—would load up Mr. Johnson's bags with pounds of free food. Turkeys, hams, sack of potatoes
—she'd stuff 'em all in. And as Mr. Johnson, his arms filled with his
hefty bounty, headed out the electric-eye door, there'd be Johnny
Walker with his telephoto lens to document another miraculous recovery.

Sometimes, though, Johnny's schemes left him a little red in the
face. Like the time he was hired by a contractor who was being
sued for shoddy workmanship. The plan Johnny came up with involved his posing as a reporter and going to interview the lady who
was making all the fuss. Once he was in her home, he'd get her to
hand over her copy of the home improvement contract. He'd say
he needed it for his story; he'd return it the next day. Only, somehow the contract would disappear. Now how was the lady going to
continue to sue the contractor if she didn't have proof of their original agreement?

Only the scam backfired.

When Johnny called to set up the interview, he made the mistake
of telling the woman that he was working with Fred Talbot, a *Ledger-
Star* reporter who had been writing articles on contractor abuses. The

woman, after agreeing that Johnny could come by, had second thoughts. She called Fred Talbot at the *Ledger-Star*.

So when Johnny the reporter came by, Fred Talbot and a *Ledger-Star* photographer, John Shealy, were hiding behind the bar in the living room. They let Johnny go into his pitch, how he was Talbot's right-hand man, how he also did writing for the Reverend Jerry Falwell's publications, and how he just needed to borrow the contract for a day.

That's when Talbot and his photographer, flashbulbs popping, jumped out from behind the bar.

That was one case Johnny had to run away from.

Some people, however, held more of a grudge than others. When Johnny kept on hounding Edward Garcia, showing up at his house on Indian River Road in all sorts of disguises, the Garcia family got a lawyer. Stephen Swain, representing the Garcia family, hit Johnny with a suit demanding hundreds of thousands of dollars damages for illegally invading their property while posing as a "Boy Scout leader looking for a campsite, a surveyor purporting to survey the land, a bird-watcher attempting to take pictures of wildlife and a Catholic priest."

To which Johnny (at least while he was in Denny's downing the $1.99 Build-A-Breakfast with one of his operatives) replied, "Screw 'em if they can't take a joke." Though he did seem upset about the failure of his bird-watcher disguise. "It was a pretty good one. I wore binoculars. Even had a picture book. Never thought they'd see through that one."

Yet while people saw the PI lurking beneath the bird-watcher's getup, no one saw the spy hiding in detective cover. This level of Johnny's convoluted life continued, too, at full pitch. In February he flew his own plane across country to San Diego for his meet with Jerry. Like schoolboys boning up for a final, the two spies lay on the floor of Jerry's den, tech manuals spread before them, and tried to determine why the KWR-37 was not decoding. Johnny had promised Ivan Four-Eyes he wouldn't mention this problem to his agent; however, a broken promise was pretty small in the scheme of things, Johnny figured, if he could get the crypto breaking. Besides, he liked the challenge. He wanted to show the Russians that he and his network could solve something the whole KGB couldn't. And in the "Dear Friend" letter he left on March 11 in the Maryland woods he did just that. So much for problems with the KWR-37.

But it was at his next meet with Jerry, in July in San Diego, that Johnny received some information he knew would really interest the Russians. He could hardly wait to share it.

Eight days later, on July 15, 1978, Johnny, the world traveler, was in Vienna. He was walking that night near a festively lit Schönbrunn Palace, the two tall fountains in the front courtyard cascading noisily, when a voice called out, "Hello, my friend."

The routine with Ivan Four-Eyes was the same as on the night of the blizzard. Johnny gave him the film cartridges, and then the Russian disappeared. When he returned, empty-handed, the handler and his asset took a stroll. It was a perfect Viennese summer's night; the cool breezes off the nearby River Wien were a delight. They talked like old friends.

It was only as the debriefing was ending that Johnny announced he had some additional news.

"Jerry's been transferred," he said.

That seemed to take the Russian by surprise. For a moment he seemed unable to continue. At last he managed to ask, "Where?"

"The *Niagara Falls*," Johnny revealed with a triumphant grin. "My old ship. And it gets better. He has the same billing—CMS custodian."

"I think," agreed Ivan, "we are very lucky."

The future, indeed, was looking bright to Johnny that summer. Two weeks after his return to Norfolk, Laura visited him. She had gotten A's in both her correspondence courses and was now on her way to Fort Jackson, South Carolina. Johnny took her to dinner, introduced her to all his friends, gave her a clock radio as a graduation present, and kept telling her how proud he was of what she had accomplished.

On the August day she left Norfolk, Johnny drove her to the Greyhound station. He parked and, carrying her bag, walked with his daughter to the bus. As passengers started boarding, Johnny handed Laura, to her amazement, a $50 bill. "I know how awful it is to be in the service and to be broke," he told her. Then, equally amazing, just as she was to board, he gave her a hug.

"You're the only one of my daughters to amount to anything," he said, his farewell voice finding an appropriately sentimental pitch. "I got high hopes for you."

22

One evening not long after Laura had gone off to the Army, Johnny was working in his den when the phone rang. He picked it up and heard an unfamiliar male voice.

"This Johnny Walker? The private investigator?"

Johnny, who had been doing his spy accounts, quickly switched lives. "You got him."

"You the same Johnny Walker who served on the *Bolivar* with a Bill Wilkinson?"

"What the hell is this all about?" And Johnny's mind is racing: Could Billy have stumbled onto something? Could he have run to the FBI or the Navy with his suspicions?

"Well, Mr. Walker," the voice got around to explaining after Johnny, in just a flash, had imagined at least a dozen possible disasters, "it's about the Ku Klux Klan and a chance for you to do some detective work. A little checking up on your old friend. You interested?" And he added, "I'll pay well."

Quickly, Johnny's mood seesawed back to normal. He invited the caller to the house on Old Ocean View Road at seven the next night.

Yet as soon as he hung up the phone, Johnny felt near to busting a gut. This was really too much. Here were the feds or maybe NIS (as all sailors call the Naval Investigative Service) reaching out for him to go poking into the intrigues of Billy Wilkinson, once coconspirator in The Bamboo Snack Bar and now Grand Dragon of the Invisible Empire, Knights of the Ku Klux Klan. I mean, Johnny decided, Mr. Mysterioso on the phone has to be working for the government: Who else could have gotten his hands on the *Bolivar* service records? Who else would care what the KKK was up to? Oh, it should be a pretty interesting meeting tomorrow night. Then, not allowing himself to waste too much time toying with the possibility of his working undercover for the United States, Johnny returned to his bookkeeping. His travel expenses had to be carefully documented if he wanted to be reimbursed by the KGB.

In the months before receiving the phone call, Johnny, who thought it was part of his job to keep up with what was going on in the Navy, had been reading a great deal about the Klan. SAILORS WEARING SHEETS CREATE RACIAL INCIDENT ABOARD AIRCRAFT CARRIER was one headline. SHIPBOARD RACIAL FIGHTS SPARK NAVY KLAN PROBE was another. Then there was the report that a cross had been burned aboard the carrier *America,* and a follow-up article stating that the Navy was particularly concerned about the Klan's success in recruiting Norfolk-based Atlantic Fleet sailors.

But Johnny really got to thinking about the Klan after the *Virginian-Pilot* started running stories about a scheduled KKK rally ten minutes away in Virginia Beach. One day it's the Anti-Defamation League demanding that the Navy discipline any sailors who attend. The next day it's the Navy Department declaring the event off limits for naval personnel. And in all the stories there's a big deal made of the shindig's featured speaker—Grand Dragon Bill Wilkinson. So that's what Billy's up to, Johnny read with some interest. More than a decade had passed since their days in Charleston, and Johnny had often wondered what had become of his drinking buddy.

Still, he wasn't curious enough to attend the rally. He made do with the *Virginian-Pilot* account: "The Ku Klux Klan," Wilkinson had declared, "is fighting for free enterprise and whites' rights." The Klan was "fed up with government preference for non-Aryans," he told his "cheering supporters."

Which goes to show, Johnny reasoned, that he wasn't the only tape ape who had served in the shack of a nuclear submarine and then gone off and done something with his life. And when, perhaps ten days later, he received that strange call, it just reaffirmed to Johnny how far his old buddy had come up in the world.

The man who arrived for the meeting with Johnny was in his early thirties, clean-cut, and even wore a suit and tie. A real flag-waver, Johnny judged with approval. A Mr. Squeaky Clean. He gave a name, which Johnny, who had been around some, didn't pay much attention to. Later, he also gave an office phone number; when it turned out to be an answering service, Johnny wasn't surprised by that either.

The man had a cop's confidence. He didn't beat around the bush. Right away he told Johnny the setup: Johnny was to contact Bill Wilkinson and announce his heartfelt ambition to join the Klan. Billy would undoubtedly welcome his old shipmate on board; he'd even make him some big mucky-muck in the Virginia organization, Mr. Squeaky Clean predicted in his airy, yet assured way. Then, once Johnny was a card carrying KKKer, the next phase of the operation would commence. Johnny was to work as an undercover informant. By hook or by crook, he was to obtain the name and address ("If you can find out their shoe sizes, I want to know too," the man joked, or at least Johnny thought it was a joke) of every Virginia-area Klansman. For his services, Johnny would receive $1,000 in cash, $500 as soon as he accepted the offer and the remainder after he had formally joined the Klan.

That kind of an assignment up your alley? Mr. Squeaky Clean concluded, keeping his pitch low-key; he might just as well have been asking about the weather.

Johnny answered with utmost sincerity: "I'm your man." While he thought to himself: And you can run off and telex that to your bosses in Washington, too.

• • •

The ceremony took place in the living room of Bill Wilkinson's house in Denham Springs, Louisiana. Johnny, dressed in his new white robes, the pointy hood over his head, raised his right arm and made one more pledge of allegiance he had no intention of keeping. When the initiation was over, Bill, wearing a robe with a grand dragon's Maltese cross stitched over his left breast, gave his new recruit a Knights of the Invisible Empire membership card. He also announced that he was immediately promoting Johnny to Kleagle, the highest rank in all of Virginia.

And so Johnny added one more disguise and one more identity to the multilayered masquerade his life had become: He was a Russian spy posing as a patriotic detective now posing as a Klansman. Yet, he believed in nothing; therefore, he betrayed nothing. His only loyalty was to the elaborate game he was playing; and in that great adventure —his only reality—the one rule was to win.

The Kleagle returned to Norfolk and immediately threw himself into this new role. He called Debbie Atkins at radio station WNIS in Portsmouth and said he was the Ku Klux Klan's state organizer. Bet I'd be an interesting guest for your show, he suggested. It took a little convincing, but she agreed.

Johnny showed up for the program looking, he felt, like a Klan leader. He wore a sky-blue polyester suit, an uncommon bit of formality for Johnny but a dressy touch he felt his lofty title deserved. He also brought with him two bodyguards, guys with beer-barrel bellies and long hair. One wore a National Rifle Association T-shirt, and went around showing off hairy forearms as thick as telephone poles. Both men carried rifles. They insisted they had to patrol the woods around the station while the Kleagle was on the air, Johnny's orders; and another example of the meticulous staging that went into all his performances.

Once on the air, Johnny, Atkins found, was a curiously jolly Klansman. He was there to tell the world that he had irrefutable evidence that blacks were intellectually inferior to whites. He also had proof that the Holocaust had never taken place. But he hadn't come to argue. His manner was that of a man who knew what was what, and if you didn't believe him, it was your loss.

When the show was over, he collected his rifle-toting bodyguards, and after thanking Atkins for her time, he drove off.

And that was the end of Johnny's public Klan career. His secret role lasted a little longer. Within two months of the broadcast, he called the answering-service number Mr. Squeaky Clean had given him. He proceeded to read off the roll of the entire Virginia cell. There were twelve names.

Naturally Johnny, who was accustomed to grander intrigues, was disappointed. It wasn't until years later that he learned this brief walk-on role was, after all, an escapade worthy of Johnny Walker. It seemed that while he was ratting on his buddy, the Grand Dragon was also ratting on him: Bill Wilkinson was a paid informant for the FBI. That meant, the way Johnny worked it out, that while some government agency (the NIS most probably, he decided) was paying him to join the Klan, another arm of the government was paying Billy to recruit Johnny. So, actually, Johnny had been a spy posing as a detective posing as a Kleagle for an FBI informant posing as a Grand Dragon. It was pretty funny, each side thinking they were putting one over on the other. Anyway, the way Johnny added things up, he had gotten the best deal: He was the only player getting paid by the KGB, too.

23

For her sixty-seventh birthday, Johnny took his mother to Europe. It was Margaret's first trip abroad, not to mention her first time on a jet, and the journey was the grandest adventure of her life. She had grown up in a home where Italian was spoken at the dinner table and Pope Pius XII's portrait hung over the living room sofa; the chance at last to walk through a land that had existed so vividly in her imagination made her rejoice.

They arrived in Rome on June 21, 1978, and that afternoon Margaret asked her son to take her to the Vatican. As soon as she entered the Holy See, excitement rushed through her like the shock of a miracle; just being this close to His Holiness was a blessing. At St. Peter's Margaret crossed herself, lit a candle, and, head bowed low, went on her knees to pray. She prayed for the souls of parents, for her sons, and for her grandchildren. She thanked God, the God who had tested her faith with years of hardship and misery, for sanctifying her old age with the comfort of a son like Johnny.

For, as she would always remember, the emotion as strong in her memory as the holy glory of the Sistine Chapel or the jubilant moment she first sighted the shining dome of St. Peter's, throughout that trip it was Johnny's presence as much as anything else that gave her joy. How proud she was of the successful man he had become.

For Johnny, too, the trip was a triumph. As a child in the apartment above the movie theater, he would often lay awake, restless and thoughtful, while his brothers slept. Wrapped tight in the scratchy khaki Army surplus blanket he had bought with money from his paper route, the Night Walker show soft background music, he would create Paradise: A land without raging, drunken fathers; a land where mothers never weep or do without; a land where he is everyone's hero. And now this childhood someday was today. It was his creation. Not James's. Not Art's. But his. His gift to his mother.

So perhaps it was only fitting that on the last leg of the trip, after Rome, after Naples, and after they had checked into the room in the Vienna Hilton with its windows looking directly out onto the Stadtpark, Johnny received his reward. One that was totally unexpected.

The walk-and-talk was a love fest. The KGB man, his glasses disguise as lame as ever, Johnny noted, was quite pleased with the quality of the product Johnny was delivering since Jerry's posting to the *Niagara*.

I bet you are, Johnny felt like saying. Last December, Johnny had met with his agent in the Philippine Plaza Hotel in Manila. Seventy-two hours later Johnny flew into Chicago carrying photographs of the diagrams of the KW-7, KY-8, KG-14, KWR-37, and KL-47 crypto machines. Jerry had also photographed advance key lists; the Soviets would now be able to break naval messages in "real time"—at the same moment as they were sent by American ships.

The Russian continued: Whitworth's access is truly remarkable. Again Johnny, choosing to play the flattered asset, simply let his control's compliments continue to pour. Though he could have yelled: Remarkable? It's perfect. Jerry's the CMS custodian. He can run through the crypto vault grabbing whatever catches his fancy. It's like he was one of those souped-up housewives barreling down the aisles on "Supermarket Sweep." Better, maybe. Since I had the same duty, we already know what's worth loading up on. We got our tradecraft down. It's foolproof, Ivan.

As the two spies continued their evening stroll through Vienna's 13th district, the streets of this industrial section as nearly empty as its dark buildings, it became clear to Johnny that his handler had something up his sleeve. The Russian's manner was bubbly and coy; he might have been a child bursting to share a secret. Which left Johnny thinking: You're a real sharp secret agent, Ivan. Can't even keep a secret, can you?

But, the Department 16 officer managed to hold back. It wasn't until after the money had been exchanged—Johnny and Jerry were earning $4,000 a month each—that Ivan, a father bringing out the scrumptious dessert now that his obedient boy had finished all the vegetables, made his announcement.

Even though Johnny had seen something coming, he was still taken by surprise.

"In recognition of your outstanding contribution to world peace," began Ivan, finding his official voice, "you have been awarded the rank of admiral in the Navy of the Union of Soviet Socialist Republics."

Smiling proudly, he shook Johnny's hand. But, still not satisfied, he shrugged as if to say the hell with cover, and he kissed Johnny once on each cheek.

"Congratulations, Admiral Walker," said Ivan.

Johnny, genuinely taken aback, could only repeat, "Admiral Walker." Then, he, too, broke into a grin.

No doubt about it, Johnny liked how it sounded.

Admiral Walker needed his mother's help.

It was the morning after his promotion and mother and son were in the room overlooking the Stadtpark. They were busy packing for an afternoon plane from Schwechat that would fly them to New York. There was so much to do; the airport bus was leaving in a half hour; and Johnny, a master of timing, launched into his pitch:

Mom, you know I carry a lot of money in my business. Well, flying is prime time for crooks, pickpockets. I was thinking, though, that maybe you can help me out. What say you wear my money belt? Nobody's gonna expect a sweet lady like you to be carrying a fortune. How about it?

What mother could refuse the best son in the world?

So in a moment Johnny was strapping around his mother's waist the belt filled with the cash he had received last night from the KGB. Margaret, embarrassed, quickly pulled her sweater over the belt.

After a minute, you'll forget you have it on, Johnny reassured her.

By the time Margaret arrived at Kennedy Airport the next morning, her son's prediction had proved accurate. When the customs officer asked if she had anything to declare, Margaret truly answered no. She was waved ahead. While Johnny, next in line, moved toward the officer and was ordered to open his Samsonite two-suiter. But Johnny had nothing to hide; it was another successful operation. His sixty-seven-year-old mother was the ideal accomplice. Just as he knew she would be when he had invited her to Europe in the first place.

A little over a month later, on August 13, 1979, Jerry came to visit his control.

Q. And what happened when he was in Norfolk and the two of you met?

A. We conducted our normal spy business in preparation for the September drop to the Soviets.

Q. What did he give you?

A. That was still the *Niagara Falls* material. That was really the best he produced throughout the whole period of cooperation, the best cryptographic.

Yet later that same sticky Monday afternoon, the two men still locked in Johnny's den, Jerry sitting as always in the ladder-back chair, Johnny in the big swivel chair behind the desk, it was suddenly crisis time; and the dissolution of the spy ring became a grave and likely possibility.

There are, basically, two sorts of field agents. Both operatives see shadows, hear footsteps, and plot out the casual movements of each day as though they were trapped behind enemy lines. The difference, however, is that one agent—the perfect spy—relishes every tense minute; it is the way he needs to live: his is a natural talent. For the other agent, it is a struggle to continue; courage or greed or romance can be called on to fight his fears for only so long: his complicated life will, eventually, become too much.

From the start, Johnny understood that it was just a matter of time before Jerry would want to escape.

Jerry, who never made any decision easily, moved into his story slowly. As he spoke, the red, white, and blue curtains in Johnny's den flapped weakly with every small cool breath from the air conditioner; this slight, steady noise a counterpoint to Jerry's wide, hesitant circles of speech.

Just a week ago, Jerry began, he had learned that the *Niagara Falls* was going into dry dock. Overhaul, renovations—he wasn't too sure what the Navy had planned for the ship. However, he was certain of this: It was his sign, his signal. He was being told to quit while he was ahead. To take the money and run.

Oh, he went on, there were other reasons too. How long could he continue telling Brenda that the extra money was coming from some top secret work he was doing for the Navy? That lie, he admitted, tormented him.

Then there was his buddy, Roger Olson. Rog had finally gotten it together to set off and sail around the world. Maybe he should join him. Maybe that was the sort of challenge he should be chasing.

Anyway, it came down to this. He was putting in his papers requesting transfer to the fleet reserve. Once they were approved, his retirement would become effective in a year. He'd be out of the Navy by September 1980. And also out of the spy business.

Johnny, a patient handler, didn't argue; that would have only created a solid opponent for Jerry's vague logic. Instead, he gave Jerry $12,000 in cash, the agent's KGB salary for the last three months. In $50 bills, it was a heavy bundle. It would feel, Johnny hoped, even heftier to a sailor whose total annual salary as a chief petty officer was $10,702.

Well, where they posting you? Johnny coolly wondered.

The package of money lay like a boulder in Jerry's lap.

The Communications Center at Alameda, Jerry answered.

Well, Johnny asked at last, you gonna keep on cooperating till your papers go through?

. . . Just till my papers are processed, Jerry agreed.

So Jerry would quit; or he would not quit. Johnny decided it would be a fool's game to try to predict. Yet in the days that followed, Johnny, slow and cautious, did begin to understand that it was high time to move beyond Jerry. There would be risks; yet there was also the prospect of a greater game. Of course, it was an idea, an ambition that Johnny had long been nurturing. And now, prompted by Jerry's threats, its time had finally come.

24

"**B**lood is supposed to be thicker than water," Johnny would one day write in an attempt to explain his behavior in the months that followed his conversation with Jerry. And looking at it that way, what occurred was, perhaps, natural and inevitable. But then again, if it hadn't been for two incidents beyond Johnny's control, his plan to become the Godfather of spies, as he called it, would never have moved forward quite so quickly.

The first event was a marriage.

From the start, the marriage had a lot working against it.

The couple was broke. Laura was an E-2 stationed at Fort Polk in Louisiana. Mark, the way Laura recalls things, was a dealer who had a habit of smoking up all the profits. He'd convince some heavy to front him a stash, promising to cover his debt as soon as he had sold a fistful of nickel bags. Only Mark couldn't seem to get it together; either he wasn't cut out to be a salesman, or maybe he liked weed too

much. By the end of the week there'd be two goons pounding on the
door demanding they get paid or they're gonna kick some ass. It was
a rough business. Army paychecks can only go so far. The couple was
thousands of dollars in the hole. And the hole just kept on getting
deeper.

Love can conquer all, though, Laura had always wanted to believe.
However, the hurtful truth was, Laura was never too sure of Mark's
love. The more she gave it thought, the more convinced she grew that
Mark was still pining for his ex-wife. It truly messed her up to think
Mark was simply settling for her; she had grown up feeling like a loser
in a household of competing women and now being the consolation
prize just seemed more of the same.

Still, when she came right down to it, it was pride that convinced
Laura to marry. She was pregnant, soon she'd be starting to show,
and there was no way she was going to allow herself to wind up like
her sister Cynthia. The idea of raising a child on her own was too
gross even to think about.

Anyway, the sex was terrific.

So that summer, in August 1979, Laura Walker and Mark Snyder
went to a justice of the peace near Fort Polk and got married.

A month later they headed north to tell their parents the news. It
only made things worse.

•

"That was a real dumb-ass thing to do, running off and marrying a
junkie," Johnny, inflating his son-in-law's small-time pot dealings to
suit his anger, lectured his daughter. They were sitting in Knicker-
bocker's, a Norfolk steak house he'd go to when he was in the mood
for something fancy, only tonight the place brought no comfort.
Johnny was angry. In fact, he had worked himself up into such a state
that he was way past easing into any sales pitch.

The way he saw it, he was riding to his daughter's rescue. Johnny
was, he would say, giving Laura the chance to get in "the mainstream
of American life." Her life was "the pits." The family business, the
good father reasoned, was her only shot at a future. He was doing her
a favor.

So, pushing aside his $6.99 New York strip, Johnny just came right
out and said it: "How would you like to earn some money while
you're still in the Army?"

It would sure come in handy, Laura told her father.

And that's when Johnny said something about prison. Either her father said, "You're already in prison. You have a two-year hitch with the Army, and that's prison." But then again, maybe he said, "Would you be interested in making a great deal of money even if it meant you might spend two years in prison?" To this day, Laura's not sure. At that moment everything became jumbled, out of sorts. But whatever her father said, it scared her, and fear surely must have shown across her face. Because Johnny, once more on guard, began to back off.

But Johnny wasn't leaving the field. He only retreated to the salad bar. He helped himself to another mountain of Boston lettuce, and, giving the tongs a real workout, crowned this pile with a fringe of raw onion slices. (Onions were one of his favorite vices; he was forever popping Tic Tacs as a sort of penance.) A couple of spoonfuls of Thousand Island dressing, pink and gluey, was the final touch.

Fortified and calm after this strategic interlude, he returned to the table and fired his only other shot. From the start, before he let a father's anger get in the way of business, he knew he had only two approaches to play: money and love. So much for money.

He tried love. His kind of love.

"You're a loser," he started in on his daughter, convinced he was proclaiming the sad truth. "You're a failure like all my kids. You'll never amount to anything," he continued, recklessly salting a lifetime of wounds.

Laura was trembling from the attack.

Then, miraculously, her father held out the possibility that all was not lost. He would kiss her wounds. She could win his love. All she had to do was cooperate. "Let me help you make a lot of money," Johnny nearly begged.

His daughter was listening, she wanted to please him, she needed the money—all signs were go. But Johnny, as though flirting with Laura's affection, held off. Instead, a concerned father, he asked about her work. He wanted to know what exactly were her duties at Fort Polk. What were her prospects for advancement? Say into Fort communications? An area like that would give you access to classified information, I bet.

Of course, Laura agreed. And she thought: Maybe my father is truly interested in me. And she also thought: Just don't hurt me.

So, his hand played, the mood set, Johnny, in command, told his daughter how things could be: "I know people who'd be willing to pay you for classified information. You could help them, and you could help yourself. We'd all make money."

Laura was stunned. It made no sense. Yet it also made perfect sense. Everything was at once explained: her mother, her father, her family. In that instant she, too, had become a keeper of the secret; and also in that instant, she, too, felt and understood its power: Things could never be the same.

But, like a patient given a fatal diagnosis, she struggled against the truth. To have jumped to her feet, to have shouted, "Go to hell," to have stormed off, would have only served to convince her that the impossible was undeniably true. Besides, he was her dad.

In desperation, she tried the next best thing.

But I'll be out of the Army in a couple of months, Laura argued with an intensity that took her by surprise. They won't let me stay in once I really start to show.

She even, reaching frantically for whatever came her way, attempted to slip off with the help of a joke: The Army doesn't make uniforms for pregnant soldiers, you know. Even camouflage fatigues won't hide this belly in a couple of months.

Johnny, the spymaster, was beyond jokes.

"You can always get an abortion," he told his daughter. "That'd solve everything."

Laura would never forgive her father for that.

Still, she didn't say no. And she didn't say yes. "Wishy-washy" was how she would describe her response.

Whatever. Johnny wasn't concerned. Everything he was saying made perfect sense to him; how could his daughter not come around to seeing things his way? Give her time, he told himself, she'll have to come aboard. What else has she got to look forward to? In his mind's eye he clearly saw Laura and her junkie husband crawling down a long, dark road—until they reached a sign announcing DEAD END.

Johnny'd wait.

Right or wrong never entered into any of his plans. All he saw were opportunities. Same, he was convinced, as everyone else.

So, just after he asked the waitress for the check, he promised Laura, "The offer's always open. If you ever change your mind, it will still stand."

It was the least a father could do for his daughter.

That night when Laura told her husband about her father's proposition—and she would swear on the Bible that it happened this way; Mark, just as firmly, would declare she was all wrong—she was still shaking. Mark, she said, plain lost it. He started screaming, cursing. Totally out of control. He threatened, Laura claimed, to punch Johnny Walker in the face.

But, according to Laura, it was only after he called her father a "traitor" that she broke into tears.

And now that the very word she had been thinking all afternoon had finally been spoken, its echo would not stop: *Traitor. Traitor. Traitor.*

She didn't know what to do. But of course she did. It was just easier not to act. Or perhaps it was harder: Her silence (and love) made her an accomplice. The only thing she knew for sure was that what she had to do was impossible; Johnny was her dad. So Laura did the only thing a daughter was able to do—nothing.

The second event that hastened the pace of Johnny's recruiting was similarly gloomy—a bankruptcy.

On December 31, 1979, Walker Enterprises, the car-radio business the brothers had started three years ago, officially passed away. Despite its brief life, it had managed to leave behind some impressive debts: a secured note—the brothers' homes were the collateral—for nearly $20,000 with the F&M Bank; $18,000 to the Clarion Corporation for merchandise; and a whopping $31,000 to the Internal Revenue Service.

Art Walker was overwhelmed. He felt as if he had slipped from the top rung of a ladder and was drifting helplessly toward a very hard fall.

Rita, the girl he had first dated when they were juniors at St. Patrick's in Scranton, would often tell the story about the time she and her husband Art had their biggest blowout. It started up over a lawn mower, but as Rita would be the first to tell you, it was really about something else.

It was a summer's morning and there was Art all set to mow the lawn; somehow, what with all the running around lately, things had gotten pretty scraggly-looking. Only just as Art was about to head out to the garage, one of the neighbors came by.

"Hey, Art," he asked, "my mower's on the fritz. Can I borrow yours?"

"Be my guest," said Art automatically.

Two minutes later the neighbor, pushing the mower in front of him, was heading to his yard, and Rita was fit to be tied. She tore into Art, calling him a patsy, a man who can't say no, who's always getting pushed around. She even brought up another sore point: How when the kids were younger—there were two boys and a girl, the two oldest in college—Art could never spank them? She'd have to lay down the law because Art, Mr. Nice Guy, couldn't hurt a flea.

Art, who never argued, simply shrugged. It was his way of saying, I am what I am.

Only now, he saw that he was crumbling to sand under the pressure of all his debts. Since leaving the Navy six years ago, he had shaped out a life on Chickasaw Court in Virginia Beach. He was president of the Civic League, a Little League coach, the man who shot the starter's gun at the Labor Day Swim Meet—and now everything was going to be taken away. He could say good-bye to the L-shaped redbrick ranch in Carolanne Farm (the "farm" named in the 1960s after the developer's daughters); there were already two mortgages, not to mention the secured loan, out on the place. He'd have to pull his kids out of college, and the thought of doing that just made him want to cry. And how was he ever going to tell Rita precisely how bad things had gotten? He'd rather die.

They had gotten so bad, that one afternoon in January 1980, when

Johnny picked Art up for lunch, there was no way Art could even think about eating. His arms and legs weighed a ton. There was no point to anything, and he knew things would never get better.

Still, Johnny somehow managed to get his brother into the pickup truck. He drove to Charlie's Waffle House on Newtown Road. They were sitting in the parking lot. Art, beyond caring, was slouched right up against the door; it was as if he wanted to roll himself up into a ball and disappear.

"I could cry," Art told his brother, and he was that close.

"Come on, let's walk," said Johnny, his long-lost pal.

The moment was, of course, a recruiter's dream. But for Johnny, it was also something more: It was the chance to save Art, the older brother who had always pulled him out of jams; and it was the opportunity to reveal—at last!—to someone whose praise Johnny coveted what a grand and exciting adventure he had made out of his life.

They had started walking across the Waffle House parking lot when Johnny, without preliminaries, told his brother, "I have friends who will pay for classified information." There was no need to beat around the bush; Johnny had the confidence of a man about to make good on a long-imagined ambition.

"Now I know where you get your bucks," was all Art could manage.

By the time they walked into Charlie's it was pretty well settled. Johnny, though he knew he was fooling no one, had waved a few false flags around. He said his friends had connections to publishers, gave *Jane's Fighting Ships* as an example. Art shot him a look, but he kept on listening. He never once made as if he wanted to run off. He even seemed interested when Johnny told him it would make sense to get a job where he'd have access to military secrets. Some civil service job, or maybe something with a defense contractor.

Not that Art had agreed to anything. But, Johnny observed, as soon as they sat down in the restaurant, Art ordered a stack of pancakes. He attacked them like a starving man.

· · ·

Over the next month Art began looking for a job. He went to the hiring office at Norfolk Naval Base. Only low-level, GS-3, GS-4, spots were open. So Art went to the federal building downtown and filled out an application he hoped would get him a position with a higher rating. Meanwhile, his brother was telling him, forget the government. "Think high tech," Johnny advised. "Those big manufacturers making missiles and satellites, that's where all the jobs are," said Johnny.

While Johnny went on about the "military-industrial complex" and Art still waited to hear from the feds, Rita spotted an ad in the *Virginian-Pilot*.

"Here's one," she said over breakfast one morning, the paper in her hand. "And look at this—it's just up the street from your old office on Greenwich Road."

On February 19, 1980, Art went for an interview with the VSE Corporation, a nationwide engineering company that held extensive research-and-development contracts with the Navy.

Ronald Baptre, the personnel interviewer, talked with Art for nearly twenty minutes. After Art left his office, Baptre filled out in longhand the answers to a series of questions on the VSE Pre-Selection Employment Appliction:

Describe applicant's attitude (stating those things you feel applicant personally holds as most important in a position): willing and cooperative attitude.

Describe applicant's reaction to technical interview: pleased.

What do you think impressed applicant most on this interview?: job opportunity.

Three days later, on Washington's birthday, Art was hired. His pay was $6.25 an hour and he was assigned to "United States Navy carrier and ship maintenance planning."

His work involved trips to the Norfolk Naval Base; however, some days he'd arrive at the base and the guards would give him a hard time about certain areas being off limits. Other times Art would be working on a project and he'd get pretty far into it only to have to pass it on to someone who was cleared. So it made sense for his department manager to apply to the Defense Industrial Security Clearance Office (DISCO) for a classification for Arthur L. Walker, Lt. Cmdr., USN, ret.

VSE CORP
ATTN: DOD SECURITY SUPERVISOR

FM DISCO, COLUMBUS, OHIO
DISCO-C-212-0122   SUBJECT: LOC ISSUE
LETTER OF CONSENT ISSUED BY DISCO TO—
EMPLOYEE NAME: WALKER, ARTHUR JAMES
SOCIAL SEC NR: 210-26-2064
CLEARANCE LVL: SECRET
CLEARANCE DTE: 30JUL80
THIS IS AUTHORITY TO GRANT ACCESS TO DOD CLASSIFIED
    INFORMATION AT LEVEL INDICATED ABOVE. THE LETTER
    OF CONSENT WILL FOLLOW BY MAIL.

And by the time Johnny learned of his brother's security clearance, he had some other news: Jerry Whitworth had written to the Navy Department to withdraw his request to retire.

25

With Jerry's posting to the Naval Communications Center at Alameda, Johnny soon found himself caught between the conflicting lunacies of his agent and his control. It was an uncomfortable place to be. Jerry was scared stiff; the Russians were suspicious; and Johnny was near to telling both of them where to get off. Yet Johnny, the spy in the middle, was also a resourceful professional: He set out to make things right for everybody.

Jerry's desk was his problem. When he had first learned of the duty, it had seemed ideal: He was CMS custodian; he managed the Autodin Center which handled message traffic for the worldwide Defense Communications System; and he had access to a variety of crypto circuits, including the keys for the KW-26 machines which encrypted Autodin transmissions to military bases throughout the world. As Jerry gleefully wrote to his handler, he was the "chief in charge of Tech Control—the heart of Naval Communications." The problem, though, was his desk.

Jerry's desk was in the back of the Communications Center—wedged right between two other desks. Behind him sat Frank Olea; in front of him sat Keith Hamlin. And Jerry could feel their eyes on him every minute of his tour. On the *Niagara,* there was a crypto vault a spy could disappear in, and still, each click of his Minox would boom about his hideout. At Alameda, a cramped and friendly place, the rapid noise of the camera's shutter would turn a dozen heads as though he were spraying the room with a machine gun. He didn't dare.

So it was a very shaky agent Johnny confronted when he flew into Oakland on January 18, 1980. As soon as the two spies got in Jerry's Toyota, Johnny could see he was in for a rough visit. They weren't even out of the airport parking lot before Jerry was telling him he had pretty slim pickings.

Johnny, who these days saw his network growing by leaps and bounds, was in no mood to put up with Jerry's fears. "Just save it for the debriefing, okay," he growled, cutting his operative off. Jerry drove the rest of the way to his home in San Leandro without saying a word. While Johnny, feeling the silence, was thinking: This is great. I'm running a spy who pouts like a ten-year-old.

The den in the town house Jerry had bought last year was a loving replica of Johnny's—same big desk with its leatherette swivel chair, same uncomfortable ladder-back opposite the desk, and same row of ship photographs framed on the beige wall. And, just as in the house on Old Ocean View Road, it was Johnny who now took the seat behind the desk.

It was a very short debriefing. Jerry had been telling the truth: He didn't have much to show. Oh, there were a few copies of low-level documents, task-force information mostly, that Jerry had been able to slip into his attaché case when no one was looking. But that was it.

"You know," Jerry announced after his brief report, pausing only to tug on his beard and put on a hangdog face that made Johnny want to throttle him, "maybe I should've quit, after all. Maybe I've just plum run out of luck."

While Johnny, biting down hard on his tongue, wanted to scream, No chickenshit, you've just plum run out of guts.

Johnny, though, kept his opinions to himself. He wasn't ready to throw in the towel. Not by a long shot. There had to be a way to make Alameda work. There had to be a strategy, a twist of tradecraft that would solve all their problems.

And if there wasn't, he'd just have to invent one.

How about a van? Johnny suggested.

It was that same depressing January afternoon and the two spies were still in Jerry's den.

Huh? said Jerry. He really never could keep up with the way his friend's mind worked.

But by now Johnny was off and running. Yes, he lectured, the words flying from him in his enthusiasm. You say you can't use the camera because there's no vault at Alameda. No hideout, no photos. I read you. Well, if I'm still understanding things right, it's no biggie to shove a few papers into your attaché case and bring 'em on home. There's no security check at the front door, right?

The guard just salutes, said Jerry, still wondering where all this was going.

Well, then, you could sneak a key list out . . .

No way, Jerry interrupted in his slow, mourner's drawl. Alarms would be ringing so loud you'd hear 'em in Norfolk. They check the crypto inventory at the end of every shift.

However Johnny was ready: That's why you're gonna return the key lists before your shift is over. No one will ever know you borrowed them.

Johnny now had Jerry's complete attention as he continued: That's where the van comes in. It'll be a photo studio on wheels. Same way I've been using my van in my detective cases. No reason why you shouldn't be able to stroll out of the office at lunchtime with a key list in your attaché case, and go for a rest, nice and private, in your van. Course you'll be snapping pictures, not zzz's. An hour later, the key list is back where it belongs and no one's the wiser.

What do you say? Johnny concluded, quite pleased with himself.

Jerry, perking up a bit, admitted, It could work.

. . .

It was a silver-blue van with maroon curtains on the windows. It cost $11,310.30 and it had a Formica table in the back that folded out if you wanted to have a picnic; or if you needed a backdrop to photograph top secret key lists.

The van would be parked in the Alameda base lot, a short walk from the Communications Center. "It's a lifesaver," Jerry made a point of telling all his new buddies, including Frank Olea. "At my last checkup the doc discovered ol' Jer had a bum ticker, ordered me to take it easy. Laid down the law, all right. So I figured better safe than sorry. And wouldn't you know it, the doc was right. A little bit of rack time at lunch, and I'm a new man. The van's a humdinger of a place to stretch out. Especially if I remember to pull the curtains tight. Can't have any of that bright California sunshine keeping me up."

It seemed a real shame to Frank that a guy as young as Jerry had cardiac problems. He looked in good shape, but you never know. One thing did strike him kind of odd: Why a man going off for a snooze would take his attaché case with him to bed. But that was none of his business, anyway.

Q. At this time, what was Jerry Whitworth's duty assignment in the Navy?

A. The Communications Center at Alameda . . .

Q. What was he producing at that time from that duty station?

A. His production there was excellent for cryptographic. He had two circuits: an Autodin circuit, plus a line to Stockton which was covered by the KW-7.

Q. And how consistent was the crypto he got for those circuits?

A. Excellent. Near 100 percent.

Yet, just when Johnny succeeded in getting Jerry's end of the operation back on track, the Russians got on his case. After a dozen years as a KGB star, Johnny felt he didn't have to take this crap. So he just let it rip. Of course, he would later admit, having to walk through the streets of Vienna in another goddamn blizzard might also have played a part in finally pushing him over the edge.

On the night of January 26, 1980, when he caught up with Ivan

Four-Eyes, there was a building snowstorm and not a word of welcome. Ivan greeted Johnny with only a succinct question: Why was Whitworth transferred?

I already told you in the letter I left at the drop in the States, he answered sharply. The *Niagara*'s in dry dock.

But Ivan was not put off. The Department 16 officer condemned him with the steely eyes of a Gulag jailer. His words had the cadence of a final decree: Whitworth was assigned to the ship for three years. All American Navy postings are for three years. You will explain to me why this was changed.

Why? I'll tell you why, Johnny shouted. The goddamn ship needed goddamn repairs. That's why.

But the Russian was firm: I am asking you, why was Jerry transferred?

Johnny stood there, dripping with wet snow, and thought this was all too crazy. One week he's baby-sitting a mopey Jerry, the next week he's getting the third degree from a KGB man who doesn't even have the brains to come in out of a storm. He'd had it.

"You dumb assholes," Johnny shouted, not caring if all Vienna heard him, "he lost his fucking access. I explained that. Am I dealing with idiots?

"And one more thing," he said, his voice no longer a shout, but still as strong and steady as a pointed gun, "I'm freezing my chops off. I'm going to get a cup of coffee."

Ivan Four-Eyes stood there as Johnny marched off through the snow; he was as motionless as the statues flanking the entrance to the Schönbrunn Palace across the road. After half a block, a distance that for all an angry Johnny knew he had covered in one furious leap, he turned back toward the KGB man. "You coming?" he called.

. . . Yes, I think I will, said Ivan.

The Russian made it clear he would not discuss business in the café, but the twenty minutes out of the snow was victory enough for Johnny. When they returned to the street, the snow had stopped, and Johnny was warm from two cups of strong, black coffee. He was prepared to listen, and to explain.

Johnny, taking things step-by-step, went through the story of Jerry's transfer one more time. This time Ivan understood. In fact, he added, he had never doubted Johnny's story. It was his bosses who had been suspicious. He would inform them there had been no need to worry.

Since Ivan was being so friendly, Johnny figured the time was right to tell him about Jerry's van. Particularly about what it had cost. The $11,000 had come out of his pocket. But it was a business expense, and he was hoping the KGB would cover it.

Of course, said Ivan, the now generous handler. And speaking of money, he went on, there was another issue. It was the feeling in the KGB that it had become very risky to carry large sums of cash through customs. With all the imperialist concern over terrorism, said the annoyed Russian, airport security has been greatly improved. Therefore, perhaps it would be safer to make all payments at the dead drops in the States. Do you agree?

Yes, said the suddenly happy spy, glad that he'd never have to take his mother to Europe again.

Jerry Whitworth, a man of roller-coaster moods, was also back to being a happy spy when Johnny met with him in May. "Follow us," Jerry and Brenda announced as they led Johnny and his girlfriend Pat Marsee out of the Oakland arrivals building. "We've got a real treat for you."

With a bit of ceremony, Jerry opened the side door to his van. "Da da!" he chimed. Inside, candles flickered across the narrow space; the curtains had been drawn tight. On the table, now covered with a white cloth, was a platter displaying a wedge of Brie. Next to the cheese, two bottles of champagne were chilling in an ice bucket.

Everybody had a pleasant buzz on by the time the van pulled up to the stucco town house in San Leandro.

The next day, when the agent and his handler finally had a chance to be alone, Johnny gave Jerry reason to celebrate—$100,000 in cash. It was all in $50 bills and Johnny had picked it up twelve days ago in the woods outside Washington. The KGB hadn't made a payment since February 1979, and now, with this fortune, Jerry was paid in full.

"I've never held a hundred grand before," Jerry said. He was scooping up handfuls of $50 bills and tossing them in the air like confetti. "I don't know how I'll spend it."

· · ·

Jerry learned that spending money was not very difficult at all. Four days later, on the first of June, he took his VCR into EID's TV to be repaired. The man told him it would take two weeks. Fine, said Jerry and he handed over the machine. But then, just as he was heading out the door, Jerry decided two weeks was a long time. He bought a new VCR for $1,218.

He had the time of his life going through $47,853 over the next six months.

Except by December, Jerry was wanting out again. A team of NIS had been poking around Alameda looking into a rape case. Yet just their presence gave Jerry the willies. Then when he was assigned for three months to Stockton to help install a new communications system, Jerry was certain the NIS was on to him. Which, of course, was absurd. But Johnny was having a hell of a time convincing Jerry of that.

In fact, as Christmas came around, the only thing bringing Johnny some cheer was that this year he'd be spending it with his son. Mike, at his father's suggestion, had given up on Maine and moved in with Johnny. The boy cut his hair, promised to get stoned only now and then, and Johnny, without a word of complaint, enrolled him in a private school. So far things had worked out really well between the father and son, and Johnny had high hopes for the future.

26

So as Johnny headed toward his forty-fifth birthday, he began to discover the joys of fatherhood. He and his nearly eighteen-year-old son would make the rounds of all the squid bars challenging each other to chugalugs. Other nights they'd hit the topless strip and then it'd be a contest who'd be the first to yell to the bimbo bouncing onstage Johnny's favorite come-on: "Sugar, long as I got a face, you got a place to sit." Or maybe it'd be just an evening at home, *The Devil and Miss Jones* on the VCR in the family room and the two of them getting nicely stoned on weed. They were sitting there, lounging at opposite ends of the plaid couch, when one night Johnny promised his son, "Someday, I'll tell you how I make my money." Mike, who thought his father was the coolest, figured Johnny probably dealt a little dope on the side. Which was fine with him: What better source could a guy have than his dad? While Johnny never imagined he could ever feel so close to any of his children.

. . .

Johnny, though, was not only a father, but also a grandfather. He had never seen Laura's son, already more than a year old, and by now he was real eager. Of course, the unfinished business between him and his daughter had something to do with it, too.

It worked out nicely because Laura and her husband were living these days in Hayward, California, about a twenty-minute drive from Jerry. He could make a pickup from his agent; and then have a recruiting session. Paid for courtesy of the KGB. It was all so convenient that Johnny decided his scheme had to be blessed.

Johnny couldn't believe he had forgotten his camera. It was just too stupid. And the more he worked his lapse over in his mind, the angrier he got at himself.

Truth be known, he had never expected to feel this way. But if the kid sitting on his lap wasn't the cutest, he was darn close. Johnny was convinced Christopher had his granddad's famous smile. How could Johnny head back to Norfolk without a picture? Something to keep in his wallet; maybe he'd even flash it at Art or some of the guys at the Lone Pine. The hell with what it cost.

Laura, he instructed his daughter who was at the wheel, I got to buy a camera. Head for the nearest mall.

So while Johnny hunted for a .35 millimeter, Laura sat in the car and decided that there was no understanding her father. Last time they had spoken, just before she had left the Army, he had torn into her but good, telling her what a screwup and a loser she was. How she had blown the big chance he had offered her. Then last night he calls up out of the blue, and says he's twenty minutes away at Uncle Jerry's; why don't I come on by in the morning and bring his grandson with me. He wants to talk. And now, the same man who used to call his kids rug rats is crazy over my son. Who knows what's going to happen next?

But while Laura found it hard to admit even to herself, she did have an idea about what Johnny wanted to talk about. It terrified her.

. . .

"Smile," Johnny insisted.

Christopher refused to cooperate. He wouldn't stop crying.

"Goddamn it," he ordered his daughter, "will you get that kid to lighten up."

Christopher, though, had a mind of his own. He didn't take to coaxing.

Johnny, who never liked a struggle, decided to pack it in. They were sitting on a bench in a park in San Leandro. It was a cool January day, and the park was nearly empty. Christopher, at last, found a reason not to cry; he occupied himself with climbing down from the bench and heading toward the grass. Laura watched him from her seat.

Johnny was no longer following his grandson's antics. There was, he abruptly realized, switching roles without the least effort, more important business at hand. He placed the camera on the park bench; it was Laura's only clue that a new act was about to begin.

"There's an age limit," he suddenly announced. "My man in Europe is concerned that you're getting older. You're going to be too old to get back in the Army if you wait any longer."

Laura was afraid to refuse her father. "What about Christopher?" she tried.

"I'll take care of the kid," Johnny said; and Laura thought of the four children whom he had never taken care of. "I'll even adopt him. Hire a nanny to watch him."

Johnny went on to explain what his daughter would have to do, while Laura attempted to keep her eyes and thoughts locked on Christopher crawling by the seesaw. He told her his people were looking for all kinds of information. "Anything is valuable." But best of all were codes, "any kind of codes you could get your hands on." He told her there was really nothing to it: "You can photograph the documents on the premises, or you can take 'em home to shoot and then return 'em the next day. It's simple.

"We'd be partners," he coaxed. There'd be good money for both of them: Laura could expect to make $500 a month plus bonuses for each document she produced. "A genuine partnership," he repeated, holding out once again this promise of a father's love.

But Laura still found it impossible to say yes. Or to say no.

Johnny gave it one last shot: Look, I know you could use some money. Right?

There was no doubt about that, Laura had to agree. Her husband had declared bankruptcy a month ago.

How about I help you out? he suggested. Would, say, $1,500 come in handy?

Laura said without any hesitation, It'd make all the difference.

Johnny promised to send a check. The money to him was a down payment, three months advance on the salary he'd be paying his daughter. For Laura, however, the money was a loan. She needed to believe that.

As they were leaving the park, Johnny got further proof, he was convinced, that things were going his way. Christopher offered his grandfather the biggest smile in California, and Johnny grabbed his new camera, focused, and shot off nearly a roll of film.

Yes, the afternoon had worked out just perfect.

Three weeks later, on February 13, 1982, Johnny went to Vienna prepared to tell Ivan Four-Eyes about his plans for his brother, Art, and his daughter, Laura. He was also prepared for the weather: He wore electric socks. But he wasn't prepared for what the Russian had in store for him.

When the KGB agent greeted Johnny that night, there was another man accompanying him. "I want you to meet my successor," Ivan Four-Eyes said.

The new Russian, Johnny judged, was built to last. He was a dark mountain of a man as broad as the Kremlin wall. And about as friendly as a galloping cossack. When Johnny went to shake his hand, Ivan the Terrible came close to yanking it off. He still hadn't spoken, and Johnny was uncertain he knew how. The fact that he had managed to learn to walk on his hind legs seemed miracle enough.

Ivan Four-Eyes, though, was full of speeches. His mood was sentimental. He recalled his meets with Johnny, starting with the one in Casablanca. There were, he said, so many memories. Theirs had been a genuine friendship. And as a memento of all they had done together, Ivan Four-Eyes had brought Johnny a present.

You didn't have to do that, Johnny argued weakly.

No, I insist, said the Russian. He reached into his pocket and handed Johnny a red Paper Mate ballpoint pen.

Thanks, Johnny lied. But it did give him some pleasure to see that Ivan the Terrible's eyes were now glowing with envy.

It didn't strike Johnny, then, as the best time to break the news that he had been recruiting new agents. He left the face-to-face without saying a word to either of the Ivans about his "Godfather operation." It made more sense, anyway, to wait till Laura had reenlisted; then he'd tell the Russians. Besides, if things worked out, by then he'd have another piece of big news to share. For on that same February day that Johnny was in Vienna, his son was in a naval recruiter's office in Norfolk signing his preenlistment papers. Mike would join the Navy in September.

But even in the most carefully planned espionage operations, there are unforeseen events. Five months later, on July 2, 1982, Laura came home to an empty apartment. On the kitchen table was a shoe box filled with bills. On top of the pile was a note. It was from Mark, her husband. He wrote that the rent was due and he was leaving. There was a page crammed with reasons and excuses, but Laura read through these jumbled sentences quickly. She was searching for something else, and she was afraid she would find it. Her instinct was right. Mark had saved it for the bottom of the page: "I'm taking Chris. I'm sorry I had to do this but I can't live without him."

Five days later Mark finally called. He swore—or at least this is how Laura remembers the call—he would tell the FBI about her father if she ever tried to take Christopher from him.

PART IV

RUS

27

In Natagutskaya Station, the railroad settlement town near the foothills of the Caucasus Mountains where he was born, it is easy to live out a small, anonymous life. Certainly, that seemed his destiny: He worked as a telegraph operator, a movie projectionist, and a sailor. Then, in 1936 he joined the Komsomol, the youth branch of the Communist party. He was twenty-two, and his ambitions suddenly had opportunities to pursue.

Within four years, he was assigned to Karelia, a territory in the northwest corner of the Soviet Union. When the Great Patriotic War came, Finnish troops claimed much of the land, and he fought against them. It was hard, guerrilla combat, and he proved brave and resourceful. His valor was noticed and praised by Otto Kuusinen, the leader of the Finnish Communist party. Comrade Kuusinen became a valuable friend.

It was on Comrade Kuusinen's recommendation that he was appointed to an administrative post with the Central Committee. He performed so successfully that he won a diplomatic assignment to Hungary. The next year, at forty, he was appointed ambassador.

As columns of Russian armor were preparing to move into Hungary in November 1956, his role as ambassador was to reassure the new nationalist government of Imre Nagy that the Soviet Union was neutral. By the end of the month Soviet tanks had rolled through Budapest and Nagy had been arrested.

The next year he was rewarded with an appointment to the Central Committee. He was chief of the department that controlled the Communist parties of Eastern Europe and China. The position gave him an opportunity to travel, to participate in Politburo meetings, and to demonstrate his skills to an influential audience.

After ten years with the Central Committee, in 1967, Yuri Vladimirovich Andropov became chairman of the KGB.

He had been KGB chairman for nearly a year when Warrant Officer John A. Walker, Jr., walked into the Soviet embassy in Washington hoping to sell a KL-47 key list.

For the next fourteen years, Yuri Andropov personally directed his Department 16's handling of John Walker.

His decisions were ultimately responsible for an espionage operation that succeeded in leaving United States forces vulnerable to a Russian attack. If war were to be declared, Soviet military theorists firmly believed—an opinion that, in time, would also be seconded by an American admiral and a secretary of the navy—the Soviet Union would now hold a strategic advantage. Or, if the Soviet Union decided to launch a first-strike attack against the United States, Russian nuclear submarines could destroy a devastating portion of the American Fleet within the first hours of combat; victory—if there can be one in the aftermath of a global, thermonuclear war—was now a feasible Soviet military scenario. And, while peace continued, international political decisions could be made not only from strength, but also, in many cases, with prior knowledge of the strategies of American diplomatic and military leaders.

Yuri Andropov was a hero of the Soviet Union: He had unlocked the gates guarding the armory of American secrets.

On November 11, 1982, he was elected general secretary of the Central Committee of the Communist party of the Soviet Union. Yuri Andropov was ruler of the party, and, therefore, ruler of the nation.

The next day, on the front page of *The New York Times* a dispatch from Moscow speculated about the long-range consequences of Premier Andropov's leadership. Yet in the offices of the Central Intelligence Agency, there were many intelligence professionals more concerned with understanding the past than with predicting the future:

What, these backbeaters anxiously wondered, had the head of the KGB accomplished that would have brought him to the most powerful position in the Soviet Union?

Thoughts about the past and predictions of the future were also on Barbara Walker's and Shalel Way's minds that same winter. The two women, a deck of Tarot cards spread between them, were huddled around a kitchen table in a Maine farmhouse. It was an icy, moonlit January night. "A night," declared Shalel, "of psychic destiny." Which, the way Barb looked at it, was maybe laying it on too thick. But then again, it was a night that set in motion events that would finally give the CIA backbeaters an answer. One they were hoping not to find.

Shalel Way had a gift. Since she was four, she "always knew what people were thinking." It had taken her awhile, though, to realize it was selfish not to share this talent. In her "gypsy days," as she dubbed them, she had played guitar in San Francisco, planted trees for the state of Arkansas, and headed a "utopian" commune in the Maine woods. But now that she was twenty-seven, Shalel and her six-year-old son, Brefney, had returned to her hometown of Skowhegan. She was making a living holding Tarot-psychic readings.

"All questions answered," she promised. "Future, spirit guides, and even stock tips are accurately unfolded." Over the past eleven years her readings had proved to be 95 percent accurate. She had kept careful track.

Barbara knew Shalel's parents, Larry and Mary Ann Vique, real well. It was the Viques who had first told her about their daughter. They could tell Barb was having a rough go of it; maybe Shalel could help her get a handle on things.

Barbara, never one to check out even her horoscope in the paper, was ready by now to try just about anything. The secret had made a hell out of her life, and she didn't see any way out it. She wanted help.

Still, when she saw the feather sticking out of Shalel's headband her expectations nose-dived.

But Barb was game. She sat at one end of the Formica kitchen table, while across from her Shalel dealt the Tarot cards into two rows. "The cards," Shalel explained, "work through dreams. People

dream their futures and through the cards a dream's meaning is revealed.''

At last, she picked up one of the cards and held it directly in front
of Barbara's face. "The significator," Shalel called it.

"Is it familiar?" Shalel asked.

The card showed a tower perched on a mountain. Lightning bolts
were attacking the tower. Bodies—victims—hurled through space.

Barbara answered, "That's my dream."

It was the first time Barbara had told anyone about her dream. She
rose from the table and began to pace. Talking all the time: "In my
dream it's a skyscraper. Like the Empire State Building, sort of. It's
all in flames. People are trapped inside. Some are diving from the
windows. I can hear their screams. But it's too late. They're being
burned alive."

Barb's face was wet with tears. She was standing by the kitchen
sink. Above the sink was a mullioned window and an opaque plastic
sheet was nailed across it for weatherproofing. From where Shalel
was sitting, Barbara appeared framed by the moonlight that filtered
through the heavy plastic. Synchronicity, Shalel decided.

When Barb found the will to continue, it was as if she had completed the running of a long race; she was drained, exhausted, but not
daunted. "You have to understand," she said, "it's not a fire in my
dream. It's Armageddon. The end of the world."

Shalel nodded, waiting. She would always believe she knew what
was coming next.

"What's so horrible, so goddamn terrifying," Barbara went on in
her flat, logical way, "is I can stop it. Me. I can save all those people. . . ."

And once she had gone that far, there was no point in holding
anything back: "Shalel, it's not a dream."

"I know," said Shalel, coaxing. She added, "You have to do something. You must try to save all those people."

Barbara answered, "I will. I'm really going to get him for this.
That's my country."

It was a vow.

She would not allow herself to cry. Instead, her words had that
perfect calm that comes with a resigned anger: "I can save this country, all right. All I have to do is destroy the people I love most in the
world."

28

When Rachel Allen was twelve, her stepfather held a .44 to her head. He shoved the nozzle into her ear and told her, "You call the cops and I'll pull the trigger."

The trouble had started that evening when he had come home drunk. Not that there was anything strange about that; ever since the auto accident had messed up his back and cost him his job as a security guard, he couldn't seem to make it through the day without drowning his sorrows. Only this evening, he was also packing a real attitude. He tore into Rachel's mom something fierce, going on about how she was his wife so he'll damn well sleep in her bed. It was scary. But when Rachel heard the slap—and Rachel knew his temper too well; her stepdad had bloodied her nose after their last set-to—she decided there was no reason to put up with this. The twelve-year-old picked up the phone and announced she was calling the cops. Next thing she knew, there was this gun at her head.

Rachel was shaking, but she told him, "Put that damn thing down." Her stepfather wouldn't. He held it hard against her ear all the time she was talking to the police. After she finished the call, the gun seemed a little pointless, so he put it down on the bed. By now he was crying, and so was Rachel.

He spent the night in the drunk tank, and the next morning when he came home his bags were packed and lined in a neat row in the garage. That was the way that marriage ended.

Seven years earlier, the marriage between Rachel's mom and natural father had just sort of petered out. Maybe it had been a bit of unfocused thinking from the start. Dora Kartafelt was the daughter of Orthodox Jews from Brooklyn, New York. Carl Earl Allen was the son of Southern Baptists from Smithfield, North Carolina. Carl, twenty-one and a naval dispersing clerk after five years in the service, was in New York City awaiting deployment to Panama when he met Dora, a nineteen-year-old secretary working in the Chrysler Building. Two weeks later they were married.

Neither of their parents were too happy about the match. But the Kartafelts saw it as a sin. That really hurt Dora. For her own sake, and, in time, for her children's. The Kartafelts, though, were not to be turned. Years later, when one of their nephews became a transsexual, the Kartafelts were still willing to accept Joan into their home; after all, he had been Bar Mitzvahed as John. But the three Allen grandchildren—Rachel and two older brothers—had been brought up to go to church on Sundays. That was unforgivable.

When Dora and Carl's marriage came apart, they were living in Chesapeake, Virginia. He had retired from the Navy, never making it past clerk, first class, and was now working as a government auditor. Dora got the house, the three kids, and, it seemed to her, all the bills. She took a job as a patty packer; that meant eight hours a day preparing sandwiches that would be sold in vending machines and in 7-Elevens. It paid minimum wage. She'd stick with it for the next ten years.

After her second divorce, Dora's life settled down; all that was left was the job at Stewart's Sandwiches and her kids. The boys were a bit of a problem; smart, one was even a member of the National Honor Society in high school, but they always seemed to be making trouble for themselves. Either they'd be running away, or they'd be smoking pot. Two divorces had worked them over good.

. . .

Rachel was Dora's blessing. She had become a sad-faced, serious girl. The kind of kid who cleaned up her room simply because if she didn't do it then her mother would have to. Always very adult. She didn't complain, not even when she had to wear a neighbor's daughter's hand-me-downs. And when she started high school, no one had to tell her to get a job in the afternoons. She just went to the Taco Bell and signed on. Her grades didn't suffer too much; she had made up her mind to go to college and that was that.

"I don't have to worry about you," Dora would tell her daughter whenever Rachel started to apologize for coming home late from school or work. Rachel, as was her way, did worry some about her mom. It was unfair for her mother to work so hard, and then for the family to have to do without. She thought about that a lot.

What with her job and schoolwork and helping out around the house, Rachel didn't have time for a lot of friends. Most of her free time was spent reading; she loved mythology.

In her four years at Great Ridge High School, she had one date. She asked her chemistry lab partner to take her to the junior prom. He was six feet four and she was five feet two. When they got on the dance floor, they attracted quite a crowd.

She didn't mind not dating. All they ever seemed to talk about in her hygiene class was sex. The films were worse. The thought of being manhandled by some teenage boy with galloping hormones scared the poo right out of her.

She didn't go out with any boys all through her freshman year at Old Dominion University, either. Which was just as well; she had signed up for the university's biology program—she still wasn't sure whether she wanted to be a doctor or a research scientist—and that was challenge enough. Then there was her job at Kinney Shoes in the mall. Also, she was now living with her father and his wife; they were close to ODU and had a Toyota she could use. Her life seemed about as full as it could get.

. . .

Then, as she began her sophomore year, it started bothering Rachel that she had never dated. She decided it was because she was too gross; no guy wants to go out with a porker. So she stopped eating. Really stopped. She'd have a glass of orange juice for breakfast, and then she'd only drink water for the rest of the day. On Sundays, though, the family went to the Western Sizzler after church. Her father made her come along. She'd fill up a plate with lettuce from the salad bar and pick at it just to please him.

In three months she went from 119 to 87 pounds. She looked a lot less because she had made a point of buying clothes that were a couple of sizes too large. She was convinced she was a real load.

After Christmas, Rachel met a guy. David was in her skin-diving class and he was twenty-five, six years older than Rachel. She couldn't believe how happy she felt to be, at last, in love. He'd take her out to dinner and make sure she finished everything on her plate. In one month she gained six pounds, and she didn't mind at all.

Rachel wanted to marry him. But just as the term was ending, he told her he had another girlfriend back home. Maybe it would be better if she started dating other people this summer. Rachel said she couldn't, so David told her she had to understand that it was over between them: She might as well forget about him.

The pain was unbearable. All she could do was think about David. She had been brought up to believe you don't sleep with a guy unless you intend to marry him and it came as a real shock that not everyone felt the same way. With all her sadness, she didn't even realize she had stopped eating again.

After her finals, though, she went out and got a summer job. She was a hostess and a cashier in the lounge at The Lone Pine Inn. She worked from 5:00 P.M. to 2:00 A.M. six days a week and that suited her fine.

Things were always jumping. There was a smoked-glass partition as soon as you walked into the Lone Pine and it served to divide the place in half, more or less. On one side was the restaurant; the prime rib dinner for $7.95 was a bargain and it brought in a lot of families. While in the dim-lit lounge where Rachel worked, you got a mixed crowd; singles looking to meet somebody over a beer would be shoulder to shoulder with the Virginia Beach executives who stopped in for a quick one after work each night and, part of the ritual, kept putting off heading home to the wife and kids.

The only downside to the job, Rachel felt, was having to deal with all the guys who were coming on to her. But they were mostly old goats, in their forties maybe, with their shirts pulled so tight across their guts that the buttons would be close to popping. It was kind of pathetic, Rachel thought, if they really believed a nineteen-year-old girl would be interested in the likes of them. So she never took their come-ons too seriously, and in no time at all she got pretty good at blowing them off.

One guy, however, was pretty persistent. He had a toupee and aviator glasses and a beard and a roll of pudge just above the belt buckle of his jeans. He'd come over to the register where Rachel worked and he'd stare and then he'd shoot her this real slick dick smile. She felt like telling him, "Look all you want, buddy, 'cause that's the most you're ever gonna do." The first couple of weeks he had kept on asking her out for a drink when she got off work, but she laughed him off. Then he started coming by with a girlfriend, a blonde not more than two years older than Rachel, so Rachel figured he had moved on to greener pastures. And that was a relief. Now when he'd ask for change to play Pac-Man, she'd tell him, "I'm only gonna give you three quarters for your dollar. You come to me at the end of the evening and I'll give you the rest. That way you won't spend all your money on those silly games." She'd put on a stern, maternal voice, and it always made him laugh.

He told her he was a private detective. Rachel said she thought only people in movies had jobs like that.

"No way. And in real life the PIs are braver and more handsome than the ones in the movies," said Johnny Walker.

Rachel also got to know Art Walker. He was another regular at the Lone Pine. He'd come in and right away he'd say to her, "I haven't had my hug today." She'd give him a hug, and not think twice about it. Course it wasn't the sort of thing she'd ever dream of doing with Johnny; that would be gross. But Art was so kind and friendly that hugging him was simply nice. All the girls did it. Just as every-one called him "Uncle Art." He was a teddy bear. You had to like him.

. . .

So one Saturday night while Rachel was working in the lounge, Johnny came up to her. She could tell he had a bit of a buzz on.

"Just how old *are* you?" he asked as though he suddenly made a great discovery.

"Nineteen," said Rachel.

"You know, I have a son your age."

"That's nice." And she was thinking: Then why don't you go home to him?

But Johnny's wheels were spinning: "Look, I've got an idea. We're all gonna be out on my houseboat tomorrow. Why don't you come by and meet him. You kids might hit it off. What do you say? About four?"

"Maybe," said Rachel, figuring if she kept things vague it would cause less of a hassle than a flat-out no.

The next day, Father's Day, June 21, 1982, after Rachel and her dad and his new family had returned from Sunday lunch at the Western Sizzler, the phone rang. Rachel was the first to reach it.

"Well," asked Johnny Walker, "you're still coming out to the boat this afternoon? Right? I promised my son."

Rachel copied down the directions and then wanted to know, "How'd you get my number?"

"Us private detectives have our ways."

Rachel's father wasn't too keen at first about his daughter's running off somewhere on Father's Day. But by three-thirty he had settled into his favorite chair and was watching a baseball game on the living room TV. He told her to do whatever she thought best.

It was only as Rachel was driving out to the boat that it occurred to her that maybe she was being played for a fool. There'd be no one but Johnny Walker on the boat. Him in a pair of swim trunks with his gut hanging out. If he tried to touch her, she'd show him he had made a real bad error in judgment.

Except when she got to the dock, she could see P.K., Johnny's young blonde, stretched out on a blanket soaking up the sun. So she relaxed. The boat, too, was a surprise. Rachel had no idea what a houseboat was going to look like and the fact that it was sort of square tickled her.

As soon as she got on board, Johnny handed her a gin and tonic and, bubbling, said, "Glad you made it. Mike'll be thrilled. Let me get him."

But before he could call for his son, Mike came up from below. He was in a pair of cutoffs and he wasn't wearing a shirt, and Rachel could see he had a surfer's tan. To cover his surfer's body. Oh, he was short, maybe five feet five, but Rachel was only a small drink of water herself. Best of all, he had this dark curly hair, like David's. Rachel had a thing about dark hair. Yes, no doubt about it, he was cute. Real cute.

"What high school you go to?"

Rachel was trying to find something to talk about with Mike. He kept on flashing her this grin, so she knew he was interested, but the conversation had been getting nowhere. The other night Johnny had told her his son was still in high school; he had lost two years after he had gotten into some trouble in Maine. Rachel, remembering this and now desperate, was ready to try anything to get the ball rolling.

But Mike was putting her off: "You wouldn't know it. It's just a small place. It's private," he added as though that explained everything.

"Try me," Rachel said. "I've lived around here all my life. Maybe I have heard of it."

"Ryan High," he said without much hope.

"My stepsister goes there!" Rachel was near to rejoicing. Why she knew dozens of kids at Ryan. They were always coming by her dad's home. Mike knew them, too.

From there, the talk just flowed.

Though, Rachel would one day admit, she was also thinking: Ryan? Mostly money goes there. And his father has a boat and he says he has a plane. Who knows?

That night the four of them went back to the house on Old Ocean View Road for a spaghetti dinner. There was a lot of red wine and a lot of laughs. Johnny and P.K. packed it in early. It had been a long day in the sun. But Mike asked Rachel if she wanted to check out a little TV. Sure, she agreed.

They went off to the family room and started watching a movie about a dog. "He's a stupid puppy. Let's bag it," Mike was insisting before the first commercial. But Rachel was genuinely fascinated. Besides, she was in no hurry to go home.

When the movie was over, Mike walked Rachel to her car.

"I had fun," he told her. "Would it be okay to give you a call?"

"That'd be great," she said.

Three days later she was still waiting for his call. And for three days she hadn't eaten a thing. She had just met him, and now she was missing him that much.

Then on the evening of the third day, he came into the lounge. They sat at a table and talked and Mike had a couple of drinks. After he had paid up, he said he was going surfing tomorrow. Would she like to come along?

"Love to," Rachel said.

"I'll come by about eleven," he promised.

Later, when she went to her Toyota in the parking lot, she found a long-stemmed red rose wedged under the windshield wiper. There was also a note: "See you tomorrow."

She couldn't sleep that night she was so excited.

Mike picked her up the next morning and they drove to Virginia Beach in his yellow Mazda flatbed truck. All he wanted to talk about was surfing. He told her how he used a Canyon board, they were the best. Though Shawn Thompson was not bad if you had to make do. But WRVs were not cool at all; they were kid stuff, for Sunday surfers. And, he told her, he was definitely not your weekend-variety surfer. His board was a tri-fin board, not a faggot's single fin. Gave you zoom. That way when you're getting tubed—riding with a hu-mongous wave hanging over you like a wet curtain of doom, he ex-plained—the rush is dynamite. And all the while he was talking, he kept on rewinding the cassette on his tape deck so that the same song played over and over. "I Wanna Be Sedated" must have filled the cab of the little yellow truck at least a dozen times in a row. Full blast.

"Joey Ramone is the coolest," Mike announced, his hand pounding out the beat on the dashboard as he drove.

". . . Uh-huh," said Rachel.

Even though Rachel was sitting on the beach she couldn't help feeling excited as she watched Mike, now in his wet suit, paddling out for a wave. Then, when he got to his feet, and this gigantic wave was breathing down his neck and the board was zipping through the water, she, too, was up on her feet and cheering before she realized it. He was her man, and she was so proud.

On the way back from the beach, Mike told her he had to work a case for his dad. Did she want to come along?

So for twenty minutes they tried to follow some lady in a red 280 Z who maybe was going to a motel. But once they got out of traffic, the lady put the Z into fourth and there was no way the little yellow pickup could stay with her.

"Solid gone and that was all she wrote," said Mike. "That's the way it sometimes is in surveillance work." It was an apology, but Rachel wasn't disappointed at all. It had been just about the best day of her life. It wouldn't take much for her to fall in love with her surfing detective.

That night, when she left work at the Lone Pine and headed to her car, she found another long-stemmed rose under the windshield wiper.

No, she decided, it wouldn't take much at all.

Their next date was to go see the X-Rays who were playing at the Wave, a club down by the beach. But Mike told her she first had to "get a new look." He took her to the mall and bought her a red miniskirt, a black leather vest, and a pair of black fishnet stockings.

After her shift at the Lone Pine, she went into the ladies' room and changed. She felt silly, even trampy, when she looked in the mirror. But when she came out of the john, Mike was waiting and he gave her a big kiss. "Très hot," he said. And that was all that mattered.

Course, he was wearing mascara and black eyeliner, but after a while Rachel hardly even noticed.

When the Fourth of July got near, Mike told her a bunch of his friends were going down to Cape Hatteras for the weekend. They'd watch the fireworks, have a few beers, camp out. Did she want to come along? It should be fun, he promised.

Rachel knew exactly what kind of fun. She told her dad she was spending the weekend at a girlfriend's house.

The two of them spent Saturday and Sunday at the Frisco Campgrounds. They didn't really hang out too much with Mike's buddies. In fact, they never really seemed to leave the back of the little yellow truck.

For the rest of the summer Mike and Rachel went everywhere together. He tried to teach her how to surf, and she tried to teach him how to scuba dive; once Johnny came along and videotaped a lesson, yelling to his cautious son, "Don't be such a pussy." Or they'd go out to the houseboat on a Sunday afternoon for gin and tonics, and afterward Johnny would take them to Mama's, an Italian restaurant in Tidewater. When they went to hear The Motels at Peabody's and all the punkers started trashing the place, Rachel had the time of her life. And some nights after her shift they would just drive to Sandbridge, watch the ocean, share a six-pack, and talk until the sun came up.

Every time Mike said, "I love you, bunny," Rachel became the happiest woman on the planet.

In September, just as Rachel was starting her junior year, they had their first fight. They were having breakfast in the house on Old Ocean View Road when Mike told her, "I have to tell you something."

Rachel didn't like his tone at all.

"I'm going into the Navy," he announced. "Look, if I could get out, I would, but they won't let me. I signed up last February. Before I met you. It was my dad's idea. Hell, I didn't know what else to do. I couldn't get into college. There's nothing I can do about it now."

Rachel had one question: "When do you ship off?"

"In December. The fourteenth."

Rachel was quiet for a moment, and all of a sudden her eyes were wet with tears, and finally she managed to say, "What do you want me to do while you're gone?"

"That's a good question." Rachel could tell Mike was hurting too. But he wasn't ready to make things easier. "I just don't know," he said after some thought.

"Well, when you get some answers, tell me."

Rachel ran from the house. She couldn't believe he hadn't asked her to marry him.

For two weeks they didn't speak. Rachel cried whenever she was alone. She never felt like eating. Then after classes one afternoon she went to her car and found a rose under the windshield wiper. A note said, "Thinking about you."

That seemed to settle things. They spent every day together until he was to go to boot camp at Great Lakes, outside of Chicago. They had an early Christmas. Mike gave Rachel a gold ring with a green stone set in the middle; it reminded her of the picture she had seen in *People* of Princess Di's emerald. Mike told her it was "a promise ring."

On the night before he was to leave, Rachel stayed at Mike's house. It must have been after 2:00 A.M. when she woke up and discovered he was not in the bed. She found him downstairs in the family room. The lights were off and Mike was crying.

"I just want to run away," he told Rachel through his tears. "I'm scared. I don't want to join the Navy. I don't. I wish my father hadn't made me."

So Rachel hugged him, and held him, and he cried and cried in the dark.

29

Rita was in a state about Art. Her husband was sleepy all the time. Men do like to sleep, she realized, but this wasn't normal. He'd come home from his job at VSE, and he'd fall asleep right at the kitchen table. While she was talking to him. But that wasn't all. One night he sat down to watch TV and the next thing she knew his hands were up around his throat and he was gasping for air like he was choking. It scared Rita half to death.

Art said it was nothing, but she laid down the law: He had to go see a doctor. So Art went for a MEDCOR checkup. The Navy doc listened to his heart, and gave him a blood test, and told him as far as he could tell Art was healthy as a horse. Do you smoke? the doc asked. Two packs a day, Art admitted, a little shamefaced. Well, that must be it. Cut down on the cigarettes and you'll be a new man.

But Art couldn't stop smoking; it was easier to give up on doctors. It was about that time the nightmares started. Each night the same awful scream would come bursting from Art, the wail ripping through the entire house. "Like he was in agony," was the only way Rita could describe it. It tore her apart, too.

Things were bad enough, then, before Art decided a drink or two might help. Art, the sailor who never liked the taste of liquor, who never had a drink at home unless there was company, now kept a glass and a bottle of scotch next to his TV chair. The alcohol just took him lower.

But worst of all was the night Art came home looking for his shotgun. He told Rita he wanted "to blow his brains out." He was drunk, yet Rita was certain he was serious. She sat with him and tried to get him to talk. He wouldn't tell her anything. All he did was cry. When he fell asleep, she went to the medicine cabinet in their bathroom and removed the razor blades, the scissors, and a bottle of aspirins.

She didn't know what else to do. And she didn't know what was wrong.

How was Rita to know she was watching her husband become a spy? Each stage of Art's misery was his acknowledgment of another level of betrayal. Like so many little lies, his treason had been gradual; until it was too late, and the only way out was with a shotgun.

In the beginning, was the first theft.

As soon as he took the job at VSE, Johnny's prodding began. Art decided he might as well get his brother off his back; after all, Johnny had covered his share of the debt to the bank. What would be the harm if he gave his brother a look at some documents? *Unclassified* documents. The distinction was very important to Art.

So at the end of his shift one afternoon, Art put the electronics section of a ship's information book and the technical manual index for LHA class ships into his briefcase. They weren't classified; he'd return them the next day. Where was the crime?

That evening, briefcase in hand, he went to Johnny's house. His brother took a quick look at the documents and made a face. "Nothing here's classified," Johnny complained to his brother. Still, Johnny made photocopies of a few pages from the tech manual. "You never know what people will pay for," he told his newest operative.

The next day Johnny met Art after work and handed him a white envelope. Inside was $6,000. "Up-front money," Johnny called it. Art should consider it payment for the "look" last night and an advance against more important deliveries in the future.

When Art went home that night he fell asleep at the kitchen table. It was the first time, and when Rita woke him up he thought she was kidding.

"If I'm going to do this shit," Art told his brother later in the week, "I need some methodology." The $6,000, he was convinced, had gone a long way toward solving all his problems.

"Tradecraft is what we call it," corrected Johnny, completing the first lesson.

The next lesson took place in the den on Old Ocean View Road. "The primary method," Johnny instructed his asset, "is photography." A lot of agents, Johnny went on, use a Minox. But for Art's purpose, Johnny was recommending a Kodak 110 camera. It's much easier to focus, he explained. All you do is put the documents on a desk and sight them through the viewfinder until the writing's legible. Then you can snap away. Try it, he told his brother.

Art, camera in hand, played spy. "Simple," he agreed.

"But how do I get stuff now?" Art demanded. "What's the methodology for getting my hands on it?"

Johnny, a patient control, told his brother a good field agent has to make things up as he goes along. "You look and see what you've got, and then you use your own ingenuity."

"But that could be difficult," Art moaned.

"Yeah. You've got to think. You've got to charge on. You've got to do it," Johnny urged.

But Art knew he didn't have to do anything. He was not a field agent. That was just crazy Johnny talking. Still, he told himself, it might be interesting to see if he could shoot a photograph. Just for the fun of it. But certainly nothing classified.

So one night he took some ship plans home with him. The plans were unclassified; he didn't even have to sign them out. But he would later say, "it was pretty challenging because they are very large and there are lots of pages." After a little practice, he got the Kodak 110 down pat. There was nothing to it, just like his brother had said.

When he was done he left the film at Johnny's office. He also put a note on his brother's desk: "Film in drawer."

He hadn't done anything really wrong, so he didn't see any reason to keep it a secret.

And he had no idea why he had started drinking.

Every now and then Johnny was mentioning the $6,000. Art, grateful, decided, he would explain, he might as well "see what I can do."

On September 21, 1981, Art went to the VSE security officer and signed out for the damage control book for the USS *Blue Ridge*. The *Blue Ridge* was the command and communications ship for the Pacific Fleet. The booklet was classified confidential.

Art went back to his desk and removed what he considered the most vital sections of the book—information regarding tank capacity, troop carry capacity, and ship stability. He placed these pages—they were about an inch thick—into his briefcase. He made sure to return the rest of the damage control book to the security officer. Then he went to lunch. Taking his briefcase with him.

He never got a chance to eat. He went to his brother's office and began photographing the pages. He used two rolls of film, and when he was done he left the cartridges in Johnny's desk drawer.

When he returned to the office, he checked out the book again and put the photographed pages back in. At four-thirty he returned a complete book.

Where was the big deal? he asked himself.

Years later, however, he got an answer when the senior intelligence officer for the Atlantic Fleet described the damage control book as a "bible for sabotage." "A Russian saboteur could determine where to place a single mine that could sink the ship or how to poison the crew through the ship's drinking water," he stated.

At the time, though, Art was more concerned about his mysterious nightmares.

For a while, Art didn't photograph anything. Why should he? he told himself; he wasn't a professional spy. But in April 1982, a project he was working on gave him access to computer tapes of ship casualty reports for the LHA class of ships from 1976 to 1980. These CASREPs on the Navy's newest assault vessels—each ship could carry 2,000 marines and 30 helicopters—were classified confidential.

Maybe this was the sort of thing Johnny was looking for, Art decided.

He took a chunk of the computer pages home with him in his briefcase. That night he photographed them in Johnny's office.

The next day at lunchtime he put the rest of the printout in his briefcase. Johnny was waiting outside in his van. They drove to the K-Mart parking lot; finding a space there would be no problem.

Johnny arranged the pages on one of the gray velour seats in the back of the van, and his brother began taking photographs.

But Art's heart started pounding. He thought he was going to have a heart attack in the back of the van in the K-Mart parking lot. "I can't do it, Bubba," he told Johnny.

So Johnny took over. Only Johnny, with a professional's pride, wouldn't use the easy-focus Kodak. He took his time and aimed his Minox C.

Somehow, that made Art feel more at ease. If Johnny was taking the pictures, then Johnny was the spy. Not Art. He wanted to believe that very much.

Only that night he woke up screaming again.

"Once you start sinning," Art would one day explain, "you either stop sinning or you just keep going and going and you carry this guilt around, subconsciously perhaps, but there is always a bit of tenseness. It's one of those things that you push back inside, you know, that makes you worse for it. It eats on you and it would be nice to tell someone, but who can you tell?"

That was Art's life as a spy.

He earned a total of $12,000 for his work. Part of that money, about $5,000, he returned to Johnny as a partial repayment toward the business debts his brother had covered.

The rest he kept in his briefcase. He didn't want Rita to know about it. He said, "It was my Happy Hour money. I bought some stuff . . . a gas grill, a new hairpiece, brakes for the car."

And he wanted to blow his brains out.

30

And while on both coasts the agents, despite swirling fears and doubts, continued their missions behind the lines, their control went off to Atlanta on the trail of a rock star.

Johnny, just as he was starting to recruit his brother, had made another career move. He had left Wackenhut to become a partner with his former boss, Phil Prince, in Confidential Reports, Inc. This new detective agency was, of course, more cover. But, much cleverer, it also created new opportunities: The agency gave polygraph examinations to sailors who needed evidence to refute the Navy's spot checks for drug use; it paid—under the table, naturally—at least a half-dozen Norfolk police officers who provided motor vehicle, criminal, and credit information about clients; and it was hired to sweep for electronic devices the offices of VSE, on Art's recommendation, and the Newport News Shipbuilding Co., the contractors for the Navy's fleet of Tomahawk missile-armed attack submarines.

"The trademark of the professional investigator," the military-brown Confidential Reports brochure explained, "is integrity, ability, and dedication." The same qualities which, conveniently enough, are found in the professional spy. In time, Johnny had no doubt, these two roles would merge: The naval contractor's office being swept would also simultaneously be bugged; the sailor with the drug problem would be a cinch to blackmail; and the cop who was willing to break the rules for a price would break larger laws for larger fees. Johnny, who got most of his ideas from television anyway, envisioned Confidential Reports becoming "the base of operations" for his network; "like that headquarters they had on 'The Man from U.N.C.L.E.' " was how he saw it. The fact that Phil Prince didn't have the slightest idea about this grand scheme only made the cover that much better.

For now, though, as he waited for his ring to solidify into a family operation, he threw himself into another set of opportunities that came his way through his detective agency—Johnny's Jewels, as Debbie Coursen, the Confidential Reports' office manager, called them. And that was how he wound up on the way to Atlanta hoping to deliver a message from a redhead with a great pair of legs to Mick Fleetwood of Fleetwood Mac.

The Case of the Reluctant Rock Star ended with a bullet. The redhead had hired Johnny Walker because she was in love with Mick Fleetwood. She had—or so she claimed; she did have a tendency to exaggerate that Johnny fully understood and excused—spent a night with Mick after the group's last show in Norfolk. She told Johnny, who tried to keep his grin under control, that she loved Mick and she was certain Mick loved her. She knew Mick wanted to be with her, but his managers and roadies were keeping them apart. Could Mr. Walker just deliver a message to Mick? If only Mick knew where he could reach her, if only he had her phone number, he'd come to her, she insisted. She was sobbing a river of tears.

Now, now, said Johnny, as he got up from his desk and put a consoling arm over her shoulder while also managing to take a good look at her majorette's legs. I think I can help you, he promised.

That night he took her to the Lone Pine for dinner, his treat. After dinner he took her to his house for a nightcap. You're in no shape to be alone, he advised her. She must have agreed because she stayed the night.

Next week, however, after he tracked the group to Atlanta and tried to confront Mick Fleetwood or at least his manager, things didn't work out as well. The KGB spy who had penetrated the Atlantic Fleet Submarine Communications Room couldn't get past the lobby of Fleetwood Mac's hotel. Neither Mick nor his manager would take a call from the house phone. The best Johnny could do was leave the redhead's message with the desk clerk.

Johnny never knew if the rock star received his message; however, he did learn that the redhead never spoke to Mick. After waiting for his call for two weeks, she tried to kill herself. She took a pistol and fired it point-blank into her chest. The bullet missed her heart and nicked her lung before exiting. When Johnny visited her in the hospital, she told him she had found God. Six months later she was working at the Christian Broadcasting Network in Virginia Beach as a volunteer. She still visited Johnny from time to time, though.

But more often Johnny had to settle for the opportunities that came his way from a juicy divorce case. "These divorcées are great for business," he told his partner. "Yeah," said Phil, not too happy about the way things were going, "monkey business." Yet Johnny, proud of his routine, would keep his office door open so his associates could listen as he reeled in the brokenhearted:

CLIENT: My husband is having an affair.

JOHNNY: A pretty woman like you? Impossible!

CLIENT: . . . it's true. When I confronted him, he slapped me.

JOHNNY: Why, you don't need that. You don't need a man who abuses you. Not a pretty woman like you.

CLIENT: It's just that my husband doesn't care about me. That's why he's sleeping with someone else. I want you to find out the bitch's name.

JOHNNY: Well, in my experience, and I've worked hundreds of cases like this, more important than finding out anybody's name is trying to get back together with your husband. You do want to stay together?

CLIENT: . . . I'm not sure.

JOHNNY: Course you do. And the way to do it is to make him jealous. Get back at him the way he's been hurting you. Give

him a dose of his own medicine. You understand what I'm
saying?

CLIENT: I think so.

JOHNNY: Maybe, and this is difficult for me to say, it's a problem of your sexual habits. You do enjoy sex, don't you?

CLIENT: . . . Yes, but . . .

JOHNNY: Well, maybe you got to try some new techniques.
Learn some things.

CLIENT: I . . .

JOHNNY: Look, I don't know exactly how to ask this—Do you
enjoy oral sex?

And at this point Johnny would usually have to get up from his desk
and close the door to his office. The laughter from the next room
would be getting too distracting.

Not all of Johnny's Jewels, however, were one-night stands. He
and P. K. Carroll, who at twenty-two was younger than two of his
daughters, were pretty much a couple; which is one way of saying
Johnny was with P.K. when he wasn't off two-timing her. She was a
thin blonde with a pixie haircut and, oddly, a linebacker's angry,
competitive tension. It would take a lot of people by surprise when
she came on like a barroom sailor on Cinderella Liberty. For a slight
girl, they'd say, she sure knew how to carry herself.

P.K. had met Johnny in 1981 while she was in the Navy and was
attending fire fighting school. It was tough-guy work, all that "holding
the wild hose" and "dogging down hot doors" on flaming ships. She
liked it fine, only it gave her too much free time. That's how she
happened to perk up when she came across an ad in the *Virginian-
Pilot:* The Confidential Reports agency was looking for part-time investigators.

Phil Prince interviewed her and, after hearing about how she had
served with the Shore Patrol before going off to fight fires, hired her
on the spot. He also invited P.K. to his partner's forty-fourth birthday
party. That afternoon she went with Phil to pick up cold-cut platters
at Farm Fresh and nothing better to do, she stayed for the fun. "It'll
be a good way to meet the clients," Phil told her.

By ten that night the party in the agency's offices was down to empty bottles, but a group was going back to the birthday boy's house. "Why don't you come along?" Johnny Walker asked P.K.

In the family room on Old Ocean View Road, with *Insatiable* on the VCR, P.K. proceeded to put away a fair amount of bourbon. She had never seen a blue movie before and to her surprise, it was turning her on. When Johnny, her employer and host, asked her to spend the night, she figured why not? No biggie.

A year later she was out of the Navy and living with her mother in Seattle when who should call her but her old boss. "Been thinking of you," said Johnny. "How about you coming back East and working for us?" So she soon was working part-time for Confidential Reports and living, a little more than part-time, in Johnny's house. But P.K. had a future full of full-time plans. She was training to join the Norfolk Police Department. "The best idea in the world," Johnny told her. She was also trying to move into the house on Old Ocean View Road on a permanent basis. "We'll have to think about that one," said Johnny. But he had bought her a ring, a ruby surrounded by a circle of ten tiny diamond chips. It cost him $500 and he called it their "unengagement ring."

A newspaper ad also attracted another part-time investigator to the agency. In time, she would become Johnny's best friend, his partner, and his victim. The way Johnny looked at it, theirs was a love story. It wasn't because they were lovers, though Johnny got a charge out of giving people that impression. But because Laurie Robinson, model and private eye, was the one woman who, though she never knew all the details, could have understood the risky game of Johnny's scattered ambitions. In her own way, she was a player too.

Before she had married the weight lifter with the twenty-one-inch biceps and after she had divorced the rock soundman who tried to kill himself with an overdose of Quaaludes, Laurie had been married to a spy. Of course by then she had also caught her mother having an affair; was beaten bloody by her Marine colonel father; had run away from home and, nearly fifteen, called herself Jenny and lived on her own in Washington for two years; had a school for the emotionally disturbed closed down after the director shot her full of Thorazine and tried to rape her; ran away from a foster home after her "dad" climbed into bed with her; worked as a bartender in a half-dozen clubs; drove a silver-blue Corvette with a T-top and a gold stripe; gave the eyewitness testimony which helped convict a member of the Greek Mafia of arson; and did runway and bikini modeling. But in all her twenty-seven years, the brief marriage to the spy was the most exciting time of all because the Marines had to come and rescue her.

Laurie, twenty, had met the spy when she was bartending in Washington. He was Iranian, and, Laurie felt, when people used words like tall, dark, and handsome, they must have been thinking about Hussein. He was also polite; she had never known a man who held the car door open before. And he was a real sharp dresser, his suits nipped tight in the waist and the top three buttons always undone on his pastel-colored silk shirts. He told her he worked at the Iranian embassy. That was true. But after she went with him on two occasions to a dumpster in a Maryland alleyway where, each time, he picked up a duffle bag, he told her the rest of the story: He worked for SAVAK, the Iranian Secret Service. "This is my business, baby. It don't concern you. You don't see nothing, baby."

Which was fine with Laurie. Anyway, she was in love, sort of.

When Hussein and one of his friends asked her to join them on a trip to Iran, she quickly decided it was an adventure she didn't want to miss. The two men had talked of palaces and servants. And, for a change, she could afford not to work for a couple of months; there was about $5,000 left from the insurance settlement she had collected after the MG she had been driving went off the side of the road and she had come *this* close to dying.

"Count me in," she told them.

The trip was a ton of fun. There were servants to wash her feet. She stayed at a villa on the Caspian Sea. She went to the palace and talked with the shah at a polo match. But she shouldn't have smoked the dope. It was raw opium, real mind-bending stuff, and she lost two whole days. For those two days, everything was kind of whiffy. When she came out of the fog, she was in Hussein's parents' house in Tehran and he was telling Laurie she was his wife. He had the marriage certificate to prove it.

Now that Laurie was Hussein's wife, he expected her to act like a proper Iranian woman. If she wanted to shop at the marketplace, she now had to dress in black, with a veil over her face.

"Come again?" Laurie told him. "I think I'll just catch the next plane to the U.S. of A., thank you."

"But you can't leave, you are my wife. Besides, how will you buy your ticket?"

"I have money," Laurie said.

"That's our money now," said Hussein. "I'm holding it."

And me too, Laurie thought.

Two days later Laurie had a chance to make her escape. She waited till Hussein had left and then snuck out through the servants' entrance. Her plan was to head for the American embassy. But she couldn't find it. She couldn't work the phones. And she couldn't find anyone who could speak English. Finally, on Queen Elizabeth Street, she saw a school and ran inside.

The man who ran the school was a former U.S. Air Force colonel. He was only too glad to help a lady in distress. He called the vice consulate at the American embassy, an old buddy. Five marines were dispatched to rescue Laurie.

But as soon as the marines started to lead Laurie out of the school, Hussein and three of his friends appeared.

"If you take my wife, I will kill you. I will kill anyone who takes my wife," Hussein started shouting at the marines. One of his friends began pounding on the embassy car.

The marines unholstered their sidearms.

Guns drawn, Hussein yelling ferociously, Laurie was escorted by five marines to the car. Fifteen minutes later, without a shot fired, she was inside the embassy.

For nearly three weeks Laurie was, in effect, a hostage in the American embassy. It took that long for an arrangement to be worked out between the Iranian government and the U.S. State Department. According to the final settlement, Hussein would be allowed to reenter the United States, and his wife would be allowed to leave Iran.

On the day of her departure, Laurie was taken to the airport under the protection of another armed escort of marines. Hussein, somehow, was there waiting for her. "Baby, let me talk to you. I just want to talk to you, baby," he was shouting. But the marines held him off.

The next day she was back in New York.

And the day after that she was living with her grandmother in Virginia Beach. It didn't take her long to get a job working nights behind the bar at Rogue's. Her days were spent with the crowd everyone called "The Beach Group." There was always a volleyball game, a keg, and good dope. What more could you ask out of life?

But as she was closing in on thirty, Henry, the soft-voiced weight lifter who worked as a bouncer at the club, gave her something to think about. "You still want to be serving drinks when you're forty?" he asked her. It was the first time she had ever looked that far ahead, and what she saw didn't make her comfortable. Worse, if she spent another ten years in the sun, Laurie worried she'd be one big wrinkle. No doubt about it, she decided, it was time to find a new line of work.

"I wanted something different. Not your nine-to-five job because I'm not a nine-to-five girl," she would explain. "I kept on thinking about it and always saw the same fantasy in my mind—Charlie's Angels. You know, the TV show was hot then. I envisioned myself like Farrah Fawcett. As one of the Angels. It was my fantasy. That's what life's about right? Fantasy."

When Johnny Walker interviewed her for the job, he asked her why she thought she'd make a good detective.

"Because I can con anybody out of anything," Laurie answered without a second's thought.

She got the job.

Two years later, Laurie became Johnny's partner in Confidential Reports. Phil Prince had left because he just didn't feel like working with Johnny Walker anymore; though if he had made a scene, Johnny had a surprise for Phil—he had bugged the ex-marine's office. The tapes, gossip mostly, were insurance Johnny never had to use; Phil was glad to walk.

Laurie and Johnny, meanwhile, were having the time of their lives. They both loved the games. As Johnny would write to her one day, "I could never get over the fact that we were *paid* to run around and have fun. I guess I love you and what was great was that I could feel that way without sex involved . . . or any contact at all. I could have stayed on the road with you permanently at $150 a day + expenses . . . "

Only years later, though, would Laurie stop and think about some of the games they had been playing. The background checks especially were giving her real pause.

The way Johnny had explained it to her, the client was a Midwest construction company. A number of sailors, officers, had applied for jobs with the company and Confidential Reports had been hired to determine if these naval officers could be trusted. "Run-of-the-mill BI" was how Johnny described it. Still, when Johnny and Laurie worked a case, they liked to add a certain touch of intrigue to the investigation; otherwise what was the point, right?

Johnny came up with the Free Dinner Scam; it was their "foot in the door." Laurie would hang out at the officers' club on the Norfolk Naval Base until she could strike up a conversation with the mark. "You know," she'd say after the second drink, "I work for a restaurant promotion company in the Tidewater area that's trying to give away free dinners. All you have to do is give me the list of the men in your command and their Social Security numbers, and I'll pick two numbers out of a hat. The lucky sailors'll get a free night on the town." And all the while the officer is thinking he wouldn't mind a night on the town with this five-foot-ten brunette. As Laurie remembered, "Ten out of ten times, it worked. I made contact with the subject."

The next phase of the operation required what Laurie called "charm." "I would just hang around the officers' club talking to the guy until he said something like, 'You know, you're an awful nice-looking lady,' and then I knew I was home free. We'd go out to dinner or for drinks and basically they'd be telling me how wonderful they were and I'd be asking them about their life and career." In all that conversation, of course, Laurie would never get around to telling the officers she was married to a weight lifter. She thought it might spoil the mood.

Her instructions from Johnny were clear. He wanted to know if these officers were susceptible to blackmail. "Find out if they have anything to hide," Johnny ordered. The client, the way he outlined it, wanted men he could trust, not men who had histories that could be used against them.

Laurie filed "at least ten" background reports on Navy officers for Johnny. She covered a lot of territory: "I wrote up reports on a commander who bragged he had access to the war room. Then there was one, an officer on a carrier, who told me about how he was cheating on his wife, and if the Navy ever found out, that would ruin his chances for promotion. There was even a lieutenant commander, a guy with a fairly high security clearance, who was addicted to gambling—horse racing, Atlantic City, the Bahamas. This guy went where the action was."

Yet these days, a detective out of a job and living in another world, Laurie has to wonder if she was playing talent spotter for Johnny's next batch of recruits. If things had worked out differently, would Johnny have made his sales pitch to a lieutenant commander who liked the horses?

But at the time, Laurie was just wrapped up in the hush-hush fun and challenge of each new case. Things were going so well, in fact, that a local radio station gave Johnny an award. He was the "Hometown Hero" of the month for his work in tracking down missing children.

Which was sort of funny, because it was P.K. who called up the radio station in the first place and told them all about Johnny.

But there was something ironic about it too. And not funny at all. Because Johnny's daughter, Laura Walker Snyder, was missing.

The last time Johnny had spoken to Laura she told him about Mark's threat to turn her father in to the FBI if she tried to take back her son.

"I can't believe you'd tell your junkie husband about my private life," Johnny had shouted into the phone.

He then asked, "Do you still love him?"

Mark had just taken her child. "No," she answered.

"Well," Johnny said, "how would you feel if he weren't around anymore?"

"Wouldn't bother me," said Laura. Her father could kill her husband for all she cared.

But nothing happened to Mark, and Laura remained separated from her son. Then, on July 4, 1983, exactly a year and two days after her husband had run off with Chris, Laura decided she could no longer bear the pain of living without her child. It wasn't right. She didn't even know if Chris remembered her. She couldn't go on like this. She called her mother in Maine for help.

Mom, Laura announced, I have to get my son back. I'm going to go to Maryland and take him. He's mine. We belong together. If Mark wants to call the FBI, let him. I've suffered enough.

Barbara screamed through the phone, No. You can't do that, she insisted. It'll ruin all our lives. Your father will have to spend the rest of his life in jail. We'll all suffer. You can't take the risk.

Laura, tearful and hopeless, hung up. She could either be a mother to her son; or she could destroy her family. The choices overpowered her. Either way, her life would be torn apart.

So Laura let her anger run. She, aching all the way, followed its hard mood: If that's the way her mother felt, the hell with her. In fact, the hell with all of them—her mother, her father, her husband, the secret. She would just run away, disappear. And try to forget.

She ran away, but she couldn't forget.

31

Jerry Whitworth, too, would have liked to run, but he couldn't find the will. Instead, he decided to buy a new camera.

In August 1982, he had been promoted to senior chief petty officer. It was an honor for a career sailor, but it was rotten luck for a spy. His new duties at the Naval Communications Center in Alameda gave him little access to crypto. Jerry, whose nerves were stretched so tightly these days that he was picking up ominous signs in even his wife's smiles, saw this as his perfect way out—out of the ring, out of trouble, and, in six months, out of the Navy. He planned to put in for his retirement.

But when his control came to San Leandro at the end of August for their scheduled exchange, Johnny reminded Jerry about what he'd be giving up. He urged Jerry to put in for a seagoing command. One last three-year deployment at sea, one last shot at glory days like they enjoyed aboard the *Niagara,* at new $100,000 stacks, at a fresh round of champagne celebrations in the back of the van. Go out in a blaze of glory, he urged his asset, and we'll both get seriously rich.

By the end of the day, Jerry had come around to seeing things

Johnny's way. Partly, this was because Jerry's convictions were only as strong as the last argument he heard. But, that is not to say the pull of friendship didn't have something to do with Jerry's change of heart; his control was his best buddy and pleasing him mattered greatly. So Jerry, a man of many motives, called up his detailer. Within the week his transfer came through: As of October 2, 1982, he would be assigned to the USS *Enterprise,* a nuclear-powered aircraft carrier.

Since he was going back into the field, the agent decided to get his equipment in working order. On September 23 Jerry went to Pacific Camera. The shutter on his Minox C had been jamming.

"Take a lot of pictures, don't you?" the man behind the counter asked.

"Guess so," Jerry said nervously.

"You must," said the man. "The shutter mechanism is plum worn-out."

Jerry had to laugh; he had been a very busy spy.

This was no simple repair job, the man brusquely went on, no doubt upset that his amused customer failed to see the enormity of the problem. The camera, he explained with undisguised glee, would have to be sent to the factory. Wouldn't be ready till mid-October.

Jerry had no choice but to buy a new camera. He bought a Minox C for $399 in cash. But he made sure he got a receipt; he'd need it to be reimbursed by the KGB.

Also on that same day, Jerry, who never failed to be organized, telephoned Olden Camera in New York. He said he was going on a trip and he wanted to order all the Minox film the store had in stock. Five days later the package from Olden arrived at his home in San Leandro. "Sorry," read the note scribbled on the invoice, "only 20 rolls."

It would have to do. He was going to be at sea for six months and he planned to bring home a lot of souvenirs.

It was a long, hectic cruise. This was his first tour as senior chief radioman, and his responsibilities were a real weight on Jerry. He now ran a shack with fourteen men on a carrier that often received 2,000 messages in a single day. Things would go pretty much nonstop during each of his eight-hour shifts; and, worse, his new duties kept him away from crypto material on a daily basis. He had to think up all kinds of excuses to disappear into the vault. That didn't help his nerves at all.

The endless cruise on the *Enterprise,* though, did give Jerry a chance to see the world; and, after all, that was why he had joined the Navy in the first place. It was pretty exciting—Africa, Australia, Japan. So whenever he could grab a minute, before hitting the rack or going off for chow, say, Jerry would talk into a cassette recorder. When the sixty minutes were filled with the cluttered details of all he had seen and done and thought, he planned to send the tape to his best friend. Jerry, cynical but not a cynic, truly believed Johnny would be interested.

"And we were in Masai country," Jerry spoke into the recorder, his tone a pilot's authoritative twang, "and these Masai people still live the way they've always lived. The exception being they do a lot of trading with the tourists and there are certain places where they have outlets for their wares which is mostly, uh, necklaces and things like that, spears and some things that would be considered art-work, I guess . . . But we had a damn flat right in the middle of their country . . ."

". . . so after Mombasa, then, our next port of call was Australia. Perth was wonderful. Absolutely wonderful. I stayed ashore the entire time. I stayed at the Hilton. Rented a car for two days and drove around the countryside and went to the, uh, a preserve there. Actually, it's a national park where they have water activities and asso-ciated activities, uh, lots of barbecue areas. They also have a kind of minizoo there. Primarily for the koala bears and Brenda is very fond of koala bears so I made a special effort to get some good pictures of koala bears. . . ."

". . . I went to Nagasaki yesterday, the first time I've been there. I always did want to check that out. Uh, it was a good tour, except the weather was lousy. Raining all the time. And, uh, I did, I don't know if 'enjoy' is the right word, I did appreciate the tour very much. I enjoyed the new things I saw and especially the atomic bomb mu-seum. It was, uh, very informative and worthwhile. . . ."

". . . We've been playing a lot of games with the Russians while we were in I.O. (Indian Ocean). There was a Russian carrier *Kiev* . . . It was down there and we played a lot of games with her. And now we're up in Japan and Korean area and we've been surveilled every day by the Russians. Every day. Flashed messages all over the place. They've been disrupting our flight operations too. Which pisses off the air devils. It kind of makes me laugh to tell you the truth. . . ."

". . . Well, I'm feeling pretty tired now. I'm taking a fade. So I'll talk to you later when I'm more alert . . ."

"Well, I'm back, Johnny, and I've had my nap. I have a feeling that a bunch of this tape—and I haven't gone back to listen to it—it's gonna be kind of a bore because I was so tired. . . ."

Yet even while Jerry was at sea, he still found time to spend the cash that was crowding his safe-deposit box. By now Brenda, who still believed the money was earned by secret work Jerry did for the Navy, had also joined the sprees. Her say was real important to Jerry. She was studying for her doctorate in nutrition and Jerry counted on her to teach him about the fine things in life. Brenda's accomplishments, the touch of class she brought to his life, made Jerry, the sailor with *The Fountainhead* in his duffle, love her more.

On December 6, Brenda sent a telegram to the *Enterprise* telling her husband she had learned of a special offering of Dali prints. She had bought one. It had cost her $1,597. Should she buy three more at a special price?

Jerry wasn't a big Dali fan. His instructions were to buy only one more print.

In fact, if things had been left to Jerry, after the money had been spent on necessities like computers, skin-diving equipment, and a new Toyota, he would have been happy to plow all the cash into new investments. His dream of becoming a stockholder, of being another one of those shrewd guys he read about in *Barrons* who were constantly making killings in the market, had turned serious. True, since 1978 he had lost $29,997. But he liked the action, and Jerry was always one to hope.

On March 11, 1983, while he was aboard the *Enterprise* and on his way to Japan, Jerry, always thinking, sent a telegram to his wife:

"I'd like you to buy 10 Krugerrands ASAP. Use cash. Associated Foreign Exchange with an address in San Francisco is a good place to buy. Discretion, please."

Of course, in between running the radio shack, touring, and deciding how to spend his money, Jerry was also a secret agent.

Q. Can you describe the material that you received?
A. Yes. Cryptographic was somewhat of a disappointment. It was sketchy at best. So he augmented that with a large supply of messages, which he described as a year's worth.

These messages—including intelligence flashes, operational communications, operational orders, and letters of instruction—provided the details of FLTX-83-1. It was information, a Navy expert on strategic planning would one day testify, that could "give the Soviet Union a distinct advantage in any large-scale naval battle."

It was the Pacific Fleet's largest series of maneuvers since World War II. Navy Secretary John Lehman's "forward strategy," the policy of moving American warships into "high threat areas" near the Soviet Union, had never been so boldly practiced. For three weeks starting in March 1983, the forty-ship FLTX-83-1 armada conducted naval exercises closer to the Soviet Union than ever before.

The sea and air surrounding Alaska's Aleutian Islands—450 miles from Russian military outposts on the Kamchatka Peninsula—were filled with constant activity. There were three aircraft-carrier battle groups accompanied by Air Force B-52 bombers, advance warning aircrafts (AWACs), and F-15 fighters. American nuclear attack submarines began operating for the first time beneath waters that were the normal patrol area of Soviet submarines. And there were more than 23,000 American military men involved. Including Jerry Whitworth, the senior chief petty officer who ran the message center on the *Enterprise* during the entire exercise.

Throughout the maneuvers, American tactics were aggressive. They became truly provocative, though, as FLTX-83-1 was ending. On April 4 a formation of at least six planes from the *Enterprise* and the *Midway* violated Soviet airspace with a flight over the island of Zeleny in the Kurile archipelago. After the official protests from the Soviet Union were filed, the State Department suggested, off the record, that the overflights were a navigational error.

But there was no official Navy admission of the incident, and certainly no attempt at an apology. Rather, when Admiral James D. Watkins, chief of naval operations, testified to the Senate Armed Services Committee a year later, he contended, "Our feeling is that an aggressive defense, if you will, characterized by forward movement, early deployment of forces, aggressiveness on the part of our ships, is the greatest deterrent we can have. And the Soviets really understand that . . . Kamchatka is a difficult peninsula. They have no railroads for it. They have to resupply by air. It's a very important spot for them, and they are as naked as a jaybird there, and they know it."

This was not true. By the time the admiral appeared before the Senate committee, the Soviet positions were no longer as defenseless as the admiral imagined—Jerry Whitworth had provided the Russians with the strategy an American attack force would employ. This knowledge now made the defense of a "difficult peninsula" a tactical possibility. Perhaps, the whiz kids in Trends and Intentions were guessing, the Russians would even have the advantage.

There was also, some American intelligence officials believe, another consequence of the FLTX-83-1 messages that Jerry Whitworth photographed: These communications confirmed to the Soviet Union that the violation of their territory by American jet fighters was not an accident.

On June 12, 1983, John Walker left a garbage bag in the Maryland woods filled with copies of message traffic from the *Enterprise*. Nearly three months later, on September 1, a Korean Air Lines civilian jet flying off course passed over the Kamchatka Peninsula. A Russian SU-15 interceptor jet fired two missiles, each with 70 pounds of high explosives, at the plane. The 269 people on board were killed.

Secretary of State George Schultz announced the destruction of Flight 007 in a 10:45 A.M. television appearance: "The United States reacts with revulsion to this attack. Loss of life appears to be heavy. We can see no excuse whatsoever for this appalling act.''

In the months that followed, however, numerous excuses, rigorous theories, and farfetched speculations would be offered in attempts at understanding the Soviet Union's decision to shoot down a passenger jet. It would not be until the incident had passed from many people's minds, nearly four years later, that National Security Agency back-beaters would suggest another factor that could have contributed to the Soviet Union's aggressiveness: Information passed by John Walker to the KGB encouraged the Soviet Air Defense Force to be-lieve Flight 007 was a deliberate provocation.

"We burned them with the overflight during FLTX-83-1 and thanks to Walker they knew it for sure,'' an NSA officer suggested. "You embarrass a guy, he's bound to get a little trigger-happy. It would make sense to me that the message traffic Johnny Walker passed on helped to create a shoot-first-and-ask-questions-later attitude in the Soviets. It was just bad luck for them that this time it was a civilian jet.''

But Jerry, as his long cruise continued, wasn't thinking of how the photographs he was taking would be used. He was simply tired. As the tape in his cassette was winding down, so was Jerry:

". . . so I'm very disappointed in the ship. I don't like it. And it's a ballbuster spiritually and otherwise. I'll just be glad when we get back to the States . . .''

32

The sandbar was the final sign. As the *Enterprise* sailed into San Francisco harbor at the end of its six-month cruise, the carrier landed on a sandbar. It was stranded. For the more than 5,000 men on board looking forward to liberty it was a restless, grumbling nineteen-hour ordeal. But for Jerry Whitworth it was liberating. He stood on the flight deck catwalk in the midst of a crowd of curious sailors caught up in watching the little tugs struggling to rescue a 60,000-ton gray hulk, and he felt wonderfully free. Even happy. His mind for once was set: He would give up his career and his trade. He had two masters and, a true double agent, he could proudly say he had served them both well. Until now. Now he'd retire from the Navy and from spying. Because now, more than any moment in his long doubt-filled voyage, he was certain of his fate: If he continued he would wind up beached like the *Enterprise,* and then it would take more than a fleet of tugs to free him.

Large decisions, he reminded himself as he stared out toward the Golden Gate Bridge, are reached in strange ways. That had been the story of his life. And the telegram in his pocket, he now understood, had been telling him all along that he was on the brink.

303

• • •

A few days before, on the twenty-fifth of April, he had received a cable from Brenda. He had kept it in the pocket of his khakis ever since. It made his heart race:

"My darling . . . I long to have you home. Look for the white 1957 Rolls-Royce, a chauffeur and me, the lady in red. Come Thursday A.M. I'm going to show you how a real homecoming should be. The backseat of a Rolls is only the beginning, so get some rest. You've got a meeting with destiny. Smack, smack. Your yearning woman."

But now Jerry, no stranger to codes, understood the true significance of the Lady in Red's message. *A meeting with destiny,* Jerry read for at least the dozenth time. Brenda, though she didn't know it, was on the money about that, all right. In his energized state, filled for once with resolve, everything fit neatly: It was destiny that had made him a spy and now it was destiny (that sounded a lot more grand than a goddamn sandbar) that was telling him to quit.

He couldn't wait to tell his yearning woman the news. Or at least the flash that he was shoving off from the Navy. He'd become a stockbroker, the money would be rolling in. So what if his Krugerrands were nose-diving. Gold would soon be zooming. He knew these things.

Jerry was in such a bouncy, happy-go-lucky state when Brenda and the rented white Rolls met him on the dock that he didn't even bitch about the expense of having to pay for the day spent on the sandbar: $438.78 might be a bundle for some sailors, but not for a man who just had a meeting with destiny. Jerry, suddenly a sport, threw in a $20 cash tip for the chauffeur. The Rolls had a right-hand drive and he thought that any driver who didn't get flustered by that kind of inconvenience deserved a reward.

It was really, he would always recall, a wonderful homecoming.

It was only later that Jerry began to worry about his control. He wanted to believe it would be as simple as saying, "I don't love you anymore." But it turned out to be as complicated as that, too: Jerry still wanted Johnny's affection—only not at the going price. There was also another concern: He understood that Johnny, his best friend, was quite capable of killing him.

So on June 3 when Johnny came to San Leandro for the scheduled exchange, Jerry was prepared. He lied. The lies, however, were only smoke, cover for the big scam Jerry was pulling on his control. It was a maneuver—"insurance," Jerry would call it—that Johnny never suspected.

After all the practice, Jerry had become quite good at deceit.

Johnny arrived at the June 3 meet with worries of his own.

First, his last trip to Vienna, the face-to-face back on January 15, had been a disaster. Johnny had been set to tell his new handler he had worked out a way to keep wishy-washy Whitworth in the ring—offer Jerry a million dollars. It might sound like a lot of money, Johnny was ready to argue, but the KGB should look at it as a $100,000-a-year salary for the next ten years. If he could persuade Whitworth to remain in the Navy for another decade, he planned to suggest, a million dollars would be a bargain for what they'd be getting.

But Johnny never got the chance to make his pitch. From the moment they met, Ivan the Terrible began to tear into Johnny. He ranted about the poor quality of Whitworth's Alameda product. Then, from out of nowhere, he brought up old suspicions about Jerry's sudden transfer from the *Niagara* three years ago. He even went on about Johnny's showing up late in Casablanca, and that's when Johnny knew his handler was off the wall. Either this new Ivan was trying to lay down the law at his first meet, Johnny decided, or the KGB was getting truly paranoid. No matter. It was bad news all around. And certainly not the time to bring up a million-dollar deal. Johnny would just have to wait; and hope that Jerry didn't do anything dumb in the meantime.

Second, there was Laura—and her husband. That was a real dangerous situation. Unguided missiles, no doubt about it.

And last, there was Gary. For a while, it had seemed like incredible luck. Johnny's father, the old Night Walker, had remarried and moved to Temperanceville on Virginia's Eastern Shore. One of his kids—Johnny's half-brother—was in the Navy. Gary Walker was a helicopter crewman assigned to an antisubmarine warfare squadron. And

ASW information, Johnny knew, was money in the bank. But it got even better: Gary was based in Norfolk and had taken an apartment in Willoughby, a couple of blocks from where Johnny kept his houseboat. Naturally Johnny worked it out so that his long-lost half brother and he got to strike up a friendship. Only thing was, when Johnny finally made his offer and said he knew a way of making money that might be a little shady, Gary shot him down. Didn't want to hear another word. It was a real disappointment, and Johnny didn't have much hope of things ever working out.

So, all this weighing on him when he came to San Leandro that June day, the last thing Johnny wanted was more headaches.

Jerry didn't provide them. Or so Johnny thought. Jerry's haul from the *Enterprise* was quality. Jer had taken a foot-high stack of documents—not only photographs, but also the actual messages—off the carrier. There was, however, a small problem. Jerry was in the midst of moving, Brenda was transferring to the University of California at Davis for her dissertation research, and the dumb movers had packed up everything. Including most of his take from the *Enterprise*. But not to worry, Jerry explained. He had the crypto key lists film, and a bunch of the stolen papers, maybe a third of the pile, were still unpacked in his den.

Johnny was suddenly suspicious. He didn't know whether to buy that story about the movers. But Jer, like a carny barker giving a rube a taste of what was waiting inside the tent, waved a couple of messages at his control. Johnny read them; and just as quickly as his doubts had popped up, they now vanished. The papers were solid gold: It was message traffic detailing the penetration of Soviet territory by a pack of F-14s. That'd get Ivan the Terrible to back off, he silently celebrated.

The rest of the messages, Jerry told his friend, would be no problem. Johnny could pick them up before his next drop; they'd certainly be unpacked by then.

Jerry, to Johnny's continuing delight, was even upbeat about the future. In October, he told Johnny, the carrier's assistant communications officer was being transferred. Jerry figured that he had a pretty good chance at taking his place and becoming CMS custodian. That meant that next May when the *Enterprise* was scheduled for another long WESTPAC deployment, he should be able to get his hands on top-quality crypto. Anyway, he was on the *Enterprise* till October 1985, and he planned to make the most of it.

"Sounds great," said Johnny.

Only it wasn't.

Johnny's first surprise came in the mail. Four months later, in October 1983, he received a printed invitation to a party at the Oakland Hyatt Regency celebrating Jerry Whitworth's retirement from the Navy.

That bastard has finally done it, Johnny fumed.

Still, in January Johnny flew to California to pick up the remaining photographs of the *Enterprise* documents. There was more money to be made off Jerry, he told himself. He just had to play him right. As he drove up to the olive-colored trailer in the Rancho Yolo Mobile Home Park that Jerry was now leasing, Johnny promised himself he would keep his anger in check.

It didn't take him five minutes to break his promise. Jerry told him that he hadn't gotten around to photographing the rest of the documents and Johnny started raging.

"Don't fuck with me," he threatened. "This is serious stuff. You double-cross the people I'm working for, and they'll kill you. Who do you think you're working for, some little guy in western New York?"

For once Johnny wasn't acting. He was scared. Scared of what Ivan the Terrible was going to say if he showed up empty-handed in Vienna next month. Whitworth's sudden retirement was going to shake up the Russians enough; he didn't want to give them anymore reasons to be suspicious.

Johnny's fear got to Jerry. He took one look at his old buddy and he could imagine Johnny going for his neck.

Look, he told Johnny, I have the documents here. I just need to photograph them.

"You damn well better," Johnny warned.

Only Jerry insisted that the photographic session not take place in the trailer; he was wary of Brenda's coming home from school and catching them. So the two of them, both on guard, the tension sparking like an electrified fence strung up between them, went to a motel.

It took over an hour. They acted as a team, and the cooperation gave them a chance to work off their anger. Jerry set up on a wooden dresser a high-intensity lamp he had brought from the trailer, and then played cameraman. Johnny, the carton full of stolen documents resting next to him on the bed, fed Jerry a new page each time he heard the shutter click.

When they were done, Johnny was feeling pretty good about things. Maybe there was a chance that Jer would come back into the fold, get a civilian defense job or something. Anyway, at least there wouldn't be any more surprises.

The last surprise was the biggest. Johnny believed it could get him killed.

Ivan the Terrible broke it to him at their next face-to-face on February 15: The film Johnny had delivered last June—Whitworth's first batch of key list photographs from the *Enterprise*—was worthless.

Worthless? Johnny repeated, in no mood to play straight man for another of the Russian's thickheaded accusations.

But it was not a joke. The Russian announced that the film was shot out of focus. Each photograph was illegible, nothing but gray fog. The Russian's voice was a hard, lashing whisper: "What kind of game are you two trying to play? This could be very dangerous."

At that moment Johnny could imagine a KGB hit team sighting him in their rifle scopes. He waited for the bullets.

Yet in that instant, the moment before his execution, he was certain he understood what Jerry had been up to: Jerry had fogged the pictures because he knew he was going to retire all along and he was afraid the KGB—or Johnny—would then refuse to pay him the money he was owed. That's why, for the first time, Jer had risked taking the actual documents off the ship. Pay Jerry the money he had coming to him, let him live in peaceful retirement, and Jer would keep his end of the deal. Jerry could shoot the photographs anytime; after all, Johnny had seen the carton full of documents. The fogged pictures, Johnny realized, were Jerry's insurance that he wouldn't get double-crossed. He wasn't out to screw Johnny or the Russians, he was simply making sure they wouldn't screw him. It was actually pretty ingenious, thought Johnny.

And now that Johnny had worked all this out in his mind, he set off with the passion of a man fighting for his life—which he had no doubt he was—to convince the Russian. He even, as he wrapped up his story, told Ivan he had hopes of Jerry's coming back into the network.

The Russian listened. His face was stone. "This is a very dangerous situation, very dangerous," he kept warning. But there were no bullets.

He also issued a new order to his agent: From now on, Walker would refrain from mentioning the names of his operatives in any conversation or correspondence. It was bad security. Instead, the KGB devised a code name for each member. He would repeat it and Walker would memorize it. It was best not to have any written record. Agreed?

Yes, said Johnny quickly. And he felt the rifle aimed at his back being lowered. For the time being.

On the plane back to New York, Johnny, never one to follow orders, wrote the code he had memorized the day before into a small loose-leaf notebook. He started at the top of the page:

D = Jerry. *He's not out of it yet,* Johnny thought.
K = Art. *He's jumpy, but he's still game.*
F = Gary. *A dead end, but it didn't hurt to keep the Russians hoping.*

It was Johnny's last entry, though, that gave him the most hope. It was his newest recruit, and the future of his network:
S = Mike.

33

$\mathbf{M}$ike was watching. Mike was waiting. Mike was ready. Just as his father told him he would be.

Four months ago, after he had come back from his shakedown cruise aboard the carrier *America,* something made Mike mention to his dad that he had seen his first classified document. He was just making conversation, the two of them shooting the bull over a beer, but he had this feeling his dad would be interested. Johnny was. Not that Mike saw him jump up or give a shout or anything. He simply told his boy, "Yeah, there's a lot of jobs in the Navy that require clearance." Yet Mike could tell his dad was pretty pleased. Sons know that about their fathers.

Still, it wasn't until about a month later, in July 1983, that Johnny told Mike what was on his mind. They were sitting in Johnny's den, and that made Mike feel good to begin with; the den, after all, had always been his dad's "inner sanctum." Just sitting there, talking man to man, meant Mike, the not quite twenty-one-year-old yeoman, was a grown-up. Mike was going on about how this fire-breathing chief was really on his case; though, of course, the point of the story was not so much to complain but to show his dad he really was a sailor, he really lived in a world where there were chief petty officers, and most of all, he really wasn't a kid. Mike kept up his moaning about his job at the Oceana Naval Air Station down in Virginia Beach, how it was mostly clerical crap, typing memos, handling the registered mail, things like that. But he did have a secret clearance, and that was a kick. In fact, he told his dad, he was kind of surprised he had been cleared without a hassle; when he first signed on, the Navy had come down hard because the preinduction physical had shown enough "unauthorized substances" in his bloodstream to get the lab technicians high. "I sure cleaned up my act pronto," he insisted. Though he didn't really have much of a choice. Hell, he moaned to his dad, you can't even afford good grass on a yeoman's pay. That's when Johnny, sitting in his leatherette swivel chair, leaned across his desk and said, "Well, I can pay you if you deliver classified material to me from your work space."

It just came out. It was like when Mike learned about sex for the first time. He always somehow knew it was out there, it was just that the details were never too clear. Then when he found out everything, it made a whole lot of things fall into place.

Mike never really had to say yes or no; Johnny took it for granted that his son would go along with him, and he was right. So it wasn't much later that, without much fuss, the training sessions began. Father and son would huddle in Johnny's "workroom," one of the girl's old bedrooms on the second floor. First week was the Minox drill. Johnny would spread out a long row of papers; and, in his warrant officer's voice, he'd explain to his recruit how the camera had to be held precisely eighteen inches from the object to be photographed, and how the film speed should be set at 110. Then he'd make Mike, never too good with his hands and even worse with his dad hanging over him, try it. It took a lot of trying. The "scenarios," as Johnny called them, went a lot better. Johnny would play the officer and Mike the young spy. "Sailor," Johnny's voice would boom, "what are you doing with those documents? They're classified." Mike, who had inherited the talent, would put on an innocent face and find a confident manner and launch without a moment's hesitation into a fallback story about how he must have forgot, or how he was on his way to the burn bag, or how he was sorry, sir, he was just about to take them to the chief. Other times, Johnny would pass on stray bits of knowledge, and he spoke with such authority that Mike knew his dad could only be talking from hard-won experience. "You always got to listen," he'd tell his son. "No matter what you're doing, you got to be able to hear footsteps." Then, almost on tiptoes, Johnny'd walk across the room and Mike, keyed to the noise, would swear that he was hearing the pounding beats of a kettle drum. Johnny also lectured Mike about patience. "Every time the chief goes to the safe, catch a number. It'll take time, but in a week you'll have the entire combination. Just don't rush things." And so the training went, one generation passing the family business on to the next.

Then, all of a sudden, it was December and Mike was at his desk in hangar 200 and the time had finally come to become his father's son. He listened. He waited. He watched. His father hadn't told him about the squadron of F-14s that would be going through a landing drill in his belly. His father hadn't told him that his shirt would become a river of sweat. But his father said that for all spies, for all men actually, there was a moment when you either had to do it—take the leap, or live forever with being a coward. Either you had the guts, or you didn't.

So Mike did it. He reached into the burn bag and pulled out a thick document. He didn't look at it too carefully. But it was stamped SECRET across the top of the page and beneath that there was a picture of a jet plane. He held it in his hand for a second as though he were waiting for it to explode. He looked up and the chief was still jabbering away on the phone. That wasn't an M-16 spraying him; the admin officer was only typing up his latest memo. Alarm bells hadn't gone off. And since he was this far along, Mike, trying to be cool, which was difficult since his hands were greased in sweat, stuffed the document under his jacket. He knew he looked like he had gained a hundred pounds, but as he walked out of the office no one seemed to notice. Twenty yards to his truck. Then five yards. He started the engine, and no one stopped him. Wave to the guard at the gate, his dad had told him. But don't overdo it; not too friendly, don't want him to think you're a homo. Mike, though, forgot about the wave. Eyes straight ahead, the document under his jacket scalding his chest, he drove through the gate. No one cried "Halt." There were no rifle shots. Nothing. Yet it wasn't until he turned onto Princess Anne Road that he realized he was home free. All right! Far fucking out! So he popped a cassette into the tape deck, turned the volume all the way to the right, and as the music blasted through the little yellow truck he was certain the Ramones were singing just for him.

In twenty minutes he was in the den on Old Ocean View Road. Johnny bolted the door and Mike handed him the stolen document. His father looked at it and said it was good. "Took a lot of guts," Johnny acknowledged.

At last Mike was a man. He was also his father's son. And he was a spy.

Mike got married just about a week later. Rachel made all the arrangements. It was one more secret.

When Mike had gone off to boot camp, Rachel thought she would never survive. It didn't get any easier after he was based back in Norfolk, but shipping off to sea all the time. There was no point to anything unless she was with Mike. She had to know that they would be together forever. When she told Mike she wanted to get married, he said he felt the same way.

She tried easing into the subject with her dad. "Wait till you finish school," he told her. But that was more than a year off. "You can either give me a ceremony, or you can give me a hard time," she told him. "Only don't be surprised if you come home one day and I'm moved out." Her father said, "Don't you dare, young lady."

Mike didn't get much further with his dad. "What do you want to do that for?" Johnny asked. "You screw women, you don't marry them."

But on a Sunday two weeks before Christmas, December 10, 1983, Mike and Rachel went to a justice of the peace in Sandbridge. Rachel had waited tables Saturday night at Chi-Chi's, a Mexican place, so she would have enough to pay for the ceremony. On Sunday morning, a wet, cold, nasty day, Mike went surfing while Rachel sat in his truck and watched. When he came out of the water, they started drinking champagne; Rachel had been sure to buy three bottles the night before because she knew the liquor stores would be closed on her wedding day. After they finished the third bottle, Rachel asked

Mike, "You sure?" "Positive," he shot back. So they went and did it.

That night they moved into an apartment near the beach that Rachel had rented a couple of days before. A mattress was their only furniture.

"This is all I ever wanted," Rachel told her husband.

"Hey," said Mike, "a stereo wouldn't be half bad."

They put off seeing their parents till Christmas. When Rachel had first called her dad and told him, he had hung up the phone. But on Christmas he gave them $100 and said he knew everything was going to work out. Johnny gave them $50 and a popcorn popper. "Welcome to the family," he told Rachel.

34

Payday was coming! All the spies were excited.
Mike, who had his heart set on a new Subaru wagon with four-wheel drive so he and his tri-fin board could plow straight across the beach to the ocean's edge, was really keyed. He had been a spy now for almost four months and had made a half-dozen dives; the last time around he had even dared to have a go at the safe. "No guts, no glory," his dad snapped at him after Mike had admitted he was finding excuses, so of course after that there was no chickening out. Still, it had taken him nearly a week of watching to get all the numbers in the combination, and then when he finally spun the dial, he was shaking like some pimply Ryan sophomore about to pay $10 to lose his cherry. He had to run through the whole thing three times before he got it right. The moment he heard the safe *click!* open, he damn near had a cow. He had earned his Subaru, all right. So on April 14, 1984—the day before he knew his dad was going to pick up the money—Mike put in a call to his handler.

"Hey, guy," he asked, "everything all set? the money coming tomorrow?"

Johnny exploded: "We don't talk about this on the phone. Ever."
Then he slammed the receiver down so hard that Mike was sure it had
cracked in two.

Johnny's mood, no doubt, wasn't helped by the fact that his son
wasn't the only spy eager to count his money. Jerry Whitworth was
in town and he was expecting a windfall. Jer, though retired, had not
been paid for the last fifteen months, a period stretching back to his
tour at Alameda. The way he figured it, the KGB owed him at least
$60,000.

But Jer, knowing the way to Johnny's heart, hadn't simply shown
up in Norfolk empty-handed. He had reshot the first third of his haul
from the *Enterprise* and brought the film along with him. "No chance
these are fogged," he assured Johnny. Though, despite all the room
Johnny was giving him, he wouldn't admit that he had purposefully
bungled the shooting the first time around.

"Let's just drop it," Johnny said at last. He wasn't sure he could
pull off a part where he had to huff and puff because someone was
lying.

Anyway, he went on graciously, that was in the past. Or so Johnny
promptly agreed once Jerry volunteered that he had come prepared to
discuss the future.

Jerry, who loved to tug on his beard and mull things over, had spent
a lot of time thinking about what he was going to do now that he was
out of the service. He had traveled across country to Norfolk by train
and, very Navy, had used the solitary time to line up his options like
so many steps in an Op Order. Becoming a stockbroker, he announced, was last week's idea. His new thoughts—plans that came to
him as houses and farms and fields flashed by his window like the
rapid heartbeat of America—were jotted down on the back of his
Amtrak ticket. Now, sitting on the familiar ladder-back chair in Johnny's den, he took the ticket from his pocket and, with a military
cadence, began to read:

One (Jerry was lost if he couldn't do things by the numbers). Get a
civil service job.

Two. Get a position at NCS Stockton hopefully in near future. Most
likely that would be a GS 5/6 crypto operator in the tech control
division.

Three. Also I will check out the Air Force in satellite area.

Four. I plan to make myself known to a large segment of government and civilian organizations just to see what is out there. An example: CIA.

Five. Brenda's situation. Graduates December '84 (Ph. D.). I'm committed to giving her first option on location (within reason); consequently where we go from Davis is unknown at present.

Six. In sum: There are a lot of ifs but I won't bite off my nose.

When Jerry finished reading, he looked across at Johnny expecting to see a big, pleased grin. He was disappointed. All this good news was too good. It was exactly what Johnny wanted to hear. And that's what bothered Johnny. He had fallen for this hopeful line before— only to get screwed. Johnny hadn't forgotten that sitting opposite him was the same sneak who had slipped him fogged film to pass on to the KGB and who had retired without any warning.

But Johnny, as always, kept his true thoughts to himself. He told Jer, "They all sound pretty good to me. I'll pass it on to my friends at the drop tomorrow. They'll be glad to know they can count on your getting back to business." Yet Johnny, the disillusioned spymaster, knew all he could count on Jerry to be was wishy one day and washy the next. It was a real pain.

That's why when payday came, Johnny had to laugh.

Mike was the first person he let in on the joke. On April 16, just back from Maryland, he called up his son and told him to come on by the house.

When Mike got there, Johnny told him to take a seat at the kitchen table. They had a cup of coffee, a little father-and-son chitchat about married life, and then it was business. The den was off limits this morning; Johnny explained it was filled with papers from the drop site that didn't concern Mike. Mike gave a small nod, but in his mind he was sure of one thing—the den was stuffed with money. And his imagination raced a little quicker after Johnny disappeared only to return with a stack of twenties.

Johnny counted off fifty of the bills and passed them to his son. "Your share. A thousand dollars."

Mike held the fortune in his hand. A red Subaru, that would be bitchin', he told himself.

Johnny, no stranger to greed, didn't miss the glow in his boy's eyes. "Be careful with your money. Don't blow it."

Mike, excited, told him how he was going to make a down payment on a car.

"Well," Johnny said, "you gonna have to earn a lot more money if you want to pay off that car. So maybe it's time I teach you how this business is run. Let me show you something."

Johnny retreated to the den and this time came back with a piece of paper. He put the page on the kitchen table, but he made sure to cover most of it with his hands.

"Just read this part here," he instructed his son.

In between Johnny's spread hands, a single sentence was exposed. It had been printed by a dot matrix computer. Mike read:

"S: Photographs were good. This man receives $1,000."

"That's you," Johnny told his son the secret agent.

This is real cool, Mike thought: I have a code name.

But Johnny, grim, went on. "This is what happens when you screw up." He revealed another paragraph of the letter to Mike:

"D: The photographs were bad. This man receives no money."

"Let this be a lesson," Johnny preached; "you only get paid for what you steal."

He was the wise father passing on the secret of his success.

Jerry had a fit. He ranted. He cursed. He bellowed.

"It's not fair," he kept repeating. "Not fair."

Johnny agreed; what did he have to lose?

"I deserved to be paid," he moaned. "You got to tell them that."

Johnny agreed to that too; it didn't cost him anything.

But Jerry, rarely insistent, wanted Johnny to promise that he would argue his case. "When's the next drop?" he asked.

"January," Johnny admitted. Though he would never think of telling Jerry it was in Vienna.

"Well, you have to tell them all I've done," Jerry hounded. "All I got off the *Enterprise*." And just to make sure Johnny would know what to say, he wrote it out on a piece of lined paper. It was a short brief:

"I got *all* 'S' [Secret] & above & important 'C' [Confidential] GEN-SER [General Service] TFC [traffic] of the 12 mos."

Johnny read the page and, nothing if not a born salesman, beefed up the argument. He wrote:

"Pic of new device—roll dispenser.

Includes flag, Battle Force Cdr. [Commander]"

He promised his old agent that the pictures Jerry had of the new NSA roll dispenser for crypto material would be a real strong selling point.

"They were just playing with you," Johnny said. "Getting back at you for fogging up the film the last time. I'm sure they'll pay you." But the truth was, he had no idea how Ivan the Terrible would respond. It might even serve Jerry right if he got stiffed. Anyway, it really wasn't his problem.

Jerry's anger was building. All the way across country, as the train moved closer to California, as the width of the entire country spread between him and his ex-best friend, his temper seemed to fan out too. He brooded and brooded till he was ill with despair. He couldn't forget and he couldn't forgive. It was the unfairness of it all, that's what was really working him into a state. He had been loyal—to them, at least—and how did they repay him? With nothing! Zero! When he was owed $60,000, money that was going to buy Brenda's and his future. He could not understand their betrayal. It broke his heart. And his rage might just as well have sprung from jealousy it was that wild, that self-righteous, that wounded, until—

He decided to get back at them.

On May 7, three high-pitched weeks after his trip to Norfolk, he waited till Brenda went off to classes and then sat himself at his Formica desk in the rear of the trailer. He put a blank page into the IBM Selectric and, at last, began to type:

Dear Sir:

I have been involved in espionage for several years, specifically I've passed along Top Secret Cryptographic Key Lists for military communications, Tech manuals for same, and etc.

I didn't know that the info was being passed to the USSR until after I had been involved a few years and since then I've been remorseful and wished to be free. Finally I've decided to stop supplying material—my contact doesn't know of my decision. Originally I was told I couldn't get out without approval, this was accompanied with threats. Since then I believe the threats were a bluff.

At any rate the reason for this letter is to give you (FBI) an opportunity to break what probably is a significant espionage system. (I know that my contact has recruited at least three other members that are actively supplying highly classified material.) (I have the confidence of my contact.)

I pass the material to my contact (a US citizen) who in turn passes the material to a contact overseas (his actual status—KGB or whatever—I don't know). That is not always the case tho, sometimes US locations are used. A US location is always used to receive instructions and money.

If you are interested in this matter you can signal me with an Ad in the Los Angeles Times Classified Section under "Personal Messages (1225)." What I would expect to cooperate is *complete immunity* from prosecution and absolutely no public disclosure of me or my identity. I will look for an Ad in *Monday editions only* for the next four weeks. Also, I would desire some expense funds depending on the degree that my livelihood is interrupted.

The Ad: Start with "RUS:", followed by whatever message you desire to pass. If your message is not clear I'll send another letter. If I decide to cooperate you will hear from me via an attorney. Otherwise nothing further will happen.

Sincerely,

RUS

Jerry, a remorseful D and now a hopeful RUS, then took the letter to be photocopied. That way it would be harder to trace; he had learned quite a lot from nine years in the field. When this was done, he drove to Sacramento—the postmark would be a false clue; more tradecraft—and mailed the letter. It was addressed to:

Agent in Charge
FBI
450 Golden Gate Ave.
San Francisco, CA 94118

On Monday, May 21, just above the instructions to "Go, CHI-CAGO CUBS, go!" a three-line message appeared in the Personal Announcements section of the *Los Angeles Times:*

RUS: Considering your offer.
Call weekdays 9 a.m.–11 a.m. 415/
626-2793 or write ME, SF.

The number reached a newly installed phone in the office of John Peterson, a special agent assigned to the Soviet Section of the FBI. His phone never rang.

RUS, so like Jerry, sent two letters that summer promising to "come clean," but sentiment came easier than action. The FBI, though, remained eager:

"RUS: Haven't heard from you, still want to meet. Propose meeting in Ensenada, Mexico, a neutral site. If you need travel funds, we'll furnish some at your choice location in Silicon Valley or anywhere else. Please respond to the above."

Yet it was on the same August Monday the FBI's proposal appeared in the *Los Angeles Times* that, across the country in Virginia Beach, the secret was also being threatened. Someone else was convinced she had been treated unfairly. Someone else wanted money.

Barbara Walker had been drinking. When she couldn't find any vodka in her daughter-in-law's apartment, she made do with the Triple Sec. It was a full bottle and soon the clear liquid was level with the top of the label. The liquor gave her conviction.

"Rachel," she ordered her daughter-in-law, "I want you to drive me to the Federal Building downtown."

"Come on, Barb . . ."

It had been that kind of week for Rachel. Barb, in town for a vacation and to get to know her new daughter-in-law better, had seemed
fine at first, real upbeat; earlier that summer she and Cynthia had
moved from Maine to Cape Cod and that seemed to have helped her
mood. Then someone, maybe it was Margaret, had to let it slip out
that Johnny was shacking up with a twenty-four-year-old blonde. It
went downhill from there. Fast.

One afternoon Barb, really in her cups, kept repeating, "I'm just
afraid of what's going to happen, so afraid." Rachel, her patience
tattered by now, shot back, "Just spit it out, okay?"

So Barbara did: "John is a spy. He's been hurting you and he's
been hurting me."

"Sure thing," said Rachel. When she happened to mention it to her
husband, Mike said, "Yeah, Mom should really write for Hollywood."

And now, two days later, she wanted to go to the Federal Building.
Rachel didn't know what to do with her. Rachel was glad when Barb,
just like that, changed her mind. "I'm going to Johnny's office," she
announced.

Barb, as determined as any boxer climbing into the ring, marched
into the offices of Confidential Reports and demanded to see Johnny
Walker.

"Let me check if he's free," Laurie Robinson told her.

So Barbara slapped Laurie across the face and, all in one swift
motion it seemed, continued down the hall to her ex-husband.

As soon as she saw Johnny, she started screaming. Everybody
could hear it.

"You owe me alimony," she insisted. "I want ten thousand dollars."

"Tone it down," Johnny advised.

But she didn't. She kept on threatening to "tell everything," to
"tell it all," unless Johnny gave her what she was owed. "Ten thousand," Barb repeated. "Alimony."

Johnny, who had been there before, just let her run. It wasn't until
her hand was wildly played that he took over.

"You don't want to do it, you don't want to do it," he said as if he were reciting a prayer. "Too much is at stake for the entire family. You wouldn't do it to your children." His final warning came out almost as a whisper; after all the thick noise the four soft words seemed to float one by one in the air: "Think of your children," he said.

She did, and she surrendered. When Barb left the office, both Johnny and she were convinced the secret was invulnerable.

RUS agreed. He wrote his last letter to the FBI during the week that Barbara returned to Cape Cod:

". . . Since my last note to you I've done a lot of serious thinking and have pretty much come to the conclusion that it would be best to give up the idea of aiding in the termination of the espionage ring previously discussed."

35

T hen, just when the FBI had given up hope of finding RUS, when Jerry had returned to thoughts about getting a job with the CIA, and when Barbara was convinced the secret would never be revealed, the prodigal daughter returned. Laura, after sixteen months of hiding, after losing her child and finding God, called her mother and asked for help.

Barbara had spent the day—November 23, 1984—unloading trucks. From 6:30 that morning till her shift ended at 2:30, she had been working the loading dock at The Christmas Tree Shop. It was, she decided, a hell of a way to spend her forty-seventh birthday.

She wasn't one to whine, but that day she was really low. The work was hard, November was the busy season, and it all, especially on her birthday, seemed a rotten deal. She had grown up dirt-poor, white-trash Johnny, damn him, had always sneered, and now after nearly a half-century of chasing around the country and raising four kids, she had come full circle: a gray-haired grandmother stranded in a windswept tourist town lifting crates for $3.50 an hour.

She had paid a hell of a price for keeping the secret. No doubt about that.

When she clocked out at the close of her shift, her arms ached. There was this tingling line of pain, starting at her waist and heading toward her biceps, that she would get by the end of each day. She trudged down narrow Main Street in West Dennis, the town bundled up in the heavy gray of a Cape Cod winter, thinking about a long, hot bath. And, of course, a birthday cocktail.

The top-floor apartment she shared with Cynthia and Tommy, now seven, was on the wrong end of town, too far away to see or even hear the ocean. The downstairs of the white stucco building was occupied by The Word, A Christian bookstore. They were friendly people and Barb, still a country girl, liked that. She threw them a wave as she climbed the stairs.

The bath was a bit of hope, but the first vodka and water was salvation. Things were once again possible.

Cynthia prepared dinner. The chicken was overcooked and dry. For dessert, though, there was a cupcake—strawberry icing, Barb's favorite—with a candle stuck in its middle. Cynthia made a big deal, turning out the lights as she brought it in. Tommy sang, "Happy birthday, dear Grandma . . ." I'll drink to that, Barb decided. So she did.

After dinner, everything mellow, Barb was sitting in the living room listening to Tommy practicing the violin, when the phone rang.

It was Laura.

Out of the blue. The last person she ever expected.

"Help me, Momma," Laura begged.

She was calling from Fredonia, New York. She was attending Peter Piccolo's School of Hair Design in nearby Buffalo. And, in the past sixteen months, she had found God. God had heard her cries and saw her tears. God had told her the time had come to regain custody of her son Chris.

"Help me, Momma," Laura begged again before hanging up. "You've got to make a choice."

Barbara poured another two inches of vodka and looked at the phone. It was a long night.

In the end, the future won out: Her hopes for her grandchild, for the life he could have ahead of him, made her previous fears seem like wasted promises.

"Operator," Barbara said into the phone, "can you give me the number for the FBI in Boston?"

She was filled with a decisive joy as she dialed. Try to get the story straight, to start at the beginning, she lectured herself. The number was ringing. She wanted to be formal, careful. She hoped the liquor wouldn't sneak up on her.

"FBI," announced the voice on the other end.

"I want to report something," said Barbara.

". . . Yes?"

A moment. Then another. Finally—

"I want you to know my ex-husband is a spy."

PART V

WINDFLYER

36

On January 7, 1983, the Soviet embassy in Washington submitted a DS-1497 notice to the State Department's Office of Protocol. The form was a "Notification of Appointment of Foreign Diplomatic Officer."

Three days earlier, according to the information on the DS-1497, Aleksey Gavrilovich Tkachenko had arrived at John F. Kennedy International Airport in New York. He was thirty-eight years old, a native of Moscow, and for the past five years had worked in the Soviet Union for the Ministry of Foreign Affairs. He was now assigned to the Soviet embassy in Washington. His title was third secretary.

When his wife and children arrived a week later, an additional form was filed with the Office of Protocol. His wife, Olga, was thirty-five and would be working at the Soviet embassy as a secretary. There were two daughters, Oksana, twelve, and Masha, six.

Copies of the DS-1497 forms were sent to the FBI. The Washington Field Office's CI-2 squad immediately instituted routine surveillance on the new diplomat and his wife.

The couple took an apartment in the Hamlet Hill development in Alexandria, Virginia. They paid $520 a month for two bedrooms. The Soviet Mission rented the furniture. It was bulky and rococo and finished in a plastic grained to resemble mahogany. Burnt orange wall-to-wall carpet already covered the living room. The Tkachenkos added a few touches to give the narrow, low-ceilinged rooms a homey feeling: Above Masha's bed was a crayon rainbow she had drawn, and on the hall mirror a blue-and-white bumper sticker was fixed at a jaunty slant. The bumper sticker read, PRESIDENT REAGAN—BRINGING AMERICA BACK.

The CI-2 watchers decided electronic surveillance of the apartment was unnecessary. After months of looking at the new diplomat they had found nothing worth pursuing. His desk at the embassy was in Siberia, far off from the crowd of KGB residency spooks on the top floor. He didn't do any talent spotting; there were no reports of his showing up at local colleges to use the libraries, or ever finding the urge for a beer in a bar down the road from a military base, or calling up a left-wing journalist to talk about détente. And he certainly wasn't a pavement artist, one of the small army of low-level hoods who used diplomatic cover in between working backup on mainstream residency operations.

The most the watchers could come up with on Aleksey Tkachenko was his look—he had the look of a soldier. For a Russian serving on the embassy circuit, a tour where the nightly rations often were foie gras, Beluga caviar, and iced Stolichnaya, he was surprisingly fit. He had the build and heft of a man who made an effort to stay in shape. Then there was his hair. None of that long sideburned, East European hipster look some of the Ivans affect once they come to swinging America. Tkachenko had the close-cropped brown hair of a soldier.

Big deal, the watchers ultimately decided. Since when is good taste a crime? Did any Russian who jogged have to be a Moscow Center hood? The final verdict about Tkachenko was that, amazingly enough, he was what he claimed to be—a diplomat. His file was graded Persil: (after the popular German detergent): investigated in depth, but found to be of no intelligence value.

This was a mistake. Aleksey Gavrilovich Tkachenko was a Department 16 operative. He had been trained at the Surveillance College in Leningrad, and now he had been sent to Washington to serve as a

handling officer. His job was to choose drop sites, write up procedures, deliver cash, and retrieve products for shipment. He was the
postman for the most significant espionage operation the KGB had
ever run in America. His asset was John A. Walker, Jr.

37

It was the one thing Barbara never expected. After she had made the call, she decided there was no point in going to sleep. She was certain the FBI, lights flashing, brakes screeching, would soon be pulling up to her house. She prepared herself, rehearsing what she would say, how she would act. When no one had knocked on her door by six that morning, she realized she was being silly: The FBI had more important things to do than question her— they were off in Norfolk arresting Johnny and Art. She might as well go to work; they'd come for her at The Christmas Tree Shop. When her shift was over and the FBI still had not shown, she rushed to buy an afternoon paper. In her mind she read the screaming headlines: SPY RING BUSTED; EX-WIFE SAVES NATION. There wasn't a line.

That night she sat on the edge of the flowery couch, a vodka and water in one hand as if for balance, and leaned toward the TV. She followed every word from Tom Brokaw's lips. He, too, seemed totally unaware that last night she had done something extraordinary. Barbara couldn't believe it. Throughout the sixteen years she had struggled to find the will to make that call, she had tortured herself with grim visions of the inevitable consequences—the men she loved in handcuffs; or there would be a shootout, Johnny, his .38 blazing, refusing to surrender without a fight; or Art, whipped by guilt, would simply reach for a bottle of sleeping pills. But in all her wild and despairing dreams, she had never imagined that this would happen— Nothing. It made no sense. In desperation and confusion, she called Laura.

"I've turned your father in," she announced as soon as her daughter answered the phone.

Laura was stunned. There was no relief, only excitement.

"I've called the FBI and turned your father in," Barbara repeated. "I did it for you, so you could get Chris."

The FBI, Barbara went on, would probably soon be calling; she had given them Laura's number. Though, Barbara admitted, for all she knew the G-men might decide to swoop down on the spies first; the safety of the country, after all, was at stake. Just make sure you listen to the news tomorrow, Barbara advised her daughter. In the meantime, she said, all we can do is get ready.

So that night, November 24, 1984, two women, one a loading-dock worker at The Christmas Tree Shop, the other a student at Peter Piccolo's School of Hair Design, prepared themselves for the role they would play in putting an end to a KGB spy ring. They waited for the FBI to call. And they waited.

It wasn't until eleven days later that the FBI got around to calling Barbara. Agent Walter Price of the Hyannis Field Office asked if he could come by.

"I'm waiting," Barb barked into the phone.

When he got to the apartment above The Word bookstore on the evening of December 5, he found that Mrs. Walker had been waiting with a bottle of vodka. Or at least what was left of it. Well, he thought as he took out his notebook, we're off to the races tonight.

"You get to speak to a lot of kooks in this business," he would later recall, hinting at his mood as the interview continued. "Everybody's got some crazy story to tell the FBI. But it's our job, so you listen.

"I sat there taking notes, and she sat there talking and drinking. And I remember thinking she sure got a lot of details, and she does sound pretty intelligent. But no, I don't think I was convinced she was telling the truth."

The next day, though, he typed a 302 report. He had been an agent for fifteen years and despite what he was certain was an off-the-wall tale about picking up garbage bags full of cash in the Maryland woods, discipline prevailed. His report detailed, point by crazy point, all of Mrs. Walker's allegations.

At the bottom of the page he typed in the file designation—65–0. The "65" signified it was an espionage report. The "0" meant nothing in the interview required further investigation.

The report arrived in the Boston Field Office two days later. It was placed in the Zero File.

Barbara and Laura still waited. Their fears were leaping all over the place. It was very rough going.

"Maybe they thought I was crazy," Barb tried out on her daughter. With genuine embarrassment, she admitted that perhaps she had had a drink or two the night the FBI came by; to calm herself, she explained. Maybe, Barb suggested, Laura should call Agent Price. It couldn't hurt.

All through Christmas and into the New Year, Laura thought about calling the FBI. It was one thing to urge her mother to turn in her father; it was another to pick up the phone and do it. She also thought about Chris, and about what Christmas had been like without him. At last, on January 24, 1985, she called.

The night she decided to make the call had not been a good one to begin with. Laura was having man trouble. She had just moved to Buffalo and the guy whose house she was living in was acting weird. Real supermacho, saying how it was his house, his furniture. Laura knew he was falling in love with her, but she wanted no part of a setup like that. The thing was, she had no money, no place to go, so she had to make do. She'd put in a hectic day doing rinse jobs at Peter Piccolo's only to come home to some guy who was trying to jump her. It was too much. And now she had to call the FBI.

Yet, she managed to make the call. She actually had Agent Price on the line and she could hear herself saying that her father was a traitor. But in the middle of the most difficult conversation of her life, the guy she was living with came into the kitchen and started yelling at her. Right while she was on the phone with the FBI. How could anyone have expected her to keep things straight? Worse, when she called Barb and said she didn't think it had gone too well with Price, her mom started dumping on her, too. Laura just burst into tears. She was so stressed out she wanted to die.

Things were just hanging in the air, going nowhere.

In every well-oiled bureaucracy, however, there is always one more spin of the wheel, one more procedure in an infinite process. Eventually, the system, its supporters promise, will justify itself. Such in its own slow, cumbersome way was the case with the FBI.

In February a supervisor at the Boston Field Office was making the quarterly review of the Zero File. It was a grim chore. There was, as always, the usual collection of lost and desperate stories—the pensioner who hears Radio Moscow through his molars; the cleaning lady who's certain Martians have taken possession of her body. And now the interview with an alcoholic loading-dock worker at The Christmas Tree Shop who insisted that her husband, the private detective, was actually the head of a Soviet spy ring.

Yet, amazingly, the Boston supervisor saw something in the report Agent Price had filed. It wasn't so much any specific detail of Barbara Walker's story as the *totality* of the details. Crazies spin wide, vague stories that trail off into a sputter of hunches. They generally do not invent tales of clandestine exchanges made after completing a complicated, but precise route. He immediately sent a flash summary of Agent Price's 302 to Washington headquarters. As an afterthought, he also decided to route a copy of his summary to the Norfolk Field Office; Mrs. Walker had claimed her ex-husband was still living in the area.

The Washington Office ignored the flash from Boston. Norfolk did not.

The AIRTEL from Boston with a 65 designation arrived on the desk of Joseph Wolfinger. He had put in fifteen years with the bureau and since 1972 had specialized in FCI—foreign counterintelligence. For the past three years he had run the Norfolk office's eleven-man FCI squad.

He read the summary carefully. Where one agent saw a convoluted yarn about twists and turns in the woods he saw something else—textbook KGB tradecraft.

He reached for his phone.

On March 7, Special Agents Paul Culligan and Chuck Wagner from the Buffalo Field Office interviewed Laura Walker Snyder in her living room. She had just returned from beauty school and was still dressed in her uniform of black pants and white lab coat. Agent Wagner sat in an orange, velveteen armchair. Agent Culligan brought in a plastic-covered chair from the kitchen. Laura sat on a wooden coffee table; it was uncomfortable, but she was between the two men and that, somehow, was more important. She couldn't wait to begin. The agents had their notebooks open.

Just as she started to tell her story, the phone rang. No, she told the caller, she couldn't talk now. She'd have to call him back. He said that'd be impossible. He was leaving in the morning. Well, she said, it was just one of those things, but right now she was very busy. She hung up, and quickly went back to talking to the FBI.

She told the two agents all she could remember. She explained about her son; she recited her story about her husband's threats; and she described each of her father's attempts to recruit her.

This report was not placed in the Zero File.

Before the week was over, the FBI gave Barbara Walker a lie detector test. As the needle jumped with her every breath, she answered an hour's questions. It had all started, she said, in 1968. Her ex-husband was involved. Also her brother-in-law. Perhaps an old Navy buddy of John's on the West Coast. She doubted there was anyone else.

When the blood pressure cuff was removed and the examination was over, the agent turned to her and said, "You have difficulty dealing with lies, don't you?"

That was the story of my married life in a nutshell, she felt like telling him. Only now it didn't matter. She was free.

So, nearly four months after Barbara's birthday phone call, nearly seventeen years after she had first learned of her husband's treason, the FBI was finally on the trail of Johnny Walker.

The Norfolk FCI squad had been officially on the case for nearly a week when it occurred to them that the investigation needed a code name.

Bob Hunter, the special agent selected by Wolfinger to manage the day-to-day operations, came up with "Family Affair." "Can't say it doesn't fit," he tried.

The problem was, shot back Dave Szady, it fit too well. Might give the whole shooting match away if it leaked, he continued. And Szady had the final say. He had seniority; he normally worked out of Washington where he was in charge of coordinating FBI operations against Soviet military intelligence.

The squad of agents threw around other code names. It was a good game.

They were getting nowhere, though, until Szady suggested "Windflyer." Name of a horse I had one day at Bowie," he told them.

"How'd it run?" asked Hunter.

Szady answered, "In the money."

"Let's hope your luck holds," said Hunter.

In all the Operation Windflyer 302s, a file that in time would be nearly two yards high, there was no mention of the call Laura received in the midst of her first interview with the FBI. At the time, it didn't seem important to her, or to the agents. It was only later, after it was too late, that Laura recalled it was her brother Mike who had telephoned on that evening in March. He was leaving in the morning for a six-month Mediterranean cruise aboard the aircraft carrier *Nimitz*. It never occurred to Laura that the next time she would talk to her brother he would be in jail.

38

In the chill Norfolk dawn of March 8, 1985, Mike walked toward the gangplank of the *Nimitz* carrying his Canyon board under one arm and his duffle bag under the other. He was going to sea for 206 days and he was prepared. He had his surfboard because he had heard there were some killer waves hitting the coast of Israel. And he had his duffle because it was the easiest way to smuggle stolen documents off the carrier. The only thing was, he was in a real funk. That morning he and Rachel had another set-to. It was a hell of a way to leave things just as he was heading off for six months. But the girl simply refused to understand he didn't have much choice: His dad was pressing him.

Three weeks after his wedding, back in January of 1984, Mike was transferred from the fighter squadron based at Oceana in Virginia Beach to the *Nimitz*. He was made a departmental yeoman. That meant, basically, he was in charge of giving out the Ping-Pong balls in the rec room. It wasn't the sort of duty that brought smiles to his control.

But for Rachel the first eight months of her marriage were the happiest in her life. They moved from the beach and took an apartment on Hampshire Avenue in Norfolk. The rent was kind of high, $375 a month, so Rachel went off to work tables at Chi-Chi's after her classes. It was a busy time for both of them.

Still, they found time to walk hand in hand when Rachel would hurry to the carrier to catch her sailor on his meal break, cuddle in front of the TV with a bowl of popcorn for the late-night Chiller Thriller flick, and go roller skating in the park on Sundays. Then there was Sparky.

It hadn't taken Rachel long to start in on Mike about getting a dog. She told him she wanted something around when he was off at sea and, always very practical, a puppy seemed like a lot less hassle than a baby; besides, there'd be time for that. Mike was all for the idea. He wanted a beach dog, a black Lab that would run with him through the surf and catch a Frisbee in its mouth. Rachel had her heart set on a Dalmatian, a little black-and-white cutie like the ones in that Disney movie, *101 Dalmatians*. So they compromised. Sparky was a Dalmatian pup, but from the start Mike tied a paisley bandanna round its little neck and taught the dog not to be afraid of the water. They both loved the dog; Rachel even carried pictures of Sparky in her wallet. When Mike made the down payment on the red Subaru wagon with money he told his wife he had earned doing free-lance detective work for his dad, the couple figured they had everything in the world going for them. "All my life I was waiting to be happy, and then it had finally happened," Rachel remembered.

In September, just as the *Nimitz* was coming out of dry dock and heading off on a ten-day shakedown cruise, Mike's request for a change of duty was approved. He was transferred to the Administration Office in the carrier's Operations Department.

". . . I had daily access to classified documents," Mike would recall. ". . . I routinely handled messages regarding U.S. Navy exercises, ship coordinates, Navy operations, and Defense Intelligence Agency messages which contained mainly information about various countries in the world. The messages would come into my office on the MPDS [Message Process Distribution System] which was linked to the Communication Center on the ship . . . I also routed messages which contained information regarding U.S. tracking of Soviet submarines. I was responsible for routine messages and deciding who would get them. I was also responsible for deciding whether the messages were of any value or whether they should be thrown in the trash.''

It was so easy, there was so much to take, that he couldn't think of any real reason not to go back to work for his father. Anyway, there were thirty-seven payments due on the Subaru.

In his den one night during the week after Thanksgiving, Johnny sat at his Apple computer and inventoried his son's latest shipment of documents: Fleet Tactical Library Cover and Deception manual; Air Strike Operations; Surface Strike Operations; Planned Maintenance Subsystems; Countermeasure Set AN/SLQ-17; Nuclear Tomahawk Land Attack Cruise Missile (TALM-N); Force Management Plan; Nimitz Mediterranean Deployment Mid-Cruise Report; Anti-Ship Missile Defense (ASMD) Doctrine: Satellite Vulnerability; Electronic Warfare Countermeasures; Maintenance Instructions, *Nimitz*; Vulnerability Reports of Recon Satellites; Satellite Vulnerability CIN-CLANTFL; New U.S. Naval Mines; Destructor MK 36 and MK 40 Mines; Open Ocean Surface Threat Commander Tactical Wing Atlantic; and thirty-three Naval Intelligence flashes sent to the carrier.

I'm gonna have to get that boy a bigger duffle bag, he thought proudly.

Mike's captain, John Findley, Jr., was also pleased with the job the sailor was doing: "Seaman Walker is an outstanding, alert and bright yeoman striker. *Hard charging, completely dependable,* and unhesitant in the assumption of responsibility, he has willingly volunteered for additional duty and responsibilities . . . A *dynamic leader—self starter*. Exemplary in conduct . . . Seaman Walker is highly deserving of this 4.0 evaluation."

• • •

Only Rachel understood. The clues, like the soft, regular drip of blood from a wound, were unavoidable.

At first, though, she refused to let her mind follow the trail. In the fall of 1984 when she noticed a stack on the kitchen table of naval documents, the one on the top of the pile stamped CONFIDENTIAL, she asked her husband, "What's this all about?" It seemed odd; she had grown up a Navy brat and you pick up things along the way.

"Nothing," Mike snapped; and he might just as well have slammed on the brakes the way his tone and abruptness made her jump. He tried to apologize by adding breezily, "Just some stuff I need for work I'm doing with my father."

There were a lot of questions she could have asked—if she wanted to know the answers. So she tried, "Hamburgers okay for dinner?" For some reason, she suddenly wanted to believe it was the largest dilemma in their lives.

The next time was not so easy. Margaret and her new boyfriend, a Navy lieutenant, had come by the apartment. The lieutenant was heading to the john when something on the bedroom dresser caught his eye. It was a Navy publication. "Hey, Mike," he called out, "what the hell is this doing here?"

Rachel listened as Mike struggled: "It's . . . uh . . . uh . . . something I'm doing. For the chief. The chief knows. Yeah, he told me to work on it at home." Rachel realized she was praying Margaret's boyfriend would believe her husband; and, for the first time, she understood there was no reason he should.

"Well," the lieutenant, not ready to come down too hard on Maggie's brother, warned, "you shouldn't be doing this, Mike. You can get in big trouble, anyone catch you with this. You read me?"

"Yes," said Mike, "I read you."

I don't, Rachel lied to herself.

So everything had to wait until the morning when Rachel, putting together a wash, began to hunt through Mike's duffle for dirty skivvies. When Mike came home that evening, the wash had not been done and a wide circle of papers lay strewn across the bed.

"What have you been doing?" Mike cried out as if scalded. "This is none . . ."

Rachel, instantly weary, cut him off: "Tell me, Mike, please tell me." Yet she silently begged: Just don't tell me the truth.

Instead, he said, "Sit down, bunny, we have to talk."

Mike sat on the bed, near the papers. Rachel, eager to flee, kept marching across the room; but there were four walls, and anyway she was already trapped. Both of them were scared. They might as well have been talking about death.

"I can get busted for this," Mike began. "What I'm doing's illegal, but it's for my father," he explained with a son's logic. "It's part of his detective work. He's paying me for it."

Rachel begged her husband to give it up. "You'll get in trouble, Mike," she pleaded.

"I'm careful. I know what I'm doing."

"Mike, please . . ."

"Bunny, don't you understand, it's for my dad."

"Please, Mike. For me. Stop for me."

Neither one ever said the word "spy."

That night Rachel slept on the living room couch. She didn't want to be in the same bed as Mike. She had told him he would have to choose. "Who means more to you—your father or me?" she had challenged.

"It's not that simple, bunny."

"Choose, Mike," she had begged. Choose me. Choose us. Choose our life.

"Don't do this to me, bunny."

But she already had. And it was his choice, more than anything else, that hurt. It was, Rachel felt, his worst crime.

She got used to the couch.

It wasn't long before Rachel decided to get off the pill. They were sleeping apart more often than not so it seemed the right time. It was the sort of decision, though, Rachel felt she should share with her husband.

"Well, I don't want children," Mike said.

Now that he had come out and said it, Rachel agreed.

"I mean not just now, but never," said Mike.

His wife said, "That's exactly what I meant—never."

They gave each other all kinds of reasons, how in the Navy you can't be sure of your future assignments, how you're always moving, how both of them had come from broken Navy homes. Yet there was one reason, as if by unstated agreement, they refused to mention. It was, in fact, the only reason. All the rest were only so many excuses for why they never wanted the power and responsibility of being parents.

It was Mike's idea to have the vasectomy. Rachel understood immediately and agreed. The Navy doctors, however, were reluctant to perform the operation on a twenty-two-year-old sailor. What if you change your mind next week or next year? suggested the surgeon.

"I'll never want to be a father," Mike promised.

At twenty-two, married less than a year, Mike had a vasectomy. He would never be a father; and, more importantly he felt, he would never have a son.

The night before Mike shipped off on the *Nimitz,* Rachel brought it up again. Perhaps it was the sight of her husband packing his duffle that scared her; or perhaps she just knew what he was going off to sea to do.

"Promise me you won't do it anymore?" she asked.

"Bunny, I'm careful . . ."

"This could hurt us so, Mike . . ."

"I'm careful . . ."

"Don't you see, Mike, how dangerous this is?"

"Look, my dad knows how to take care of things. After this cruise I'll get out. I'll quit the Navy. We'll move to California. We'll get a house on the beach. You'll see . . ."

Her husband, the man she loved most in the world, was going away for six months and on their last night together Rachel slept on the couch.

· · ·

In the morning, Rachel drove Mike to the dock. They were hardly talking. Mike took his surfboard and his duffle out of the rear of the red station wagon.

"C'mon," he asked, "walk me to the ship."

"No."

He waited. At last he started walking off toward the carrier.

"Hope you have a nice cruise," she called out to him. "Maybe you'll even grow up."

Mike didn't turn around. He just kept walking, a short sailor weighed down by a surfboard under one arm and a duffle bag under the other.

Rachel watched him through her tears.

39

Mike, alone at sea, wrote to his wife nearly every day.

Dear Rachel,

Hello bunny, I love you. How are you today? Good I hope, things are just fine with me. We are underway again and steaming hard for the eastern side of the Med. We will operate in the area just north of Greece for about two weeks, and then in port Haifa.

I am looking forward to liberty there. I would love to catch a few waves. I miss surfing so bad. . . .

Anyway, I really had a good time in Toulon. I wish you were there to help me with my French. Communication was done in sign language. You would have loved the way they dressed. These people know how to punk out. I mean they have it on the States. I bought this radical yellow plaid jacket . . .

I guess you had a good time at the U2 concert. I wish I could have been there. I heard some U2 while I was in France and I got a little bummed out. I would just like to see you now with all your friends. Speaking of music, I was really surprised to hear the music they listened to there. I was in this little bar and they had a juke box with all the cool songs, Ultravox, U2, Oingo Boingo, etc. . . .

I met this guy the other day, he's from Arizona, not California, but he lived in LA for a while, anyway he is really cool. He doesn't act like a total idiot in front of people, sounds like he has a pretty decent girlfriend and he surfs. I think I am going to hang around with him during the cruise. . . .

I look forward to the day that I can hold you, I'm not talking about making love, just holding. I miss your touch something awful. I think that the first night we are together . . . we should just hug and kiss and save the more intimate things for another day. Do you get that feeling sometimes?

Well bunny, now that we are underway again I will be writing a little more. I kind of slacked off for a couple of days. Thinking of you often, I love you.

Michael

S also kept in communication with his control.

Jaws,

Hey guy, how are you doing? . . .

I asked you in my previous letter what I should do about the increasing amount of photos I have been acquiring. Do you have any suggestions? At the rate I am going I will have over a hundred pounds of souvenirs. I have run out of space and sooner or later I will have to weed out the ones that are not so important to me. Currently I have two boxes that weigh about 15 lbs. apiece. Looking for a little advice . . .

Would I be asking too much if I were to ask what the status is of my previous photos? I would like to know if they were developed yet, and if so how did they come out?

Not much more to write about. I will keep in touch.

Michael

. . .

After her husband had been at sea for a month, Rachel also took an alias. She called herself "Roxanne," same as the girl in the Police song who walked the streets for money. It was her dancing name, the name she used when she put on her Rambo outfit with the camouflage G-string and got on the runway at Donald's. That's how she met the guys from Elvis From Hell and went off with them to shoot their video.

Looking back at it all, Rachel would shake her head and say the whole thing was real low-life. But it was the quickest and easiest way she knew to make money. And at the time, nothing was more important than making money. If she could earn enough to meet Mike in Naples in June, she was sure the two of them, an ocean away from his father, would be able to work things out. Rachel had decided to talk tough to Mike. She would even threaten divorce. That would make him stop. She just needed to be alone with him, to thrash it all out before there was any real damage.

40

In Johnny's world, all was calm. Or so he thought. While Jerry considered resuming his role of RUS, while Barbara and Laura met with the FBI, while Rachel tried to convince Mike to end his cooperation, and while Art thought about putting a shotgun into his mouth, the ring's control believed things were going just great. In fact, Johnny had returned from his Vienna face-to-face in January 1985 full of triumph. And, given his narrow view of the dramas that were intersecting his complicated life, it was understandable: He had gone to the mat with his handler on two issues, and to his surprise, Johnny had won them both.

The first victory was actually one for Jerry. Johnny had argued his agent's case for compensation before the glum sidewalk court of Ivan the Terrible and the verdict was unequivocal. "Tell Jerry he will be paid. Make him understand," Ivan ruled, and he made sure to repeat his finding at least four times.

The other coup, though, was all Johnny's. The night of the meeting, January 19, was another bonechiller. The professional fieldman was decked out in his spy gear of parka, ski hat, gloves, scarf, boots, electric socks; and still Johnny was freezing. After more than a decade of shivering on the streets of Vienna, Johnny had plain had it. Look, he challenged the KGB man, this doesn't make sense. Don't you guys have a place nearby we can go to. This is insane.

Incredibly, Ivan the Terrible agreed. He told an amazed Johnny that now that you mention it, there has to be a better way of meeting than stomping around in the ice and snow. Perhaps, he said, their next meeting could be across the border in Czechoslovakia. Immediately Johnny's mind filled with a warm picture of a cozy safe house, fire burning, a plate of sausages on the table, and a bottle of schnapps for a thirsty spy.

"Yeah," said Johnny, "anything's got to be better than whispering in a goddamn blizzard."

The Department 16 agent concluded this first segment of the meet with the assurance that the procedures for the Czech face-to-face and Whitworth's money would both be left at the next drop in Maryland. And now having given (and given in), he also hoped to receive. He had two assignments for Johnny.

The first involved Johnny's daughter-in-law, Rachel. In his last "Dear Friend" letter, Johnny, always selling, had announced that Rachel was going to graduate with a science degree. Did Johnny think he could persuade Rachel to join the Navy?

There's a chance, said Johnny who was confident he could persuade anybody to do anything.

Well, the Russian continued, now as eager as any suitor rushing to make his intentions known, the plan at Moscow Center was for Johnny to try to place a member of his ring in the Navy's SOSUS research program. Rachel, with her science background, seemed like the perfect candidate.

"She might be at that," Johnny agreed. (Though, of course, he was unaware that this potential recruit was these days wearing a plastic pistol around her waist as she got funky on the runway at Donald's.) The prospect of a member of his ring—and a family member, to boot —involved in the Navy's submarine underwater detection system seemed like a real growth opportunity. "I'll talk to Rachel," he promised.

The KGB's other plot involved Art. Ivan the Terrible, in his long-winded, grave way, went through a detailed plan hatched in Moscow Center. It involved, the best Johnny could follow, some James Bond device the Soviet whiz kids would manufacture for Art. When Art, through his work at VSE, noticed that ships were suddenly being taken out of dry dock before their scheduled repairs were completed, he was to press the button on this electronic device on the double. Once the button was pressed, if Johnny was still tracking Ivan's story, an alarm would go off in KGBland: The United States is placing itself on a higher defense posture; war must be in the wind.

I'll try out the idea on Art, said Johnny. Though he felt like telling the Russian to make sure the device had only one button; two buttons would require more cooperation than his brother seemed willing to give these days. But, Johnny realized, there was no percentage in sharing that with Ivan.

As the face-to-face ended, the Department 16 control handed Johnny the procedures for the next drop in Maryland. He asked his asset, "It's set for the nineteenth of May. Should that be a problem?"

"Can't see why," said Johnny blindly.

When he returned to Norfolk, Johnny, who was still confident Jerry would soon be back in the ring, was quick to spread the good news. He, sticking to the photography word code he used with all his agents, wrote:

"Had a buyer for the photography equipment you asked me to sell. We haven't agreed on a price yet, but the age of the equipment will cause us to receive less than I had hoped. Also the fact that the accessories are no longer available will affect the outcome. . . . Anyway, I expect to get a final offer early summer, and we'll be in touch."

Dear Johnny,

. . . It was nice to hear from you . . . I was beginning to wonder if a jealous husband had given you the Goetz treatment (smile).

How am I really doing? I won't deny it, there have been many reflections on my decision to retire and subsequent decisions. And still, I can't say I'm entirely happy with the outcome. When it gets to the bottom line tho, I believe that once Brenda & I are into our new careers I'll be happy with my strategy and that it

will succeed. This period (Oct. 83 to now) has been rough on my
mental health at times. . . .

Take care.

Always,

Jerry

Which, Johnny decided, was typical Jerry: unhappy on the one
hand, and undecided on the other. Johnny, however, had no doubts
about the bottom line: As soon as the money ran out, Jerry would
come out of retirement.

Meanwhile, Johnny went on to his next bit of spy business. He
called his daughter-in-law.

He asked Rachel if she was interested in joining the Navy's SOSUS
program, never telling her, naturally, that the idea had originated in
Moscow Center.

Rachel agreed to drop off her résumé, never telling him, naturally,
that all she wanted to do after the long evening with the guys in Elvis
From Hell was get off the phone and go to bed.

And, while Johnny thought he was putting one over on Rachel, and
while Rachel believed she was humoring her father-in-law, a third
party was having the last laugh on both of them. The FBI was monitoring John Walker's phone.

Yet the FBI's investigation continued so secretly that only later was
Johnny able to understand the significance of two seemingly unrelated
incidents that spring. At the time, both events seemed simply odd—
which, Johnny had good reason to believe, was normal for the perpet-
ual chaos that was the condition of his life.

Out of the blue, Laura called him in April. Johnny was surprised.
He would have been even more surprised if he had known that before

making the call Laura had pushed the "record" button on a tape recorder provided by the FBI.

When the Windflyer agents heard the tape, they were disappointed. Laura, the new operative trying to catch an old one, had tried her best to hook her father. In a rapid-fire, almost screechy recital she had cast all her lines: She was thinking of getting a job in the Army reserves. Or perhaps at Eastman Kodak, which had a lot of defense contracts. Oh, Laura also added in a thunderously obvious afterthought, she forgot to mention she had taken a preemployment exam at the CIA.

Johnny, who had set enough traps in his time, knew something was up. He never imagined it was the FBI, but he did believe Laura had some scam going. Clearly enjoying himself, he danced around the bait. He talked with his daughter for fifty-five hectic minutes and in the entire transcript there wasn't one direct, incriminating admission of espionage. John Walker, the Windflyer team grumbled, had outsmarted them.

They were wrong. Buried in the last pages of the thick transcript was a small suggestion by Johnny. He told Laura that since she was living in Buffalo she should find the time to visit his favorite great-aunt. He was really fond of the woman, and he knew his daughter would be too. Why don't you go visit her? he urged.

The suggestion was dismissed by the FBI as irrelevant to the scope of their investigation. It was a corner of the transcript that, in those early weeks, was never underlined, never circled, never discussed.

At the time, the FBI was still wrapped up in trying to make its case.

So they enlisted another double agent.

When the Windflyer team first learned Barbara Walker was coming to Norfolk for Easter to visit Margaret, many of the agents felt the operation was as good as dead. If Laura with her freight-train subtlety hadn't already alerted her father, well then you could count on Barbara to finish things off. After a few pops, Barbara would probably tell her husband the FBI was waiting outside so would he please hurry and type up a confession.

But that was only one school of thought. Other agents, particularly

Bob Hunter, believed the ex-wife was the best way to throw Walker off the scent. If Walker suspected anyone of plotting against him, it had to be Barbara. If she could now convince him there was nothing to worry about, Windflyer could continue to build its case.

There was, however, one very large leap of faith in Hunter's plan: Barbara, a skittish actress who had a hard time following scripts, would have to give the performance of her life.

She did. Even in spite of the scare Johnny gave her.

Johnny took his ex-wife to McDonald's for dinner.

"If I didn't have to leave the Navy because of your threats," he told her between swallows of a Big Mac, "I could have made a million dollars more."

"Well," Barb said, "I would never have turned you in. I don't have the nerve." She delivered her lines precisely as they had been written.

And, also as had been planned, Johnny believed her because he needed to.

"I've talked to all the children except Margaret," Johnny continued. "They all agree you mustn't say anything." Barbara nodded; it was as if her ex were reading from the FBI's script. Then Johnny added, casually enough, "If you do, you would ruin Michael's career."

And suddenly, for one tense moment, the action seemed to be moving in a direction that neither Barbara nor the FBI had ever anticipated. *Michael?* Barbara's mind was close to screaming. *What have I done?* But, despite her panic, she found the inspiration to ad-lib, "Are you saying Mike's working for you?"

"No, no," Johnny quickly corrected her, "I'm not saying that at all. It's just that he's up for a secret clearance and if you say anything, you'll ruin his chances."

I can live with that, Barbara thought. Reassured, she returned to the script.

An hour later Johnny was driving Barbara back to Margaret's house. As he pulled into the driveway he turned toward his ex-wife and, grinning like a man who had survived a duel, told her, "I knew you wouldn't turn me in. I knew you wouldn't want to see your fifty-year-old husband in jail."

• • •

Perhaps distance, though, brings perspective. Mike was on an aircraft carrier heading toward Greece when he wrote his wife:

"You mentioned something about my mother coming down. Did everything go okay? I hope so. I received a tape from my father and he said she was down for Easter. Did you spend any time with her? I understand it was not a very good visit from my dad's point of view. My mother continues to ask for money. I get the feeling something is going to happen."

4I

There was, the Windflyer team realized, more than simply whim in Supervisor Dave Szady's decision to christen the operation with a racehorse's name. In every successful undercover investigation, as in every lucrative day of handicapping, the hours of preparation are endless. Research, surveillance, and plotting are, in both occupations, the stuff that gets you, tickets in hand, to the win window. Yet, a dicey fact of life in both the field house and the field office, all the homework in the world is nothing but good intentions coming into the stretch. Heading toward the wire, you need luck. And so far Windflyer had not been blessed.

After four months of living with Johnny Walker, after listening to his calls, and probing—discreetly, of course—into his life and career, the FBI had little to show. They could make the case the man was a sleazy private detective and a rotten father, but that was a long way from an espionage conviction. In all the hours of telephone transcripts, there had not been one admission of spying. In all the days and nights of watching, they still had not caught him in the act. Windflyer was near to breaking stride. Then the agents got lucky.

A death provided the break. On May 16, 1985, the FBI was listening as Johnny received a call announcing that his great-aunt in Buffalo had died. The funeral, Johnny was told, was on Sunday; when should they expect him to arrive? I can't, Johnny explained. I have business, important business, down in North Carolina on Sunday. I'm sorry, but there's no way I can get out of it.

A half-hour later, Johnny received another call. This relative really tore into him: What do you mean you can't come to the funeral? Your aunt was like a mother to you. You have to be there. Forget about your big deal business. Get someone else to take care of it.

Look, Johnny answered, and if he wasn't ashamed, he was doing a good job of acting, this business is something I simply can't postpone. Only I can take care of it. Any other day, you know I'd be there. But on Sunday I have to be in Charlotte.

When he hung up, the FBI had the clue they had been waiting for —only the agents didn't know it. It wasn't until later that afternoon when one of the surveillance team happened to mention the great-aunt's death to Bob Hunter that things began to fall into place.

"Just like Walker to flake out on going up to Buffalo for his great-aunt's funeral," the agent grumbled. Hunter thought about it for a moment; and then, with an unnerving rudeness that even caught himself by surprise, snapped, "No, it's not like him at all."

Ten minutes later the Windflyer team was rereading the transcript of Laura's call. And now they zeroed in on the small section where Johnny urged his daughter to visit his favorite aunt. The same great-aunt whose funeral he now was too busy to attend.

Must be pretty important business Walker has scheduled for Sunday, Joe Wolfinger, a cautious supervisor, tried out on Hunter.

But his agent was too excited to be coy: "Joe, it's finally coming down. Sunday is drop day."

In the meantime—four days that were an eternity—the FBI could only wait. Life, relentless, continued.

On Thursday, three days after she had graduated from Peter Piccolo's School of Hair Design, Laura made her escape from the apartment in Buffalo. The guy she had been living with had gotten out of control. The only way she could get him to back off was by going to bed with him. And that only bummed her out worse; she felt like a prostitute. So now, while he was at work, she was packing up and running away. She would move in with a friend, Marie Hammond. It was a six-hour drive to Marie's house in Canton and she couldn't wait to get on the road.

On Friday, Bob Hunter kept a long-standing appointment to address his son's government class at First Colonial Beach High School. He ended by telling the students that any day now they might be reading about one of his ongoing cases. Can't tell you about it yet, but when you see the headlines, you'll understand what I'm talking about.

Later that day, Johnny stopped by Art's house. He was lending his brother a 35-millimeter camera so Art could take pictures of his son's college graduation that weekend. Johnny gave his brother the camera and left. He didn't want to hang around because he knew Rita couldn't stand him.

On Saturday, Jerry Whitworth took his examination to become a securities trader. He had failed the test the first time, but he had his hopes for this go-around. Though he might have been a little jumpy if he had known FBI agents had him under twenty-four-hour surveillance. He had become a prime suspect in the Windflyer investigation. There were even some people in the San Francisco office who were certain Whitworth was also the mysterious RUS.

On Saturday, too, Johnny called Rachel. He apologized for not being able to attend her graduation from Old Dominion tomorrow, but he had important business out of town. Maybe he could make it up to her by giving a special graduation gift? Well, Rachel quickly leaped in, she was trying to get enough money together to visit Mike when the *Nimitz* docked in Naples next month. Could Johnny help her out? Her father-in-law said he'd see what he could do.

And that night, Johnny sat in his den and wrote a letter on his Apple computer:

Dear Friend,

This delivery consists of material from "S" and is similar to the previously supplied material. The quantity is limited, unfortunately, due to his operating schedule and increased security prior to deployment. His ship departed in early March, and they operated extensively just prior to deployment. The situation around him looks very good, and he is amassing a vast amount of material right now. His last correspondence indicated that he now has material that would fill two large grocery bags. Storage is becoming a problem. As is obvious, I did not make a trip to Europe to pick up material for this delivery.

His schedule does fit fairly well with our meeting, and I plan to meet him during a port call which will give me two days to make it to our meeting. I will arrange to pick up the best of his material and deliver it in bulk; photographing it on the road does not seem practical. . . .

"D" continues to be a puzzle. He is not happy but is still not ready to continue our "cooperation." Rather than try to analyze him for you, I have simply enclosed portions of two letters I've received. My guess? He is going to flop in the stockbroker field and can probably make a modest living in computer sales. He has become accustomed to the big spender lifestyle, and I don't believe he will adjust to living off his wife's income. He will attempt to renew cooperation within two years.

"F" has been transferred and is in a temporary situation giving him no access at all. He is having difficulty in making a career decision in the navy. He is not happy and is experiencing family pressure with our father who is 73 and in poor health. He married a younger woman who has a significant drinking problem. "F" feels obligated to support them. He may come around, and good access is possible.

"K" and I have discussed your proposal, and I will pass on some extensive details when we meet. Briefly, he is involved in carrier and amphibious ship maintenance planning. He would instantly recognize unrealistic schedules or see that ships were "off their normal schedules." This may provide a basis for information we seek. Otherwise, he has no useful material.

So I will see you as scheduled and hope I will make the Primary date with no problem. I'm sure you have access to S's port schedule and can anticipate my moves in advance. I am not providing his schedule in this note for the obvious reasons.

Good luck . . .

And then it was Sunday.

42

The day, more luck, broke with watcher's weather. It soon became a warm, bright May Sunday, the sort of pleasant, cloudless afternoon that was made for going places; and for following where people were going. The ground teams would have no trouble blending in with the caravans of Sunday drivers out celebrating a sunny day of rest. While 4,000 feet above, the single-engine surveillance plane would have perfect visibility. The only hitch was, Johnny Walker didn't seem to be going anywhere.

Early that morning of the nineteenth, there had been a false alarm. At just minutes after seven, at a time when most of his neighbors on Old Ocean View Road hadn't picked up the Sunday papers from their doorsteps, Johnny was bouncing out the door and heading toward his van. He was dressed in jeans and a blue golf shirt with a tiny alligator lounging across its left breast; on his feet were ripple-soled sneakers decorated with galloping kangaroos. As he hurried to his silver-and-blue Chevy Astro van, the word was passed to the watchers: Wake up, gentlemen. It's game time.

It wasn't. Johnny led them down Tidewater Drive straight to Mc-

Donald's. While Agent John Hodges banked his tiny plane into wide circles above the Golden Arches, the suspect had breakfast. Bob Hunter, a coffee in hand for cover, was close enough to see that his prey was gobbling an Egg McMuffin and hash browns; the agent, a jogger, had a brief, troubling flash that cholesterol would ambush Walker before he had his chance. But in a moment, looking none the worse for the meal, Hunter rejoiced, Johnny was heading to his van. The surveillance teams got ready, set, and then followed Johnny straight back to his driveway. He disappeared inside the house.

The watchers watched. Old Ocean View Road was waking up. Families were going off to church. Two hours later, the families returned. Soon barbecues were being lit, the smell of charcoal carrying through the clear spring air. Kids zipped along on their bikes. There was the constant thud of a baseball being thrown with determination into a mitt; a voice yelled, "C'mon, burn it in there." And Johnny hadn't budged. His house was silent. The curtains were drawn. The watchers watched.

Finally, just before two, Johnny emerged. He was dressed as earlier, except he had on a black nylon windbreaker. It was the sort of jacket a man might wear if he expected rain; or if he expected trouble. There wasn't a cloud in the sky, so the watchers passed the word: Walker was packing his .38 under his coat.

Johnny walked toward his van. Three steps, and he stopped abruptly. He looked left, then he looked right. There was an airplane above him; a truck down the street; and a Chevy Cherokee just across the way. But Johnny didn't see anything unusual. He got into his van and drove off.

The FBI was right on his tail. Things were looking good. Yet it didn't take more than ten minutes for the Windflyer team to be caught totally by surprise.

From his plane, John Hodges was the first to report the new development. Walker was not heading south to Charlotte. The van was moving north on Interstate 64. Toward Richmond? Washington? Johnny's destination was now anybody's guess.

Wolfinger played it safe. He stopped at a pay phone and called the Washington Field Office. "Windflyer may be coming your way," he reported.

Within minutes a coded signal went out over beepers throughout Washington. It announced: Report on the double to the Windflyer Command Center! More than sixty agents stopped whatever they were doing—later they would compare notes about abandoned golf games, half-painted houses, and exasperated wives—and, without much explanation, headed off on a Sunday afternoon to help trap a spy.

Johnny, his radio tuned to a jazz station, hadn't noticed a thing. He was now barreling along Interstate 95 at a steady sixty; there was no longer any doubt that he was going toward Washington. Above him the plane had him perfectly beaded. The car teams, getting cocky, were bored with hanging two or three lengths back. For a while a couple of the watchers rode alongside of Walker; it was good for a laugh.

Then, after about an hour and a half on the road, just as Johnny led his band into Woodbridge, Virginia, someone started shooting at the FBI. Or at least that was what the agents, for an impossibly tense interlude, believed. But it wasn't gunfire; it was—perhaps more frightening—spontaneous combustion.

Agent Beverly Andress was driving a hundred yards behind Johnny's van when, in the middle of sending a message, her transmitter burst into flames. Her fellow agents watched as instantly her car was filled with smoke. Had Walker shot at her? Should they return the fire? Should they pull Walker over?

In a moment, however, Andress was out of her car and signaling a thumbs-up to her buddies. They didn't know what had happened— later it would be worth a joke about Bev's talking into her cigarette lighter by mistake—but they knew enough to let things keep on going.

So they followed Johnny's van as he took the Beltway around Washington and, crossing the Cabin John Bridge, entered Montgomery County, Maryland. It was there that Johnny lost them.

Montgomery County is horse country. White-fenced acres of roll-ing, emerald-green meadows parallel twisting, dirt roads for miles

until the fields end in thick stands of woods. It's the sort of country
that attracts weekenders from Washington, tweedy people who repair
the crumbling stone fences and talk at cocktail parties about brood
mares. It's also the sort of terrain that's perfect for what, in another
sort of fieldman's trade, is known as "dry cleaning": You can spot a
tail on the open stretches of the road, and then you lose him in the
woods.

And that's what Johnny did. He doubled back along Cloppers Road,
cut over into Whites Ferry Road, and floored it on Query Mill
Road. By 4:45 there was no sight of the van. The plane was useless;
the thick spring foliage was a green umbrella covering the narrow
roads.

Confidence collapsed into anxiety. Bob Hunter, directing the surveillance teams in the area, worried that Walker had made them and
bolted. A new plane arrived from Washington. It flew in wider and
wider circles. It couldn't find the van.

It was six. Then seven. It got dark. Some of the agents decided
there was no hope. The show was off. Walker had run. Or maybe he
had changed his mind. Or maybe he had been on his way to meet
some woman all along; that would be very Johnny, the agents knew.
Then again, this could be part of his tradecraft, full of starts and stops,
twists and turns; wasn't that how his ex-wife had described his behavior when she had accompanied him on a drop? We waited this long,
Hunter decided, we'll wait a little longer.

Hardly anyone spoke; what was there to say? It was dark. They
were tired. They knew the past four months had all come down to this
night, this chance. They waited.

Suddenly, at 7:48, Agent James Koluch, his voice as dull as a dis-
patcher's, spoke into his walkie-talkie: The suspect is in view. A cheer
went up at Windflyer Control. The agents in the field felt a rush, the
kind football players get before a kickoff. Everyone was now certain:
A drop was about to go down.

The only light in the woods was from Johnny's van. Silhouetted in
this strong, almost eerie illumination, Johnny walked from his van and
headed toward a utility pole. He was in a field near the intersection of
Dufief Mill and Quince Orchard roads. The crunch of his steps was

the loudest sound in the slow spring night. And agents in camouflage outfits lay belly down in the woods and watched him through infrared binoculars. They saw him lean a 7-Up can against the base of the pole. Johnny then hurried to his van; he moved awkwardly, a man not used to exercise. The van sped north.

A decision had to be made, and quickly: Should they grab the can, a container big enough to hold a roll of film; or should they wait, take their chances, and hope they'd be able to retrieve it when the operation was completed?

The Windflyer team was still smarting from losing Walker for three full hours. This made them cautious. They decided to grab the can. It was the wrong decision. The 7-Up can did not contain any microfilm. It was only Johnny's safety signal. It said: Everything is fine, proceed to rendezvous point.

Its absence screamed an entirely different story.

Minutes after the can was retrieved, Koluch broadcast another flash: a 1983 blue Malibu sedan, license number DSX-144, was entering the area.

At Windflyer Control the license number was immediately fed into a computer. DSX signified the vehicle was registered to the Soviet embassy; the 144 was assigned to Aleksey Gavrilovich Tkachenko. He was listed as third secretary at the embassy and, according to the CI-2 vetting, of no intelligence importance. That appraisal was instantly changed.

The Department 16 legman, as his file was being sped to Windflyer Control, continued to drive slowly down the dirt roads of Montgomery County. His wife was next to him in the front seat and one of his daughters was in the rear. It was good cover; like his asset, he, too, believed espionage should be a family trade.

The Russian was also well trained. He stuck to the rules: no 7-Up can, no drop. By nine he was hurrying down River Road and heading back toward Washington. He would need to send an emergency flash to Moscow Center: The drop had been aborted.

• • •

Johnny, though, did not know his handler—and his money—were speeding away.

Agent Bruce Brahe, dressed in camouflage fatigues and lying (he would find out tomorrow) in a patch of poison ivy, watched as Walker got out of his van. Johnny, in no hurry, walked toward the woods at the intersection of Partnership and Ferry roads. Something was in his hand; then Johnny moved out of the glow of his van's headlights and his actions were lost to the FBI. When he returned to the van, though, he was empty-handed.

Had the drop just gone down?

As soon as Johnny drove off, Brahe, flashlight bouncing in the darkness, ran to the area where he had just seen Walker. He looked around. The woods were filled with a spy's hiding places. He picked up a log. It was light enough. He was certain it was a phony. He searched for the opening. When he couldn't find it, he tried breaking the log in half. When that failed, he tried slamming the phony log against the tree. When he was certain the log was just a log, he threw it deep into the woods. Exasperated, he continued his search, kicking rocks, knocking trees. He was making a lot of noise, and he wasn't having much success.

Finally, at the base of a pole with a NO HUNTING sign he saw a brown paper bag. He kicked it. And he knew! The sound he heard was not the soft thud of week-old garbage. This was a hard, fresh clang. He shined his light on the bag, and removed two soda bottles. The caps had been replaced on the empty bottles. Better, the bottles had been rinsed out. Encouraged, he stuck his hand deeper into the bag and found a package. It was an inch thick and wrapped in a white plastic garbage bag. The corners of the bag were folded like hospital corners on a bed and taped with white adhesive.

Brahe grabbed the bag and stuck it under his arm as though he were a halfback heading into the end zone. He ran at full speed into a cornfield a hundred yards off. Other Windflyer agents were waiting there. Within minutes the garbage bag was on its way to FBI headquarters on Pennsylvania Avenue.

Espionage experts in the FBI laboratory undid the package's hospital corners. They found the "Dear Friend" letter; and beneath it were 129 documents stolen from the *Nimitz*.

Johnny, however, still wanted his money. At 10:30, then at 10:47 he drove back to the contact point. The FBI agents could see the glow from his flashlight darting through the woods. He searched the area methodically: Nothing. An agent, crouched behind a tree, was close enough to hear him curse in desperation. But Johnny drove off. He parked in the Quince Orchard Shopping Center and tried to think this thing through. This had never happened before. Had he gotten the date wrong? Or was the KGB double-crossing him? Were they taking their revenge for Jerry's fogged photographs?

Yet in all his anxious, scattered thoughts, it never once occurred to him that the FBI might be on to him. Just as it would have never occurred to him that the couple locked in a late-night embrace in the car a stone's throw away were agents James McKay and Katie Southern.

It must have been 11:30 when he returned to the drop site. The plastic bag holding his money was still not there.

Johnny realized something was very wrong.

It was late, after midnight, so Johnny checked into the Ramada Inn in Rockville. He registered as John Johnston. It would be the last identity he would ever invent.

While Johnny slept in room 765, the FBI prepared to make its move. Agents Hunter and Koluch were in room 750. They put on bulletproof vests and they checked their revolvers. Before they stepped out into the hall, they made a promise to each other: They were going to take Johnny Walker alive.

At 3:30, as the two agents crouched on the bright geometrically patterned carpet near the seventh-floor elevators, Agent William Wang made a call to room 765.

"Hello, Mr. Johnston," the agent said, "this is the front desk."

". . . yes?" said Johnny, foggy with sleep.

"Is your van the blue-and-silver Chevy with the temporary plates?"

"What's up?" In an instant Johnny was awake.

"Well, there's been an accident. A guy ran into it. He's at the desk now so if you could come down with your insurance forms, we can clear this whole thing up."

"I'll be down," said Johnny. But he didn't like the sound of this at all.

The two agents waited by the elevator. Their guns were drawn. They kept listening for the sound of Johnny's door to open.

When it did, Johnny didn't walk to the elevator. He went to the service stairs. Slowly he eased the door open. He looked down the stairwell. He looked up. It was empty. Still, something didn't seem right. He returned to his room.

In the hallway the agents waited. Was Walker on to them? Would he come out firing? Should they bust into his room?

A minute passed. And another. Bob Hunter was gripping the gun in his hand with all his might. Then they heard the door to room 765 swing open and, without any hesitation, Johnny went to the elevator.

Hunter and Koluch, guns drawn, yelled, "FBI! Stop!"

Johnny drew his .38, turning toward the agents.

"Drop your weapon," Hunter ordered.

They were five yards apart. Johnny hesitated, and then let his gun drop to the carpet.

He was grinning.

Koluch slammed him against the wall.

"You're under arrest," said Hunter, "for violation of the espionage laws of the United States."

And with Johnny's hands cuffed behind his back, Agent Koluch ripped the toupee off the head of the man who had betrayed his country. It was the most he could do.

At 6:20 that morning, Rita answered a knock at her door. It was the FBI.

"Your brother-in-law, John Walker, has been arrested for espionage. Can we come in and talk with you and your husband?"

Rita was still in her nightgown. "I'd like to put on my robe first," she said.

"No," contradicted one of the agents.

And just as he spoke, Art called from the bedroom. "What's all the racket?"

Rita told him.

"Let them in," he said at last.

While the FBI agents were interviewing Art at the Norfolk Field Office, Mike was sitting in the master of arm's office on the *Nimitz*. The carrier was anchored off the Israeli coast, and NIS Agent Hitt was busy searching through the yeoman's belongings. Mike waited, and filled the time with a letter to Rachel: "At this time I have no idea what has come up, although I would imagine it is pretty serious . . . If I end this letter on an unhappy note please contact my father as soon as possible."

Mike never got to send the letter. Agent Hitt found fifteen pounds of classified documents hidden behind an air-conditioning unit near the sailor's bunk.

At just about the same time—11:00 A.M. in California—Jerry was also thinking about Johnny Walker. He was writing his friend on his new IBM computer. It was a friendly, conversational letter, full of his plans to buy a new house and news of Brenda's job prospects. He also wrote, "The camera situation is probably settled, but in case one or more are still wanted I'm amenable to anything reasonable."

Jerry's writing was interrupted by a knock on the trailer door. It was two FBI agents. He, too, never got to mail his letter.

PART VI

CELEBRITY

43

The New York Times

AT LEAST 135 U.S. AGENTS FOLLOWING UP CLUES
IN NAVY SPY INQUIRY

By Philip Shenon

June 25, 1985—The search for members of a Navy spy ring
has turned into one of the largest espionage investigations in
American history, involving more than 100 agents of the Federal Bureau of Investigation and more than a dozen bureau
field offices, officials said today.

They said the investigation also included 35 Navy intelligence agents, Federal prosecutors on both coasts and several
Justice Department employees. The investigators have followed up on leads that have taken them as far afield as Oklahoma and Louisiana. . . .

. . .

U.S. NAVAL INVESTIGATORS SERVICE
REPORT OF INVESTIGATION (RUC)   11 JUN 85
ESPIONAGE
I/WINDFLYER
REQUESTED BY/ FBI NORFOLK, VA.
MADE AT/ BEEVILLE, TX./ J. Y. NICHOLS, SPECIAL AGENT

SYNOPSIS

1. Mrs. Janice Styron Donnell was interviewed after she alleged to possess information that might be pertinent to the CWO John Walker, Jr., investigation. . . .
   Interview of J. S. Donnell
2. Mrs. Janice Styron Donnell, Beeville, Tx. . . . was contacted at her residence and related the following:
   Mrs. Donnell said her husband retired as an RMC from the U.S. Navy in 1952 and is deceased. Mrs. Donnell said that in 1942, while her husband was overseas with the U.S. Navy, she took a job with the U.S. War Department at Bluthenthal Air Base, near Cherry Point, NC, as a motor pool driver. She recalled that during this time frame she was dispatched to drive some civilian agents (possibly CID) to a large three-story ocean-side house. She recalled that the agents searched the house and found a radio set concealed in a closet on the second floor and the only person at the house was a man named "Walker" (NFI), approximately age 60. She said that from her observation she concluded that the house was used as a warehouse and that Walker was utilizing bi-wing pontoon aircraft to ferry food provisions to German U-2 boats that were operating off the Atlantic coast. She said that Walker was, in her opinion, a "full-blooded German" by judging physical characteristics and accent. Mrs. Donnell said that she had not thought of the man's name in years until reading of the recent USN espionage case involving CWO Walker. Mrs. Donnell offered that this case may go back further than suspected and offered that CWO Walker may have been a descendant of the Walker she met in 1942. Mrs. Donnell

said that out of her allegiance to the U.S. Navy and the U.S. she felt obligated to report this matter.

3. Files of NISRO New Orleans contain no further information of pertinence to this matter other than that reported herein.

And Mrs. Donnell from Beeville, Texas, was just the starter. Johnny Walker and his three operatives—a ring of career sailors— had served at twenty-two duty stations, had lived in a half-dozen Navy towns, and had hung around a fair share of squid bars. A lot of sailors knew them, and today's headlines jarred a fleet of memories. The 135 investigators were kept plenty busy.

44

Things were totally out of control. Laura thought she just might bottoms up a bottle of pills one night, so she could get out of waking up in the morning. It was all too much. It had been bad enough when, without any warning, just as she was chopping onions for tacos, she heard Tom Brokaw from the other room: " . . . arrested for espionage, John A. Walker, Jr. . . . " Laura had started it, but now that it was over she couldn't stop crying. The next day, though, when two FBI agents showed her a copy of the "Dear Friend" her dad had written, she really fell apart.

"Maybe you'll give us a hand. Got any idea who these guys might be?" asked Paul Culligan in his friendly, laid-back way. Then he gave her the letter to read.

She only had to skim it. "K" was Uncle Art, and that was a surprise and a heartache. But "S" was Mike, and that was devastation. Her baby brother! What had she done! Guilt grabbed her tight and wouldn't let go. She wanted to cry, but was too lost. Everything was without any reason.

When she saw Mike on the news being led off a Navy transport jet at Andrews Air Force Base, it was like a dream. How could it be real? He was in jeans; he had on his red Converse high top sneakers; he looked about sixteen with his floppy brown hair cut short; and his arms were in chains. He was a spy. He was her brother. She had done this to him.

She hated herself, and she hated her life.

There was no peace. When she went to get the dog's hair cut with Marie Hammond, whose house in Canton she had moved into two days before Johnny's arrest, the press surrounded her. They were shoving microphones at her, yelling questions nonstop, knocking on the windshield of the Toyota. She felt she was being treated as if she were the criminal; and that only helped to reinforce her hopeless feeling that she had done something very wrong.

She didn't know what to do; and for days couldn't do anything. Marie decided she had better step in.

"Laura," she said, "no way you're gonna get through this by yourself. You need a lawyer. And you need someone you can talk to. I know someone who's both of those things."

"I'll try anything," Laura promised. "Who?"

"Pat Robertson—the head of the Christian Broadcasting Network."

In 1959 God had told Pat Robertson, a lawyer and an ordained Baptist minister, to start a Christian television station. Twenty-five years later, his Christian Broadcasting Network (CBN) was the third-largest cable network in the country. His hour-long talk show, "The 700 Club," was watched daily by approximately 4.4 million Americans, in addition to millions of viewers in 45 countries around the world. In 1985, more than 600,000 "700 Club" supporters contributed $139 million to CBN. And Pat Robertson, the television evangelist, was seriously considering—and, if the polls were accurate, being seriously considered by the voters—running in the 1988 Republican party primaries for president.

Marie Hammond, who never failed to watch "The 700 Club," believed Pat Robertson had brought Jesus into her life and had filled her days with love and hope. She insisted Laura call him. "He'll know how to help you," she pledged. She gave Laura the toll-free National 700 Club Center number in Virginia Beach.

. . .

The voice at the other end of the phone prayed with Laura, but it wasn't enough. It didn't help. Laura needed, she decided, to speak to someone who actually talked with God. She knew, instinctively, only Pat Robertson himself could help her. She made up her mind to refuse to give up until she got through to him; it was as if, she would later say, the Holy Spirit was urging her on. But after a half-dozen calls, the closest Laura got to Pat was his secretary, Barbara Johnson. Barbara offered to pray with Laura, but she refused. Laura only wanted to speak to Pat. Finally, after Marie got on the phone, Barbara agreed to put a note on Pat's desk. "Pat will call you," Barbara promised before she hung up.

Pat Robertson didn't call. Jackie Mitchum, one of the "700 Club" staff members, did. She told Laura that someone from "The 700 Club" wanted to interview her. Would Laura be willing to come down to Virginia Beach? All expenses paid, naturally.

Laura was delighted. The chance to get away from Canton, from the press surrounding the house was, truly, a godsend. The opportunity to be counseled by Pat Roberston himself, though, was a miracle.

Laura, Marie, and Marie's thirteen-year-old son, who was bankrolling the trip with the money from his paper route until the expense check came, caught a plane that afternoon. It was a pretty unpleasant flight. One of the flight attendants at La Guardia recognized Laura's name. She told Laura her brother and father should be hung. No, hanging was too good for them. They should be drowned. Laura wondered how anyone could be so cruel. She felt worse than ever. The plane landed at Norfolk at about eleven-thirty that night and the travelers were met by CBN's Ken Green. Laura was worn out, but Ken was bubbling.

"I know all the networks have been trying to get you," he said. "We're thrilled to have you on the air. This is a feather in CBN's cap."

Laura immediately wanted to go home. She felt used. She had come down to Virginia Beach to be counseled, to meet Pat Robertson, not to appear on a TV program. If she had realized this was the kind of interview Jackie Mitchum had been talking about, she would never have agreed. "These people don't care about me at all," she moaned to Marie.

"You've gone this far, there's no backing out now," Marie told her.

When they got to the hotel, there was a basket of fruit and a bottle of wine in the room. Marie and her boy rang up room service. "See, this isn't so bad at all," Marie said.

Laura prayed with Ken Green before he left and that helped.

The next morning Laura was driven to the CBN studios. She was taken to a room where a man brushed her hair into place and helped her apply makeup. As Laura waited in the Green Room, she no longer felt like a criminal. It was incredible, but after all she had been through, people were suddenly treating her as if she were a movie star. When she was called, she went onstage. A microphone was hooked to her dress, the crew bowed their heads in prayer, and then the taping began. Danuta Soderman, one of the "700 Club" regulars, asked the questions. Laura was very calm. She sounded like a straightforward young woman who was trying very hard to hold back tears. Seven minutes had been scheduled for the interview; it lasted twenty. The CBN staff was quite pleased.

It was only later that Jackie Mitchum told people that when Pat Robertson saw the tape he became very nervous. "That woman has to be an impostor," Jackie recalled his saying. "She's too pretty, too self-confident. She must be an actress." He ordered CBN's security staff to investigate. It held up the broadcasting of the interview for a couple of days.

After the interview was over, Laura, almost feeling like herself again, told Jackie the saddest part of this whole thing was that she was still separated from her son. She wanted Christopher back, but she didn't know how to get him. She didn't even know where her husband, Mark, was living.

Jackie took her upstairs to talk with Guy Evans, a CBN attorney.

Guy solved half the problem in an instant. I'm sure your husband's been subpoenaed by the Baltimore grand jury that's investigating the case, he said. Just call the federal prosecutor down there. He'll have Mark's address.

Laura had no trouble getting through to Mike Schatzow, an assistant U. S. attorney. Just two months ago she had tried to trap her dad on the phone. This time she was trying to put one over on the government. But now she was sitting in the offices of CBN; she had God on her side. She told the prosecutor she had lost her husband's address. Could he help her out? Schatzow was only too glad.

Laura hung up the phone and let out a victory shriek. She was jumping up and down and she was hugging Marie. Then, her mood coming down like an express elevator, she considered the obstacles. Chris was living with his dad in Laurel, Maryland, wherever that was. She didn't have a car. She didn't have any money. She didn't know what she was going to do.

Guy Evans offered to help. He said CBN would lend her a car and give her $500.

Laura, Marie, and Jonathan, Marie's thirteen-year-old, left Virginia Beach that night. Laura was convinced they were on a mission from God.

Laura saw her son! It was Saturday morning, June 15, and she was parked on Old Stagecoach Road across from the address Schatzow had given her. Chris was playing on the lawn, a thin, blond-haired, brown-eyed boy. Her son! And then, just as soon as she spotted him, Mark called the boy to come inside. She had been *that* close.

Next, as if on signal, thunderclouds began to roll in. Laura could feel them. If it started to rain, Chris certainly wouldn't be coming back out. She gripped Marie's hand and the two women prayed. The clouds passed.

They waited in the sunshine. Jonathan had joined some children playing on the lawn. Make a lot of noise, Laura had told him, so Chris will hear and want to come out. Jonathan whooped it up. A half hour passed. Jonathan was getting hoarse. Then Chris came down the stairs.

Jonathan wasted no time. He grabbed Chris's hand and led the boy toward the car.

Laura ran to them. "I'm your mother," she said as she hugged and kissed her son. In a moment, Chris was on her lap and Marie, foot hard on the pedal, was driving off. "I've missed you so, I've missed you so," Laura told the son she had not seen in three years.

"Do you know who I am?" she asked her five-year-old. They were in the car, Marie still driving like a bank robber, and they were returning to Virginia Beach

Chris nodded. "You and Daddy used to fight all the time in California," he said.

He started crying. "Take me home or Daddy will whip me," Chris begged. "We have to go back. We're going on a picnic today. Daddy won't know where I am."

Laura tried to make her son feel better, but it just wasn't working. Still, when they stopped at a McDonald's and Chris had a cheeseburger, she wanted to believe the worst was over.

Laura called Mark as soon as she arrived at the hotel in Virginia Beach. "I saw the whole thing," Mark told her. He had been watching from the balcony as she had driven off with Chris. He had already called the police. And, he told her, the police had called the FBI.

Laura, near the end of a long day, didn't panic. She called Paul Culligan, the Buffalo FBI agent who had that nice way about him. Paul said he had already gotten a flash on the incident. But there was nothing to worry about. Mark and she weren't divorced. No one had legal custody of the boy. She had a perfect right to take her son anywhere she wanted.

Everything suddenly seemed to fall into place. All she had been through—the arrest of her father, her brother, her uncle—had been worth it. Laura had her son.

Celebrating, she called Jackie Mitchum to thank her for her help. The "700 Club" office said Jackie was in California for a TV special. Laura reached her in Los Angeles.

Jackie didn't know who Laura was.

Laura explained.

"This is a tremendous story for the Christian community," Jackie decided. She told Laura she wanted her and Chris to fly out to Los Angeles for a taping. This time with Pat Robertson himself. Marie and her son could come along.

The next day the four of them were on a plane to Los Angeles.

They checked into the Century Plaza Hotel. Jackie arranged a trip to Disneyland. There was also a luncheon at the hotel for born-again Hollywood stars. Laura couldn't believe how many people she recognized. There was even one of the women from "Dynasty." And then in the middle of the luncheon Pat sent word that he wanted to see her.

It was, she would say, sort of an anticlimax. She didn't need counseling anymore. She had her son. An old boyfriend had seen her on "The 700 Club" and was flying down from San Francisco; they had plans to sit on the beach and unwind. It was hard to believe that less than a month ago her father and brother had been arrested for espionage. Now she was famous.

They made her bring out Chris for the taping. He sat on Laura's lap. When the cameras started rolling, Pat announced to the audience how God had fulfilled His promise to Laura and had returned her son. Pat, smiling, tried to get Chris to speak. Chris wouldn't. Pat tried again. Chris turned away. Johnny Walker's grandson refused to be recruited.

45

Art broke. His collapse was similar to his recruitment—he confessed in stages.

On the morning of May 20 when agents Carroll Deane and Beverly Andress came to his door, Art poured coffee for everyone and went off to speak with them in his den. Rita, still in her nightgown, stayed in the kitchen with another team of agents.

Art said he had no indication of his brother's spying. Oh, about four years ago, Johnny had mentioned he was doing some contract work for *Jane's Fighting Ships*. Said it wasn't a bad way to make money. But, Art claimed, he ignored his brother. "Never have I passed on anything," he insisted. "It's something I wouldn't even consider. Even for my brother."

When the agents told him he might want to get an attorney, Art said he didn't need one. "I have no concern along those lines," he stated. "I'm clean," he kept repeating. It was as if he was trying to reassure himself.

The next morning Art was waiting at the FBI offices in the Federal Building for the agents to arrive. He had on a sky-blue leisure suit and he looked lost in it; it was as if he had shrunk overnight. Even his voice was smaller. He told the agents he had been thinking about what he had told them yesterday and he "wanted to talk to help his situation." "I don't see where clamming up and getting a lawyer would do any good," he went on. He realized he'd probably lose his job anyway.

The agents looked at each other: That was the least of it, buddy. But if he was only prepared to go one step at a time, they were willing to sit back and let him slowly walk himself to the edge.

They talked for hours, and by the end of the afternoon Art had told them he had given his brother unclassified documents. He also admitted he had known Johnny was a spy.

Art, again unsummoned, returned to the FBI offices on Wednesday with a list of things he wanted to discuss. Let's start at the beginning, he declared. But once he began, he forgot his list and rushed straight to the end: Yes, he had photographed classified documents for his brother. As Art, with a doctor's matter-of-fact detachment, described his thefts, he smoked Camels nonstop. A fresh one was lit with the stub of the cigarette already in his mouth. He was surrounded by smoke; it was a thin, gray screen between him and his interrogators. He had received $12,000 he finally told the agents. For some reason, the money seemed the hardest part of the story to confess.

When he was finished, they asked him to take a lie detector test. Art, shaking, agreed. So, he was asked if he had ever spied while on active duty. If he had recruited Johnny. If he had provided a foreign intelligence service with information other than the documents he had already cited. He answered no to all these questions. At the end, he seemed out of breath. The examiner described his answers as "deceptive."

Six days later, on May 28, Art drove his wife to Baltimore. She was scheduled to testify before the grand jury, and he didn't want her driving alone. Still, he wasn't very good company. Art's troubles seemed to be choking the life out of him; he was gasping, unable to breathe. He thought he would suffocate. He decided maybe things would get better if he just told the truth. The complete truth. He wanted to be able to breathe again. In the car, on the way to Baltimore, he told Rita about his affair with Barb. He wanted to be honest with her, and he was also trying to save himself. If people would forgive him, then maybe he could stop struggling and breathe.

He, forever the uninvited guest, waited in the hallway outside the grand jury room while Rita testified. He was standing there, staring into space, when he decided there was no longer any point. He couldn't continue like this. Bob Hunter, the FBI agent, was nearby, so Art asked him to tell Mike Schatzow he was willing to appear.

When Art took the stand, he was astonished that words were coming from his mouth. He had previously doubted he had the strength. He could hear his words, but his voice was unfamiliar. He felt cut off from life, and he was reaching back toward it.

Q. You can just get up and walk out. Do you understand that?
A. Yes, sir.
Q. You don't have to say anything before you go to walk out. You can just get up and walk out. Do you understand that?
A. Yes, sir.
Q. You have the right to be represented by an attorney. Are you represented by an attorney?
A. No, I am not. . . .
Q. Let me ask you some questions now. During what . . .

Art told them everything.

The next day, May 29, four FBI agents came to the house on Chickasaw Court and arrested Arthur Walker. He had been up all night wondering when they would come. He spent the entire night listening for the sounds of their cars.

When they marched in, Art handed them a letter that had come in yesterday's mail; he wanted them to know straight off he was on their side. The letter was from Johnny. It had been written in the Baltimore County jail. Art had refused to open it; he thought that would impress the officers. One of the agents read it aloud: "Don't worry, Art. I'll take care of things. I'll tell them you weren't involved, that you had nothing to do with it. Which is the truth." Then they led Art away in handcuffs.

He was charged with seven counts of espionage and placed in solitary confinement. The light in his cell glowed around the clock. A closed-circuit camera stared at him. Art was lonely, but he was no longer choking.

In prison, he thought a lot about God:

"The priest here, he's a little older than me—in his sixties—and real nice and I made a confession and he gave me communion and, man, it had been a long time. We had a chitchat and I mentioned that I had been an altar boy when I was age seven or eight for quite a few years and that John was one too, and I liked it. Everything was in Latin and it was fun. And he says, 'Do you remember any of it?' And I said, 'I don't know.' And he gives me the first line—'*Introibo ad altare Dei.*' And the response popped right out of me—'*Ad Deum qui laetificat juventutem meum.*' He grabs my hand and shakes it and that was really neat, really neat."

It wasn't much of a trial. His lawyers had tried to plea-bargain. They were willing to plead guilty to conspiracy, which carried a life sentence. The way Sam Meekins, one of his court-appointed attorneys explained it, "Art was more a patsy than a spy." The government wouldn't listen. "You don't put a knife in your country's back and come in and ask for some kind of deal . . . " countered Stephen Trott, an assistant U.S. attorney general.

Art waived the right to a jury; the thought of twelve of his neighbors staring at him seemed more punishment than he could bear. Still, throughout the five-day trial one of the government's exhibits was propped against the jury box. It was a blowup of a photograph of Johnny Walker. Art's eyes were drawn to it. He didn't want to look, but he couldn't help himself. It really spooked him.

Otherwise, he was a model defendant. He was the first on his feet when Judge J. Calvitt Clarke, Jr., entered the courtroom; well-trained, he stood at ramrod attention. When one of the government's witnesses, his supervisor at VSE, Emil Popa, took the stand and couldn't recognize the defendant without his customary toupee, Art helped out. "Over here, Emil," he called. Art, as always, wanted everyone to like him.

On August 9, 1985, Judge Clarke took fifteen minutes to consider the proceedings and then found Arthur Walker guilty on all seven counts.

The sentencing was three months later. Art, stammering, yet still standing at attention, told the court: "I'd like to take this opportunity to apologize to all the citizens of our country who—for what I did breaking my oath, dishonored myself, devastated my family. Nobody could be sorrier for anything that they ever did than I am, Your Honor."

"All right, sir," responded Judge Clarke. And then he sentenced Art to three life terms in jail plus another forty years, the sentences to run concurrently. There was also a $250,000 fine.

Johnny, meanwhile, was hanging tough.

On the day after his arrest, he called P.K. collect. "I'll probably never see you again. Just pretend I got hit by a truck." A few days later he called Laurie Robinson: "I've always been prepared for this. I always knew Barbara would push the button sooner or later."

When he sat down with the FBI on July 2 for his first formal interrogation since his arrest, he told the backbeaters the "true story of how I became a spy." He said he had bumped into a Yellow Cab driver one night at the Norfolk Naval Base. The cabbie told him a guy could make a few bucks selling classified papers. If Johnny was interested, he should go down to a corner bar and ask for "Joe." Johnny did. Joe put him in touch with some other people. And that was that.

The backbeaters, fuming but game, turned to damage assessment. Well, they asked, what specific documents and crypto material had Johnny passed to the Russians? Johnny told them not to quibble: "If I had access, color it gone."

Other than that, Johnny wasn't talking much. "I had to preserve my defense at this point," he later explained.

As for prison, he was sending out signals that he'd have no trouble doing the time.

Dear Laurie,

. . . Everything is going well with me. It is almost a vacation. You remember me bitching about the 3-piece suits and traffic and endless tension. Well, I sure as hell dropped out, but not quite as planned. The jail is really fine: air-conditioned, 3 or 4

movies a week, TV, radio, too much food. I spend a lot of time
in the library and have tackled four big books I have been putting
off for years. In fact, you won't believe this . . . there is even
sex! Since I am regarded as the nation's biggest criminal in 30
years, it makes me a goddamn celebrity. People ask for my au-
tograph. Well, the librarian just had to have the *ultimate* auto-
graph . . .

Well, kiddo, I'm heading for the movie. Will you be my pen
pal?

As ever & love,

Jaws

Johnny, though, didn't plan on spending too much time in prison.
He still had a few tricks up his sleeve.

46

Margaret couldn't get the scene out of her mind. She'd lay in bed, staring at the pink ceiling, thinking about it. Wishing. Just before her life had fallen apart, she had gone to the movies with some friends. They had waited on line at the Cinemax to see *Back to the Future*. It was a pretty funny flick, and Michael J. Fox was kind of cute, but she went off to work the next day and never gave it a second thought. Then, after her family name became a curse and nothing seemed important anymore, one scene from the movie suddenly started playing and replaying in her head; it had popped into her mind from out of nowhere, and now she couldn't get rid of it.

It was the scene where the Michael J. Fox character comes home after his trip back in time. He walks into the same house, he has the same parents, the same kid sister, but nothing's the same—everything is the way it should be; not the way it was. The parents are no longer losers, the sister is no longer a joke—things have worked out and it's —shazam!—one big, happy family.

That was the scene in her mind. And that was her wish. Except her life was stuck in the present. It was tearing her apart. She hated her

387

father for what he had done; and she hated herself for hating him: he
was her dad. She just wanted to come home one day like Michael J.
Fox and find that—shazam!—everything was the way it should be.
But life wasn't that kind of movie. And even wishing became hard
after she got the call from Johnny about "The System."

"It's an emergency." Johnny announced when he reached his
daughter in September, less than four months after his arrest. "You
have to come down here right away. We have to talk," he ordered.
Margaret recognized his frantic, scheming voice, and took a deep
breath.

"What's up, Dad?" she asked.

"We can't talk now. Not on the phone. You have to come down
here."

So that Sunday Margaret drove down to the Federal Detention
Center in Rockville, Maryland; Rachel, hoping to see Mike, came
with her. As soon as the two women walked up to the glass screen in
the prison interview room, Johnny, full of business, commanded,
"Margaret and me got some personal affairs to discuss. If you don't
mind, Rachel, we'd prefer to be alone."

But when Rachel left, Johnny didn't have much to say. He held a
long finger up to his lips signaling "quiet." "The rooms are probably
bugged," he added as an explanation. Then, from underneath his
shirt, he took out a pile of papers. He held one of the pages flat against
the glass screen. Margaret read one word—"Escape."

He held the pages up one after another and Margaret, sitting across
from her dad, quickly read them; it was as if Johnny had written his
plot on cue cards. Margaret was immediately in a state. She expected
guards to swoop down on her and cart her off. It was all too weird,
she kept telling herself. Her role in the plan—as best she understood
it, that is, and things were rolling by rapidly—came down to this: Two
men, one a former marine, were going to call her up and ask for her
help. They would identify themselves by referring to "The System."
Whenever Margaret heard the code word, she was to obey the caller
instantly.

There was one other matter. Margaret was to pay these callers
$200,000. She should cash in his life insurance to get part of the

money. The remainder would be raised by selling something Johnny had for her.

Uh-oh, Margaret thought. What is he getting me into?

Johnny, though, coolly signaled for a guard to come over. "Could you give this envelope to my daughter?" he asked. The guard opened the envelope and found nothing suspicious; it was passed to Margaret.

"You should be able to get a hundred, two hundred grand easy for this," he told his daughter. Margaret was as scared as she had ever been in her life.

It wasn't until the evening that Margaret found the nerve to look at what was in the envelope. There were twelve legal-size pages. At the top of one page, Johnny, in his cramped, narrow hand, had written the address of *Playboy* magazine. Margaret, fascinated, started reading. It was an interview between an anonymous questioner and Margaret Walker; or that's what the editors at *Playboy* were supposed to think—Johnny, sitting in his cell, had written both parts. The substance of the dialogue, too, was fiction; yet reading the long, rambling sentences, Margaret had the sad feeling that her dad, writing about himself with third-person objectivity, truly believed the flattering "truths" he was inventing. It was as if Johnny Walker, like the Michael J. Fox character, had been able to snap his fingers and—shazam!—enter a reality that suited him:

Q. Was it dangerous?
A. Silly question—I'll bet half the intelligence agencies in the world would have loved to eliminate him. I know he was in dangerous situations as a private detective and was shot at more than once. He told me that PI work was safe in comparison.
Q. How start & why?
A. JW always a political conservative and hater of communism. He joined the John Birch Society in about 1959 . . . The US government was basically liberal and socialist. As such, government never told public the full extent of Soviet threat. He would read top secret reports on a certain subject, then the

opposite in *Time* which showed government not only lied to public, but made world more dangerous by doing so . . .

JW was also more religious than most thought. He was a devout catholic with 11 years of catholic school; he was an altar boy as a child. He believed strongly in the bible and believed, as many, that the prophecies of Revelation would come to pass in his lifetime. As war in the Middle East intensifies, and the chance for Soviet involvement increases, world peace could be improved by making Soviet secrets *public*. In short his motives (I believe) were to screw the Russians while keeping the world safer . . .

Q. Why involve family?

A. Why not? Blood is supposed to be thicker than water. Family members should provide a safe nucleus where one could feel safe from being compromised . . . Laura agreed, accepted money, then declined. JW made a mistake with her, but with his ex-wife having knowledge, it probably didn't matter. She would never accept that they had "fallen out of love." She just had to get her revenge. She threatened him for years (to turn him in). I don't know how he was able to live with her "big threat" hanging over his head. My mother never could get on with her life after divorce. It is sick to hate someone 10 years later—hate enough to send to prison for life, or even death. She is now a complete alcoholic.

Q. Did your mother know Michael was involved?

A. How could she not? If JW made a recruitment pitch to daughter Laura while she was in Army, wouldn't he also recruit son in Navy? . . . If mother was concerned about Michael's possible involvement and arrest, why didn't she simply ASK him? or my Dad? That is the most unforgiveable thing she did, to destroy my brother's life.

Q. What now?

A. Dad is prepared for his fate. I guess he always was ready for arrest with someone like B lurking behind him, I guess Dad never expected her to destroy Michael as well.

The courts have already been brutal to Art, we can expect the worst for JW & M.

Margaret read, and her anger grew. Even from prison her father was reaching out, trying to manipulate her life. He would not let up.

Of course, she wouldn't send these lies ("I never saw him hit B and I don't believe he ever did"; that line in the "interview" really had her seeing red) to *Playboy*. Of course, she wouldn't get involved in "The System."

Yet Margaret understood she was already involved, and that only turned her mood fiercer. She was her father's daughter, and she was now his latest coconspirator. Her choices—her share of the inheritance, at last—were either silence or betrayal. She could allow her father to escape, and it never occurred to Margaret that Johnny would fail; or she could turn her father in to the FBI. She hated him, and all he had done; but he was her dad. She lay in bed, staring at the pink ceiling, hoping things would change; yet after all the shazams! in the world nothing was different. She didn't have her father's gift. And it was destroying her.

But Johnny was jumpy. When he got the feeling that Margaret wasn't moving fast enough on "The System," he called Laurie Robinson. He told Laurie that she was to contact Dan Rivas, a sailor who used to do free-lance work for Confidential Reports. There'd be $100,000, maybe $250,000 for Dan and her to split if they would help him out. "I've got everything arranged. I need Danny up here immediately," he said. "Only the two of you can help me pull off what I've got planned," Johnny pressed. "Time is of the essence, of the essence," he ranted. He promised to call back in a day or two. He sounded, Laurie thought, very desperate.

Laurie hung up the phone and almost had to laugh, it was so damn, achingly sad. Here she was out of work, broke, the FBI talking tough about her to the papers, saying that maybe she knew more than she was admitting, all because she had the bad luck to be Johnny Walker's business partner. No doubt about it, Johnny had ruined her life. And yet—this was the punch line—he was still her friend. What was she supposed to do? Run to the FBI, or simply run?

Behind her house was the barn where she kept her two horses, Brandy and Whiskey. For no reason at all, she went out back and started grooming them. The smell of the hay was comforting. She rubbed Brandy's white nose; he was her favorite. She started brushing his coat. She made it into slow and careful work. Moving the wire brush back and forth kept her busy. Until, scaring herself, she suddenly shouted, "Damn you, Johnny Walker." She broke into tears, and she hugged Brandy tighter and tighter.

When Johnny called on September 16, she taped the conversation. The next day she delivered the cassette to the FBI.

47

But Johnny was relentless. He waited patiently; took a bead on all the angles; and then, timing his shot perfectly, found another "System."

In the weeks following his arrest, he had been a man—and a symbol—easy to despise. "They should be shot," decided Defense Secretary Caspar Weinberger. Senator Strom Thurmond, chairman of the Judiciary Committee, agreed: "People on Capitol Hill are really disgusted and frustrated when a citizen is willing to sell his country down the creek." And Senator Patrick Leahy, the ranking Democrat on the Senate Select Committee on Intelligence, said, "The Walker case has made a number of people finally understand the dangers of espionage. They know we're not talking about some bad James Bond movie."

Johnny, however, didn't panic like Art. He was patient, even disciplined. He knew they would come around. After all, he had something they wanted. It was the same commodity he had always pedaled—information.

• • •

The damage assessment teams were worried. For the professionals who concerned themselves less with the sensation and more with the aftermath of scandal, anger was a luxury. Johnny's if-I-had-access-color-it-gone quip had not been funny at all: It was probably true. The NSA and the Navy were eager to know what specific information Walker had passed to the Russians. Johnny, in no hurry, continued to stonewall them.

The prosecutors in the Justice Department had other, anxious concerns. Without Walker's cooperation, Whitworth might be able to beat an espionage conviction; the evidence against Jerry was largely circumstantial unless Johnny would testify against his buddy.

However, all these problems and concerns became nothing but small troubles after a diligent CIA backbeater circulated a disturbing document. It was the transcript of an interview with a recent defector.

In July, two months after Johnny's arrest, Admiral Vitaly Yurchenko, deputy chief of the First Department of the First Chief Directorate of the KGB, had walked into the U.S. embassy in Rome and announced he wanted to defect. Within a week, he was sitting in the dining room in a CIA safe house not too far from Washington while four American agents threw questions at him. It did not take long for the interrogators to ask about the Walker ring.

There was a tape, of course, of the interrogation, and according to those who have heard it, Yurchenko's voice was wonderfully mellifluous, even charming, as he toyed with his new friends in the CIA. The Walker ring, he began, no, he had no direct knowledge of the case. But, contradicted one of the backbeaters, you were the principal KGB security officer at the Soviet embassy from—there was a rustle and a pause as the agent checked his papers—1975 to 1980. If it had been a major operation, surely you would have known about it?

Well, responded Yurchenko, I didn't know about it. And then, like the cat caught coughing up the canary, he revealed—until it was over. Then I heard plenty.

It was a Department 16 case, explained the defector, chiding his ignorant questioners. They would never inform another department of an ongoing operation. But after it ended, when the KGB backbeaters were trying to understand why Walker had been arrested, he was given a peek at the file. And, a professional gloating over the success of his comrades, Yurchenko proceeded to tell the agents in the safehouse dining room what he had learned.

The transcript of his lecture was quickly classified top secret; however, a summary of sorts by John Martin, chief of the Internal Security Section, Criminal Division of the Justice Department, captured the distressing spirit of its revelations:

"From his briefings, Yurchenko learned the KGB regarded the Walker/Whitworth operation to be the most important operation in the KGB's history.

"Yurchenko stated that the information delivered by Walker enabled the KGB to decipher over one million messages. . . .

"The KGB officers who handled the operation received important promotions and decorations for their success. One of these officers secretly received the Hero of the Soviet Union award after the Soviet Navy expressed its delight over the success of the operation. Two other KGB officers involved with the Walker/Whitworth operation were awarded the coveted Order of the Red Banner. . . .

"Yurchenko was informed by a high KGB official that the information learned from the Walker/Whitworth operation would have been 'devastating' to the United States in time of war."

It was this defector interview that left Johnny holding all the cards.

Johnny moved. He cut his deal. He insisted it include his son. The Justice Department drew up a settlement contract for both spies to sign. It terms were: Both John and Michael Walker would cooperate "fully and truthfully" with the government and would testify against Jerry Whitworth. In return, John Walker would be sentenced to two life terms and a 10-year term, to run concurrently. Michael Walker would serve two 25-year terms and two 10-year terms, to run concurrently.

Under federal law, the father will be eligible for parole in 10 years. The son in 8 years and 4 months.

Mike's attorney predicted his client would be out of prison before he turned forty.

"It's theoretically possible," shot back Mike Schatzow when asked about the spies' being paroled, "just as it's possible this building might fall on us. I think the chances of both happening are about the same.''

Barbara waited restlessly for the dawn on October 28, 1985, the day Johnny and and Mike were formally to plead guilty at the Baltimore Federal Court House. She had not slept. She was in a Holiday Inn near the courthouse and she had been crying all night. She lay in the dark sobbing, thinking about Mike. Yesterday she had visited him in the Harford County Detention Center. She had been on one side of the glass partition, he had been on the other. She wanted so much to touch him. They had to speak through phones.

Eleven months ago she had made a decision: For love, for her daughter's future, for the sake of her grandchild, she would tell her secret. She knew there would be consequences. Two men she loved —Johnny and Art—would be destroyed. She was resigned to living with this responsibility, this pain.

But she never, *never* imagined her son was also part of the secret. And for this, she could not forgive herself. This she could not endure.

Barbara continued to sob. Sleep was hopeless. Perhaps, she decided, she would feel better, more in control, if she could get her thoughts in order, if she could write them down. That had helped before. She got out of bed and searched for a piece of paper. She could not find any. Then she noticed a brown paper bag; inside had been last night's dinner, a ham sandwich. The bag would have to do. She began to write:

> Sometimes you are alone in life. It is 5:21 a.m. and I am sitting in a motel room in Baltimore . . . I know only God can know and understand what my pain for my son is. I wonder what it would be like to cry forever.
>
> I have always thought my children are part of me and that my children were conceived in love because I dearly loved their father. I know that I can never tell him this because I know he is responsible for the terrible fate of my son . . .
>
> God, I hurt. Do you know what it's like to live everyday knowing the decision I have made has done this to my son? My baby. And I did this to him. May God have mercy . . . ''

She continued writing until there was no more space on the paper bag. It was time to leave for the courthouse. But she decided not to go. She could not bear to see her son standing there, a prisoner, next to his father, another prisoner. Instead she flew back to Cape Cod.

The next morning she was on the loading dock at 6:30. Another Christmas was coming, and things would soon be very busy.

48

The secretary of the Navy was furious. The day after the sentencing agreement with the two spies was announced, Navy Secretary John Lehman, Jr., began fuming. And fuming. Until, according to what a Justice Department official told *The New York Times,* he "went off the reservation."

"We in the Navy are disappointed at the plea bargain," he asserted in a statement to the press. "It continues a tradition in the Justice Department of treating espionage as just another white-collar crime, and we think that it should be in a very different category." "The acts," he went on, "were traitorous acts and ought to be treated differently than insider trading."

Which only made the secretary of defense, who had approved the deal after being persuaded by John Martin's arguments, furious. Two days later it was his turn to go "off the reservation."

Caspar Weinberger issued the sort of statement that newspapers described as "a rare public criticism of a senior official": "Secretary Lehman now understands that he did not have all the facts concerning the matter before he made injudicious and incorrect statements with respect to the agreement. Secretary Lehman now has all the facts and is in complete agreement with the government's decision."

And so the feud began, the Navy on one side, the Justice Department on the other. It was just Laurie Robinson's luck that she'd wind up in the middle.

The feud seeped down into the ranks. The naval investigators, like their boss, were enraged. They felt the Justice Department—and its agents, the FBI—had allowed John Walker to betray the Navy—and get away with it. They decided to make a case against the confessed spy that would not be covered by his plea bargain. The NIS set out to prove John Walker was a murderer.

Still, it was Johnny, having fun in prison, who originally put the idea into their angry heads. It had occurred to him, now that he was busy shaping his life into the stuff of legends, that a master spy should have some notches in his gun. He started telling stories; reality, even the high-pitched sort that energized his daily life, was never sufficient for him. He wrote to P.K. that someone was once "on to him" and he had no choice but to "take him out." He told Mike in one of their jailhouse conversations how he had admitted to his handler in Vienna that someone was suspicious of his activities. The Russian, Johnny confided, issued an order: Kill the suspect. It would be, Johnny had the Russian saying, proof of Johnny's loyalty. Johnny, naturally, obeyed; and never one to skimp on the details that help a yarn along, he created for his son's enjoyment a vivid death scene in the foggy, predawn woods of Germany.

Of course, Johnny's storytelling did not go unnoticed, which was fine with him. The NIS read his mail; they heard his jailhouse conversations. They grew eager. Here was their case; even the Justice Department couldn't allow Walker to cut a deal on murder. Their enthusiasm was intensified by the confident, detailed authority with which Johnny spun his tale about the shooting in Germany. It was so real, it had to be true. The agents, the honor of the Navy goading them on, never understood that truth for Johnny was a cumbersome situation. It didn't have too much to do with actuality, but that didn't mean Johnny didn't believe his inventions with all his heart.

To complicate matters, which was the normal course of events in

Johnny's intersecting worlds, one of his buddies was also talking to
the NIS about murder. Dan Rivas, the Confidential Reports' free-
lancer, the man Johnny described as "the best investigator in the
world, next to myself," the man he was hoping would rescue him
from prison, was also trying to work a deal. Rivas had been court-
martialed by the Navy after bugging the Norfolk flight tower where he
worked; it had been, he explained apologetically, part of a prank to
embarrass his bosses. It had backfired. Now, he was hoping the Navy
would restore his rank if he would tell them all he knew about Johnny
Walker. The Navy brought the sailor from his new post in Okinawa to
Washington to tell his stories.

The FBI listened to Dan, and then told the NIS that "Rivas was all
theirs." "He exaggerates," said an FBI official. "Other things he's
said don't check out. A lot of people think he doesn't know what he's
talking about. Still, the Navy has bought him hook, line, and sinker."

So, the NIS wound up investigating the case of the murdered go-go
dancer. And then the strangled radioman. Not to mention the case of
the suspicious suicide of a police officer.

The body of Garland Joyner, Jr., a thirty-nine-year-old police detective, was found on the morning of March 18, 1984, floating facedown
in Warwick Creek in northeastern North Carolina. His revolver, four
rounds missing, was found in the water. According to the medical
examiner's report, Detective Joyner, who was right-handed, held the
gun backward in his left palm and pulled the trigger with his thumb.
The body was extensively bruised, but these contusions were dismissed as consistent with his falling into the creek. The death was
officially ruled a suicide.

The detective's widow, however, with the hope of collecting insurance money that was denied to her because of the suicide verdict,
hired a lawyer, Billy Franklin, to dispute the medical examiner's rul-
ing.

It was a matter of chance that the same Billy Franklin was asked by
the Norfolk Police Department to administer a lie detector test to
probationary policewoman Pamela K. Carroll on the day following the
arrest of her boyfriend for espionage. Billy, in his slow, deep drawl,
started asking P.K. questions about her relationship with John

Walker. While P.K. was calm, even confident, in her answers, Billy, to his surprise, found himself growing agitated. Something the woman said had jarred him, only he couldn't quite figure out what it was. It was after the examination was over that it came into focus—a brown Confidential Reports business card had been found on the creek bank across from Joyner's body.

This bit of evidence, slim and circumstantial, was passed on to the intelligence assessment teams. The NIS ran with it. They learned Joyner was also working as a contract agent for the Bureau of Alcohol, Tobacco and Firearms and, at the time of his death, was investigating a gun-smuggling ring. When Dan Rivas was told this, he suddenly recalled, "Hey, hey, hey. Johnny had approached me with a scheme to smuggle three hundred thousand dollars worth of Uzi machine guns to Latin America. Maybe we got something here?"

The NIS decided perhaps there was something, too. As their investigation continued, there was more encouragement. A suit by Mrs. Joyner to collect $130,000 in life insurance payments that were initially denied her because of the suicide ruling was settled out of court. The insurance company agreed to pay $125,000.

The go-go dancer was also a sailor with access to classified information. Carol Ann Molnar had been assigned to the Armed Forces Staff College in Norfolk. And at nights, under another name, she danced topless at the squid clubs.

On the afternoon of February 8, 1983, a friend of Carol Ann's called the police and reported her missing. She had last been seen at 3:00 A.M. on February 6 on the stage at the Galleon Club in Norfolk. Her car was soon found, but the dancer remained missing until May 1. On that morning, her body washed ashore beneath the piers near the Naval Air Station. She had been shot.

The murder was never solved. Neither the Norfolk homicide detectives nor the NIS agents assigned to the case were able to establish any convincing leads. The case was abandoned, and it most probably would have remained forgotten if Johnny Walker had not been arrested. Yet in the weeks following May 19, 1985, NIS investigators retrieved the Molnar file. A number of coincidences had gotten them thinking.

First, Carol Ann worked for over a year at the Staff College in an office with Pat Marsee, the same Pat Marsee who had flown to Casablanca in 1977 to meet Johnny.

Then, there was where she was found. Carol Ann's body drifted ashore a couple of hundred yards across from where Johnny docked his Thunderbird Drift-R-Cruise houseboat.

And, there was also the clubs she danced in—Bob's Runway, the Wayside, the Galleon. These bars were all on Johnny's late-night circuit.

But it wasn't until the day before Christmas, 1985, that all these coincidences came together for the NIS into a theory of sorts. On that day two agents were on Okinawa interviewing Dan Rivas. When they showed him a photograph of Carol Ann Molnar, Dan, after some thinking, said he recognized her. He had been with Johnny in a hotel bar in Northern Virginia when the girl in the photograph—who was a real looker, by the way, he added with a grin—showed up for "an appointment." When Dan left the two of them at the bar, they were "busy talking about something."

It was then that one of the NIS agents reached into his briefcase and took out a black ski mask. "Recognize this?" the agent asked.

"It's mine," said Dan matter-of-factly. "I kept it in the back of Johnny's van. We used it for nighttime surveillance work on divorce cases, things like that."

The ski mask had been found in the backseat of Carol Ann Molnar's car.

But there also was another ski mask. And another murder. And another story from Dan Rivas.

When Dan was brought to Washington by the NIS, the agents asked him about Pamela Ann Kinbrue. A watch engraved with the initials PK had been found in Johnny's house. The FBI was convinced it belonged to P. K. Carroll. The NIS was not so certain.

The body of Pamela Ann Kinbrue, a Navy radioman, was discovered on March 26, 1982. She was found in her automobile, hands bound behind her back. The car was submerged in the Chesapeake Bay, near a ramp used for seaplanes. She had been strangled until unconscious, and then she was drowned.

The only clue to the murderer was a ski mask found in the back of the car.

"You ever hear of this Pamela Kinbrue?" an NIS investigator asked Dan Rivas.

Dan considered the question for a moment. When he seemed sure of his facts, he announced that Johnny Walker had said he had killed her.

After being interviewed by the NIS in Washington, Dan went down to Virginia Beach to visit Laurie Robinson. Laurie and her husband, Henry, were real glad to see him; Dan was a reminder of the old days when things were hectic, but still a lot of fun. Yet, Dan was acting really weird, even for him. He was walking around the house carrying an attaché case. Laurie, a detective, noticed there was a circle of perforations on the side of the case.

"You're not going to believe this," she told her husband, after finding an excuse to drag him out to the barn, "but that jerk is taping us."

"Laurie, since we got married, I've learned to believe anything."

Never adverse to a good plot, Laurie decided she'd play along. "We'll give him something to tape all right," she told Henry.

Later that night as they sat in the narrow living room, Laurie told Dan about a case she had worked on with Johnny. "Operation Rainstorm," she called it, the name popping into her mind because when she glanced out the window it looked like rain. She, a quick worker, cooked up a story about Johnny's buying nuclear secrets from a bunch of submariners. Can't imagine, she told Dan, why the damage assessment boys have never asked me about Rainstorm. But, she said, that was their problem.

Dan sat on the green couch listening to his friend, his attaché case resting on the coffee table.

Two weeks later when Laurie appeared before a federal grand jury in Norfolk investigating John Walker's possible involvement in three unsolved murders, the prosecutor asked her about her knowledge of Operation Rainstorm.

"I don't have the slightest idea what you're talking about," she told him. And she didn't.

The prosecutor proceeded to introduce a transcript of Laurie's conversation with Dan Rivas. It was written on stationery headed, "U.S. Naval Investigative Service."

"Oh that," Laurie exclaimed. She told the grand jury that the entire conversation with Dan was a put-on. She didn't know he was working with the NIS. She thought he was being goofy. Operation Rainstorm was just something she made up.

Well, said the prosecutor, if it's just something you've made up, how do you explain this: "Operation Rainstorm" was the code name of a top secret antisubmarine warfare exercise . . . .

Jesus, thought Laurie.

An exercise, the prosecutor continued, in which Chief Warrant Officer John Walker, Jr., was a key participant.

Laurie, who had married one spy and gone into business with another, had done it again.

And while Laurie tried to explain the accident of her choosing the name "Rainstorm," and while the NIS continued to investigate three murders, Johnny prepared himself for the most public performance of his life.

49

San Francisco, a city of life-styles, was well represented in courtroom 2 on the 17th floor of the federal courthouse throughout the trial of *United States of America, plaintiff,* v. *Jerry Alfred Whitworth, defendant.* The defense team consisted of one New Left lawyer, another who wore a gold stud in his left ear, and an investigator who was formerly a *Ramparts* correspondent. The prosecution was led by an assistant U.S. attorney suffering from alopecia areata; all his body hair—including his eyebrows and eyelashes—had started falling out, perhaps coincidentally, after Interpol had informed him he was the target of a vengeful Colombian cocaine dealer's hit team. The coprosecutor had taught school in a Chicago ghetto, married and divorced a policeman, went to law school, and now was living with the man who had alopecia areata. The judge, John Vukasin, was nicknamed "Judge Vacation"; an article in *The Los Angeles Daily Journal* explained by quoting a public defender: "He takes a lot of vacations and when he's here he isn't here." And sitting daily at the defense table to the right of the judge was the slim, sad figure of Jerry Whitworth. Before the trial, Brenda had bought him two suits: one

405

gray, one blue. Both were too short, the sleeves not quite reaching his wrists. He made sure to alternate the suits; one day he would be in his blue outfit, the next day in his gray outfit. His one maroon tie never varied. He watched the proceedings grimly, taking notes, never speaking.

It was a long trial. It started in March 1986 and didn't end until July. There were over two hundred witnesses and more than two thousand exhibits. The pages of transcripts and exhibits and motions and discovery information piled on top of each other would reach past the hoop on a basketball backboard if anyone were interested in creating such a tower. FBI and NIS agents had flown all around the world to gather evidence. The prosecutors had gone off to sea on an aircraft carrier, had traveled to Vienna. Witnesses were flown in from Papua, New Guinea, and Germany. For example, there was the testimony of plaintiff's witness Siegfried Jaedicke, of Giessen, Germany.

Q. Is it possible to determine, by examining a Minox camera, whether it has been subjected to heavy usage?

A. Yes.

Q. How can that be determined?

Mr. Tamburello (for the defense). Your Honor, once again, my objection is foundation, in terms of whether or not expertise is required. And what "heavy usage" means, in light of the fact that we're dealing with an interpreter, I don't know if he's a technician. From what I understand, he's not. I don't know if he was a manufacturer of the camera. My understanding is he's not. If he's an engineer; I don't know.

Mr. Farmer (for the prosecution). I'll cover that.

The Court. Go ahead.

Q. (By Mr. Farmer) Mr. Jaedicke, what qualifications do you have to examine Minox cameras for technical signs of wear?

A. I am manager of the customer service department . . .

The Court. How long have you been involved in supervising repair of cameras?

The Witness. Since 1971.

The Court. About how many cameras have you supervised repair or maintenance on?

The Witness. We have constantly repairs . . .

The Court. How many cameras have been repaired while you had this responsibility?

The Witness. Exact numbers are not known to me.

The Court. Approximately?

The Witness. Fifty or a hundred.

The Court. Fifty or a hundred cameras since 1971?

The Witness. I think I misunderstood. I am misunderstood because I'm not repairing them myself. I supervise the repair . . .

The Court. Only 50 or 100 cameras have been repaired under your supervision in the last 15 years?

The Witness. A higher number of cameras is being repaired, but these . . .

The Court. I understood you to say that you are in charge of customer relations. And, included within that, is camera repairs; is that correct?

The Witness. Which is true, but which I do not personally do myself.

The Court. Don't do what yourself?

The Witness. The repair of cameras.

The Court. Don't do what yourself?

The Witness. I do not generally repair the cameras themselves.

The Court. People under your supervision and direction repair the cameras; is that correct?

The Witness. Yes.

The Court. So for 15 years you have been in charge of people who repair cameras; is that correct?

The Witness. Yes . . .

The Court. All right. That's what I was—what we have to find out is whether or not you have had sufficient experience to testify about the wear and tear of cameras . . .

The Interpreter. Vielen Dank.

The Court. What did you say?

The Interpreter. Vielen Dank.

Mr. Larson (for the defense). Your Honor, considering the hour, and not trying to be a pill—

The Court. Pill?

Mr. Tamburello. Yes . . .

And so the trial went for over one hundred days. It cost the government more than one million dollars.

All the Walkers appeared. Art, sitting rigidly in his chair and staring deep into the distance; Mike, pale and nervous, and looking like a teenager caught shoplifting; Barbara, who got sick when she first stepped into the witness box and had to leave; Laura, who told the court she had traveled to San Francisco with the "woman that is writing my life story"; and Margaret, who wore a ribbon in her red hair and made sure the prosecution and the defense had to pull every response out of her. The high point of the trial, though, was Johnny's appearance.

On April 28, John Walker took the stand. He declared to the world that he had recruited his friend, his son, and his brother as spies. He was smiling as he spoke, as though repressing a secret hilarity. It was as if he were trying to convey one last lesson to Jerry across the courtroom: Betrayal is easy, a fact of life.

Johnny was on the stand for over a week. The defense called him a liar:

"Your common sense tells you that when a man comes into this court, raises his hand, takes the oath, swears to tell the truth so help him God, and then looks you in the face and tells you a lie, you have to be very seriously concerned about the rest of what he said.

"Now I submit, ladies and gentlemen, that when Mr. Walker took that oath, when he raised his hand, when Lani, the clerk, swore him in, that man had no sense at all of the meaning of an oath. He doesn't owe allegiance to any God. The only God that he owes allegiance to is himself. . . ."

The prosecution didn't argue: "Now, John Walker is of course every bit the bad person that the defense has held out. . . . He is a master of deception. John Walker's a dog!"

• • •

On July 24, 1986, the jury found Jerry Whitworth guilty of seven counts of espionage and five counts of tax evasion. A month later he was sentenced. Judge Vukasin called him "a zero at his bones." "He believes in nothing."

Jerry was asked if he wanted to speak. He rose slowly. His legs appeared to be rocking, as if he were on the deck of a ship. "Except to say I'm sorry," was all he managed to get out.

The judge then read the sentence: 365 years in prison, and a $410,000 fine.

There was another, less public result of the four-month trial. The experience helped to bring the Walker family back together again—though, of course, in their own fashion.

As the trial was beginning, the Walkers were fighting viciously. The issue was money—the money to be made from the sale of the Walker Family miniseries.

From the start, Johnny had been thinking big bucks. He wrote to P.K., "We have already been approached, but the first offer was too low at $750 thousand for book & movie rights. We're looking at $5 million minimum into a trust with Mags in charge. We plan to help those who were hurt by this, particularly Mike . . . and others." He hired a Washington law firm that had represented some of the Watergate criminals in their entertainment ventures.

Barbara, meanwhile, was off pursuing her own deal. She was represented by a Boston law firm and by a man she described as "Bob Dylan's agent." Her personal adviser, however, was the Cape Cod realtor who owned the building where she lived, the two-story house with The Word bookstore on the ground floor. He announced that he was "reviewing all of Barbara's offers." Prospective authors and producers were required to send a list of their credentials to his realty office.

Barb, though, did attend some meetings on her own. For one, she was flown to New York by a producer and taken to the Plaza Hotel in a black Cadillac limousine. "I hate black," she told the producer. The next day she was driven around the city in a white limousine.

Laura hired her own ghostwriter. She wanted to tell "a Christian story."

Rita hired a Norfolk lawyer, a former Navy man, to handle all of Art's offers. He suggested that the price for an interview with Rita would be about $5,000.

Margaret and Rachel decided to sell their story as a team. Mike told Rachel whatever she wound up doing, he'd go along with.

It was a real competitive situation. Each of the Walkers wondering who was going to get the best deal, who was going to get the biggest contract, who would land the TV miniseries. Throughout the negotiations, Margaret was the one daughter and sister everyone was still talking to.

"You can forget about me doing any movie where Barbara or Laura are involved," Johnny told his daughter.

"I wouldn't work with your dad for all the money in the world," Barb told her daughter.

"I'll stick with Rachel," Mike told his sister. "Whatever she decides, I'll do. I owe her."

And Art said he really didn't want a movie at all. "Wouldn't it be better if people just forgot about us?"

So each of the Walkers was pretty set in his ways. "I'll make my own movie, I got plenty of story in me," Barbara announced, though any of the family members might just as well have said it.

But that was before the networks' and cable stations' Rights and Permissions offices sent a distinct message to all prospective producers—the project cannot proceed unless the producer has secured the rights from *all* the principal Walker family members.

The chances of a miniseries sale didn't look too good after that.

But Johnny, as always, was plotting. He had put together a package of agents to sell to the KGB; certainly he could put together a package of spies to sell to an agent. He just needed the opportunity to talk to everyone, to work on his operatives. The Whitworth trial gave him his chance.

For over a month, while they waited to testify in the San Francisco courtroom, Johnny, Art, and Mike were transferred to the Oakland City Jail. Mike and Art shared a cell; Johnny was just down the corridor. They got to spend a lot of time together. Johnny did a lot of talking.

Mike was the first to call his sister.

"Margaret, I'm backing out of the deal with you and Rachel."

"How can you do that? You gave us your word."

"Look," he explained, "Dad knows what's what. I got to listen to him."

Not long after that, Art spoke to his wife. Johnny would be advising him from now on. Whatever deal Johnny arranged, he'd be part of it. He told Rita, Johnny would get the best deal for all of them.

When Barbara learned that all the men in her family were about to make an agreement with Phoenix Entertainment, she hurried not to be left out.

"I didn't go along with your father. I signed my own deal," Barbara explained to her daughter.

"But, Mom, that was the same producer Dad signed with."

". . . well, you didn't expect me to walk away with nothing after all I've been through, did you?"

And then came the call Margaret had been anticipating.

"Hey, Mags . . ."

"Look, I thought you weren't going to make a deal without me. I thought you were going to put me in charge. I thought you weren't going to work with Mom. You lied to me."

"Would I lie to you?" asked Johnny Walker.

Margaret was breathing hard and fast. She could not speak.

"Hey," her dad said at last, "I did what I thought best for the family."

Which is not to say Johnny hadn't learned from experience. The five-million-dollar movie and book package he was trying to put together for his family was a lot sweeter than the last deal he had cut for them. It was about five times the entire sum the ring had earned from the Russians: Mike had received a total of $1,000; Art, $12,000; Jerry, $332,000; and Johnny, over seventeen years, approximately $750,000. A lot of people thought the KGB had made out like bandits.

• • •

The New York Times

WEINBERGER SAYS THE WALKERS GAVE SOVIETS MUCH KEY DATA

By Michael R. Gordon

April 16, 1987—Defense Secretary Caspar W. Weinberger said today that the John A. Walker Jr. spy ring had given Soviet officials information on a wide range of highly sensitive subjects . . .

"The Soviets gained access to weapons and sensor data and naval tactics . . . and surface, submarine and airborne training, readiness and tactics," Mr. Weinberger said.

Mr. Weinberger said the classified information provided to the Russians also enabled them to learn about the location of American ships and transit routes for those ships. The Russians also learned about military intelligence activities.

"The information stolen by Walker enabled the K.G.B. to decipher more than one million messages," said Mr. Weinberger. . . .

Mr. Weinberger said the K.G.B. considered the Walker family spy ring to be "the most important" operation in its history. . . .

"We now have clear signals of dramatic Soviet gains in all areas of naval warfare, which must now be interpreted in light of the Walker conspiracy," he said.

EPILOGUE

"HOPE YOU'RE NOT A SPY/ GEE, YOU'VE GOT NICE THIGHS"

The only light was directed toward the stage, so Rachel, sitting in the back of the club, was hidden. She was nervous; she wasn't sure she should have come. All day, after her stepsister had told her they were playing at the Cafe Local down by the beach, she had been toying with the idea of checking them out. First, she had decided she wasn't going to go because, well, it was finally over; and then, she realized she had to go because no way was it over. There was still something to take care of. If she could find the nerve.

The five guys in Elvis From Hell were tuning up. The Local was very hot and crowded. The spotlight burned on Chris's, the lead singer's, face; Rachel thought he looked ready to howl at the moon.

He told the crowd he was about to sing a song about a hometown boy and his wife. The band behind him by now was revving like the fleet of cars at the starting line of the Indy 500. The name of the song, he said, was "Wife of a Spy." He put his lips so close to the mike that Rachel for a moment wondered if he was about to kiss it. Then, he started to sing:

"Rachel was a Walker;
Michael was a talker.
She had no idea
To Russia he would squeal.
She liked to get her kicks
As one of Donald's chicks.
She would shake her tail
And documents he would sell. . . ."

Rachel listened. She had the woozy sensation of seeing the last fourteen months—the weeks, the days, the hours—since Mike's arrest spread like so many impossible moments before her. Elvis From Hell played on, and her mind went its own way. . . .

Oh, she had been one of Donald's chicks, all right. She had been strutting her stuff for the money that was going to get her to Italy, and to her husband. She was going to straighten Mike out once and for all, lay down the law about the work he was doing for his dad. But Mike never made it to Italy. Instead, she got a call from her mother, frantic, telling her, "Rachel, put on the news. Hurry." The man on the TV was talking about a father and son spy ring, and Rachel knew she had run out of time. She would never be able to fix things now.

When she heard that Mike was being flown in to Andrews Air Force Base, she drove on up. It was a five-hour trip, but she wanted a glimpse of him, to wave or something. She couldn't get close. An officer told her Mike was being taken to the FBI office in Baltimore; she rushed back to the red Subaru and headed off. In Baltimore, she got lost. She drove into a gas station and asked some guy if he knew where the FBI was—which, of course, she realized later was a pretty dumb way of going about it—and he looked at her like maybe she was public enemy number one, so she broke down in tears. She was crying her eyes out. She was lost, and she didn't know what to do. The only thing she could think of was to call the FBI and ask for help. They sent a car for her.

When Mike was brought into the room, he had on jeans and a surfing T-shirt. And he was handcuffed.

"Hi, bunny," said Rachel.

Mike looked at his wife and whispered, "I'm in serious trouble now." He covered his head with his shackled hands like a man trying to protect himself from falling debris.

"I don't know what's going to happen," he said after a while.

They both started to cry.

Rachel was with her husband for nearly thirty minutes. When she left, the FBI asked a teary-eyed Mike if he was willing to make a statement. He admitted everything. At the time, he just wanted to make up for all the pain he had caused his wife. He wanted to repent.

It was only later that Rachel would accuse the FBI of using her. "They wore Mike down with me," she complained. But by then she was coming to terms with the fact that a lot of people had used her; this was just one more nasty item in a long list.

Take for example, she thought, those bastards up on the stage.

". . . We talked her into leaving,
In us she was believing.
In front of the lens
She danced three hot numbers;
Rachel, my dear, what a silly blunder . . ."

She couldn't understand why they were going on like this about her. Real hip dudes. Sure, just so long as they could make a buck. The bastards.

". . . Hey, girl, you dance so well.
You had that look
And we could tell.
The tape we made we tried to sell
But guess what—
Detective Love."

At least there was some justice, she thought. Served those creeps right. It was even sort of funny. Hey, if *Playboy* called tomorrow and wanted to do a centerfold on the wife of a spy, be my guest. That's how she was feeling these days. But at the time, it really had her twisted.

It started about a month after the arrest when Laura telephoned. Laura was famous now. She was working for CBN. And Rachel wasn't too fond of her. Rachel understood what Laura had done, but that didn't mean she had forgiven her for Mike.

Laura wanted to know if Rachel had ever made any kind of videotape.

. . . No, said Rachel, waiting.

Laura asked if she was sure about that.

Rachel was in no mood to be interrogated.

Laura, though, continued. Didn't Rachel recall a rather suggestive dance? A dance while she was wearing, said the born-again sister-in-law, "erotic attire."

Oh that tape, Rachel told her. She didn't have to explain anything to Laura.

Well, Laura went on, CBN had been approached by the father of one of the guys who had made the tape. Said he was going to sell it to the *National Enquirer* unless CBN bought it first. He wanted $50,000.

By now Rachel had just plain lost it. That was all her father needed. One day he picks up the paper to read his son-in-law is a spy; the next day he gets to see pictures of his daughter in her camouflage G-string. Rachel was crying hysterically.

Laura told her not to worry. CBN, she said, would get the tape. They'd buy it. All Rachel had to do was sign a release.

A release, Rachel started shouting. Are you trying to blackmail me too? Is CBN trying to latch onto another Walker? Well, they can forget about that. She hung up the phone in a huff.

But before Elvis From Hell could sell the tape to the *Enquirer* and before CBN could stop them, the FBI did. The tape was confiscated from the band by Agent Love. It was evidence in an espionage investigation, he said. It couldn't be sold.

Which served all the schemers right, Rachel concluded.

Chris, his face twisted into a pout, was heading back into the chorus when Rachel walked out:

". . . Hope you're not a spy,
Gee, you've got nice thighs . . ."

She had heard enough. She had put up with enough. Her mind was set.

When she got home, it was late but she knew if she waited till the morning she might change her mind. She found a pad and a pen, and tried to find the words. She thought about telling Mike about the song; the old rock dog would probably get off on it. But, there was no point anymore. Instead she began to write:

"I do love you, but we know it would never work. We are in two different worlds now, they can't seem to get together."

She was telling her husband, the person she loved most in the world, she wanted a divorce. It was the only way. She was twenty-two, and she had lived a lifetime. She just wanted to go away.

She wrote about destiny, and learning from each other; and after a page and a half she almost convinced herself this just was another Navy romance that had gone on the skids.

For a moment she considered telling Mike the rest of her news. How last month, when she was laid up again with female trouble, she had told the doctor to take care of business. The doctor warned that after a tubal ligation she'd never be able to have children. That's fine with me, she agreed. There was no way she would ever want to bring children into this world. She didn't want to love anyone ever again. She was certain a child would only betray her; or, in time, she would betray the child. It was what life was all about. She was twenty-two, and it was the one lesson she had learned.

She decided not to tell any of this to Mike. Her problems weren't his anymore. She put the letter in an envelope and found a stamp. It was very late, but she knew she wouldn't be able to sleep unless she dropped it in a mailbox.

"C'mon, Sparky," she called, "take a walk with Momma."

As she walked to the mailbox, the letter slipped from her hand. She watched it floating to the pavement when, in an instant, Sparky jumped up and caught it in his mouth as if it were a Frisbee.

"Good dog." She gave him a hug. "Your daddy'd be so proud of you," she told the Dalmatian. "He taught you well."

Then she took the letter from the dog's mouth and put it into her pocket. She turned toward home. It was late. She might as well wait until morning to mail the letter, after all.

A NOTE ON SOURCES

In all spy stories—as, similarly, in many love stories—there are at least two versions of the truth: that of the betrayer and that of the betrayed. In the attempt to tell the history of the Walker family—which is both a love story, of sorts, and an espionage case with international implications—the search for truth is further complicated by the varied and often conflicting needs and responsibilities of the assorted personalities and institutions involved. Consider the obstacles a writer faces in his attempt to tell "what actually happened":

In such a bitter and unhappy family as the Walkers, a thousand small and large crimes have hardened attitudes and distorted memories. A wife's angry and vivid recall, for example, is dismissed as vengeful by her self-protective spouse. Or, a daughter's painfully articulated accusations against her father are viewed by the accused as a shiftless brat's rantings. It would be impossible to emerge from such a home without some ax to grind, some wrong one is determined to avenge, some sin or embarrassment one is eager to cover up. It was a family where growing up and living together was a shattering experience; it would be naïve to believe that truth—that is, objective

421

reality—was not, therefore, scrambled in the minds of the family members.

Then, since this story is not only about family secrets but also involves state secrets, there are government institutions—and their agents—intent on keeping a thick layer of mystery over the activities of the Walker spy ring. The motivation of these close-mouthed organizations—the FBI, the NSA, the NIS, the CIA; agencies whose daily trade is secrets—is often an understandable concern for national security; the Walker ring had, after all, disclosed to the KGB, according to Rear Admiral William Studeman, the director of Naval Intelligence, information that had "powerful war-winning implications for the Soviet side." However, on occasion it has been self-interest rather than larger, patriotic considerations that has encouraged these agencies to turn up their trench-coat collars and offer, for the record at least, a terse "no comment" to a badgering reporter. For example, there was the FBI's official reluctance to discuss the four-month delay in following up on Barbara Walker's initial phone call, or its error the night of the arrest which allowed the KGB agent—and, perhaps more significantly, his "Dear Friend" letter to Walker—to escape. Similarly, the Navy refused to discuss, for attribution at least, how relatively low-ranking sailors like John Walker and his son—Mike also had a history of drug use—were allowed access to such crucial defense secrets. Also, there was another element which made dealing with these organizations difficult: Their agents live in a hush-hush world and it suits both the demands of their job *and* their personalities to throw a cloak of secretiveness over their complex intrigues.

Another problem which further complicated the search for truth was the character of many of this story's principal participants. Treason is a habit, a way of life. For a man like John Walker, the "truth" is simply a pragmatic device: he often employs it to create the reality he needs, rather than to describe what actually occurred. His account of his life ranges from the self-serving—he testified under oath at the Whitworth trial that he never struck his wife—to the fantastic; that is, his jailhouse conversations with his son about a murder in Germany or his seduction of the prison librarian were both pure invention. He is a man with a remarkable imagination and little conscience: a perfect spy, but not a very reliable source. Other members of his family and some of his friends—Navy buddies and Happy Hour drinking partners—have also let the truth get a little ragged. Often it is because they have something to hide—they are guilty and ashamed by their actual or tacit complicity in John Walker's treason. Or—a more curious phenomenon but also one that is fitting in a tale about an American scheme—occasionally these "friends" are as eager as Johnny Walker to invent stories. They want to share, however vicariously, in his notoriety.

Yet, this is a true story. This book is a factual account of the activities of John Walker and his family and friends.

To re-create as accurately and as objectively as possible what actually happened I have established a number of research standards:

All directly quoted dialogue is just that. Either it was specifically recounted by at least one of the participants or a witness in an interview with this writer, or it was told to a federal investigator, or it was actual courtroom testimony.

When I explore what an individual is thinking or feeling, it is no casual narrative device, but a reporter's using the facts as he discovered them to describe a scene as accurately and as completely as possible. For example, when I write about John Walker's anger and fears after Whitworth passed "fogged" film to the KGB, it is based on specific comments Walker made at the Whitworth trial (pp. 26-3042, 25-2927, and passim in the transcript) and was further detailed by Walker in conversations that were related to me by the government agents involved in his debriefing. Or, when I write (at the end of part 1) that Walker was looking out the bus window, eager to begin his life as a man when he left Scranton to join the Navy, this small incident was related to me by both James Walker and Joe Long; both men had the scene *and* the emotions re-created for them in conversations and letters they had with John Walker. And when Rachel Walker's reaction to dancing on the runway at Donald's are depicted (in the Prologue and Epilogue), this description is based on lengthy taped interviews with Rachel.

Another standard I have used to help give some order to complex and often contradictory "facts" is to adopt the dates that are on the naval service records of all the participants in this story as the actual dates when certain events occurred. (These service records were helpful in other ways, too. A case in point: When James Walker told me the story about his brother and the rifle at the Roosevelt Theatre, he couldn't—understandably after thirty years—remember the theater manager's name. However, on Arthur Walker's enlistment papers the manager, Mr. Robert Kilcullen, was cited as a reference. My mentioning this jarred James's memory.) And, all dates for espionage activities used in this book conform not to Walker's mercurial memory but rather to the dates determined by federal prosecutors and submitted in court records.

I applied these standards to shape this book from what, after nearly a year and nine months of research, became—quite literally—a room full of tall piles of source material.

My primary source of information was the 117 interviews I conducted. In the course of my research I spoke with nearly all the Walker family members: These ranged from brief telephone conversations with John Walker and longer ones with Michael to lengthy personal interviews and phone conversations with Barbara, including one marathon call that lasted over three hours during which she shared what she had written in a Baltimore motel room the morning before her son's sentencing. Other interviews include at least nine taped hours with Rachel Walker as well as four interview sessions of significant length with Laura Walker Snyder. Friends of John Walker also granted interviews. I conducted, for example, at least twenty taped hours of interviews with Laurie Robinson, while Bill Wilkinson talked with me on two occasions, Don Clevenger at least five times, and Dan Rivas on eight different occasions.

Members of various government agencies—specifically the backbeaters who interviewed Walker and Whitworth—also granted numerous interviews. These men requested anonymity and were often difficult to track down. A small story: The National Security Agency —which played a key role in this affair and yet has refused to discuss publicly the Walker case in any significant detail—became more accessible after a study of the court papers of a 1984 case involving cryptographic material stolen by sailors on the USS *Peoria* revealed the names of NSA damage assessment experts who would, a year later and in greater secrecy, be assigned to analyze the consequences of the Walker ring. The FBI was also reluctant to discuss the case for the record in much detail; however, John Wagner, special agent in charge of the Norfolk Field Office, gave a valuable interview and tour of his facilities and Special Agent Robert Hunter was a source of fascinating, but nonclassified information; for example, how the Windflyer name originated. Government sources at other agencies also gave lengthy, detailed interviews (and have provided such documents as the Naval Investigative Service report that is quoted in the opening of part 6). I have promised to repay them by keeping their identities secret.

Another valuable research tool was the stacks of government documents (some remain classified) and investigative reports (including confidential FBI 302s of the interrogations of the Walkers) and legal affidavits (including previously undisclosed grand jury minutes) that I have collected in the course of my research. Directly quoted dialogue in the book is often taken from these FBI summaries of interviews with the members of the ring or their families.

Letters, many never published before, were also used in the telling of this story. For these exclusive letters I am particularly grateful to Joe Long, who volunteered the twenty-three letters he exchanged with John Walker over a period stretching back thirty years; to Margaret Walker, who provided solely to this writer the long, rambling autobiography John Walker composed in prison, which is cited throughout the book; and to Rachel Walker, who shared her husband's Navy and prison letters.

A large and rich source of information was provided by the transcripts of the two trials in the Walker case—that of Arthur Walker and the much more involved trial of Jerry Whitworth (this transcript totaled 6,206 pages in 56 volumes). John Walker took the stand at the Whitworth trial for over a week (the Q. and A.'s throughout this book are taken from the trial transcript), and all the Walker family members testified at length. Also, FBI agents, naval officers and NSA officials offered valuable background and technical information at these trials. And, in the course of these legal proceedings a mountain of exhibits —ranging from the security clearance "Faxgram" sent by DISCO to the VSE corporation quoted in part 4 to the rotor decryption device described in part 2—were introduced.

The various books, newspaper articles, and government publications I consulted on topics ranging from cryptography to ASW warfare were a final source. Of the more than one hundred books and naval department extracts and "backgrounders" consulted, a few works were particularly valuable: James Bamford, *The Puzzle Palace;* John Barron, *The KGB Today;* Seymour Hersh, *"The Target Is Destroyed"*; David Kahn, *The Codebreakers;* and Jeffrey Richelson, *The U.S. Intelligence Community.* The newspaper reports that I relied on most frequently were the well-written and detailed accounts in *The*

New York Times by Phil Shenon and Stephen Engelberg; the many articles in *The Virginian-Pilot and Ledger-Star* by Tony Germanotta, Jim Morrisson, and Patrick Lacey that time after time were scooping papers around the nation on breaking news; a thoughtfully written and meticulously researched background report on Jerry Whitworth by Nancy Skelton in the *Los Angeles Times;* and the accounts in *Scranton Times* by Francis DeAndrea that first revealed the details of John Walker's arrest record. I also consulted two books about the Walker case: *Family Treason* by Jack Kneece, which was most valuable for an amusing summary of John Walker's Navy hijinks; and *Breaking the Ring* by John Barron, which reported new details about the FBI's apprehension and debriefing of Walker.

The specific sources for the information in each chapter of this book are as follows:

Prologue

Author interviews: Rachel Walker (RW); Michael Lance Walker (MLW); Laura Walker Snyder (LWS); Ed Whitby; Chris Esterley; FBI sources.

Documents: FBI transcript of conversation between John Anthony Walker, Jr. (JAW), and RW (as related to author).

Chapter One

Author interviews: James Walker, Joe Long (JL), Mrs. Margaret Walker; members of the Fritsch family; George Gilbert; George Schreiber.

Documents, letters, and articles: letters from JAW to Joe Long; Navy service records of JAW and Arthur Walker (AW); St. Patrick's High School yearbook; *Scranton Times;* JAW autobiography; Scranton court records.

Chapter Two

Author interviews: Barbara Walker (BW); LWS; Margaret Walker (MW); Cynthia Walker (CW); Shalel Way (SW); Anne Crowley Nelson.

Documents: FBI interviews with BW; JAW autobiography.

Chapter Three

Author interviews: BW; MW; LWS; James Walker; Navy buddies (anonymous).

Documents and letters: JAW to JL; AW, JAW service records.

Chapter Four

Author interviews: Don Clevenger (DC); Navy buddies; Bill C. Wilkinson (BCW), James Walker, BW, MW, Laurie Robinson (LR).

Documents and books: JAW service record; *Family Treason;* naval orientation documents on submarines; *Defense Electronics* articles; *Surface Warfare Magazine* articles; Navy Department "Backgrounders."

Chapter Five

Author interviews: BCW; BW; MW; LWS; LR; DC.

Documents and transcripts: FBI interviews with AW, JAW; BW, JAW testimony at Whitworth trial; AW and JAW service records; JAW autobiography.

Chapter Six

Author interviews: FBI, NSA agents; BW; MW; BCW; DC; Norfolk naval officials; San Diego Naval Training Center instructors; David Kahn.

Documents, transcripts, and books: FBI interviews with JAW and AW; JAW, AW testimony at Whitworth trial; *The Puzzle Palace;* *"The Target is Destroyed"; The Codebreakers;* Earl David Clark, Admiral Lawrence Layman, Admiral Robert Kirksey testimony at Whitworth trial.

Chapter Seven

Author interviews: FBI, NSA agents.

Documents and transcripts: JAW at Whitworth trial; FBI, NSA debriefing reports.

Chapter Eight

Author interviews: FBI counterintelligence agents; CIA officials.

Documents, testimony, books, and articles: Raymond Carver, John Barron at Whitworth trial; *The KGB Today;* sentencing memorandum by John Martin, chief of the Internal Security Section of the Justice Department; statements in *The New York Times* by Caspar Weinberger.

Chapter Nine

Author interviews: FBI, NSA agents; David Kahn.

Documents, transcripts, and books: Clark, JAW testimony at trial; JAW FBI debriefings; Whitworth trial exhibits; *The Codebreakers;* a "statement of facts" memorandum by assistant U.S. attorney Michael Schatzow.

Chapter Ten

Author interviews: BW; LWS; MW; DC.

Documents and transcripts: JAW, BW testimony at Whitworth trial; Schatzow memorandum; BW FBI interviews; AW FBI interviews; Rita Walker testimony at sentencing hearing; AW, JAW service records.

Chapter Eleven

Author interviews: MW; LWS; BW; DC; RW; Michael O'Connor; FBI CI-2 agents; NIS agents.

Documents, transcripts, and books: O'Connor, JAW, BW at Whitworth trial; Admiral William Studeman; *Vietnam: The Naval Story,* Frank Uhlig, editor.

Chapter Twelve

Author interviews: Johnie Whitworth; Billy Phillips; Adele Olson; Willard Owens; Michael O'Connor; Sheila Robinson; Peter Massa; Russ Stetler; James Larson; William Farmer; Leida Schoggen; Shary Ratliff; LWS; MW; BW; LR; Dan Rivas.

Documents, transcripts, letters, and articles: JAW, BW, LWS, Roger Olsen testimony at Whitworth trial; Whitworth debriefing reports; Skelton in *Los Angeles Times;* bail letters written to U.S. attorney by a dozen Whitworth friends and relatives; Whitworth service record.

Chapter Thirteen

Author interviews: FBI, NSA agents; BW; MW; LWS; CW.

Documents, transcripts, letters, and official publications: JAW, BW testimony at Whitworth trial; JAW, Whitworth service records; JAW autobiography; FBI debriefing of JAW; U.S. Navy "Backgrounder" on Diego Garcia; Brenda Reis letter quoting Whitworth, submitted as trial exhibit.

Chapter Fourteen

Author interviews: Stetler; Massa; O'Connor; LR; BW; LWS; MW.

Documents and transcripts: JAW, BW, O'Connor testimony at Whitworth trial; FBI debriefing reports; Whitworth service record.

Chapter Fifteen

Author interviews: LWS; BW; MW; RW; LR; Michael Lance Walker (MLW).

Documents, transcripts, and letters: JAW, BW, LWS, MW, MLW testimony at Whitworth trial; Whitworth service record; FBI debriefing reports; Whitworth letter to JAW.

Chapter Sixteen

Author interviews: NSA, CIA, NIS agents; BW; LWS; MW; LR.

Documents, transcripts, books, and articles: JAW testimony at Whitworth trial; Norfolk, Virginia, County Court records; *The Puzzle Palace; The U.S. Intelligence Community; Newsweek,* 6/10/85; *The New York Times Magazine,* 12/7/86; *U.S. Naval Institute Proceed-*

ings, various issues; *Surface Warfare,* various issues; JAW autobiography.

Chapter Seventeen

Author interviews: Schatzow; Stetler; FBI, NSA agents.

Documents, transcripts, letters, and articles: JAW, Roberta Puma testimony at Whitworth trial; article by Puma in *The Virginian-Pilot,* 5/25/85; Schatzow memorandum; IRS documentation of Whitworth spending; Reis letter to Whitworth; debriefing reports.

Chapter Eighteen

Author interviews: BW; LWS; Anne Nelson; MLW; RW; MW; CW; SW.

Transcripts and articles: BW at Whitworth trial; *Somers Reporter* articles, Skowhegan, Maine; *Washington Post* stories from Skowhegan by Sharon LaFraniere and Ruth Marcus, 6/10/85.

Chapter Nineteen

Author interviews: FBI, NSA agents; LR.

Documents, transcripts, and books: JAW testimony at Whitworth trial; debriefing reports; hotel receipts submitted at Whitworth trial; *Breaking the Ring.*

Chapter Twenty

Author interviews: LWS; MW; FBI, NSA agents.

Documents, transcripts, and books: JAW calendar submitted at Whitworth trial; JAW testimony at Whitworth trial; debriefing reports; documents recovered from JAW's house by FBI; *Breaking the Ring; The U.S. Intelligence Community.*

Chapter Twenty-one

Author interviews: FBI, NSA agents; LR; RW; LWS.

Documents, transcripts, articles, and books: JAW testimony at

Whitworth trial; *Family Treason; Virginian-Pilot* stories; legal papers filed by Stephen Swain.

Chapter Twenty-two

Author interviews: FBI; Stetler; BCW.

Documents, transcripts, and articles: JAW testimony at Whitworth trial; trial memorandum by Stetler; James Ridgeway in *The Village Voice,* 6/25/85.

Chapter Twenty-three

Author interviews: Mrs. Margaret Walker; James Walker; RW; MW.

Documents and transcripts: AW, JAW testimony at Whitworth trial; AW interviews with FBI; JAW debriefings.

Chapter Twenty-four

Author interviews: LWS; Mark Snyder; MW.

Documents, transcripts, and articles: LWS, JAW, AW, BW testimony at Whitworth trial; Rita Walker testimony at sentencing hearing; numerous *Virginian-Pilot* stories on Arthur Walker; FBI interviews with AW; Schatzow memorandum; VSE records submitted at AW trial.

Chapter Twenty-five

Author interviews: FBI, NSA agents; Massa; O'Connor; MLW.

Documents and transcripts: JAW, MLW, O'Connor, Frank Olea, Pat Marsee at Whitworth trial; debriefing reports; IRS receipts; JAW pay record submitted at Whitworth trial.

Chapter Twenty-six

Author interviews: LWS; MLW; RW.

Documents, transcripts, and books: JAW, LWS, MLW at Whitworth trial; debriefing reports; FBI interviews with LWS; *Breaking the Ring*.

Chapter Twenty-seven

Author interviews: CIA officials; BW; SW.

Documents, articles, letters, and books: *The KGB Today;·The New York Times* articles; letter SW to author.

Chapter Twenty-eight

Author interviews: RW; MLW; BW.

Documents: MLW service record.

Chapter Twenty-nine

Author interviews: FBI agents; Samuel Meekins.

Documents and transcripts: AW, JAW at Whitworth trial; Rita Walker at grand jury and sentencing hearing; FBI interviews with AW, Rita Walker; indictment of AW; AW trial transcript passim.

Chapter Thirty

Author interviews: LR; P. K. Carroll (PKC); Henry Robinson; FBI agents; LWS; BW.

Documents, transcripts, and articles: Confidential Reports files; LR, JAW, LWS, BW testimony at Whitworth trial; *Virginian-Pilot* articles; FBI interviews with LR.

Chapter Thirty-one

Author interviews: FBI, NSA, NIS agents; Stetler.

Documents, transcripts, books, articles, and letters: JAW at Whitworth trial; receipts entered as evidence in Whitworth trial; Whitworth service record; transcript of taped letter Whitworth to JAW; telegrams submitted at Whitworth trial; *"The Target Is Destroyed"*; *The New York Times Magazine*, 12/7/86.

Chapter Thirty-two

Author interviews: FBI, NSA, NIS agents; Stetler.

Documents, transcripts, and letters: JAW, Gary Walker testimony at Whitworth trial; Reis letter submitted at trial; IRS receipts; Whitworth service record; notes recovered by FBI at JAW house; debriefing reports; Gary Walker interviews with FBI.

Chapter Thirty-three

Author interviews: MLW; RW; FBI, NIS agents; MLW classmates (anonymous).

Documents and transcripts: FBI interviews with MLW; statement of facts signed by MLW; MLW service record.

Chapter Thirty-four

Author interviews: MLW; RW; Stetler; BW; LR; MW; Sheila Robinson; PKC; Shary Ratliff.

Documents, transcripts, and letters: JAW, MLW, BW at Whitworth trial; notes recovered by FBI at Whitworth trailer and JAW house; RUS letters submitted at Whitworth trial; JAW autobiography.

Chapter Thirty-five

Author interviews: BW; CW; MW; LWS; RW; Chester Buck; Walter Price; FBI agents.

Documents, transcripts, and articles: BW, LWS at Whitworth trial; *The New York Times* interview with BW by Jane Perlez, 6/20/85; LWS on "The 700 Club"; FBI interviews with BW, LWS.

Chapter Thirty-six

Author interviews: FBI agents.

Documents: State Department "notification of appointment" forms; pictures of Tkachenko apartment taken by FBI; FBI CI-2 reports.

Chapter Thirty-seven

Author interviews: BW; LWS; Walter Price; Robert Hunter; John Wagner; FBI agents.

Documents, transcripts, articles, and books: BW, LWS at Whitworth trial; FBI interviews with LWS, BW; FBI trial memorandums; FBI agents testimony at AW and Whitworth trials; *Breaking the Ring;* Perlez in *The New York Times*.

Chapter Thirty-eight

Author interviews: RW; MLW; MW.

Documents and transcripts: MLW at Whitworth trial; MLW statement to FBI; MLW service record; documents found at JAW house by FBI.

Chapter Thirty-nine

Author interviews: RW.

Letters: MLW to RW; MLW to JAW submitted in Whitworth trial.

Chapter Forty

Author interviews: BW; RW; LWS; MW; FBI, NSA agents.

Documents, transcripts, and letters: JAW testimony at Whitworth trial; debriefing reports; AW interviews with FBI; JAW to Whitworth, recovered from house by FBI; Whitworth to JAW submitted as trial memorandum; debriefing reports; transcript of JAW call to RW; transcript of LWS call to JAW; MLW letter to RW.

Chapter Forty-one

Author interviews: Wagner; Hunter; Szady; FBI agents.

Documents and transcripts: testimony by FBI agents at AW and Whitworth trials; affidavits submitted at both trials by FBI agents; AW, JAW testimony at Whitworth trial; transcript of JAW call to RW; JAW letter recovered by FBI.

Chapter Forty-two

Author interviews: Wagner; Hunter; Szady; FBI agents.

Documents, transcripts, letters, and books: testimony by FBI agents at AW and Whitworth trials; affidavits submitted at both trials by FBI agents; AW, JAW testimony at Whitworth trial; *Breaking the Ring; Family Treason;* Rita Walker at sentencing hearing; AW, Rita Walker interviews with FBI; MLW to RW letter confiscated by NIS; Whitworth letter confiscated by FBI.

Chapter Forty-three

Author interviews: FBI, NIS agents.

Documents and articles: *The New York Times,* 6/25/85; NIS.

Chapter Forty-four

Author interviews: LWS; Mark Snyder; Marie Hammond; Jackie Mitchum; Schatzow; FBI agents.

Documents, transcripts, and articles: LWS on "The 700 Club"; CBN brochures; Michael Kramer in *New York* magazine on Pat Robertson, 8/18/86; Robertson's *The Secret Kingdom; The New York Times* on Robertson, 9/12/86; LWS at Whitworth trial.

Chapter Forty-five

Author interviews: Samuel Meekins; Hunter; Schatzow; FBI agents.

Documents, transcripts, letters, and articles: FBI interviews with AW; AW at Whitworth trial; affidavits of "version of crime" AW submitted at his trial; grand jury testimony by AW, Rita Walker; *Washington Post* interview with AW as quoted in *Family Treason;* transcript of AW trial; transcript of AW sentencing; FBI interviews with JAW; JAW letter to LR.

Chapter Forty-six

Author interviews: MW; LR; RW; Dan Rivas; John Hooker; FBI, NIS agents.

Documents, transcripts, and letters: LR, MW at Whitworth trial; LR, MW interviews with FBI; JAW autobiography.

Chapter Forty-seven

Author interviews: CIA, NIS, FBI agents; Schatzow; Fred Warren Bennett; RW; MW; BW.

Documents and articles: *The New York Times,* 7/22/85; JAW, MLW plea bargaining contracts; debriefing reports; John Martin sentencing memorandum.

Chapter Forty-eight

Author interviews: LR; Henry Robinson; Dan Rivas; PKC; Billy Franklin; Kenneth Toffy; Keith Dodgson; MLW; RW; NIS, FBI, ATF agents.

Documents, testimony, and articles: *The New York Times,* 11/2/85, 11/5/86; PKC at Whitworth trial; NIS interviews with Rivas; numerous *Portsmouth Times* articles on Joyner; North Carolina State Bureau of Investigation reports; Pitt County autopsy reports; Spencer review of autopsy; Molnar, Kinbrue service records.

Chapter Forty-nine

Author interviews: Larson; Tony Tamburello; Farmer; Schoggen; Katherine Bishop; MW; RW; LWS; BW; PKC; Tom O'Hearn; Rob Scheidlinger; various producers.

Documents, transcripts, and articles: *Los Angeles Daily Journal,* 7/21/84; Siegfried Jaedicke, BW, LWS, MW, JAW, MLW at Whitworth trial; sentencing transcript of Whitworth; IRS records at Whitworth trial; AW to PKC letter in *People* magazine, 12/9/85.

Epilogue

Author interviews: MW; LWS; Ed Whitby; Chris Esterly; FBI agents.

Documents: Song with permission of Ed Whitby; RW letter to MW.

ACKNOWLEDGMENTS

A lot of people were kinder than I ever had any reason to expect. It would be a vanity to say they made the finished book more fully realized, but without them the entire process—the research, writing, and editing that went into this work—would certainly have been more helter-skelter, and less fun. For his wise advice, thoughtful criticism, and constant prodding, Fred Hills, my editor, was a godsend; I'm really in his debt. Others at Simon and Schuster also went out of their way to be generous with their support and talents: Joni Evans, whose enthusiasm was most flattering and whose coaxing kept me at my word processor; Dick Snyder, who responded quickly and generously when I first approached him with the idea for this book; Burton Beals, a perceptive and gracious editor; and Jenny Cox, whose intelligence and kindheartedness made everything easier. My agents, Lynn Nesbit and Suzanne Gluck, were also valued supporters. And, since parts of this book appeared in a slightly different form in *The New York Times Magazine* and *Life* prior to this publication, I am also indebted to the following editors: Alex Ward, Ed Klein, and Ken Emerson at *The Times;* and Dean Valentine and Judy Daniels at *Life*. They all helped me shape the story that led to this work. Another perceptive reading of this manuscript was given by Richard Adams, who is writing the teleplay based on the Walker family for CBS; his comments were greatly appreciated. And, in putting together a project with as many ornery personalities as this one, lawyers were involved from the get-go. I was lucky I had Jerry Lurie and Rick Glickstein in my corner. When it came time to print the stack of diskettes I had dutifully filled, John Downing kindly allowed his fancy, high-speed printer to be used. And, as always, boy, do I owe Annette.

PICTURE CREDITS

ABOUT THE AUTHOR

Howard Blum, journalist and novelist, has received wide critical acclaim for his work. As a staff writer for *The Village Voice* he won Columbia University's coveted Meyer Berger Award. During his six years as a reporter for *The New York Times,* he received over a dozen journalism awards and was twice nominated for the Pulitzer Prize for Investigative Reporting. His nonfiction best-seller, *Wanted! The Search for Nazis in America,* sparked congressional hearings and resulted in the deportation of Nazi war criminals from this country. His novel, *Wishful Thinking,* was praised by many literary critics. His investigative reporting on the Walker case—which led to this book—made national headlines when his story about the spy ring appeared on the cover of *The New York Times Magazine* and in *Life.* Mr. Blum lives in New York City.